Social Studies for Elementary School Children

Developing Young Citizens

Second Edition

Peter H. Martorella
North Carolina State University

Merrill,
an imprint of Prentice Hall
Upper Saddle River, New Jersey   Columbus, Ohio

Library of Congress Cataloging-in-Publication Data

Martorella, Peter H.
   Social studies for elementary school children : developing young citizens / Peter H.
Martorella.—2nd ed.
     p. cm.
   Includes bibliographical references and index.
   ISBN 0-13-496506-X
    1. Social sciences—Study and teaching (Elementary)—United States. 2. Education, Elementary—Activity programs—United States.   I. Title.
LB1584.M346 1998
372.83'0973—dc21

97-18758
CIP

Editor: Bradley J. Potthoff
Production Editor: Mary Harlan
Design Coordinator: Karrie M. Converse
Text Designer: STELLARViSIONs
Cover Designer: Brian Deep
Cover photo: Mike Agliolo, International Stock
Production Manager: Deidra M. Schwartz
Electronic Text Management: Marilyn Wilson Phelps, Matthew Williams, Karen L. Bretz, Tracey B. Ward
Photo Researcher: Anthony Magnacca
Illustrations: Tracey B. Ward
Director of Marketing: Kevin Flanagan
Marketing Manager: Suzanne Stanton
Advertising/Marketing Coordinator: Julie Shough

This book was set in Carmina by Prentice Hall and was printed and bound by
R.R. Donnelley & Sons Company. The cover was printed by Phoenix Color Corp.

Photo credits: All photos copyrighted by the individuals or companies listed. Jim Cronk/Photographic Illustrations: p. 339; Scott Cunningham/Merrill: pp. 13, 80, 87, 114, 116, 137, 217, 252, 295, 314, 332, 369; Brad Feinkopf/Merrill: p. 346; Anthony Magnacca: pp. 5, 333; Anthony Magnacca/Merrill: pp. 46, 108, 193, 232, 356; Barbara Schwartz/Merrill: p. 177; Anne Vega/Merrill: facing p. 1, pp. 50, 58, 162, 186, 224, 260, 284, 349, 380; Todd Yarrington/Merrill: pp. 18, 33, 38, 128, 152, 277, 387.

Printed in the United States of America

10 9 8 7 6 5 4 3

ISBN: 0-13-496506-X

Prentice-Hall International (UK) Limited, *London*
Prentice-Hall of Australia Pty. Limited, *Sydney*
Prentice-Hall of Canada, Inc., *Toronto*
Prentice-Hall Hispanoamericana, S. A., *Mexico*
Prentice-Hall of India Private Limited, *New Delhi*
Prentice-Hall of Japan, Inc., *Tokyo*
Prentice-Hall Asia Pte. Ltd., *Singapore*
Editora Prentice-Hall do Brasil, Ltda., *Rio de Janeiro*

Preface

In constructing this text, my intent was to tap three bountiful wellsprings of information: teacher craft wisdom, research findings relative to instruction, and well grounded theories. Each of these streams affords both neophytes and experienced teachers abundant insights into how effective social studies instruction can be nurtured and sustained.

Craft wisdom is that residual base of rich, informed, and practical knowledge that effective teachers have shared for centuries, often through oral rather than written histories. It embodies the lode of stories and case studies that experienced successful teachers have passed along about "things that worked well for me" and "the pitfalls I have learned to avoid." Craft wisdom also includes the identification of instructional materials and resources that have been tested under real classroom conditions and found to be exemplary.

Such practitioner craft wisdom often is buttressed neither by theory nor research—much like aspects of folk medicine. Instead, it derives its credibility and permanency from the number of iterations of success that teachers have encountered in applying it. Teachers are not always sure why something worked or whether others will have similar success under different classroom conditions. What they can affirm are consistent positive results.

Research and *theory*, in turn, offer complementary insights into how teachers might most effectively teach social studies. These represent the accumulations of scholars' tested conclusions under controlled conditions and in varied settings over time. They also include scholars' hypotheses and reflective deductions undergirded by logic and evidence.

Properly focused, research and theory can yield practical applications and identify areas that require attention in our social studies classes. Researchers and theorists also can aid us in designing and selecting materials and texts that engage students and stimulate reflection. Additionally, they can provide us with models for analyzing our teaching behaviors and generating new instructional strategies.

Old friends comparing the first edition with the second will find its foundational themes intact and its point of view burnished. To wit, as a central thesis, I contend a well-balanced social studies program consists of matters of the head, the hand, and the heart. Following on this metaphor, I continue to hold that the fundamental purpose of the social studies should be *the development of reflective, competent, and concerned citizens*. I also reassert the importance of theory, research, and craft wisdom as beacons for effective social studies teaching. In this context, throughout the text, constructivist approaches that engage students in meaningful activities are emphasized.

Features of This Text

This book was designed to assist preservice and inservice elementary and middle grades teachers in becoming more effective teachers of social studies. The text is meant to be used in a variety of settings, such as group activities and workshops. Toward these ends, several steps have been taken to make it readable and understandable to audiences with different levels of experiences and needs.

Each chapter has a detailed outline on the opening page to serve as an advance organizer. Also, throughout the text, key terms appear in bold face in the text and in color in the margin to alert the reader to their importance. At the end of each chapter, two types of activities are suggested to apply and extend learning: those to be completed individually and others to be done in groups.

Numerous field-tested lessons and activities are sprinkled throughout the text. These are borrowed from a variety of sources and reflect a combination of craft wisdom, research, and theory. They cover the primary, intermediate, and middle grades. For easy reference, a list of these lessons and activities appears at the end of the Contents.

Organization

Chapter 1 offers an overview of the foundations of the social studies curriculum and advances a perspective on what exemplary social studies teaching entails. Chapters 2 and 3 explore the sources of the social studies curriculum, the relationship of the social sciences to the social studies, and alternative views concerning what the social studies curriculum should be.

Planning and instructional strategies constitute the core of the book and the focus of Chapters 4 through 8. In Chapter 9 I address the urgent and complex issue of how to prepare children to live in a global and culturally diverse world. Chapter 10 is devoted to strategies for aiding students in comprehending, communicating, and remembering social studies subject matter. Finally, Chapters 11 through 13 consider, respectively, ways to enrich classroom activities through technology, assist students with special needs, and assess the outcomes of social studies instruction.

New to This Edition

There are notable changes small and large in this revision. In order to more adequately address emerging issues concerning national curriculum standards and multicultural education, Chapters 3 and 9 have been modified. In Chapter 12, the focus on the reading–writing–listening–social studies connection and the integration of children's literature into the social studies curriculum has been sharpened. Similarly, the discussions of portfolios and authentic assessments in Chapter 13 have undergone changes. Also, the discussion of learning styles in Chapter 12 has been updated to reflect the latest work of Howard Gardner and his associates.

The most dramatic change in this new edition deals with technology applications in the social studies—a fast-moving target. Chapter 11 has been extensively updated, but with the discomforting awareness that the swiftness of new advances in computer-based technologies will outpace our capacity to keep the reader current.

To further heighten the technology strand in the book, two actions were taken. At relevant points throughout the text, examples of social studies software are cited. Also, in those sections of the text that call for the use of a computer to illustrate a point, an icon will appear in the margin as shown here.

Like its predecessor, this text ultimately must contend with a host of others in the marketplace of ideas, staking out its own claims to uniqueness, credibility, utility, and significance. In that arena, I believe the new book is well armed.

Acknowledgments

The second edition of this text has been greatly enriched by the array of insights that readers gleaned from the first edition and shared with me. The meanings they derived from interacting with my text and the life they breathed into the skeleton of ideas I presented were a delight to experience. I thank and salute them for their contributions. I also thank those who reviewed the first edition and offered suggestions for improvement in the second: Gloria Alter, Northern Illinois University; Thomas B. Goodkind, University of Connecticut; Edith Guyton, Georgia State University; Kathleen Naylor, University of Arizona; and Jesse Palmer, University of Southern Mississippi.

Brief Contents

Contents

Chapter 1

Learning and Teaching Social Studies 1

Chapter

The Sources of Subject Matter and Instructional Resources for the Social Studies   19

Chapter 3

Alternative Scope and Sequence Patterns in the Social Studies   47

Chapter **4**

Planning for Social Studies Instruction   81

Chapter **7**

Aiding Students in Developing Effective Citizenship Competencies   187

Chapter

Aiding Students in Developing and Acting on Social Concern   225

Chapter

Preparing Children to Live in a Global and Culturally Diverse World   253

Chapter **10**

Comprehending, Communicating, and Remembering Subject Matter 285

Chapter **11**

Harnessing Technology to the Social Studies Curriculum 315

Chapter  **12**

Adapting Social Studies Instruction to Individual Needs   347

Chapter  **13**

Evaluating and Assessing
Student Learning   381

Lessons and Activities

Chapter 1

Learning and Teaching Social Studies

Picture a little girl, Sarah, age 8. She is about to enter your third-grade class on the first day of school. You, the school, and the students will be a new experience for Sarah.

What does Sarah look like? Does she live in an urban, suburban, or rural area? Is her habitat a room, an apartment, a house, or a homeless shelter? Is English her first or second language? What type of family structure does she have—does it include one or more parents and other siblings? What knowledge does she bring with her? What are her dreams and fears? When she arrives at your classroom, will she be nourished, self-confident, and eager to learn? What will her day be like when she leaves the school at 3:00?

Sarah is Everychild. She represents the countless variables that effective teachers thoughtfully consider in providing nurturing and personalized learning experiences for millions of youngsters across our nation. She also embodies our aspirations for a better world and a society in which all children can reach their full potential. Within Everychild are the seeds of our nation's future.

One significant component of Everychild's increasingly complex needs intersects with the social studies curriculum. Everychild is a developing citizen who, we hope, someday will be a fellow voter and a partner in civic activities. She also may be an *elected official. If the social studies program is to help prepare children for roles such as these and others, it must provide ongoing opportunities to engage in social discourse and decision making. In the process, it must portray authentic events, people, and issues embedded in rich contextual frameworks. It also must supply Everychild with the models and analytical tools to help construct a fulfilling and contributing civic career.*

The Origins and Evolution of the Social Studies

What are the origins of the social studies? In the early history of our nation, the social studies curriculum drew heavily on the areas of history, geography, and civics. The term *social studies*, according to Saxe (1991, 1992), became the official designator for the curriculum in the late 19th and early 20th centuries. It came into use as an outgrowth of the writings of Sarah Bolton, Lady Jane Wilde, Heber Newton, and, later, Thomas Jesse Jones. Saxe (1991) noted: "From Newton and Jones we find that the initial use and sharpening of the term 'social studies' was directly tied to the utilization of social science data as a force in the improvement of human welfare" (p. 17).

Jones later served as a member of a group known as the Committee on the Social Studies. The committee, which comprised 21 members representing different social science disciplines and different levels of professional education, had been appointed by the National Education Association in 1912. Its charge was to make recommendations concerning the reorganization of the secondary curriculum.

The 1916 Report of the Committee on the Social Studies

The final report of the committee, issued in 1916, was called by Hertzberg (1981) "probably the most influential in the history of the social studies" (p. 2). One social studies educator, Engle (1976), credited the committee's report with setting the general direction of the field from that time forward.

The 1916 report defined the social studies as "those whose subject matter relates directly to the organization and development of human society, and to man as a member of social groups" (U.S. Bureau of Education, 1916, p. 9). It also laid out the broad goals for the social studies, the cultivation of the "good citizen," a theme we examine in detail in later chapters. In addition, the report sketched some guidelines for the curriculum and touched on a variety of other issues, including the preparation of teachers and text materials.

Although the report looked to the social sciences as the primary sources of enlightenment for the preparation of the good citizen, the high ideals the report embodied clearly required a broader base of subject matter. For example, it asserted, "The social studies should cultivate a sense of membership in the 'world community,' with all the sympathies and sense of justice that this involves among the different divisions of human society" (U.S. Bureau of Education, 1916, p. 9).

Legacy of the 1916 Report.   Among other things, the 1916 report reflected the diversity of disciplines that individuals on the committee represented—the dominant perspective being that of history—and the emergence of the behavioral sciences and the growth of professional associations. In addition, it represented the flowering of progressivism and the apprehension of a nation on the brink of a world war (Hertzberg, 1981). The report became the touchstone for conceptions of what the social studies curriculum should be for the next eight decades, transcending the dramatic shifts in the nation and the world during that period.

The report also gave impetus to the rise, in 1921, of the first professional organization devoted to the concerns of social studies teachers, the National Council for the Social Studies (NCSS). Sixteen years later, the NCSS would publish the first professional journal for social studies teachers: *Social Education*. More than a half-century later, in 1988, it would publish a second journal, devoted to the elementary grades: *Social Studies and the Young Learner.*

A major legacy of the 1916 report is a festering debate that continues to the present, concerning both the nature of the social studies and the subject's relationship to the social sciences. The first sentence of *Defining the Social Studies*, written in 1977, captures the flavor of contemporary debates and analyses: "The field of social studies is so caught up in ambiguity, inconsistency, and contradiction that it represents a complex educational enigma. It has also defied any final definition acceptable to all factions of the field" (Barr, Barth, & Shermis, 1977, p. 1). In exasperation, Barr and his colleagues concluded, "If the social studies is what the scholars in the field say it is, it is a schizophrenic bastard child" (p. 1).

The New Social Studies

During the 1950s, the period of the cold war, the Soviet Union ushered in the era of space exploration with its launching of *Sputnik*. It also initiated an intense and extensive reassessment of the American educational system. For the Soviets to have beaten the United States into space, conventional wisdom said, meant that something must be wrong with our schools and their curricula.

First, the science and mathematics programs came under intense scrutiny, followed by the foreign language curricula. In response, the federal government sponsored a wave of reforms aimed at improving the curricula of the schools. By the mid-1960s the social studies also were drawn under the umbrella of reform. From that point forward, through the early years of the 1970s, the social studies would witness an unprecedented period of innovation in both the development of curricular materials and related teacher education efforts.

The fruits of this period became known as **the new social studies.** The efforts at innovation were fueled primarily with funds from the federal government and private foundations. Ultimately, commercial publishers would underwrite the final stages of development and publication of some of the curricular products. Haas (1977), who was involved directly in the evolution of the new social studies, wrote, "If measured by sheer output of materials, the period 1964 to 1972 is unequaled in the history of social studies education in this country" (p. 61).

the new social studies

Driving the new social studies were more than 50 major projects (Fenton, 1967) and scores of minor ones touching every grade level (Haas, 1977). The projects were scattered throughout the nation in different centers. A firsthand observer of many of these projects and the director of a history project at Carnegie Mellon University, Fenton (1967, p. 4), wrote of them:

> They are organized in a variety of ways: one or two professors in a university run most of them; organizations of scholars such as the American Anthropological Association administer a few; others are run by school systems, groups of schools or universities, or independent non-profit corporations…. Some projects aim to turn out a single course for a single dicipline [sic], such as a course in tenth-grade geography; others are preparing units of material—anthropology, sociology, economics—which can fit into existing course structures; still others propose to develop entire curriculum sequences or to isolate the principles upon which curricula can be built.

Included in the new social studies were projects for the primary, intermediate, and middle grades, such as:

- Man: A Course of Study (MACOS)
- Social Science Laboratory Units
- The University of Georgia Geography Curriculum Project
- The University of Georgia Anthropology Curriculum Project
- The University of Minnesota Project Social Studies, K–12

Many of the projects were based on the seminal ideas in a slender volume, *The Process of Education*, written by the psychologist Jerome Bruner (1960). Particularly appealing to social studies educators were Bruner's ideas concerning the structure of the disciplines and discovery modes of learning. Bruner himself was extensively involved in *MACOS*, a middle-grades curriculum that integrated the disciplines of anthropology and biology to help children discover the similarities in and differences between humans and animals.

Legacy of the New Social Studies.   Despite the concerted efforts at curricular reform, the new social studies projects collectively failed to affect significantly the scope and sequence patterns of the social studies curriculum across the United States (Fancett & Hawke, 1982; Haas, 1977, 1986). By some accounts, the projects had no significant impact on teaching practices either (Shaver, Davis, & Hepburn, 1979; Superka, Hawke, & Morrissett, 1980).

How can we account for this? Lockwood (1985) suggested three basic reasons why, in his estimation, the new social studies had limited lasting effects: (a) Teachers perceived that adoption of the innovations would have required major changes in the scope and sequence of existing curricula and teaching practices, (b) the reading levels of the new social studies materials were too advanced, and (c) students lacked the intellectual capacities required to use the materials. Massialas (1992) argued that the new social studies lacked a research base and that projects failed to adequately address issues such as gender and ethnicity (see also Atwood, 1982; Fenton, 1991; Rossi, 1992).

There is evidence, however, that the new social studies did have some significant sporadic effects. For example, it gave rise to a larger role for the emerging social sciences. Similarly, although it failed to shake the dominance of the textbook as the primary instrument of instruction, it did stimulate the use of commercial and teacher-made supplementary materials. Further, it encouraged the use of media in teaching.

Although the new social studies did not loosen substantially the grip of teacher-centered approaches, it did open the door for a more active role for students and for greater consideration of their concerns in the curriculum. It also increased the use of instructional strategies that emphasized students' inquiry in the learning process, presaging later constructivist arguments for greater engagement of students in the learning process. The new social studies also helped establish the principle that affective concerns relating to significant beliefs, attitudes, and values should have a place in social studies classes.

Social Studies on the Edge of the 21st Century

As we approach the 21st century, several trends in elementary- and middle-grades social studies curriculum are prominent. They include integrating literature and social studies; emphasizing multicultural themes, ethics and values, and social issues; exploring issues in depth; and utilizing emerging technologies.

Teachers can use current technology to involve their students in problem-solving activities.

A dominant fundamental issue in the social studies remains how to best prepare citizens for a democratic society in an increasingly interdependent and culturally diverse world. Much of the discussion centers around which subject matter is of most worth and how to stimulate students to become active rather than passive participants in the construction of knowledge.

A lightning rod for the debate over what students should know and be able to do in the social studies is national standards (see Lewis, 1995). The standards movement was propelled by the **Goals 2000: Educate America Act,** passed by Congress in 1992. Among other provisions, the act established the following goal:

**Goals 2000:
Educate
America Act**

> By the year 2000, all students will leave grades 4, 8, and 12 having demonstrated competency over challenging subject matter including English, mathematics, science, foreign languages, civics and government, economics, arts, history, and geography, and every school in America will ensure that all students learn to use their minds well, so they may be prepared for responsible citizenship, further learning, and productive employment in our Nation's modern economy. *(The National Education Goals Report*, 1995, p. 11)

A number of professional organizations have established general guidelines for what all students should learn for all grade levels. For example, there now exist standards for history, civics and government, geography, and social studies, and those for economics are under development. In Chapter 3 and again in Chapter 13, we consider in more detail examples of these initiatives and the controversies surrounding them.

Alternative Definitions of the Social Studies

As noted, social studies educators have waged a vigorous debate over the nature of their field. From the time the term *social studies* came into popular use through the era of the new social studies and into the current decade, many have attempted, unsuccessfully, to set out a definition of the field that would embrace all of the disparate views. Consider the following examples:

> The social studies are the social sciences simplified for pedagogical purposes. (Wesley, 1950, p. 34)

> Social studies is the integrated study of the social sciences and humanities to promote civic competence. (National Council for the Social Studies [NCSS], 1993, p. 3)

> The social studies are concerned exclusively with the education of citizens. In a democracy, citizenship education consists of two related but somewhat disparate parts: the first socialization, the second countersocialization. (Engle & Ochoa, 1988, p. 13)

> The social studies is an integration of experience and knowledge concerning human relations for the purpose of citizenship education. (Barr et al., 1977, p. 69)

Social studies is a basic subject of the K–12 curriculum that (1) derives its goals from the nature of citizenship in a democratic society that is closely linked to other nations and peoples of the world; (2) draws its content primarily from history, the social sciences, and, in some respects, from the humanities and science; and (3) is taught in ways that reflect an awareness of the personal, social, and cultural experiences and developmental levels of learners. (Task Force on Scope and Sequence, 1984, p. 251)

Consider also one *fifth grader's* attempt to define the social studies:

Social studies is the hardest thing you could ever ask me to explain. I guess social studies is a class where you learn about different things that happen around the world, and do reports on stuff that happens around the world, or things like that. (Stodolsky, Salk, & Glaessner, 1991, p. 98)

None of these definitions or any others proposed have attracted a consensus. As Lybarger (1991) underscored, "One of the most remarkable aspects of the history of the social studies has been the ongoing debates over the nature, scope, and definition of the field" (p. 9).

A Working Definition of the Social Studies

As a point of reference, I use throughout the text a *working definition* of the social studies. It is consistent with the purposes of the social studies curriculum that are advocated later in the chapter.

The social studies are:

- selected information and modes of investigation from the social sciences,
- selected information from any area that relates directly to an understanding of individuals, groups, and societies, and
- applications of the selected information to citizenship education.

Social Studies and Citizenship Education

Many of the definitions that have been proposed over the years, including mine, point toward the historic linkage of the social studies to *citizenship education*. To function, even nominally, all societies must engage in some form of citizenship education. Those entrusted with the formal responsibilities for the maintenance, defense, and improvement of the society depend on some degree of citizen participation so that social, political, and economic institutions can operate.

What we now regard as social studies came to be seen as the subject that would teach students about our nation's history, traditions, achievements, and aspirations. It also was to prepare them for responsibly exercising their rights and duties as citizens. Today, as in the past, we expect the social studies curriculum to continue its historic mission of preparing young people for their roles as effective citizens.

The Context of Citizenship Education

Citizenship education in our society occurs in many forms, both outside and inside the schools. Institutions external to the school, including those of the mass media, increasingly have assumed a larger role in the process. For example, advertisements on billboards and book covers urge students to serve their country in the military, to use condoms to prevent social epidemics, and to protect the environment. Political action groups, representing every shade of the political spectrum and fueled by tax exemptions and contributions, now loom as a major force in both the political and educational process.

Citizenship education also takes place informally through the "hidden" curriculum: the policies, mores, activities, rules, norms, and models that the school provides. Within the classroom itself, civic education has several dimensions, as Oppenheim and Torney (1974) reminded us:

> Civic education does not merely consist in the transmission of a body of *knowledge*, . . . it aims at inculcating certain shared *attitudes* and values, such as a democratic outlook, political responsibility, the ideals of tolerance and social justice, respect for authority, and so on. . . . Indeed, the cognitive content of the curriculum is frequently used in order to highlight the underlying principles and ideology; thus, information about electoral systems could be utilized in order to bring out fundamental ideas about equality and majority rule. (p. 13)

Alternative Perspectives on Citizenship Education

Social studies educators generally agree that citizenship education should be the major focus of the social studies curriculum (Martorella, 1991). Beyond this general area of agreement, however, are disagreements regarding which specific purpose the curriculum should serve as a way to promote citizenship education. I characterize these different views as alternative perspectives on citizenship education.

A related debate continues over the characteristics of the ideal, or "good," citizen, who is the object of the social studies curriculum. In our discussions I use the term ***effective citizen*** to refer to this idealized type.

the effective citizen

Classifying Alternative Perspectives

Barr et al. (1977) analyzed and attempted to categorize the statements of purposes related to citizenship education that various social studies educators have advanced in the 20th century. From their investigation, the authors created three categories into which they grouped all approaches to citizenship education—social studies taught as (a) *transmission of the cultural heritage*, (b) *the social sciences*, and (c) *reflective inquiry*.

FIGURE 1.1   Alternative perspectives on citizenship education

Perspective *Social studies should be taught as*:	Description *Citizenship education should consist of*:
Transmission of the Cultural Heritage	Transmitting traditional knowledge and values as a framework for making decisions
Social Science	Mastering social science concepts, generalizations, and processes to build a knowledge base for later learning
Reflective Inquiry	Employing a process of thinking and learning in which knowledge is derived from what citizens need to know in order to make decisions and solve problems
Informed Social Criti- cism	Providing opportunities for an examination, critique, and revision of past traditions, existing social practices, and modes of problem solving
Personal Development	Developing a positive self-concept, and a strong sense of personal efficacy

Further analyses by Engle (1977) and Nelson and Michaelis (1980) suggested two additional categories of approaches—social studies taught as (d) *informed social criticism*, and (e) *personal development*. These major perspectives on citizenship education and their respective emphases are summarized briefly in Figure 1.1.

These five perspectives certainly do not exhaust all of the possible classifications. Furthermore, none of the alternative categories that have been outlined completely avoid overlap among the others. Often one category, when analyzed and discussed, appears to include all other categories of purposes. Teaching social studies as social criticism, for example, may at times include teaching for reflective inquiry.

Nevertheless, it may be helpful to clarify your own view by considering some of the emphases or dominant perspectives that each statement of purpose reflects. As you do this, you may wish to borrow elements of several categories to create a new composite category of your own.

The Enduring Goal of the Social Studies Curriculum: Reflective, Competent, and Concerned Citizens

Arguments over the purpose of the social studies frequently cannot be categorized easily into one of the five perspectives shown in Figure 1.1. For example, the NCSS (NCSS, 1993) has endorsed the following view: "The primary purpose

of social studies is to help young people develop the ability to make informed and reasoned decisions for the public good as citizens of a culturally diverse, democratic society in an interdependent world" (p. 3).

Similarly, my position does not match neatly with any one of the five perspectives, although it draws on several of them. My perspective borrows heavily from the tradition of *reflective inquiry* as developed in the works of Dewey (1933), Engle (1977), Hullfish and Smith (1961), Griffin (1992), and Hunt and Metcalf (1968).

It also includes an emphasis on learning to be an informed and responsible social critic of society, as described by Engle and Ochoa (1988). Additionally, the perspective reflects the influence of recent research in the field of cognitive psychology that addresses how individuals construct, integrate, retrieve, and apply knowledge.

The Nature of the Effective Citizen

The effective young citizens that such a perspective seeks to develop require a three-dimensional social studies program: one that emphasizes rationality, skillful behavior, and social consciousness. Further, such a program must cast citizen roles within the framework of a democratic society and its corresponding continuing needs for maintenance, nurturance, and renewal.

reflective, competent, and concerned citizens

I will characterize the young citizens who emerge from such a program as **reflective, competent, and concerned citizens.** I propose that reflection, competence, and concern, in some form, can be nurtured at all levels, from the primary through the intermediate and middle grades. Correspondingly, throughout the text, I argue that the basic purpose of the social studies curriculum across the grades is to develop reflective, competent, and concerned citizens.

Reflective individuals are critical thinkers who make decisions and solve problems on the basis of the best evidence available. *Competent* citizens possess a repertoire of skills to aid them in decision making and problem solving. *Concerned* citizens investigate their social world, address issues they identify as significant, exercise their rights, and carry out their responsibilities as members of a social community.

the head, the hand, and the heart

Social Studies as a Matter of the Head, the Hand, and the Heart.   I identify planning and curriculum that seek to develop the three dimensions of the reflective, competent, and concerned citizen by way of a simple metaphor: social studies as a matter of **the head, the hand, and the heart.** The head represents reflection; the hand, competencies (skills); and the heart, concern. The characteristics of the reflective, competent, and concerned citizen are summarized in Figure 1.2. In subsequent chapters I analyze in greater detail what each of these three dimensions of the effective citizen entails and how they may be developed through social studies instruction.

FIGURE 1.2   The reflective, competent, and concerned citizen

Social Studies as a Matter of the Head: Reflection

The *reflective* citizen has knowledge of a body of concepts, facts, and generalizations concerning the organization, understanding, and development of individuals, groups, and societies. Also the reflective citizen can engage in hypothesis formation and testing, problem solving, and decision making.

Social Studies as a Matter of the Hand: Competence

The *competent* citizen has a repertoire of skills. These include social, research and analysis, chronology, and spatial skills.

Social Studies as a Matter of the Heart: Concern

The *concerned* citizen has an awareness of his or her rights and responsibilities in a democracy, a sense of social consciousness, and a well-grounded framework for deciding what is right and what is wrong and for acting on decisions. Additionally the concerned citizen has learned how to identify and analyze issues and to suspend judgment concerning alternative beliefs, attitudes, values, customs, and cultures.

The Interrelationship of the Head, the Hand, and the Heart.   Thinking, skillful action, and feeling are intertwined. No one of the three dimensions operates in isolation. The head, the hand, and the heart are interrelated and work in concert. Reflective citizens are responsive to what their heart dictates and apply their store of knowledge and competencies to make a decision and act on it.

The relationship between head, hand, and heart often is not systematic or linear. William, a second grader watching the news on television, may learn that thousands of workers at an auto plant have just lost their jobs, causing a rise in unemployment. As a result, he asks his mother why the layoffs occurred and what will happen to the employees. After their discussion, his level of social consciousness and concern is aroused. He begins to understand the relationship between the canned goods he took to church for a Thanksgiving basket and the potential economic consequences of losing a job.

The sequence of economic analysis, however, just as easily might have begun more dramatically as a matter of the heart. Suppose, for example, that William's mother lost her job and the family was evicted because it was unable to pay the rent.

Social studies programs designed within the framework advocated in this text should offer students a balance of activities and subject matter for growth in the three areas of reflection, competence, and concern. The relative proportions of time paid to matters of the head or the hand or the heart may vary according to the level of the grade, the abilities and needs of the students, and the current needs of society. A teacher may decide, for example, that the hand should receive more weight in the social studies curriculum in the lower grades and less in later years. Some attention to all three dimensions across the grades, however, is necessary for a balanced social studies program.

The Exemplary Social Studies Teacher

the exemplary
social studies
teacher

What would a profile of an **exemplary social studies teacher** look like? What instructional strategies do exemplary teachers use? How do they engage students in meaningful learning?

One way to try to answer this question is to observe teachers recognized as exemplary and to note what they do. Brophy (1992) shared his observations from a detailed case study of one fifth-grade social studies teacher, who was given the pseudonym "Mrs. Lake." She organized the year's social studies curriculum around seven units, covering the period through the Civil War. Among her goals, Mrs. Lake wants students to enjoy school, to experience success, and to apply what they learn. Within the framework of United States history, she hopes her students will acquire knowledge of conditions in the past and how our country developed.

As you read excerpts of Brophy's rich account, focus on what you regard as Mrs. Lake's exemplary characteristics.

> She wants her students to enjoy school and feel successful there, and she also wants them to understand, appreciate, and be able to apply what they are learning. . . . Instead of a text, she uses her own lecturing and storytelling as the basic source of input to her students. . . .
>
> Mrs. Lake is a talented storyteller, and much of the initial information that students receive about historical events comes in the form of dramatic readings from historical literature (i.e., children's trade books, not texts). Much of the rest comes in the form of storytelling or explanations backed by photos, artifacts, or other props. . . .
>
> Mrs. Lake begins the year by engaging [students] in developing information about their own personal histories. She has them interview their parents or other family members and collect artifacts and source materials (birth certificates, newspaper or almanac information on what was happening in the world on the day they were born, mementos marking events in their lives). . . .
>
> A time line describing and illustrating some of the salient events in U.S. history extends across most of the front wall of the classroom, above the chalkboard. Mrs. Lake refers to this time line periodically, especially when beginning and ending units, to help students keep track of where the current topic fits within the big picture. Similarly, she refers to maps frequently to provide geographical orientation.
>
> In connection with her reading and storytelling, Mrs. Lake uses repetition, visual aids, and story mapping techniques to help students remember main themes. She emphasizes key ideas when telling stories and repeats them several times in review and follow-up activities. She posts key words (organized within "people," "places," and "events" columns) on a special social studies unit display as they are introduced, and they remain displayed throughout the rest of the unit. (pp. 147–149)

Effective social studies instruction engages students in answering intriguing questions.

As Brophy (1992) acknowledged, Mrs. Lake's teaching lacks some dimensions that would be desirable. For example, there is an absence of student engagement in the analysis of social issues. At the same time, her teaching clearly reveals many exemplary qualities for other teachers to emulate.

Characteristics of Exemplary Social Studies Teachers

In analyzing Mrs. Lake's teaching, Brophy cataloged a number of her exemplary qualities and capabilities. Building on his foundation and adding items, let us consider a broader set of characteristics that I have hypothesized and organized into two broad categories: planning characteristics and instructional characteristics.

Planning Characteristics

Exemplary social studies teachers:

1. Have clearly formulated goals, objectives, and purposes.
2. Have acquired a well-grounded knowledge base related to the social studies curriculum.
3. Select subject matter and activities that will interest and challenge students and intersect with meaningful aspects of their lives.
4. Emphasize the coverage of a small number of topics and key ideas in depth, rather than a superficial coverage of many.
5. Strike a balance in the curriculum among reflection, competence, and concern.
6. Identify a variety of instructional resources.

7. Incorporate authentic ways to assess what students have learned.

8. Provide adequate time for social studies instruction.

Instructional Characteristics

Exemplary social studies teachers:

1. Relate new knowledge to students' existing social knowledge structures.

2. Engage students in the analysis of important social issues, values, and ethical concerns.

3. Present students with intriguing questions, puzzles, and anomalies as a way to engage them in investigating social data.

4. Afford students frequent opportunities to engage actively in constructing and applying social knowledge.

5. Develop skills in the context of solving problems or answering questions.

6. Emphasize relationships among ideas, people, places, and events.

7. Provide frequent opportunities for students to work cooperatively in small groups, developing ideas and engaging in social interaction.

8. Encourage students' oral and written communications relating to social data.

This is just one list of exemplary qualities; others have offered related suggestions (e.g., Engle & Ochoa, 1988; NCSS, 1988; Torney-Purta, 1991). You may wish to add other characteristics.

Throughout the remainder of the text, I flesh out what each of these qualities represents and consider which are most important. The ultimate goal is to gain further insights into how teachers can create increasingly effective social studies programs to develop reflective, competent, and concerned young citizens.

Group Activities

1. Discuss your recollections of social studies when you were in the elementary and middle grades. Are they pleasant or unpleasant?

2. Refer to the issues of the last two years of the following professional journals: *The Social Studies, Social Education*, and *Social Studies and the Young Learner*. Read from each of two journals two articles that interest you. Be prepared to discuss the essence of the articles and the reasons they interested you.

3. Select five individuals for an interview. Ask them to answer this question: What are the characteristics of the good citizen? Summarize the similarities and differences in the answers. Then state your own answer in a sentence or two.

4. Consider the various perspectives on citizenship education discussed in the chapter. Formulate your own position. State the reasons for the position that you have taken.

5. How much time should be devoted to learning social studies in the primary grades? The intermediate grades? What is the rationale for the position you have taken?

6. Consider the list of characteristics of the exemplary social studies teacher. Would you add or delete any characteristics? Which do you consider to be the most important and why?

Individual Activities

1. After consulting the References, locate a copy or a description of a curriculum project for the primary, intermediate, or middle grades that was developed during the period of the "new social studies." Note which characteristics of the project you find especially appealing and which you regard as weaknesses.

2. Locate your state's guidelines for the teaching of social studies in the elementary and middle grades. Indicate which guidelines are specific and which are general.

3. Examine two social studies methods texts, one for the elementary grades and one for the middle grades. What does each state the purpose of the social studies curriculum should be? How does each define the social studies?

4. The appearance of the computer icon, either in the body of the text or in the activities sections, signals the inclusion of an optional computer activity. To prepare for the various computer-related activities in the chapters that follow, do the following:

(A) Obtain the use of a computer account with access to the Internet and a copy of software such as Netscape Navigator (see Chapter 11).

(B) To be sure you understand how to send messages over the Internet, select a partner and send him or her a brief e-mail message explaining the significance of the 1916 Report of the Committee on Social Studies.

References

Atwood, V. (1982). A historical perspective of social studies. *Journal of Thought, 17,* 7–11.

Barr, R. D., Barth, J. L., & Shermis, S. S. (1977). *Defining the social studies* (Bulletin 51). Washington, DC: National Council for the Social Studies.

Brophy, J. (1992). Fifth-grade U.S. history: How one teacher arranged to focus on key ideas in depth. *Theory and Research in Social Education, 20,* 141–155.

Bruner, J. (1960). *The process of education.* Cambridge, MA: Harvard University Press.

Dewey, J. (1933). *How we think.* Boston: D. C. Heath.

Engle, S. H. (1976). Exploring the meaning of the social studies. In P. H. Martorella (Ed.), *Social studies strategies: Theory into practice* (pp. 232–245). New York: Harper & Row.

Engle, S. H. (1977). Comments of Shirley H. Engle. In R. D. Barr, J. L. Barth, & S. S. Shermis (Eds.), *Defining the social studies* (Bulletin 51, pp. 103–105). Washington, DC: National Council for the Social Studies.

Engle, S. H., & Ochoa, A. S. (1988). *Education for democratic citizenship: Decision making in the social studies.* New York: Teachers College Press.

Fancett, V., & Hawke, S. (1982). Instructional practices in social studies. *The current state of social studies: A report of project SPAN.* Boulder, CO: Social Science Education Consortium.

Fenton, E. (1967). *The new social studies.* New York: Holt, Rinehart & Winston.

Fenton, E. (1991). Reflections on the "new social studies." *The Social Studies, 82,* 84–90.

Griffin, A. F. (1992). *A philosophical approach to the subject matter preparation of teachers of history.* Dubuque, IA: Kendall/Hunt.

Haas, J. D. (1977). *The era of the new social studies.* Boulder, CO: Social Science Education Consortium.

Haas, J. D. (1986). Is the social studies curriculum impervious to change? *The Social Studies, 77,* 61–65.

Hertzberg, H. (1981). *Social studies reform: 1880–1980.* Boulder, CO: Social Science Education Consortium.

Hullfish, H. G., & Smith, P. G. (1961). *Reflective thinking: The method of education.* New York: Dodd, Mead.

Hunt, M. P., & Metcalf, L. E. (1968). *Teaching high school social studies: Problems in reflective thinking and social understanding* (2nd ed.). New York: Harper & Row.

Lewis, A. C. (1995). An overview of the standards movement. *Phi Delta Kappan, 76,* 744–750.

Lockwood, A. L. (1985). A place for ethical reasoning in the social studies curriculum. *The Social Studies, 76,* 264–268.

Lybarger, M. B. (1991). The historiography of social studies: Retrospect, circumspect, and prospect. In J. P. Shaver (Ed.), *Handbook of research on social studies teaching and learning* (pp. 3–15). New York: Macmillan.

Martorella, P. H. (1991). Consensus building among social educators: A delphi study. *Theory and Research in Social Education, 19,* 83–94.

Massialas, B. G. (1992). The "new social studies"—Retrospect and prospect. *The Social Studies, 83,* 120–124.

National Council for the Social Studies (NCSS). (1988). *Social studies for early childhood and elementary school children preparing for the 21st century.* Washington, DC: Author.

National Council for the Social Studies (NCSS). (1993, January/February). *The Social Studies Professional.* Washington, DC: Author.

National Education Goals Report. (1995) Washington, DC: Government Printing Office.

Nelson, J. L., & Michaelis, J. V. (1980). *Secondary social studies.* Upper Saddle River, NJ: Prentice Hall.

Oppenheim, A. N., & Torney, J. (1974). *The measurement of children's civic attitudes in different nations.* New York: Halstead.

Rossi, J. A. (1992). Uniformity, diversity, and the "new social studies." *The Social Studies, 83,* 41–45.

Saxe, D. W. (1991). *Social studies in schools: A history of the early years.* Albany: State University of New York Press.

Saxe, D. W. (1992). Social studies foundations. *Review of Educational Research, 62,* 259–277.

Shaver, J. P., Davis, O. L., Jr., & Hepburn, S. W. (1979). The status of social studies education: Impressions from three NSF studies. *Social Education, 39,* 150–153.

Stodolsky, S. S., Salk, S., & Glaessner, B. (1991). Student views about learning math and social studies. *American Educational Research Journal*, 28, 89–116.

Superka, D. P., Hawke, S., & Morrissett, I. (1980). The current and future status of the social studies. *Social Education*, 40, 362–369.

Task Force on Scope and Sequence. (1984). In search of a scope and sequence for social studies. *Social Education*, 48, 249–262.

Torney-Purta, J. (1991). Schema theory and cognitive psychology: Implications for social studies. *Theory and Research in Social Education*, 19, 189–210.

U.S. Bureau of Education. (1916). *Report of the committee on social studies*. Washington, DC: Government Printing Office.

Wesley, E. B. (1950). *Teaching social studies in high schools* (3rd ed.). Boston: D. C. Heath.

Chapter

The Sources of Subject Matter and Instructional Resources for the Social Studies

A group of first graders is cutting out pictures of people from old magazines the teacher has provided. After they finish, the teacher will ask them to form sets of families from their collections. As needed, the teacher will offer additional pictures to ensure variety (e.g., age and gender considerations).

Eventually the children will have an opportunity to compare and discuss their sets of families and to consider what they have in common. In addition, they will be asked to try to identify other types of families. At some point they also will draw pictures of their own families.

As a concluding activity, the children and the teacher will construct a bulletin board representing all of the different types of families they have identified. When different new examples of families are encountered, they will be added to the bulletin board.

knowledge

*From reflective encounters with social data, such as in the activity just described, students construct **knowledge**. "In the social studies, what is presented by the teacher or in the textbook as public and agreed-upon knowledge or beliefs, is received by the student and given meaning in terms of his or her past experience and cognitive capabilities or structures" (Torney-Purta, 1991, p. 190). In this sense knowledge does not exist independent of learning; it arises from students' interactions with texts, images, other people, and the larger culture in which they reside.*

Knowledge Construction and Subject Matter

Knowledge is the fabric of social studies instruction. Woven into it are the facts, generalizations, skills, hypotheses, beliefs, attitudes, values, and theories that students and teachers construct in social studies programs. The threads from which the rich and intricate patterns are spun are concepts.

During knowledge construction, students activate both cognitive and affective processes. *Cognitive* processes refer generally to how individuals confront, encode, reflect on, transform, and store information. In turn, *affective* processes relate to the beliefs, attitudes, values, and ethical positions we bring to and derive from analyses. These also shape the meanings we extract from information.

Schemata and Prior Knowledge in Social Studies Instruction

schemata

Our knowledge is organized into structures known as **schemata.** The term has been defined as a mental structure that represents a set of related information (Howard, 1987). Schemata provide the basis for comprehending, remembering, and learning information. Schema theory posits that the form and content of all new knowledge is in some way shaped by our **prior knowledge** (existing knowledge).

prior knowledge

Our individual collections of schemata comprise the store of prior knowledge we bring to each new knowledge acquisition task. Students, for example, bring their map schemata to the study of spatial issues. They have certain expectations concerning the kinds of information a map contains and the types of questions a map can answer.

Schemata as elements of our prior knowledge are activated when our experiences elicit them. Perkins (1986) cited the example of how the date 1492 can serve as an important cognitive peg for analysis of parallel historical events. He suggested that such key dates in American history provide a structure for placing intermediate events. In this way dates can be not merely facts but also tools for collecting and remembering information.

When our prior knowledge conflicts with new data, restructuring of schemata may occur. New schemata arise through comparisons with prior ones and through modifications that reflect our current experiences. For example, a little boy may acquire some new information relating to Indians who lived in caves. From this encounter, he then shapes a revised schema that accommodates earlier information about different Indian habitats. On the other hand, firmly embedded prior knowledge may be resistant to transformation and require skillful challenging by a teacher (Marzano et al., 1988).

The process of knowledge acquisition also transcends the disciplinary boundaries established by social scientists and other scholars. In solving a problem, a student is less likely to be concerned whether the relevant data are drawn, let us say, from the discipline of history than whether they contribute to a solution, whatever the source. Further, disciplines themselves are in a constant state of flux, with shifting parameters.

Selecting Social Studies Subject Matter

Hunt and Metcalf (1968) argued: "Content assumes an emergent character. From the standpoint of the learner, it comes into existence as it is needed, it does not have a life independent of his own" (pp. 281–282). In identifying subject matter for the social studies curriculum, teachers must search for information that has the greatest potential for achieving their purposes and goals. The subject matter they select should enable students to construct knowledge that will be useful in their current and future roles as citizens. It should be information of real worth for successful functioning in our society.

The subject matter that fuels functional knowledge must be drawn from a number of sources, including **the social sciences,** other disciplines, and interdisciplinary areas. It also must embrace the school and the community. Together these resources constitute a vast reservoir of information for the social studies curriculum.

the social
sciences

The Social Studies and the Social Sciences

The academic disciplines of the social sciences are the touchstones of the social studies (Gross & Dynneson, 1991). Most social studies educators would concede that the field of social studies gains a significant portion of its identity from the disciplines of the social sciences: history, political science, geography, economics, sociology, anthropology, and psychology (see Figure 2.1). We consider history, which arguably may be regarded as a discipline from either the humanities or the social sciences or both, as one of the social sciences throughout our discussion. Among all of the social sciences, history and geography particularly have nourished the social studies curriculum throughout its history.

The *methods of inquiry* used in the social sciences, such as the formulation and testing of hypotheses, also are important sources of social studies subject matter. To function effectively in their daily lives, citizens often have need of the

FIGURE 2.1

Contributions of the social sciences to the social studies curriculum

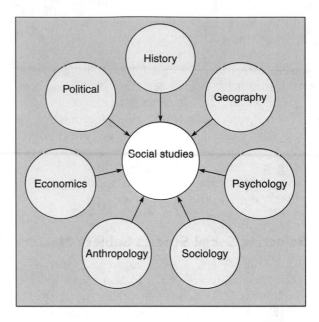

same skills as social scientists. For example, citizens frequently are called on to locate data or to verify information.

The social sciences share many commonalities—their use of the scientific method, focus on understanding and explaining human behavior, and systematic collection and application of data. Their methods are both quantitative and qualitative. Social scientists measure phenomena and draw inferences from observations. They also share an interest in predicting patterns of behavior, a concern for verification of information, and a desire for objectivity. Each social science discipline, however, claims special insights and characteristics that provide its distinct identification.

In the sections that follow, the nature and scope of each of the social sciences is outlined. To examine the social science disciplines in more depth, you may wish to consult a comprehensive reference source such as the *International Encyclopedia of the Social Sciences* (17 vols.) (New York: Macmillan, 1968). Also, dictionaries such as the *Dictionary of Human Geography* identify and define the major concepts for each of the social science disciplines.

Geography

Geographers sometimes organize their discipline in terms of five central themes: location, place, relationships within place, movement, and region. *Location* is viewed as describing the positions of people and places on the earth's surface in either absolute or relative terms. *Place* is seen as detailing the human or physical characteristics of places on the earth. *Relationships within places* refers to cultural and physical relationships of human settlements. The theme of *movement* describes relationships between and among places. *Regions* are viewed in terms of the ways areas may be identified, such as governmental units, language, religious or ethnic groups, and landform characteristics.

The concept of *place* is central to the discipline of geography. Geographers are concerned with the location and character of places on the earth's surface and the factors that have shaped these places. They have an abiding interest in how the places affect the lives of those who locate there. Foremost is their interest in why people and things are located in particular places. They attempt to relate these places to events and to explain how goods, events, and people pass from place to place.

Geographers attempt to describe accurately, from many perspectives, locations on the earth's surface. They examine, for example, what is below ground in the form of rocks and mineral deposits and what is above ground in the form of climate.

Maps and globes of all types are geographers' basic tools, as are aerial photos and remote sensing images. They also use census counts and data from surveys and fieldwork.

In addition to the ones mentioned, major concepts addressed by geographers include *population distribution, spatial interaction, environment,* and *boundaries.*

History

History includes chronicles, interpretations, syntheses, explanations, and cause-effect relationships. In essence, history is always a selective representation of reality. It is one or more individuals' chronicles or recollections of what occurred from his or her frame of reference. Such chronicles may be oral, visual, and written, and they may relate to oneself, others, events, nations, social groups, and the like. As chroniclers, historians are concerned with constructing a coherent, accurate, and representative narrative of phenomena over time.

Although absolute objectivity—the search for truth regardless of personal preferences or objectives—is unachievable, some historians, in the tradition of Otto von Ranke, regard it as their methodological goal. Others, in the spirit of James Harvey Robinson and Carl Becker, consider such a goal to be "history without an objective" and urge historians to state explicitly the frames of reference they bring to their analyses.

Because it is impossible to record everything about any event or individual, and because all records are colored to some extent by our attitudes and frame of reference, history is also a selective *interpretation* of what occurred. Often the task of recording and interpreting an event also involves investigating and reconciling alternative accounts and incorporating documents into a pattern of verified evidence. Hence history is also a synthesis and explanation of many facts concerning the past.

Historians search for the *causes* of events, as well as the *effects*. Where the relationships between the two are ambiguous, historians construct hypotheses about causal relationships. Over time, as new evidence is uncovered, hypotheses are tested and, as a result, are supported or refuted.

In addition to the ones mentioned, major concepts addressed by historians include *change, the past, nationalism,* and *conflict.*

Economics

Economics is concerned with relationships among people that are formed to satisfy material needs. More specifically, the discipline deals with production, consumption, and exchange. The object of these three activities is some set of goods (e.g., cars) or services (e.g., lawn cutting).

Because countries often differ in their systems for organizing production, consumption, and exchange, economists also compare their applications. In addition, they examine comparatively specific economic institutions within a nation, such as banks and small businesses. Similarly, they examine the international patterns of exchange or currencies and how these affect economic behavior among countries.

Within the framework of production, consumption, and exchange, economists study, document, and attempt to predict patterns of human behavior. Other issues that they consider include job specialization, incentives, markets and prices, productivity, and benefits to be derived in relation to the costs incurred. Also examined is the surplus or scarcity of goods and services in relationship to people's needs and wants.

Because these issues arise at all levels and on all scales—an international conglomerate (macro-level) or a local lawn-cutter (micro-level)—economists often examine them according to the scope of their impact. They also consider patterns of interdependence among nations and the relative levels of their imports and exports.

In addition to the ones mentioned, major concepts addressed by economists include *cost, division of labor, standard of living,* and *balance of payments.*

Political Science

The discipline of political science has its roots in philosophy and history. Works such as Plato's *Republic* and Aristotle's *Politics,* for example, are used today in college classes in both philosophy and political science. Broadly speaking, political science is concerned with an analysis of power and the processes by which individuals and groups control and manage one another. Power may be applied at the governmental level through the ballot box and political parties, but it also is exercised in many social settings. Power in some form is exercised by all individuals throughout society.

Above all, political science is concerned with the organization and governance of nations and other social units. Political scientists are interested, for example, in political interaction among institutions and the competing demands of various groups in our society as they affect governmental institutions. They analyze how different constituencies or interest groups influence and shape public policy. Such analyses include polls of public opinion and investigations of the impact of the mass media.

At the international level, political scientists are concerned with the relationships among nations, including the ways cooperation and ties develop and the ways conflicts emerge and are resolved. Political scientists trace patterns of interdependence and compare and contrast political systems. They also examine national and international legal systems and agreements between nations.

In addition to the ones mentioned, major concepts addressed by political scientists include *rules*, *citizenship*, *justice*, and *political systems*.

Anthropology

Closely aligned with the discipline of sociology is anthropology. Anthropologists, speaking broadly, say their discipline is the study of humankind. They are interested in both the biological and the environmental determinants of human behavior. Because its scope is far-ranging and the discipline has a number of major subdivisions, anthropology is perhaps the most difficult subject to define.

Culture is a central concept in anthropology, much like the concept of *place* in geography. It refers to the entire way of life of a society and the shared ideas and language. Culture is unique to humans, and it is learned rather than inherited. The totality of how individuals use their genetic inheritance to adapt to and shape their environment makes up the major framework of what most anthropologists consider as culture.

Cultural anthropologists are interested in how cultures change over time and how they are modified through interaction with other cultures. These scholars study cultural or subcultural groups to ascertain common patterns of behavior. They live among the groups, functioning as participant observers (recording observational data). Another group of anthropologists, *archaeologists*, unearth the past through excavations of artifacts from past generations and carbon-dating techniques. *Physical anthropologists* share many interests with natural scientists such as biologists, including the study of nonhuman primates and animal fossils.

In addition to the ones mentioned, major concepts addressed by anthropologists include *enculturation*, *cultural diffusion*, *cultural change*, and *traditions*.

Sociology

Sociology is the study of human interactions within groups. Sociologists study people in social settings, sometimes called *social systems*. They exercise wide latitude in their fields of investigation. For example, within various community settings, they examine behavior in such basic social units as the family, ethnic groupings, social classes, organizations, and clubs.

Sociologists are interested in how the basic types of institutions (e.g., social, religious, economic, political, legal) affect our daily lives. Other areas that sociologists examine include how the actions of individuals in groups serve to preserve or change social systems, such as worker behavior in plants or teacher activities in schools.

Sociologists attempt to abstract patterns from cumulative individual studies. From the study of cases within specific social systems, such as the various families within a small community, sociologists try to derive general principles that can be applied to all similar groups.

Because the scope of sociology includes some analysis of behavior in every major institution within society, it often overlaps with the other social sciences. For example, the work of a sociologist studying the political behavior of various groups during a national election and that of a political scientist analyzing voting patterns may intersect.

In addition to the ones mentioned, major concepts addressed by sociologists include *norms*, *status*, *socialization*, and *roles*.

Psychology

A discipline with many subdivisions, psychology focuses on understanding individual mental processes and behaviors. Modern psychology derives from earlier religious and philosophical studies into the nature of humans and the reasons for their behavior. The question of whether an individual has a free will, for example, merely was shifted into a scientific arena as psychology developed.

The boundaries of psychology are often difficult to determine because its investigations often spill over into the areas of biology, medicine, and physics, as well as into the other social sciences. Psychologists study animal as well as human behavior. Like anthropologists, they are interested in both the genetic and the learned aspects of behavior. The major branches of the discipline concentrate on investigating how learning occurs, which psychologists regard as a major determinant of human behavior.

Psychology has both an applied and an experimental side. Some psychologists, such as counseling psychologists, apply knowledge directly to the solution of human problems in clinical settings similar to a doctor-patient relationship. Other psychologists function in laboratory environments, conducting controlled experiments that may have no short-term applications to human behavior.

In addition to the ones mentioned, major concepts addressed by psychologists include *values*, *self*, *motivation*, and *learning*.

Figure 2.2 presents how a K–6 social studies curriculum can incorporate themes from each of the social science disciplines. In the example given, anthropology and sociology, which are closely related disciplines, are combined.

| FIGURE 2.2 | A K–6 social studies curriculum that incorporates themes from social science disciplines |

SCOPE AND SEQUENCE	Kindergarten	Grade 1	Grade 2
Geography	Make body map. Learn left, right, up, and down.	Make body maps and simple maps of classroom.	Define *map*. Draw own route to school.
History	Study favorite holidays, how places change, sequence of events from past to present.	Study own past. How places and people change with time.	Recall facts verbally from the past, and classify them as pleasant or unpleasant.
Economics	Learn that people work and that people need special skills to do some kinds of work.	Study work of family members. Learn how people get what they need by working.	Make lists of ways students spend money. Make economic decisions.
Political Science	Begin citizenship training. Learn sources of rules and norms.	Study sources of rules and norms. Gain citizenship training through study of national symbols.	Study persons in authority and decisions they make.
Anthropology— Sociology	Learn about the family as a group and the differing norms and preferences of families. Study the grouping of people through similarities, differences.	Study family and functions, how norms are transmitted, and how people change. Group people by their cultural traits.	Study the concepts of *behavior, communication, decision making,* and *ways of learning.*
Psychology	Explore own perceptions of self and others. Explore own feelings.	Explore own and others' perceptions, feelings, and attitudes.	Study reasons for behavior. Tell about feelings of their own or others.

FIGURE 2.2   *(Continued)*

Grade 3	Grade 4	Grade 5	Grade 6
Explore concepts and uses of maps and globes, geography of the United States, landforms, land use in cities.	Study environments, climate types, landforms; locales in four countries.	Study North American geographic regions, waterways, and climate.	Study geography, climate, waterways of China, Nigeria, Brazil, the United Kingdom, plus an overview of the continents.
Study the concept of *history*, the history of cities, and the concept of *time lines*.	Survey the historical background of four culture groups in relation to four countries.	Study a broad, chronological overview of United States history and the history of culture groups within the United States.	Investigate the history of China, Nigeria, Brazil, and the United Kingdom.
Learn how people obtain what they need in different times and places. Learn about goods and services and economic decisions.	Learn how people in four cultures fill their needs, use resources, and make choices at minimum cost.	Study the natural resources and environments of North America and learn about its technology and cultures. Study the workings of government and social welfare.	Study the basic concept of *economy*. Distinguish developed and underdeveloped economies.
Study the political divisions of nation, state, and city. Learn members of state and city government.	Survey forms of government in three cultures. Learn about form of government in Russia and its effects on Russian life.	Survey North American nations. Study the structure of United States government, meanings of democracy, and the struggle for equal rights.	Study a group decision-making model. Learn about majority and plurality rule. Survey government of four nations.
Investigate how people live together in families, communities, and national groups. Study the concept of interdependence.	Learn the characteristics of culture. Explore the concepts of *fairness, power, norms,* and *status.*	Study the elements of culture and the phenomenon of cultural pluralism in the United States. Study communication and decision-making models.	Study in more detail the concept of *culture*. Examine cultural clashes and culture contact. Study concept of *communication*.
Learn about cooperation, competition, conflict, and people's reasons for past actions.	Study the relationship between behavior and learning; copying, reward and punishment, trial and error.	Study the principles of learning through cultural and historical examples.	Examine beliefs about foreign peoples and cultures. Examine sources of beliefs.

Source: From *Looking at Me: Teacher's Manual* (pp. 15–16) by C. Cherryholmes, G. Manson, and P. H. Martorella, 1979, New York: McGraw-Hill. Copyright 1979 by McGraw-Hill. Adapted by permission.

Other Sources of Subject Matter for the Social Studies

Besides the findings and methods of inquiry of the social sciences, the social studies curriculum has drawn and will continue to draw on many other areas for data. The social studies are concerned with the application of social knowledge to citizenship roles. Many sources of information beyond the social sciences can aid in this task.

The arts and sciences, the humanities, the law, popular culture and music, data from students' and teachers' daily lives, the social life within the school and community, and the mass media are but a sample of the possible sources of subject matter that are outside the framework of the social sciences but that affect the human condition (see Figure 2.3). Subject matter within these areas that relates to the organization, understanding, and development of individuals, groups, and societies has considerable relevancy for the social studies curriculum.

Interdisciplinary Studies

In teaching social studies, we may draw on primarily the subject matter of a particular social science discipline, such as when we look to history for an

FIGURE 2.3

Other sources of the social studies curriculum

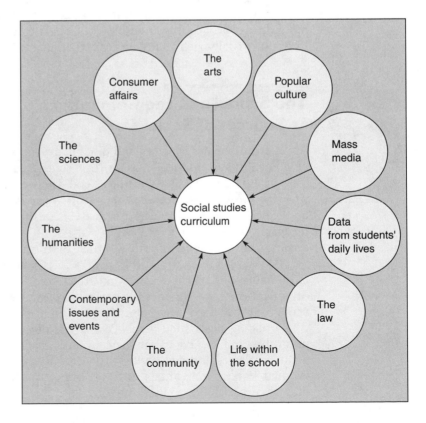

account of the first Thanksgiving. On other occasions we may wish to use an **interdisciplinary** approach, in which several of the social sciences are tapped to explain a topic or to examine an issue. This would be the case, for example, when we used the combined insights of economists, sociologists, psychologists, anthropologists, and geographers to help explain why some areas of the United States are growing more rapidly than others.

Crafting Interdisciplinary Lessons and Activities.   Although the traditional social science disciplines are important structured sources of systematically analyzed data for students' knowledge construction, often the insightful and creative contributions of scholars do not fit neatly into any existing discipline. Many areas of study and many activities can be enriched through reference to subject matter drawn from several disciplines (see Sunal & Hatcher, 1986).

As an example, investigation of urgent national and international problems, which Engle and Ochoa (1988) advocated as a curricular emphasis, typically calls for interdisciplinary subject matter. Addressing such issues as poverty, the homeless, the destruction of the ozone layer, and the imbalance of resources and wealth among nations of the world also often requires the perspectives of many disciplines.

More basically, individual social studies activities often can be enriched by combining the dimensions of several disciplines. Consider the activity in Figure 2.4 for primary-level children. It incorporates data from the arts, anthropology, architecture, geography, environmental science, and literature to engage children in a contextually rich multicultural experience.

The School and the Community as Sources of Social Data

Apart from the use of texts and disciplinary perspectives, students also need to be guided in systematically using their schools and communities as laboratories for social data (Gillis, 1991). To this end, they require assignments and activities that encourage them to view data from their daily life experiences as relevant and legitimate subject matter for analysis in the classroom. For example, a unit on crime in America might begin with students collecting objective data concerning the occurrence of crime in their own neighborhoods or communities.

The wealth of material that generally is available within every community is probably one of the least tapped resources for social studies teaching. Local organizations and businesses, for example, often cooperate with teachers in arranging field trips, guest speakers, information, and assistance.

Public agencies such as police and fire departments sometimes have special programs and speakers that they provide to schools. Other sources of speakers include colleges and universities, the Chamber of Commerce, and the League of Women Voters. Individuals in the community, likewise, generally are eager to offer their assistance to local schools.

FIGURE 2.4   Sample lesson plan

Sample Lesson Plan

Background

Though written fifteen years ago, the story of Alice Yazzie is real and not unlike that of many children in the more remote parts of the Navajo Reservation. This book is highly recommended by Indian educators and the comments by Carl Gorman in the back of the book are very helpful. The teacher can find a multitude of ways to teach about Indian children and culture in this book.

Objectives

Knowledge (Content)

Students will:

1. Recognize that Alice lives in two cultures.
2. List some ways of the Navajo that make them unique.
3. Identify the ways that Alice is learning about her Navajo culture and the Anglo culture.

Skills

Students will:

1. Listen critically to the story.
2. Compare Navajo culture with Anglo culture.

Values

Students will:

1. Recognize that Alice's Navajo world is beautiful to her.
2. Appreciate the importance of maintaining old traditions and Indian cultures.

Activities

1. In preparation for the story, have pictures of the desert and the Navajo Reservation. Such things as a model of a hogan, a small Navajo rug (or pictures), a piece of Navajo pottery, some Navajo jewelry, and pictures of examples of traditional Navajo dress will add to children's understanding.

2. Be prepared to discuss strip mining and the Four Corners power plant as well as terms used in the book, such as White Shell Woman and Blue Corn Woman. Hogan is pronounced HO'gahn. Read the book thoroughly to identify those terms or ideas about which you need to be knowledgeable.

3. Because there is so much to discuss in this book, consider reading it slowly as a series of poems as the class begins to learn more about Indian children. As you read the book, ask children to develop a classroom list of Navajo ways. For example, caring for sheep (including lambs in cold weather).

4. Begin to develop the idea of two cultures living in harmony and how Alice is learning about each culture. This should be a developing discussion, with each poem giving new examples. In multicultural classrooms, this should be a powerful and personal experience for many of the children.

Evaluation

Ask children to make pictures of Alice's world. Then have children categorize the pictures into two divisions—Alice's Navajo world and Alice's larger world (do not call this the *white* world or the *American* world). Students should be able to give reasons why it is important for Alice to learn about both worlds.

Extensions

1. If possible, develop pen pals with children on the Navajo Reservation.
2. Visit a local Indian center (visitors are usually very welcome).
3. Some museums in urban areas have extensive exhibits of traditional Navajo culture.
4. Invite a Native Storyteller or Indian parent or elder to visit your class.
5. Keep a journal by months, highlighting significant events in classroom life or in the life of each child individually. For older children, a personal journal could lead to discovery and reflection about their own unique cultural backgrounds and the traditions they keep.

Materials and Resources

Maher, R. (1977). *Alice Yazzie's Year*. New York, NY: Coward, McCann & Geoghegan.

Osinski, A. (1987). *The Navajo.* Chicago, IL: Childrens Press.

Pictures, films, and books about Navajo life. A map which shows the location of the reservation would be helpful.

Source: From "Native Americans: The Next 500 Years" by K. D. Harvey, 1993, *Social Studies and the Young Learner, 5*, pp. 2–3. ©National Council for the Social Studies. Used with permission.

Using Community Resource Persons Effectively

Typical uses of community resource persons include having individuals from different career areas report on what they do. This includes having persons work with students as mentors (see Chapter 12). It may include drawing on community members who have specialized advice concerning selected topics as well.

The South Carolina Department of Education (1987) has prepared a useful set of general guidelines for using resource speakers. The agency's suggestions appear in Figure 2.5.

A number of practical suggestions for integrating resource speakers into the regular social studies curriculum are available (Monti, 1988). Lamm (1989) pre-

---

FIGURE 2.5   Guide for using resource speakers

Locating Resources

Community/school contacts may be made through:

> Partnership coordinator in the school district
> Businesses (domestic or foreign owned)
> Local Chamber of Commerce
> College or university
> Technical education center
> Parent interest survey
> Identification of students for peer teaching
> Local speakers bureau
> School volunteer coordinator
> Clubs
> Museums

Contacting Community Resources

How?

> Personal contact
> Phone call
> Written request stating exact need
> Combination of the above

Through whom?

> Partnership coordinator in the school district
> Public relations or community relations executive (business)
> Survey information (parents)
> Local Chamber of Commerce

Preparing Students

Please remember: The purpose is to enrich and enhance, not to teach the unit!

Let the students help with preparations whenever possible. A feeling of responsibility helps ensure interest.

Students will profit from understanding of some kind of expected measurable results. They should know what will be expected from them prior to the visit. The results may take the form of one or more of the following:

> Quiz
> Puzzle or "Treasure Hunt"
> Identification list
> Report or summary
> Problem solving
> Model or project
> Interview results
> Letter

Secure materials and biographical information from the speaker in advance. These materials may include:

> Posters or brochures
> Background of speaker
> History of the company
> Photographs
> Audiovisual aids to be shown in advance

Source: From *Guide for Using Guest Speakers and Field Trips* (pp. 8–9) by South Carolina Department of Education, 1987, Columbia: South Carolina Department of Education. Copyright 1987 by South Carolina Department of Education.

Within every community are rich resources that can be tapped for social studies instruction.

pared her class for a speaker's visit by involving it in a related activity prior to the speaker's arrival. The speaker was a children's services worker from a local social service agency who was to serve the class as a resource on the problem of child abuse.

The day before the speaker arrived, the teacher gave each member of the class a card that contained one piece of information concerning a case of an abused child. Students were asked to seek out and form a group with other class members who had related information on the same child. Once each group was formed, students were to discuss what they believed would be an appropriate remedy to the case of abuse.

The following day the speaker arrived. She spent the session comparing the group's recommendations with what the services bureau typically would do in cases similar to the ones the students considered. A follow-up discussion brought out the key issues involved in child abuse cases and detailed the scope of the problem nationally and locally.

Fieldwork in the Community

In addition to bringing the community to the school to enrich lessons, students can be taken into the field to observe or to collect data. Armstrong and Savage (1976) observed that the community can function as a laboratory for students that generates a "higher degree of personal commitment and enthusiasm for social studies than can be anticipated when books, films, and other stimulators of reality are used" (p. 164). Some examples of community sites for field visits are:

Hospitals	Television studios
Observatories	Waterfronts
Historic sites	Military bases
Farms	Archeological excavations
Museums	Post offices
Construction sites	Firestations
Factories	Newspapers

Social scientists refer to the process of gathering information on-site directly, rather than secondhand through texts and other such materials, as *fieldwork*. Fieldwork often is used to collect data, to generate or test hypotheses in problem solving, and to provide clear examples of concepts.

A trip to the field does not of itself imply fieldwork or even a meaningful activity. During fieldwork, students act on what they observe or experience by relating their experiences in the field to other information they have studied or are studying and then reflecting on the connections. Fieldwork should be a pleasant change-of-pace activity for students, not merely a diversion. It is important that a trip to the field be an integral part of the school's instructional program.

Often it may be appropriate to have individual students or small groups working in the field, either during or after school hours. When an entire class is to be engaged in fieldwork during normal school hours, a great deal of teacher planning is involved to ensure a successful and productive experience. (See also *electronic field trips* in Chapter 11.)

The planning process may be viewed in three stages—before the trip, during the trip, and following the trip—as the following guidelines suggest.

Before the Trip

1. Establish clear and specific objectives for the trip. Plan to share these with the students either before or after the trip, as appropriate to your instructional strategy.

2. View the trip as a means, rather than as an end. Consider such issues as how time will be used and how variety in experiences will be provided.

3. Familiarize yourself with the major features of the site you will visit. Identify those features of the visit that will interest students and reflect *action* (people doing things).

4. Make a list of those features of the site you plan to discuss and emphasize during the trip. Then make notes on the types of comments and questions you plan to raise concerning them.

5. If possible, obtain pictures, written information, slides, and the like to introduce the site to be visited. In preparing for the visit, focus on special features you wish students to notice.

6. If appropriate, provide students with a sheet of points to consider and data to collect during the visit. If students are to engage in an activity, be sure to indicate what they are expected to do and not to do.

7. Develop a checklist of all procedural, administrative details that need to be arranged, such as confirmation of visitation date, bus plans, parental permissions, provisions for meals or snacks (if any), rest room facilities, safety precautions (if necessary), and special student dress (if needed).

8. Organize a simple file system for collecting all forms or funds required from students and parents.

During the Trip

9. Focus students' attention on those features of the trip that are most important. Have them observe and record, where appropriate, answers to such questions as:

    What things did I see?

    What people did I see, and what were they doing?

    How did _____ get done? Which people were involved? What materials were used?

10. Where possible, engage students in some activity during the visit. Where this is not possible, raise related questions, as well as provide relevant information.

11. Take pictures or slides or make a videotape to use in discussing important aspects of the trip during the follow-up.

12. Make brief notes on what seemed to interest and bore students and on the more important questions that were asked. Note those points you would like to call attention to during the follow-up discussion.

Following the Trip

13. Ask students to offer their open-ended impressions of what they learned from the trip and what they enjoyed most about it and why.

14. Review your notes from the trip and discuss important points, referring to the data students collected.

15. Review (or identify) the objectives for the trip and relate the experiences to previous learning.

16. Engage the students in additional related follow-up activities.

17. While the procedural and substantive features of the trip are still fresh in your mind, construct a file card of notes, similar to the one shown in Figure 2.6, for future reference.

FIGURE 2.6	Sample field trip data sheet

Field Trip Data Sheet

Theme or Objectives of Trip:	How a modern factory works; assembly line procedure; demonstration of computer components
Place:	Widgit Computer Works
Address:	1000 Futura Boulevard Silicon Valley, CA 10000
Telephone Number:	100/999-1000
Contact Person:	Steve Jobs
Grade Levels for Which Trip Is Appropriate	4–8
Summary of Main Features of Trip and General Comments:	Students are shown a videotape of all the plant's operations (20 minutes). Tour of all facilities covers the parts that are used in constructing microcomputers, as well as the assembly operations. Students are allowed to ask all workers questions during the tour. At the end of the tour students are allowed to work at assembled microcomputers for as long as they wish. Tour itself, without any questions, probably takes an hour. The company provided snacks for the students.
Overall Rating of Trip:	One of the best we have ever taken!
Suggestions for Future Visits by Other Classes:	It would be helpful to students to have a general discussion before the trip concerning their perceptions and stereotypes of factories.

Collecting Oral Histories

oral history

A data collection project that lends itself well to individual and small-group fieldwork is recording oral histories (Mehaffy, 1984; Mehaffy, Sitton, & Davis, 1979). An **oral history** may be defined as any firsthand account of an event. Although the emphasis in oral histories is on the spoken word, they may include both audio and video data.

As fieldwork, recording oral histories provides students with a sense of personal engagement in a stream of events (Totten, 1989). The activity also helps tie specific events and the larger sweep of history to a real person who was affected by them (Mehaffy, 1984). Further, when the narrator is a local person, the history may help tie the local community into the national history being examined in the classroom.

Procedures for Collecting Oral Histories.   Numerous collections of rich oral histories already exist across the United States, covering a wide array of topics and individuals (see Totten, 1989; Zimmerman, 1981). One of the more extensive collections can be found at the John F. Kennedy Library at the University of Massachusetts in Boston. The Southern Oral History Program at the University of North Carolina at Chapel Hill is an example of a more limited collection. In fieldwork, however, the emphasis is on students collecting their own data through actually *recording* oral histories.

Foci for oral histories include events, issues, recollections of individuals, periods, places, and biographies. Each focus requires different types of questions to bring out relevant data. Zimmerman (1981), for example, recommended detailed questioning procedures for collecting oral biographies that included items such as:

- What have been the major accomplishments in your life?
- What have been the biggest problems, mistakes, or adversities in your life?

For a class project to determine why people came to America, Taba and Elkins (1950) gave students with ethnically diverse backgrounds a basic set of questions to use in interviewing their relatives. The set could be adapted easily for application to a variety of oral history projects. The students were to investigate:

1. Who came and from what country.
2. Why they came.
3. Where they went.
4. What worries they had.
5. What they found here.
6. What kinds of work they found.
7. What adjustments they had to make.

Totten (1989) suggested that a teacher introduce students to the procedures involved in recording oral histories by having them observe the teacher conduct one in class. He also recommended that prior to the recording, students be involved in developing the set of questions to be asked.

Conducting Surveys and Interviews

Closely related to oral histories are *surveys* and *interviews*. These techniques allow students to transform the school and community into a laboratory for gathering social data. Surveys and interviews can help answer such questions as What do the third-grade students in our school think about the new social studies textbooks? and How do people in my neighborhood feel about the idea of raising taxes to build a new public swimming pool? In the case of many questions, the only conclusive way to obtain an answer is to conduct surveys and interviews.

Even in the early grades, students can begin to record oral histories and to interview individuals who play key roles in the community.

Figure 2.7 offers an excerpt of an interview that a third-grade student, Tim, conducted with a police officer in his community. The purpose was to learn more about why individuals became police officers and what their job entailed. Prior to the interview, Tim determined what his objectives were and then wrote out the questions he would use. His teacher helped refine them and suggested procedures for how he might go about arranging the interview. Tim then called the police department, indicated his objective, and set up an appointment for the interview. The actual interview took only 10 to 15 minutes and, with the officer's permission, was recorded at the police station for sharing with the class.

Community Service Projects

As students begin to explore their community through hands-on projects, they will encounter opportunities to make a contribution to its well-being and improvement. Through community service, they can gain insights into the fundamental commitment implicit in a democratic society: All citizens, even young ones, have responsibilities as well as rights. Active civic participation also can empower young citizens and contribute to the enhancement of their self-esteem when they discover that they can make a difference (Lewis, 1991; Wade, 1994).

Kids Around Town (KAT), an example of a model community service program, has been piloted in elementary schools in Pennsylvania (Rappaport & Kletzien, 1996). The core of the KAT model is a series of interdisciplinary steps:

- Introducing students to local government
- Selecting a local issue to explore

FIGURE 2.7

Third-grade student's interview

Tim:	My first question is, "Why did you want to be a policeman?"
Police Officer:	Why did I want to be a policeman? Well, I wanted to be a policeman because I thought I could help people.
Tim:	Why did you decide to live and work in Upper Dublin?
Police Officer:	Well, I don't live here. But the reason I decided to work here was I thought it would be a great opportunity for someone who wanted to be a policeman. I think it is a fine township.
Tim:	What would you be if you weren't a policeman?
Police Officer:	I really have no idea.
Tim:	Did you ever have another job?
Police Officer:	Oh, yes, I had another job. I was a mailman; before that I was in the army.
Tim:	Do you like the job of a policeman?
Police Officer:	Do I like the job? Yes, I do like the job.
Tim:	What improvements do you think could be made in Upper Dublin?
Police Officer:	As far as the Police Department goes, you mean?
Tim:	Well, I mean not just about your job, but other things.
Police officer:	Well, I don't know. I think that's up to the taxpayers and the commissioners. I think they're doing a pretty good job, don't you?
Tim:	I don't know.
Police Officer:	Don't you really?
Tim:	Well, I never really studied it.
Police Officer:	Well, sure there are improvements that could be made, but I think they're doing the best they can.
Tim:	Do you think policemen have good enough equipment?
Police Officer:	I think it's going to get better. I think we're trying. I think it's probably not as good as it could be, but it's getting better all the time. It's eventually going to get to the point where everything is OK. Yes.
Tim:	How many people commit murder a year?
Police Officer:	I really don't know. In this township, not too many. In other places, a lot more.

FIGURE 2.7 (Continued)

Tim:	About how many robberies are there a year?
Police Officer:	We have quite a few burglaries, not robberies. We have very few robberies; we have a lot of burglaries.
Tim:	What's the difference?
Police Officer:	Well, the difference is a robbery is where somebody actually holds you up with a gun. A burglary is where someone, say, breaks into your house or business or something. We have quite a few of those—in the hundreds.
Tim:	What do you think Upper Dublin would be like without police?
Police Officer:	Well, it would be like any other place without policemen, very bad.
Tim:	Are there any things that a policeman does that most people don't know about?
Police Officer:	I think there are quite a few things that people don't know about.
Tim:	What?
Police Officer:	Well, one thing—they work different shifts, which maybe some people know about but they don't really know what the job details; they don't really know what a policeman does. [At this point the interview is interrupted as the police officer takes and relays to a patrol car a call for assistance.]
Tim:	What do policemen do most of the day? What kind of things do they do?
Police Officer:	Most of the day, they ride around in the patrol car, observe traffic violations, check suspicious . . . [Another call interrupts the conversation.] They ride around in cars; as I say, they observe things. They try to check various things, in other words, businesses, places of business. They get calls, they answer all calls when people call them on the telephone. In other words, you just heard one here. Right? If someone's in the house, if the person doesn't want them in there, they go and they try their best to get them out of there and possibly to arrest them if they have to. Anything that they're called upon by the general public to do, they try to answer the call.
Tim:	OK, thank you.

- Researching the issue
- Analyzing the information
- Solving problems
- Taking action

In KAT, "Students select a public policy issue that affects them locally—for example, cleaning up litter in a community park. This issue then serves as a springboard for study and analysis, planning strategies, and actions" (Rappaport & Kletzien, 1996). Issues that students have tackled include land-use practices (third graders), the problem of abandoned housing (fifth graders), bicycle safety ordinances (fifth graders), and juvenile crime (fifth graders).

Organizational Resources for Social Studies Instruction

Beyond community resources, a number of agencies can help keep teachers abreast of new developments, issues, and trends within the field of social studies, as well provide subject matter information.

Teachers can look especially to professional organizations that have a particular interest in the social studies. The list that follows identifies some major institutions that meet this criterion:

American Anthropological Association
1703 New Hampshire Avenue, N.W.
Washington, DC 20009

American Bar Association
750 North Lake Shore Drive
Chicago, IL 60611

American Economic Association
1313 21st Avenue South, Suite 809
Nashville, TN 37212

American Historical Association
400 A Street, S.E.
Washington, DC 20003

American Political Science Association
1527 New Hampshire Avenue, N.W.
Washington, DC 20036

American Psychological Association
1200 17th Street, N.W.
Washington, DC 20036

American Sociological Association
1722 N Street, N.W.
Washington, DC 20036

Association of American Geographers
1700 16th Street, N.W.
Washington, DC 20009

Educational Resources Information Center (ERIC)
Clearinghouse for Social Studies/Social Science Education
Indiana University
2805 East 10th Street
Bloomington, IN 47408-2698

Joint Council on Economic Education
432 Park Avenue South
New York, NY 10016

National Council for Geographic Education
Department of Geography and Regional Planning
Indiana University of Pennsylvania
Indiana, PA 15705

National Council for the Social Studies
3501 Newark Street, N.W.
Washington, DC 20016

Organization of American Historians
112 North Bryan Street
Bloomington, IN 47408

The preceding organizations produce a number of materials, including guidelines and policy statements, such as the ones that are referenced throughout this text. Many also sponsor annual regional and national conferences for teachers of social studies on a range of issues in the field. Some of the organizations also publish newsletters and periodicals for teachers.

In addition to these national organizations, affiliate units within many of the states provide similar services. Regional social studies organizations cover several states. The national organizations listed can provide information on affiliates.

Professional Journals

A number of specialized professional periodicals are available for social studies teachers. Some of the periodicals are sponsored by the organizations cited. They include:

- *Journal of Economic Education*
- *Journal of Geography*

- *Social Education*
- *Social Studies and the Young Learner*
- *Teaching Political Science*
- *Teaching Sociology*
- *The History Teacher*
- *Theory and Research in Social Education*
- *The Social Studies*

Professional Development Through the Internet

In the 21st century, social studies teachers increasingly will rely on technology to supply ongoing professional development. In particular, the Internet will continue to be a major source of information on cutting-edge developments, as well as an important medium for teachers to share ideas, seek assistance, solve problems, and acquire in-service training. A growing list of institutions also offer courses over the Internet and through distance education.

Examples of electronic sources that social studies teachers currently can tap for professional development through the World Wide Web (WWW), along with their corresponding Universal Resource Locator (URL), are:

AskERIC Library: http://ericir.syr.edu

NCSS Organizational Information: http://www.ncss.org/online

H–High-S Teaching Project: http://www.h-net.msu.edu/~highs

World Lecture Hall: http://utexas.edu/world/lecture/index.html

Eric-Chess: http://www.indiana.edu/~ssdc/eric-chess.html

Social Studies Development Center: http://www.indiana.edu/~ssdc/ssdc.html

Group Activities

1. Which of the social sciences do you think should receive the most emphasis in the primary grades? The intermediate grades? The middle grades? Give reasons for your answers.

2. In your local community, make a list of the community resources that a social studies teacher could draw on. Compare your list with those of others in the group.

3. Refer to Figure 2.2, which illustrates how themes from each of the social sciences can be incorporated into the curriculum at each grade level. Discuss what additional themes you think it would be appropriate to include.

Individual Activities

1. Consult the *International Encyclopedia of the Social Sciences* (17 vols.) (New York: Macmillan, 1968). Summarize the definition provided for each of the social sciences.

2. Besides those listed in the chapter, develop a list of 10 additional concepts related to each of the social sciences.

3. Obtain a brochure that explains the structure of a basal social studies program for the elementary grades. Note the extent to which the series incorporates elements of each of the social sciences at every grade level. Also identify any other disciplines that are represented in the texts.

4. Write to each of the organizations listed in the chapter to obtain information concerning their services, materials, and conferences.

5. Access the Internet and contact each of the web sites listed in the chapter to learn what it offers. Consult Chapter 11 if you need information on the World Wide Web (WWW).

References

Armstrong, D. A., & Savage, T. V., Jr. (1976). A framework for utilizing the community for social learning in grades 4 to 6. *Social Education, 40*, 164–167.

Cherryholmes, C., Manson, G., & Martorella, P. H. (1979). *Looking at me: Teacher's manual.* New York: McGraw-Hill.

Engle, S. H., & Ochoa, A. S. (1988). *Education for democratic citizenship: Decision making in the social studies.* New York: Teachers College Press.

Gillis, C. (1991). *The community as classroom.* New York: Boynton/Cook.

Gross, R. E., & Dynneson, T. (Eds.). (1991). *Social science perspectives on citizenship education.* New York: Teachers College Press.

Harvey, K. D. (1993). Native Americans: The next 500 years. *Social Studies and the Young Learner, 5*, 2–3 (insert).

Howard, R. W. (1987). *Concepts and schemata: An introduction.* Philadelphia: Cassell.

Hunt, M. P., & Metcalf, L. E. (1968). *Teaching high school social studies: Problems in reflective thinking and social understanding* (2nd ed.). New York: Harper & Row.

Lamm, L. (1989). *Facilitating learning through the effective use of resource persons in the classroom.* Unpublished manuscript, North Carolina State University, Department of Curriculum and Instruction, Raleigh.

Lewis, B. A. (1991). *The kid's guide to social action.* Minneapolis: Free Spirit Publishing.

Marzano, R. J., Brandt, R. S., Hughes, C. S., Jones, B. F., Presseisen, B. Z., Rankin, S. C., & Suhor, C. (1988). *Dimensions of thinking: A framework for curriculum and instruction.* Alexandria, VA: Association for Supervision and Curriculum Development.

Mehaffy, G. L. (1984). Oral history in elementary classrooms. *Social Education, 48*, 470–472.

Mehaffy, G. L., Sitton, T., & Davis, O. L., Jr. (1979). *Oral history in the classroom* (How to do it series). Washington, DC: National Council for the Social Studies.

Monti, J. (1988). Guest speaker programs bring community members to school. *NASSP Bulletin, 72*, 113.

Perkins, D. N. (1986). *Knowledge as design*. Hillsdale, NJ: Lawrence Erlbaum.

Rapport, A. L., & Kletzien, S. (1996). Kids around town. *Educational Leadership, 53*, 26–29.

South Carolina Department of Education. (1987). *Guide for using guest speakers and field trips*. Columbia, SC: Author.

Sunal, C. S., & Hatcher, B. A. (1986). *Studying history through art* (How to do it series). Washington, DC: National Council for the Social Studies.

Taba, H., & Elkins, D. (1950). *With focus on human relations*. Washington, DC: American Council on Education.

Torney-Purta, J. (1991). Schema theory and cognitive psychology: Implications for social studies. *Theory and Research in Social Education, 19*, 189–210.

Totten, S. (1989). Using oral histories to address social issues in the classroom. *Social Education, 53*, 114–116.

Wade, R. C. (1994). Community-service learning. *Social Studies and the Young Learner* (pull-out), 1–4.

Zimmerman, W. (1981). *How to tape instant oral biographies*. New York: Guarionex.

Chapter

Alternative Scope and Sequence Patterns in the Social Studies

Suppose *you randomly selected 10 first-grade classes from across the United States. What type of social studies curricula would you expect to find? What guidelines were used to shape the curricula? Who was primarily responsible for determining the curricula?*

The answers to these questions are rooted in our history and constitutional framework. Because the framers of the Constitution rejected a national system of education, the matter of schools and curriculum fell to the individual states. States, in turn, often granted considerable authority in these matters to local governments. Consequently we have no national control of curriculum. Rather there exists a collection of thousands of local school districts and governing boards, each with varying degrees of autonomy over its social studies curriculum.

Existing Social Studies Scope and Sequence Patterns

**scope and
sequence**

Each state varies in the degree of control it exercises over the curriculum, including the **scope and sequence** patterns that local school districts may adopt. *Scope* refers to the topics included in the curriculum; *sequence* refers to the order in which they appear (see Joyce, Little, & Wronski, 1991).

Subject to general guidelines and standards for the social studies curriculum established by each state, a local school district often has considerable freedom in the development of its social studies program. Thus the potential for variety in the social studies curriculum scope and sequence patterns across the United States is great.

Although the principle of local control holds out the promise of diversity in curriculum offerings, in reality there is considerable homogeneity in the social studies programs in grades K through 12 across the 50 states. Typically, the pattern is as follows (Superka, Hawke, & Morrissett, 1980):

Grades K–1	Self, Family, School
Grade 2	Neighborhoods
Grade 3	Communities
Grade 4	State history, geographic regions
Grade 5	United States history, culture, and geography
Grade 6	World cultures, history, and geography
Grade 7	World cultures, history, and geography
Grade 8	American history
Grade 9	Civics
Grade 10	World history
Grade 11	American history
Grade 12	American government

The Curriculum Pattern in the Elementary Grades

**expanding-
communities
curriculum
pattern**

The existing organizational pattern of the social studies curriculum in grades K through 6 follows what has been characterized by Hanna (1963) as the **expanding-communities curriculum pattern.** This approach, which has dominated the elementary curriculum for several decades, is based on the notion that a student will be introduced during each year of school to an increasingly expanding social environment, moving from examining the self and the family in grades K–1 to the world at large in grade 6. Hanna's model also identified nine categories of basic human activities that should be addressed during each year of the social studies curriculum: expressing, producing, transporting, communicating, educating, recreating, protecting, governing, and creating (Powers, 1986).

The Curriculum Pattern in the Middle and Secondary Grades

The long-term impact of the 1916 report of the Committee on Social Studies (see Chapter 1) ironically proved to be pervasive and enduring, extending into the 1990s. Note the close similarities between the typical national pattern described in the preceding section and the following general recommendations for grades 7 through 12 from the 1916 report of the Committee on Social Studies:

Grades 7–9	Geography, European history, American history, civics
Grade 10	European history
Grade 11	American history
Grade 12	Problems of democracy

Contrary to the intent of the committee, its report became a paradigm of what the scope and sequence of courses in the curriculum should be. The committee itself had refrained from offering detailed outlines of courses. It believed that the selection of topics and the organization of subject matter should be determined by the needs of each community.

A further irony spawned by the report was that its recommendations often were viewed as being literal, timeless, and universal, applicable in all particulars to all generations and communities. The committee's intent, however, had been to sketch only general principles on which different schools could build their curricula in concert with the changing character of each time period, community, and group of students.

The 1916 committee constructed its recommendations in the context of a school population vastly different from the one that exists today. It saw its immediate task as planning a social studies curriculum that emphasized citizenship education for a nation in which the majority of students completed their education without entering high school. This short educational period meant that all of the essential elements in the curriculum needed to be provided before the 10th grade.

The Dominance of Traditional Scope and Sequence Patterns

Why has the dominant national scope and sequence pattern for the social studies curriculum endured so long? A major part of the answer lies, perhaps, in several interrelated factors: *tradition, accrediting agencies and professional organizations, preservice teacher education programs*, and *patterns of textbook selection and adoption*.

The weight of tradition bears down heavily on those who would challenge the conventional scope and sequence of the social studies curriculum. Parents and community members tend to encourage preservation of the status quo. Teachers themselves are often more comfortable with the known than the unknown.

Moreover, tradition influences the norms for accrediting agencies that examine the quality of our school districts across the country. It is also an important consideration for national organizations such as the National Council for the Social Studies (NCSS) and the National Council for Geographic Education (NCGE), which provide curricular guidelines for programs. These organizations represent thousands of social studies teachers across the United States and Canada.

Tradition also establishes some of the basic goals for preservice teacher education programs that seek to prepare teachers for existing conditions in schools, as well as for the future. Often in such programs the emphasis is on socialization of new teachers into the present curriculum, rather than on consideration of alternatives. Correspondingly, the subject matter background of elementary and middle grades preservice teachers frequently has been shaped to prepare them for the dominant scope and sequence pattern, rather than for the consideration and development of alternatives. This pattern of preparation also typically stresses traditional disciplines, such as history, and deemphasizes or ignores the newer social science disciplines and interdisciplinary studies.

basal textbooks

Basal Textbooks and the Social Studies Curriculum

Perhaps the most significant factor in influencing the standardization of the scope and sequence pattern of the social studies curriculum is the system of selecting and adopting **basal textbooks** that schools employ. The impact of textbooks on perpetuating the scope and sequence of the curriculum has been profound. The best research evidence available suggests that, in social studies, basal texts are used extensively and more often than other types of curricular materials (Shaver, Davis, & Hepburn, 1979).

A basal textbook represents the major elements that the author or publisher regards as basic to provide an appropriate social studies curriculum for a particular grade or subject. Generally publishers of basal social studies texts build them around some model or notion of scope and sequence related to the grades

Patterns of textbook selection and adoption have significantly influenced the scope and sequence of the social studies curriculum.

for which the texts have been developed. Thus adopting a basal text, in effect, means adopting the curricular pattern on which it is based.

Use of Basal Texts in the Social Studies

Teachers and schools often build on a basal text, using commercially produced and teacher-made supplementary materials, newspapers, articles, and trade books. Some teachers use no textbook at all, instead creating their own programs by following general scope and sequence guidelines. Other teachers use texts primarily as reference books. Still other teachers use a *multitext* approach, picking those units or chapters from each textbook that best meet their specific curricular needs. As we consider in Chapter 10, textbook publishers also may offer supplementary books, such as children's literature, correlated to the basal text.

Surprisingly, perhaps, basal textbook series available from major publishers display striking similarities in the scope and sequence models they incorporate. Contrary to the canons of capitalism that we might expect to operate when major corporations are competing for large profits from widely distributed heterogeneous customers, basal texts reflect more homogeneity than diversity. Although individual basal texts differ considerably in the types of activities, pictorial content, and specific objectives they include, in the main they reflect the dominant curricular pattern.

Mehlinger (1992, p. 149) noted: "Textbook publishers mainly reinforce the status quo. They exist to provide school customers with textbooks needed to teach the existing curriculum. Publishers rarely make money by launching ventures that deviate greatly from current practice." Typically, publishers provide few alternatives for educators who wish to experiment with different curriculum configurations or even to vary the grade levels at which certain subjects (e.g., world cultures) are studied (Parker, 1991).

Selection and Adoption of Basal Textbooks

How are the textbooks that appear in elementary, middle, and secondary classrooms selected? Text adoption occurs in two basic ways. One is through **local adoption,** in which local districts are free to adopt any texts they wish. The other is through **state adoption,** in which the state in some fashion selects and prescribes the books that the local districts may use.

local adoption

state adoption

Currently a majority of states permit local selections of basals. However, 22 states use state adoption procedures: Alabama, Arkansas, California, Florida, Georgia, Hawaii, Idaho, Indiana, Kentucky, Louisiana, Mississippi, Nevada, New Mexico, North Carolina, Oklahoma, Oregon, South Carolina, Tennessee, Texas, Utah, Virginia, and West Virginia.

Texts typically are adopted for a 5- or 6-year cycle. Adoption committees at the state level often include parents, teachers, college and university faculty, civic leaders, and organizational representatives. A sample form that has been used by adoption committees to evaluate social studies texts is shown in Figure 3.1.

FIGURE 3.1   Sample of a social studies textbook evaluation form

ELEMENTARY
SOCIAL STUDIES

TEXTBOOK EVALUATION
FORM

DIVISION OF INSTRUCTIONAL MATERIALS & TECHNOLOGY
DEPARTMENT OF CURRICULUM & INSTRUCTION
MEMPHIS CITY SCHOOLS – MEMPHIS, TENNESSEE

copyright 1990

LIST SECTION TOTALS BELOW

A.	TEXTBOOK DEVELOPMENT	_____
B.	PUBLISHER	_____
C.	COST	_____
D.	PHYSICAL FEATURES	_____
E.	ORGANIZATION	_____
F.	INSTRUCTIONAL FEATURES	_____
G.	INSTRUCTIONAL CONTENT	_____
H.	TEACHER'S EDITION	_____
I.	ANCILLARY MATERIALS	_____
	TOTALS – SECTIONS A–I	=====

Complete one form for each textbook evaluated for each grade level or course.

Name of Textbook _____

Name of Publisher _____

Name of Series _____

Name of Committee _____ Evaluation Date _____ , 1990

RESPOND TO ALL OF THE STATEMENTS LISTED BELOW BY USING THE FOLLOWING SCALE.

N – Not Applicable
    No Information

STRONGLY DISAGREE   0   1   2   3   4   5   6   STRONGLY AGREE
                                    AGREE

A. TEXTBOOK DEVELOPMENT

1. There is evidence that the development team of authors, advisors, and consultants includes a wide range of people (Grades 1–12 and university teachers).   _____

2. There is evidence that the text and ancillary materials were successfully field-tested.   _____

3. The field test data were used to refine and improve the text and ancillary materials.   _____

4. The textbook reflects current thinking and knowledge (consider the publication date).   _____

5. The textbook can be used successfully for the next six years.   _____

   Textbook Development Total   =====

B. PUBLISHER

1. The publisher will provide, at no cost, sufficient professional consultants to help implement the program.   _____

2. The publisher will provide, at no cost, continuous consultant services to meet school and classroom needs.   _____

3. The publisher will correlate its program to the MCS's social studies objectives within a reasonable time period.   _____

4. Reliable and quality service has been provided in the past by the publisher.   _____

5. The consultants provided at the hearing were knowledgeable and competent.   _____

   Publisher Total   =====

FIGURE 3.1   *(Continued)*

C. COST

1. The cost of the textbook is comparable to the cost of other textbooks in the field. _____

2. The cost of ancillary materials is comparable to the cost of other ancillary materials in the field. _____

   Cost Total _____

D. PHYSICAL FEATURES OF THE TEXTBOOK

1. The size and weight of the text are appropriate for the age of the student. _____

2. The type-size and style are clear and appropriate for the age group. _____

3. The binding and cover are durable. _____

4. The paper quality is good. Non-glare paper is used. _____

5. The page layout is uncluttered and balanced. There is sufficient white space for easy reading. _____

6. Provisions for emphasis (heavy type, boxes, color, italics, etc.) are clear and appropriate. _____

7. The illustrations, table, figures, graphs, charts, and maps are free from sexual and cultural bias. _____

8. The illustrations, tables, figures, graphs, charts, and maps are relevant and functional. _____

9. The cover is attractive, well designed, and appealing to students. _____

   Physical Features of Textbook Total _____

E. ORGANIZATION OF TEXTBOOK

1. The table of contents shows a logical development of the subject. _____

2. The glossaries/appendices are clear and comprehensive. _____

3. There is uniformity in lesson format within a single text. _____

4. The unit/chapter introductions are clear and comprehensive. _____

5. The unit/chapter summaries suitably reinforce the content. _____

6. There are sufficient, relevant, and well-placed unit/chapter tests. _____

7. There are sufficient, relevant, and well-placed practice exercises. _____

8. The references, bibliographies, and resources are sufficient. _____

9. There is uniformity in development from text to text within the series. (Examine the grade level above and below your committee's grade level.) _____

   Organization of Textbook Total _____

F. INSTRUCTIONAL FEATURES OF TEXTBOOK

1. The text is written in clear, simple, and logical terms. _____

2. Sentence structure and grammar are correct. _____

   (Instructional Features of Textbook continued on next page)

FIGURE 3.1 (Continued)

INSTRUCTIONAL FEATURES OF TEXTBOOK – CONTINUED

3. The style of writing improves comprehension. _____

4. The text provides sufficiently for individual difference. There are suggestions and alternative resources/activities for enrichment, as well as for remediation. _____

5. The reading level is appropriate. _____

6. Key vocabulary is made clear in context or in the glossary. _____

7. End-of-lesson questions review key ideas and vocabulary. _____

8. Atlas and gazetteer sections reinforce the lesson. _____

9. Skills are introduced, taught, and maintained throughout the text. _____

10. Skills are tied to other elementary subjects, such as reading, writing, math, etc. _____

11. The activities appeal to a wide range of student abilities and interests. _____

12. The students are sufficiently encouraged to develop skills beyond literal comprehension. _____

13. New concepts are identified in an easily distinguishable manner (boldface type, etc.). _____

14. There are opportunities for students to apply their skills to interesting, real-world situations. _____

15. There are sufficient activities for independent research and reports. _____

   Instructional Features of Textbook Total _____

G. INSTRUCTIONAL CONTENT OF TEXTBOOK

1. The objectives listed in the proposed curriculum guide under Strand I can be successfully taught using this textbook. _____

2. The objectives listed in the proposed curriculum guide under Strand II can be successfully taught using this textbook. _____

3. The objectives listed in the proposed curriculum guide under Strand III can be successfully taught using this textbook. _____

4. The objectives listed in the proposed curriculum guide under Strand IV can be successfully taught using this textbook. _____

5. The objectives listed in the proposed curriculum guide under Strand V can be successfully taught using this textbook. _____

6. The objectives listed in the proposed curriculum guide under Strand VI can be successfully taught using this textbook. _____

7. Provides thorough geographic coverage and grade-appropriate map and globe skills. _____

8. Map/Globe skills are an integral part of the lesson. _____

9. Map/Globe skills are reinforced in content-related activities. _____

10. Critical thinking skill development is provided at the lesson, chapter, and/or unit level. _____

11. Coverage of the content is adequate and balanced. _____

12. Sufficient examples of relationships between past and present are provided. _____

   (Instructional Content of Textbook continued on next page)

FIGURE 3.1   *(Continued)*

INSTRUCTIONAL CONTENT OF TEXTBOOK – CONTINUED

13. Covers important historical events and people. _____
14. Biographies of famous people are highlighted. _____
15. The content is actual and factual. _____
16. Historical events are clearly presented and supported by quotations and examples _____ from firsthand accounts.
17. Includes all social studies disciplines (history, geography, economics, civics/ _____ government, sociology/anthropology).
18. Emphasizes responsibilities of citizenship in a democratic society. _____
19. Controversial issues are treated factually and objectively. _____
20. The content is free of biases and prejudices. _____
21. The content is free of sexual and cultural stereotypes. _____
22. Contributions of the sexes and various cultural groups are reflected fairly. _____

Instructional Content of Textbook Total =====

H. TEACHER'S EDITION/RESOURCE PACKAGE

1. The teacher's edition is easy to use. _____
2. The teacher's edition is comprehensive, well organized, and contains sufficient _____ information for even the inexperienced teacher.
3. Step-by-step plans are included on how to implement the student's text in the _____ classroom.
4. Objectives are clearly stated. _____
5. Scope and sequence for each level is provided. _____
6. Sufficient, complementary assessment tools are included. _____
7. Supplementary components are referenced in the teaching plans at the appropriate _____ place.
8. Teaching techniques are suggested that improve instructional effectiveness. _____
9. Includes provision for reteaching skills and concepts related to objectives. _____
10. Sufficient activities and optional strategies are provided for enrichment and _____ remediation.
11. Answers to exercises and tests are provided on the facsimiles of the student pages. _____
12. Lists of key vocabulary are included for each unit. _____
13. Incudes a variety of strategies for teaching skills and alternative strategies for _____ reteaching.
14. The size of type is suitable. _____

Teacher's Edition Total =====

FIGURE 3.1 *(Continued)*

I. ANCILLARY MATERIALS

1. Duplicating/blackline masters are of high quality. _____

2. Printed and/or audiovisual materials being provided at no charge are of high quality and enhance instruction. _____

3. Quality printed and/or audiovisual materials are available at no charge to conduct independent inservice and to aid the individual teacher. _____

4. Transparencies that are being provided at no charge enhance instruction. _____

5. Software components are available to aid the individual teacher to enhance instruction, meet individual needs, and for remediation. _____

Testing and Management System

6. Tests are provided for assessment of facts, vocabulary, main ideas, and skills. _____

7. Sufficient, relevant, and well-placed unit/chapter tests are provided. _____

8. End of level tests (end-of-book) are provided. _____

9. Placement, diagnostic, and assessment tests provided are reliable and valid. _____

10. Reproduction rights to placement, diagnostic, and assessment tests are provided to the Memphis City Schools at no charge. _____

Workbooks

11. Workbooks are clear and well organized. _____

12. Practice relates to previously taught skills, vocabulary, and concepts. _____

13. Material extends understanding—not merely "busy work." _____

14. Include a variety of activities and response formats. _____

15. Workbooks are simple enough for independent work. _____

16. Workbooks are appealing to a wide range of students. _____

17. Sufficient amount of writing space is given. _____

Ancillary Materials Total _____

We, the duly constituted members of the Textbook Adoption Committee, do hereby certify that the information contained in this document represents a consensus opinion that is supported by the undersigned.

1. _____
    (Name, School, Date)

2. _____
    (Name, School, Date)

3. _____
    (Name, School, Date)

Source: From Division of Instructional Materials, Department of Curriculum & Instruction, Memphis City Schools, Memphis, Tennessee. Used with permission.

Criticisms of Basal Textbooks

Both the process of selecting members of the textbook adoption committees and the selection criteria they use and the recommendations they make often are politically sensitive and controversial issues. A number of reviews have charged that the textbooks that emerge from the state adoption process are, among other things, bland, overburdened with factual context, overly sensitive to pressure groups, distorted, and watered down (e.g., Apple, 1992; Brophy, 1991; Nelson, 1992; People for the American Way, 1986, 1987; Sewall, 1987; Tyson-Bernstein, 1988).

Textbooks also have been charged with ignoring critical analyses of significant social issues. One social studies teacher characterized the adoption choices in her school district in this fashion: "Recently, we had to choose between a brain-dead textbook, with no controversy and therefore no content, and one that didn't cover all the topics in the curriculum" (Needham, 1989, p. 4).

Social studies textbooks also often have been found to be riddled with inaccuracies. In 1992, for example, the State Board of Education in Texas fined publishers $647,000 after more than 3,700 errors were discovered in U.S. history textbooks (Viadero, 1992).

Implications of State Adoption Policies

The implications of state adoption policies for the 28 states and the District of Columbia that do *not* have them and permit local selection are considerable. Because the costs of developing and producing major texts are considerable, publishers have been reluctant to produce more than one for each grade level. Their objective has been to design their products for the greatest possible sales. This goal involved attending carefully to the adoption criteria formulated by the states with the largest student populations among the group of 22 having state adoption policies. The net effect has been that a minority of states have had a major impact on the textbooks that are available to all states.

However, in the wake of controversies over the nature of state adoption processes and the quality of the textbooks they provide for our classrooms, changes are occurring within the publishing industry. These changes should have major implications for the curricular choices schools have. In 1992 the *Social Studies Review* reported:

> The actual number of mass-market social studies textbooks has been gradually diminishing. Some publishers are concluding that it is no longer economic to develop and sell "one-size-fits-all" products. Educators more than ever insist on radically different themes and interpretations in their history books. Increasingly, the position of mass-market textbook publishers seems threatened, and among the headaches are the controversies that attend social studies texts. . . .
>
> The evident movement away from mass-market history textbooks surely creates opportunities for niche textbooks that seek particular audiences. The trend may benefit publishers who produce supplementary and specialized products, including collections of stories, biographies, documents, and other non-traditional source

The social studies curriculum must move beyond the textbook to include activities that intersect with students' lives.

materials. CD-ROMs and video formats will undoubtedly continue to make inroads as teaching devices. ("Textbooks Today," 1992, p. 2)

State adoption processes also are undergoing changes. Utah and Texas, for example, now permit adoptions of technology resources such as videodiscs (see Chapter 11) in lieu of textbooks.

Alternative Social Studies Scope and Sequence Patterns

As noted, the social studies texts found in our social studies classes mirror the dominant K–12 scope and sequence model that was outlined earlier. Surprisingly, although this pattern is dominant across the United States, there is no explicit national consensus among social studies educators concerning what the scope and sequence of the social studies curriculum should be. Nor is there agreement on whether it even would be desirable to adopt a single scope and sequence model for all of the nation's classrooms.

To the contrary, since the 1916 report of the Committee on Social Studies and the advent of the expanding-communities curriculum model, many social studies educators and various groups have proposed and encouraged the development of alternative patterns for organizing the curriculum (e.g., Joyce, 1972; Welton & Mallan, 1992). In the past decade, states and national groups dissatisfied with the dominant pattern of the social studies have advocated detailed alternatives and have worked through the political process to implement their recommendations. We consider briefly several such alternatives, one proposed by a *state board* (California), and two others by *national professional organizations* (NCGE/AAG and NCSS).

The California Model

In 1990 the state of California adopted its own framework for the social studies curriculum, entitled *History–Social Science Framework for California Public Schools, Kindergarten Through Grade 12* (California State Department of Education, 1988). Among other differences with the dominant national pattern, the California model places heavy emphasis on the discipline of history. The organizational plan established new social studies guidelines for each school within the state. A summary of the scope and sequence framework for grades K through 12 is shown in Figure 3.2.

Although the California model directly affects only one state, it ultimately may affect other states. Through its influence as our most populous state and the major state purchaser of textbooks, California, in the past, often set the standards for what publishers included in social studies textbooks. This meant, for example, that a sparsely populated state with a relatively small student population (e.g., Vermont) had to select its social studies texts from those designed to fit California's scope and sequence.

The National Council for Geographic Education/ Association of American Geographers Model

In the 1980s, at the same time that advocates for the study of history asserted its claim for supremacy in the curriculum (e.g., Ravitch & Finn, 1987), a strong base of support also developed for the systematic study of geography. As the number of geography departments across the United States decreased over the previous decade and surveys of student knowledge of geography revealed major deficiencies, there was growing national alarm over the prevalence of geographic illiteracy. It was argued, for example, that students were ill-prepared for an era of increasing global interdependence.

Providing leadership for this issue, the National Council for Geographic Education (NCGE) and the Association of American Geographers (AAG) in 1984 issued a set of scope and sequence guidelines that emphasized the study of geography, K–12 (Joint Committee on Geographic Education, 1984). The organizations recommended specific courses for grades 7 through 12, but only general guidelines for geographic topics to be addressed in the elementary school curriculum. Their general recommendations for grades K through 6 are summarized in Figure 3.3. Notice the relationship of these guidelines to the current scope and sequence pattern outlined earlier.

| FIGURE 3.2 | California History–Social Science Framework: scope and sequence |

K Learning and Working, Now and Long Ago

Helping children learn their way in new school role by analyzing problems, considering alternatives and appreciating democratic values. Readings: *Jack and the Beanstalk, Goldilocks, Aesop's Fables.*

1 A Child's Place in Time and Space

Developing social skills, expanding geographic and economic awareness, building a three-dimensional floor map, neighborhood studies. Readings: *Little Toot, Little Red Lighthouse, Mike Mulligan and His Steam Shovel.*

2 People Who Make a Difference

Studying people who supply our needs, farmers and laborers on wheat and vegetable farms, effect of climate on crops, urban development. Readings: *Johnny Appleseed,* folk tales, myths, legends.

3 Understanding Continuity and Change

Constructing history of region, California geography, terrain model of locality, Native Americans, classroom time line. Readings: *White Stallion, Wagon Wheels, The Drinking Gourd.*

4 California: A Changing State

Pre-Columbian times, Spanish conquest, colonial Mexico, Gold Rush, rapid population growth, new immigrants, physical and cultural geography, modern California urban growth and technology.

5 U.S. History and Geography: Making a New Nation, to 1850.

The land before Columbus, Age of Exploration, settling colonies, settling Trans-Appalachian West, War of Independence, Young Republic, Westward Ho! Readings: *Immigrant Kids, Waiting for Mama.*

6 World History and Geography: Ancient Civilizations

Ancient Civilizations to AD 500: Stone Age, Mesopotamia, Egypt, Hebrews and Greeks, early civilizations of India and China, Rome. Readings: Greek and Roman literature, Bible.

FIGURE 3.2 *(Continued)*

7   World History and Geography: Medieval and Early Modern Times

Medieval AD 500 to 1789: Fall of Rome, Islam, China and Japan, Medieval society, European Reformation and Renaissance, Enlightenment. Readings: *Pillow Book, Song of Roland, Tale of Genji, Koju-ki.*

8   United States History and Geography: Growth and Conflict

Course covers 1783 to 1914: New Nation, Constitution, launching the ship of state, the West, the Northeast, the South, Civil War, Industrial Age. Readings: *Huckleberry Finn, My Antonia.*

9   Elective Courses in History-Social Science

Semester courses: Our State, Physical Geography, Cultural Geography, Humanities, Anthropology, Psychology, Sociology, Women's History, Ethnic Studies, Area Studies-Culture, Law-related Education.

10   World History and Geography: The Modern World, 1789 to Present

Unresolved world problems, Enlightenment, Industrial Revolution, Imperialism, WWI, WWII, Nationalism, Soviet Union, China, Africa, Mexico. Readings: *We, Darkness at Noon, Krystallnacht.*

11   U.S. History and Geography: Continuity and Change in 20th Century

Progressive Era, Jazz Age, Great Depression, WWII, Cold War, American post-war society, recent times. Readings: *Grapes of Wrath.*

12   Principles of American Democracy/Economics

One semester deals with Constitution, Bill of Rights, court system, Federalism, and comparative governments. Another semester is economic systems, micro/macroeconomics, international economics.

Source: From *History–Social Science Framework,* copyright 1988, California State Department of Education.

FIGURE 3.3   Summary of recommendations for grades K–6

Grade Level	Central Focus and Related Geographic Topics

K – 2	Self in Space
	    Location
	    Characteristics of Place

	Homes and Schools in Different Places
	    Relative Location
	    Characteristics of Microenvironments

	Neighborhoods—Small Places in Larger Communities
	    Location
	    Place
	    Environmental Changes
	    Interdependence across Space
	    Interaction within and between Neighborhoods
	    Neighborhoods as Regions with Similarities and Differences

3 – 4	Community—Sharing Space with Others
	    Relative Location
	    Characteristics of Landscapes
	    Environmental Relationships
	    Interdependence and Interaction within Community
	    Community as a Region

	The State, Nation, and World
	    Location
	    Interaction of the Human and Physical Environments
	    Human Interactions within and between the State, Nation, and World
	    Global Interdependence
	    The Nature of Regions

5 – 6	United States, Canada, and Mexico
	    Location
	    Comparative Analysis of Places
	    Quality of Life
	    Human Interaction in the U.S. with Canada and Mexico
	    Physical and Cultural Regions of the U.S., Canada, and Mexico

	Latin America, Europe, Former Soviet Union, Middle East, Asia, and Africa
	    Location
	    Physical and Cultural Geographic Characteristics
	    Human-Environmental Interactions
	    Spatial Interrelationships
	    Regions and Subregions of the World

Source: From *Guidelines for Geographic Education* (pp. 11–16) by Joint Committee on Geographic Education, 1984, Washington, DC; Association of American Geographers and National Council for Geographic Education.

The National Council for the Social Studies
Scope and Sequence Initiatives

As the national organization representing social studies teachers, the NCSS has searched over the years for a consensus set of scope and sequence patterns that it could adopt on behalf of its membership and recommend to schools. Early in the 1980s, the NCSS House of Delegates called for the appointment of a committee to develop a series of scope and sequence options for the K–12 curriculum in social studies. As an outgrowth, the NCSS formed a **Task Force on Scope and Sequence**, which completed and published its report in 1983–1984 (Task Force on Scope and Sequence, 1984).

Task Force on Scope and Sequence

The task force recommendations generated considerable discussion but little consensus among social studies educators. As a result of the debate, the council invited five additional sets of authors to develop further scope and sequence alternatives (Bragaw, 1986). These were reported in a special issue of *Social Education* that appeared in November/December, 1986.

The National Council for the Social Studies Alternatives. In an attempt to resolve the scope and sequence issue, the NCSS, in 1988, appointed an ad hoc committee to make recommendations among the alternatives for the council's endorsement. Specifically, the ad hoc committee was charged with reviewing all NCSS position statements and guidelines and other pertinent materials, including reviews of relevant research. It was to derive basic principles, criteria, and guidelines that should be reflected in any social studies curriculum scope and sequence design. In addition, the committee was to identify three scope and sequence models that most nearly met the criteria it established.

In carrying out its charge and looking to official NCSS policy statements and guidelines, the committee developed 24 general criteria for evaluating a scope and sequence model. These, shown in Figure 3.4, were used to assess the various alternative models that already had been published. The committee also recognized that, with varying degrees of modifications, a number of models could meet the criteria.

Subsequently, on recommendation of the committee, NCSS endorsed three alternative models (NCSS, 1990). In doing so, it left open the possibility that many other models might exist or could be created that met the 24 criteria. Like earlier NCSS initiatives, however, the three alternative scope and sequence models that were identified generated considerable debate but, reflecting the divisions within the field, no clear consensus.

Apart from meeting the criteria established by the ad hoc committee, the three models, now almost a decade old, are quite different in their designs, emphases, and complexity. Each of them is summarized here.

The Task Force Model. One of the three alternatives selected was the model recommended by the earlier 1984 Task Force on Scope and Sequence (1984, 1989): the NCSS Task Force model. This model conforms closely to the scope

FIGURE 3.4   Scope and sequence criteria

A social studies scope and sequence should:

1. State the purpose and rationale of the program.
2. Be internally consistent with its stated purposes and rationale.
3. Designate content at every grade level, K–12.
4. Recognize that learning is cumulative.
5. Reflect a balance of local, national, and global content.
6. Reflect a balance of past, present, and future content.
7. Provide for students' understanding of the structure and function of social, economic, and political institutions.
8. Emphasize concepts and generalizations from history and the social sciences.
9. Promote the integration of skills and knowledge.
10. Promote the integration of content across subject areas.
11. Promote the use of a variety of teaching methods and instructional materials.
12. Foster active learning and social interaction.
13. Reflect a clear commitment to democratic beliefs and values.
14. Reflect a global perspective.
15. Foster the knowledge and appreciation of cultural heritage.
16. Foster the knowledge and appreciation of diversity.
17. Foster the building of self-esteem.
18. Be consistent with current research pertaining to how children learn.
19. Be consistent with current scholarship in the disciplines.
20. Incorporate thinking skills and interpersonal skills at all levels.
21. Stress the identification, understanding, and solution of local, national, and global problems.
22. Provide many opportunities for students to learn and practice the basic skills of participation, from observation to advocacy.
23. Promote the transfer of knowledge and skills to life.
24. Have the potential to challenge and excite students.

Source: From *Social Studies Curriculum Planning Resources* (p. 16) by National Council for the Social Studies, 1990, Washington, DC: Author.

and sequence pattern currently dominant (discussed earlier) across the United States. Apart from a set of basic recommendations, shown in Figure 3.5, the model also offers some optional patterns for grades 6 through 12.

The Themes and Questions Model.   The second model that emerged from the NCSS initiative was developed by Hartoonian and Laughlin (1989). They laid out an alternative based on the assumption that specific scope and sequence decisions should be made by local curriculum committees and teachers. Although the authors did not label their approach, I characterize it as the *themes and questions model* because it spells out themes and questions that local decision makers should consider in developing the curriculum. The themes for grades K through 12 are presented in Figure 3.6.

FIGURE 3.5	NCSS Task Force scope and sequence model

Kindergarten — Awareness of Self in a Social Setting

Grade 1 — The Individual in Primary Social Groups: Understanding School and Family Life

Grade 2 — Meeting Basic Needs in Nearby Social Groups: The Neighborhood

Grade 3 — Sharing Earth Space with Others: The Community

Grade 4 — Human Life in Varied Environments: The Region

Grade 5 — People of the Americas: The United States and Its Close Neighbors

Grade 6 — People and Cultures: Representative World Regions

Grade 7 — A Changing World of Many Nations: A Global View

Grade 8 — Building a Strong and Free Nation: The United States

Grade 9 — Systems That Make a Democratic Society Work: Law, Justice, and Economics

Grade 10 — Origins of Major Cultures: A World History

Grade 11 — The Maturing of America: United States History

Grade 12 — One-year course or courses to be required; selection(s) to be made from the following:
Issues and Problems of Modern Society . . .
Introduction to the Social Sciences . . .
The Arts in Human Societies . . .
International Area Studies . . .
Social Science Elective Courses . . .
Supervised Experience in Community Affairs

Source: From "In search of a scope and sequence for social studies" by Task Force on Scope and Sequence, 1989, *Social Education, 53,* pp. 380–382.

FIGURE 3.6

Themes and questions curriculum model: Themes for grades K–12

Source: From "Designing a Social Studies Scope and Sequence for the 21st Century" by H. M. Hartoonian and M. A. Laughlin, 1989, *Social Education, 53,* p. 389. ©National Council for the Social Studies. Used with permission.

Grade Levels

K	1	2	3	4	5	6	7	8	9	10	11	12
← Cultural heritage →
← Global perspective →
← Political/economic →
← Tradition and change →
← Social history →
← Spatial relationships →
← Social contracts →
← Technology →
← Peace/interdependence →
← Citizenship →

The Global Education Model.   The third model, developed by Kniep (1989), also is untitled. I refer to it as the *global education model* because it emphasizes global approaches to all social studies topics. Like the themes and questions model, it encourages local decision making with respect to the actual shape of the curriculum.

Kniep proposed that the scope of the curriculum be framed around four areas of study:

- human values
- global systems
- global issues and problems
- global history

His complex model incorporates *conceptual themes, phenomenological themes,* and *persistent problem themes.* He advocates that teachers consider these themes for curriculum organization across the grades. Kniep's conceptual themes are shown in Figure 3.7. Phenomenological themes, which are more complex, include "actors and components playing major roles in the world's systems" (Kniep, 1989, p. 401) and major historical and contemporary events. The persistent problem themes, according to Kniep, address both local and global problems shown in Figure 3.8. He proposed a complex weaving of the three types of themes throughout each grade level from K through 12.

Selecting a Scope and Sequence Pattern

For better or worse, no singular alternative scope and sequence model looms on the horizon to challenge seriously the dominant national curricular pattern outlined earlier, the one on which existing basal texts are based. Similarly, no con-

| FIGURE 3.7 | The global education curriculum model: Conceptual themes for grades K–12 |

1. **Interdependence**

   We live in a world of systems in which the actors and components interact to make up a unified, functioning whole.

   Related concepts: causation, community, government, groups, interaction systems.

2. **Change**

   The process of movement from one state of being to another is a universal aspect of the planet and is an inevitable part of life and living.

   Related concepts: adaption, cause and effect, development, evolution, growth, revolution, time.

3. **Culture**

   People create social environments and systems comprised of unique beliefs, values, traditions, language customs, technology, and institutions as a way of meeting basic human needs; shaped by their own physical environments and contact with other cultures.

   Related concepts: adaption, aesthetics, diversity, languages, norms, roles, values, space-time.

4. **Scarcity**

   An imbalance exists between relatively unlimited wants and limited available resources necessitating the creation of systems for deciding how resources are to be distributed.

   Related concepts: conflict, exploration, migration, opportunity, cost, policy, resources, specialization.

5. **Conflict**

   People and nations often have differing values and opposing goals resulting in disagreement, tensions, and sometimes violence, necessitating skill in coexistence, negotiation, living with ambiguity and conflict resolution.

   Related concepts: authority, collaboration, competition, interests/positions, justice, power, rights.

Source: From "Social Studies with a Global Education" by W. M. Kniep, 1989, *Social Education, 53*, p. 401.

sensus has emerged regarding the issue of whether it even would be desirable to have a common pattern across all school districts, with all their diversity and disproportionate needs.

The several alternative models presented, as well as others proposed (see Downey, 1986; Engle & Ochoa, 1986; Stanley & Nelson, 1986), along with the related criteria for selecting a scope and sequence, should provide teachers and schools with some basic frameworks for decision making. Ultimately the develop-

| FIGURE 3.8 | The global education curriculum model: Persistent problem themes, grades K–12 |

Peace and Security
the arms race
East-West relations
terrorism
colonialism
democracy vs. tyranny

Environmental Problems
acid rain
pollution of streams
depletion of rain forests
nuclear-waste disposal
maintenance of fisheries

National/International Development
hunger and poverty
overpopulation
North-South relations
appropriate technology
international debt crisis

Human Rights
apartheid
indigenous homelands
political imprisonment
religious persecution
refugees

Source: From "Social Studies with a Global Education" by W. M. Kniep, 1989, *Social Education, 53*, p. 401.

ment of reflective, competent, and concerned citizens depends less on the scope and sequence decisions that are made for the nation, states, and local school districts than on the curricula that teachers and students construct in individual classrooms.

National Standards

As noted in Chapter 1, in recent years the debate concerning what students should learn in the social studies and when they should learn it has shifted to the arena of national *standards*. Such standards can function as tools for individual teachers and instructional leaders to aid in designing K–12 programs, planning curricula, and engaging students in meaningful learning experiences. Standards, in effect, are extensive reference works or guidelines that social studies educators can consult to craft scope and sequence patterns.

To date, five professional organizations have worked on standards related to the social studies curriculum. Their efforts are represented in the History Standards Project, the Geography Standards Project, the National Council on Economic Education Standards, National Standards for Civics and Government, and the NCSS Curriculum Standards for the Social Studies, addressing the social studies curriculum as a whole.

All but the economics standards have been published as we go to press. For updates on the progress of the various projects and more information, write the organizations at the addresses that follow.

Center for Civic Education
5146 Douglas Fir Road
Calabasas, CA 91302-1467

National Council on Economic Education
432 Park Avenue
New York, NY 10016

National Center for History in the Schools
University of California at Los Angeles
10880 Wilshire Boulevard, Suite 1610
Los Angeles, CA 90024

National Council for Geographic Education
1600 M Street, NW, Suite 4200
Washington, DC 20036

National Task Force on Standards
National Council for the Social Studies
3501 Newark Street, NW
Washington, DC 20016-3167

Each set of recommendations from the various projects contains some type of *content standards* that indicate what subject matter themes should be included at each level and *performance standards* that specify what students are expected to learn. The statements of performance standards for the social studies and civics and government standards are the most general, while the structure of the history standards recommendations is the most complex to understand.

History Standards.   There are three sets of history recommendations: history for grades K through 4, United States history for grades 5 through 12, and world history for grades 5 through 12. Each set consists of two parts: standards in historical thinking and standards for history. Those for historical thinking are the same for each set of recommendations: chronological thinking, historical research capabilities, and historical issues analysis and decision making. The number of standards for history vary across sets. For each content standard, there is also a performance standard (see example in Figure 3.9).

Geography Standards.   As Figure 3.10 reveals, the National Geography Standards Project has identified 18 basic standards to be used across the grades. Each basic standard is accompanied by a more detailed *performance standard* (see Figure 3.11 for an example). Student proficiency in the use of the content and performance standards is to be assessed at the end of grades 4, 8, and 12.

Civics and Government Standards.   Alternately, the National Standards for Civics and Government are framed around five basic questions to be addressed in grades K through 12 (National Standards for Civics and Government, 1994). Under each basic question, two to seven related questions are grouped as Figure 3.12 illustrates. Similar to the geography standards, each subquestion is associated with a specific content and performance standard that students are to

| FIGURE 3.9 | History performance standard |

TOPIC 1

Living and Working Together in Families and Communities, Now and Long Ago

Standard 1

Students Should Understand: Family life now and in the recent past; family life in various places long ago.

Students Should Be Able to:

1A   Demonstrate understanding of family life now and in the past by:

- Investigating a family history for at least two generations, identifying various members and their connections in order to construct a time line. *(Teachers should help students understand that families are people from whom they receive love and support. Understanding that many students are raised in nontraditional family structures—i.e., single-parent families, foster homes, guardians raising children—teachers must be sensitive and protect family privacy.)* **[Establish temporal order]**

- From data gathered through family artifacts, photos, and interviews with older relatives and/or other people who play a significant part in a student's life, drawing possible conclusions about roles, jobs, schooling experiences, and other aspects of family life in the recent past. **[Draw upon historical and visual data]**

- For various cultures represented in the classroom, comparing and contrasting family life now with family life over time and between various cultures and considering such things as communication, technology, homes, transportation, recreation, school and cultural traditions. **[Distinguish between past and present]**

- Examining and formulating questions about early records, diaries, family photographs, artifacts, and architectural drawings obtained through a local newspaper or historical society in order to describe family life in their local community or state long ago. **[Formulate historical questions]**

FIGURE 3.9   (*Continued*)

- Comparing and contrasting family life now with family life in the local community or state long ago by considering such things as roles, jobs, communication, technology, style of homes, transportation, schools, religious observances, and cultural traditions. **[Compare and contrast]**

Grades K–2

Examples of student achievement of Standard 1A include:

- Present a family history through two generations in a picture time line, family tree, or oral presentation. Students could portray their own family or the history of a family portrayed in children's literature.

- Draw upon stories such as *The Sky is Blue* by Charlotte Zolotow, *Hundred Penny Box* by Sharon E. Mathis, *Tell Me a Story* by Angela Johnson, and *They Were Good and Strong* by Robert Lawson to compare family life today with family life in the recent past.

- Compare the cultural similarities and differences in clothes, homes, food, communication, technology, cultural traditions, and other aspects of family life between families now and in the past. Possible sources might include information provided by family members, family photographs, artifacts, and books such as *The Keeping Quilt* by Patricia Polacco, *Thy Friend, Obadiah* by Burton Turkle, *From Me to You* by Paul Rogers, *The Patchwork Quilt* by Valerie Flournoy, and *The Old, Old Man and the Very Little Boy* by Kristine L. Franklin.

- Create charts, illustrations, Venn diagrams, or other graphic organizers to demonstrate similarities and differences between family life now and long ago.

- Draw upon literature such as *The House on Maple Street* by Bonnie Pryor or *Since 1920* by Alexandra Wallner to compare life in a home of the past with life in a community of the present. Create charts, illustrations, Venn diagrams, and other graphic organizers with examples of similarities and differences to demonstrate comparisons.

Source: From *National Standards for History for Grades K–4* (p. 32) by National Center for History in the Schools, no date, Los Angeles, CA.

FIGURE 3.10   The eighteen geography standards

Physical and human phenomena are spatially distributed over Earth's surface. The outcome of *Geography for Life* is a geographically informed person (1) who sees meaning in the arrangement of things in space; (2) who sees relations between people, places, and environments; (3) who uses geographic skills; and (4) who applies spatial and ecological perspectives to life situations.

The World in Spatial Terms

Geography studies the relationships between people, places, and environments by mapping information about them into a spatial context.

The geographically informed person knows and understands:

1. How to use maps and other geographic representations, tools, and technologies to acquire, process, and report information from a spatial perspective
2. How to use mental maps to organize information about people, places, and environments in a spatial context
3. How to analyze the spatial organization of people, places, and environments on Earth's surface

Places and Regions

The identities and lives of individuals and peoples are rooted in particular places and in those human constructs called regions.

The geographically informed person knows and understands:

4. The physical and human characteristics of places
5. That people create regions to interpret Earth's complexity
6. How culture and experience influence people's perceptions of places and regions

Physical Systems

Physical processes shape Earth's surface and interact with plant and animal life to create, sustain, and modify ecosystems.

The geographically informed person knows and understands:

7. The physical processes that shape the patterns of Earth's surface
8. The characteristics and spatial distribution of ecosystems on Earth's surface

FIGURE 3.12   K–4 content standards for civics and government

I. What is government and what should it do?
   A. What is government?
   B. Where do people in government get the authority to make, apply, and enforce rules and laws and manage disputes about them?
   C. Why is government necessary?
   D. What are some of the most important things governments do?
   E. What are the purposes of rules and laws?
   F. How can you evaluate rules and laws?
   G. What are the differences between limited and unlimited governments?
   H. Why is it important to limit the power of government?

II. What are the basic values and principles of American democracy?
   A. What are the most important values and principles of American democracy?
   B. What are some important beliefs Americans have about themselves and their government?
   C. Why is it important for Americans to share certain values, principles, and beliefs?
   D. Why do disagreements about values and principles arise?
   E. What are the benefits of diversity in the United States?
   F. How should conflicts about diversity be prevented or managed?
   G. How can people work together to promote the values and principles of American democracy?

III. How does the government established by the constitution embody the purposes, values and principles of American democracy?
   A. What is the United States Constitution and why is it important?
   B. What does the national government do and how does it protect individual rights and promote the common good?
   C. What are the major responsibilities of state government?
   D. What are the major responsibilities of local government?
   E. Who represents you in the legislative and executive branches of your local, state, and national governments?

IV. What is the relationship of the United States to other nations and to world affairs?
   A. How is the world divided into nations?
   B. How do nations interact with one another?

V. What are the roles of the citizen in American democracy?
   A. What does it mean to be a citizen of the United States?
   B. How does a person become a citizen?
   C. What are important rights in the United States?
   D. What are important responsibilities of Americans?
   E. What dispositions or traits of character are important to the preservation and improvement of American democracy?
   F. How can Americans participate in their government?
   G. What is the importance of political leadership and public service?
   H. How should Americans select political leaders?

Source: From *National Standards for Civics and Government* (pp. 1–2) by Center for Civic Education, 1994, Calabasas, CA.

achieve. An example related to the question "How should Americans select polit-ical leaders?" is provided in Figure 3.13.

Social Studies Standards.   The NCSS content standards consist of ten themes that are to be included for each grade. They are: Culture; Time, Continu-ity, and Change; People, Places, and Environment; Individual Development and Identity; Individuals, Groups, and Institutions; Power, Authority, and Gover-nance; Production, Distribution, and Consumption; and Science, Technology, and Society. For each theme and grade level there are related performance stan-dards; note the example in Figure 3.14.

| **FIGURE 3.13** | K–4 content standards for civics and government |

H.   How should Americans select political leaders?

Content summary and rationale

Citizens need to learn how to examine the responsibilities of differing positions of authority and how to evaluate the qualifications of candidates for those positions. The development among citizens of the capacity to select competent and responsi-ble persons to fill positions of leadership in American government is essential to the well-being of the nation.

Content standards

1. Selecting leaders. *Students should be able to explain and apply criteria useful in selecting political leaders.*

   To achieve this standard, students should be able to

   • identify the major duties, powers, privileges, and limitations of a position of political leadership, e.g., class president, mayor, state senator, president of the United States

   • identify qualifications political leaders should have such as

     • commitment to the values and principles of constitutional democracy

     • respect for the rights of others

     • ability to work with others

     • reliability or dependability

     • courage

     • honesty

     • ability to be fair

     • intelligence

     • willingness to work hard

     • special knowledge or skills

   • evaluate the strengths and weaknesses of candidates in terms of the qualifica-tions required for a particular leadership role

---

Source: From *National Standards for Civics and Government* (p. 29) by Center for Civic Education, 1994, Cal-abasas, CA.

FIGURE 3.14   Example of NCSS performance expectations

Culture

Social studies programs should include experiences that provide for the study of *culture and cultural diversity,* so that the learner can:

Early Grades	Middle Grades	High School
a. explore and describe similarities and differences in the ways groups, societies, and cultures address similar human needs and concerns;	a. compare similarities and differences in the ways groups, societies, and cultures meet human needs and concerns;	a. analyze and explain the ways groups, societies, and cultures address human needs and concerns;
b. give examples of how experiences may be interpreted differently by people from diverse cultural perspectives and frames of reference;	b. explain how information and experiences may be interpreted by people from diverse cultural perspectives and frames of reference;	b. predict how data and experiences may be interpreted by people from diverse cultural perspectives and frames of reference;
c. describe ways in which language, stories, folktales, music, and artistic creations serve as expressions of culture and influence behavior of people living in a particular culture;	c. explain and give examples of how language, literature, the arts, architecture, other artifacts, traditions, beliefs, values, and behaviors contribute to the development and transmission of culture;	c. apply an understanding of culture as an integrated whole that explains the functions and interactions of language, literature, the arts, traditions, beliefs and values, and behavior patterns;
d. compare ways in which people from different cultures think about and deal with their physical environment and social conditions;	d. explain why individuals and groups respond differently to their physical and social environments and/or changes to them on the basis of shared assumptions, values, and beliefs;	d. compare and analyze societal patterns for preserving and transmitting culture while adapting to environmental or social change;
e. give examples and describe the importance of cultural unity and diversity within and across groups.	e. articulate the implications of cultural diversity, as well as cohesion, within and across groups.	e. demonstrate the value of cultural diversity, as well as cohesion, within and across groups;
		f. interpret patterns of behavior reflecting values and attitudes that contribute or pose obstacles to cross-cultural understanding;
		g. construct reasoned judgments about specific cultural responses to persistent human issues;
		h. explain and apply ideas, theories, and modes of inquiry drawn from anthropology and sociology in the examination of persistent issues and social problems.

Source: From *Expectations for Excellence* (p. 33) by National Council for the Social Studies, 1994, Washington, DC.

The NCSS encourages educators to combine the NCSS standards with those proposed by the other four projects. Following this approach, educators could construct "customized" curricula to meet local needs.

Additional examples from the standards projects are included in Chapter 13 in conjunction with the discussion of assessments.

Group Activities

1. Analyze the alternative scope and sequence models discussed in the chapter and select the one you find to be most appealing. Discuss what you consider to be its strengths and limitations.

2. Identify three basal social studies textbooks series for the elementary grades. Focus on the third- and fifth-grade texts and the titles of unit topics in each. Compare the lists of topics for each grade level. To what extent are they similar, and how are they different?

Individual Activities

1. Determine the adoption policies for social studies texts in either a local school district or at the state level (if applicable). Discuss what you regard as the strengths and weaknesses of the adoption policy.

2. Select a local school district and determine what the scope and sequence pattern is for social studies in grades K through 12. To what degree is it similar to or different from the dominant national pattern described in the chapter?

3. Through the World Wide Web (WWW), search for examples of social studies scope and sequence models. Find two models you find appealing and summarize their characteristics. Then compare the two with those in this chapter.

References

Apple, M. W. (1992). The text and cultural politics. *Educational Researcher, 21,* 4–11, 19.

Bragaw, D. (1986). Scope and sequence alternatives for the future. *Social Education, 50,* 484–485.

Brophy, J. (1991). *Distinctive curriculum materials in K–6 social studies* (Elementary Subjects Center Series No. 35). East Lansing: Michigan State University, Institute for Research on Teaching, Center for the Learning and Teaching of Elementary Subjects.

California State Department of Education. (1988). *History-social science framework for California public schools kindergarten through grade 12.* Sacramento: Author.

Center for Civic Education. (1994). *National standard for civics and government.* Calabasas, CA: Author.

Downey, M. T. (1986). Time, space, and culture. *Social Education, 50,* 490–501.

Engle, S. H., & Ochoa, A. (1986). A curriculum for democratic citizenship. *Social Education, 50,* 514–525.

Geography education standards project. (1994). Washington, DC: Author.

Hanna, P. R. (1963). Revising the social studies: What is needed? *Social Education, 27,* 190–196.

Hartoonian, H. M., & Laughlin, M. A. (1989). Designing a social studies scope and sequence for the 21st century. *Social Education, 53,* 388–398.

Joint Committee on Geographic Education. (1984). *Guidelines for geographic education.* Washington, DC: Association of American Geographers and National Council for Geographic Education.

Joyce, B. R. (1972). *New strategies for social education.* Chicago: Science Research Associates.

Joyce, W. W., Little, T. H., & Wronski, S. P. (1991). Scope and sequence, goals, and objectives: Effects on social studies. In J. P. Shaver (Ed.), *Handbook of social studies teaching and learning* (pp. 321-331). New York: Macmillan.

Kniep, W. M. (1989). Social studies within a global education. *Social Education, 53,* 399–403.

Mehlinger, H. D. (1992). The National Commission on Social Studies in the Schools: An example of the politics of curriculum reform in the United States. *Social Education, 56,* 149–153.

National Council for the Social Studies (NCSS). (1990). *Social studies curriculum planning resources.* Washington, DC: Author.

National Council for the Social Studies (NCSS). (1994). *Expectations of excellence: Curriculum standards.* Washington, DC: Author.

Needham, N. R. (1989, March). Is there a decent textbook in your future? *NEA Today, 7,* 4–5.

Nelson, M. R. (1992). *Children's social studies* (2nd ed.). Orlando, FL: Harcourt Brace Jovanovich.

Parker, W. C. (1991). *Renewing the social studies curriculum.* Alexandria, VA: Association for Supervision and Curriculum Development.

People for the American Way. (1986). *Looking at history: A major review of U.S. history textbooks.* Washington, DC: Author.

People for the American Way. (1987). *We the people: A review of U.S. government and civics textbooks.* Washington, DC: Author.

Powers, J. B. (1986). Paul R. Hanna's scope and sequence. *Social Education, 50,* 502–512.

Ravitch, D., & Finn, C. (1987). *What do our 17-year-olds know?* New York: Harper & Row.

Sewall, G. T. (1987). *American history textbooks: An assessment of quality.* Washington DC: Educational Excellence Network.

Shaver, J. P., Davis, O. L., Jr., & Hepburn, S. W. (1979). The status of social studies education: Impressions from three NSF studies. *Social Education, 39,* 150–153.

Stanley, W. B., & Nelson, J. L. (1986). Social education for social transformation. *Social Education, 50,* 528–534.

Superka, D. P., Hawke, S., & Morrissett, I. (1980). The current and future status of the social studies. *Social Education, 40,* 362–369.

Task Force on Scope and Sequence. (1984). In search of a scope and sequence for social studies. *Social Education, 48,* 249–262.

Task Force on Scope and Sequence. (1989). In search of a scope and sequence for social studies. *Social Education, 53,* 376–387.

Textbooks today: How sensitive? How accurate? (1992, Spring). *Social Studies Review,* pp. 1–2.

Tyson-Bernstein, H. (1988). *A conspiracy of good intentions: America's textbook fiasco.* Washington, DC: Council for Basic Education.

Viadero, D. (1992, August 5). Texas assesses $860,000 in new fines for textbook errors. *Education Week,* p. 22.

Welton, D. A., & Mallan, J. T. (1992). *Children and their world: Strategies for teaching social studies* (4th ed.). Boston: Houghton-Mifflin.

Chapter

Planning for Social Studies Instruction

Consider a teacher, Mr. Amato, who has visited the People's Republic of China over the summer. He wishes to share his excitement and insights with his sixth-grade students. Further, he hopes to provide them with a perspective and level of in-depth current information that the 3-year-old social studies text used in the course cannot.

The idea for a unit on modern China begins to take shape. At the outset the teacher mulls over some basic questions: How would this unit fit in with my overall purpose in teaching social studies? Why should my students be asked to learn about this topic? From these initial questions, a goal emerges that suggests an important rationale for the unit, other than that of merely sharing the teacher's interesting experiences.

How much time can be spared for such a unit? The answer to this question helps constrain the scope of the unit. Time in the elementary curriculum is always a limited resource. Further, the time required for a unit often is difficult to estimate accurately, especially for beginning teachers.

What specifically should Mr. Amato's class of culturally diverse students gain from the study of the unit? Which instructional techniques would be the most effective with them? He has a few ideas, but he will more fully flesh out the answers to these questions as he gets to know his students better.

What resources already exist to help create the unit? Some background reading and perusal of the school's and the local library's holdings indicate a wealth of information and resources. Several community agencies also have indicated they can help with guest speakers.

A search of the Educational Resources Information Center (ERIC) Clearinghouse for Social Studies/Social Science Education reference materials (discussed later in the chapter) turns up a field-tested teaching unit developed by a group of classroom teachers at the Malcom Price Laboratory School in Cedar Falls, Iowa (McClain et al., 1985). It provides Mr. Amato with several valuable items, including a simplified map of the major cities of China (see Figure 4.1) and a set of focus questions (see Figure 4.2). He will use the questions both to help structure his unit and to evaluate what students are expected to learn from it.

From the teacher's informed reflections and initial investigations flow specific objectives, related teaching strategies, student activities, resource materials, and assessment procedures. A new social studies unit is born!

FIGURE 4.1

A map of major cities of China

Source: Adapted from *China: A Teaching Unit for Primary Grades* (p. 22) by J. McClain et al., 1985, Cedar Falls: University of Northern Iowa, Malcom Price Laboratory School.

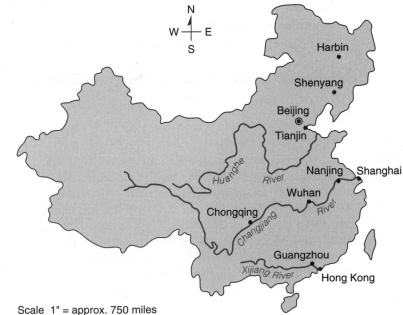

Scale 1" = approx. 750 miles

FIGURE 4.2	Focus questions

1. Where is China located?
2. What is China's natural environment like?
3. What is China's man-made environment like?
4. What are the ethnic and social characteristics of people who live in China?
5. How do people in China satisfy their basic needs of food, clothing and shelter?
6. What types of economic activities are engaged in by the Chinese?
7. How is China organized and governed?
8. How do the Chinese communicate with other people?
9. What kinds of leisure activities are used by the Chinese?
10. What kinds of transportation are used by the Chinese?
11. What kinds of values are accepted by the Chinese?
12. What changes are taking place in China?

Source: From *China: A Teaching Unit for Primary Grades* (p. 2) by J. McClain et al., 1985, Cedar Falls: University of Northern Iowa, Malcom Price Laboratory School.

Basic Issues in Planning Social Studies Instruction

One of the most difficult roles that a beginning elementary teacher has to master—and quickly—is instructional planning. For new teachers, the challenge of providing quality learning experiences for 25 to 35 youngsters for more than 4 hours a day 5 days a week in five or more subjects often appears overwhelming.

To an untrained observer, experienced teachers often make effective teaching look effortless or spontaneous. Such teachers even may profess to have done little immediate or sustained planning for their lessons. In reality, through trial and error and reflective analysis over the years, seasoned social studies teachers gradually build on their series of successful planning experiences.

Well-planned, carefully prepared lessons are a key ingredient in all successful teaching. Planning involves having a clear rationale for what we are about, a sense of what we specifically hope to accomplish if our instruction is successful, and a clear set of procedures for accomplishing our objectives. It also requires attention to the prudent use of the limited instructional time available to us during the school day. Planning involves thoughtful consideration of both the nature of what students are to learn and why and how they are to learn it.

Identifying a Purpose for Citizenship Education

All social studies planning begins with some notion of the purpose of the social studies. In Chapter 1 we considered six alternative perspectives concerning the major purpose of citizenship education—namely, that the emphasis in citizenship education most appropriately might be placed on one of the following:

- Transmission of the cultural heritage
- Concepts and methods of inquiry from the social sciences
- Reflective inquiry
- Informed social criticism
- Personal development
- Development of reflection, competence, and concern

The process of planning social studies instruction should begin with the teacher's adoption of one of these six perspectives or a new one. The statement of purpose then becomes a rudder that guides the remainder of the planning decisions. A clear connection should exist between the teacher's statement of purpose and the individual lessons, activities, and total curriculum that are developed for students.

goals

Social Studies Goals for Instruction

The general expectations for what educators plan to accomplish in the social studies curriculum over the course of the year or a shorter unit of time constitute curricular **goals.** They express in broad terms what students are to achieve as a result of some instructional program (Glatthorn, 1987). Goal statements may be different for each level of the social studies curriculum, or they may remain the same across the grades. Brophy and Alleman (1993) suggested that all aspects of the curriculum should be goals-driven, including questions, subject matter, and evaluation items.

Identifying and Stating Goals

Establishing goals is an important step toward creating a basic framework for a course of study and for leading the way to more specific curriculum expectations. Goal statements are distinguished by their *level of generality*. For example, consider the following two goals:

1. To help students understand the need for conserving and preserving the natural environment and identify ways they can play a role in conservation and preservation.
2. To help students understand that citizens have both rights and responsibilities in our society and that these have evolved over time due to the efforts of many groups and individuals.

Although these are important statements of broad concerns that teachers may wish to address in the social studies curriculum, they require further elaboration and specificity if they are to offer guidance for crafting individual lessons. For example, the first goal does not spell out what aspects of conservation and preservation will be considered. Nor does the second goal indicate the types of rights and responsibilities that will be considered.

Social Studies Objectives for Instruction

objectives

As the preceding examples suggest, goal statements provide only a general guidepost for what the social studies curriculum should encompass. Related to goals are the more particular **objectives** that the curriculum is designed to achieve. Objectives spell out specifically and clearly what students are expected to learn as the outcome of some measure of instruction (Bloom, 1956; Krathwohl, Bloom, & Masia, 1969). They may be stated for individual lessons, for a unit of study, or for the complete curriculum. The same objective also may be included in more than one lesson.

Identifying and Stating Objectives

Consider the following sample objectives. Then contrast them with the two goal statements listed earlier.

As a result of the lesson (activity), the student will be able to:

- Identify on the first trial at least five of the continents by writing in the names on an outline map.
- State in writing, after reading the text, at least three important rights that all American citizens have.
- Score at least 75% on a multiple-choice test covering the subject matter studied in the unit on conservation and preservation of the environment.
- Identify from among alternatives their value priorities.
- Briefly describe how urban, suburban, and rural communities are similar and different.
- Adopt three patterns of behavior that will help protect the environment.
- Construct a map that includes all of the features listed on the chalkboard.
- Make a commitment to become a better listener.
- Construct a pie chart that accurately represents the data on the attached sheet.

- Sort a set of pictures into two piles, one labeled "transportation" and one labeled "not transportation."
- Identify some of the ways families differ with respect to customs, foods, and types of shelter, as a result of the field trip to the museum.

Objectives and Student Learning Outcomes.   All of the sample objectives indicate some clear and specific student learning outcomes, but some are more precise than others. The first one, for example, is an illustration of a highly specific objective. Some objectives state the criteria for an acceptable response (e.g., "five of the continents" or "75% on a multiple-choice test"). Others state the conditions for demonstrating achievement of the objective (e.g., "by writing in the names on an outline map" or "after reading the text").

behavioral
(performance)
objectives

Objectives that provide this degree of specificity and describe clearly the expected behavior of the student are characterized as **behavioral, or performance, objectives.** Some topics lend themselves to the use of behavioral or performance objectives, such as identifying the location of states and listing their corresponding capitals. However, all objectives that are stated clearly and specifically can be used effectively in the social studies to plan instruction and to communicate what the expected outcomes of student learning are to be.

Writing Statements of Objectives.   Sources such as curriculum guides and basal texts often contain examples of the types of social studies goals and objectives for various grade levels and subjects. Typically, statements of objectives begin with headings similar to the following: *As a result of this lesson, the pupil will be able to* . . . . In other cases the introductory phrase is assumed, and the objective is stated in a briefer form similar to the following: *To (write) (draw) (point to).* . . .

Many lists of verbs have been identified to aid teachers in writing objectives. A sample list is provided here to suggest the range of possibilities that can be considered.

The student will be able to:

rank	identify	defend	formulate
estimate	assemble	sort	participate
predict	match	summarize	compose
rate	point to	explain	exhibit
select	organize	demonstrate	hypothesize
role-play	classify	locate	list
construct	define	draw	measure
write	diagram	modify	display
state	create	critique	contribute
justify	judge	support	order
listen	share	map	volunteer
observe	debate	convince	resolve

Organizing Subject Matter into Units

Typically, teachers are assigned only the general outline of the subject matter or a list of topics they should include in their social studies curriculum (e.g., a unit on families around the world). In other cases, the complete course of study for the entire year may be laid out (e.g., a district curriculum committee has created a series of units for the third grade). In many cases a basal text is available as a resource; in others teachers have access to a collection of multiple materials, including trade books.

Whatever structure a school provides for the social studies program, teachers should shape it to create their own curriculum based on the unique needs, interests, and talents of their students. In teaching social studies, teachers should infuse the curriculum with their own sense of purpose, goals, and objectives. They also need to include timely issues and to draw on the resources of the local community to enrich and enliven the curriculum (see Chapter 2).

Unit Planning

The subject matter of a year's course is organized into a series of **units** of study.   units
The essence of a unit is a series of sequenced and related learning activities organized around a theme, issue, or problem, along with goals, objectives, resources for learning, and procedures for evaluation. Resources in units include bibliographies, primary source materials (firsthand accounts), computer software, text-

Unit activities should include a mix of things for individual students and for groups to do.

books, readings, posters, work sheets, simulation games, transparencies, drawings, guest speakers, field trips, films, videotapes, videodiscs, audiotapes, artifacts, maps, periodicals, microfilm, and microfiche. Units may extend for any length of time, but typically they require from 2 to 6 weeks to complete.

Sample Unit Topics.   Some illustrations of unit titles are:

- "Understanding Our Behavior"
- "Communities and How They Change"
- "Ways That Each of Us Is Special"
- "The American Family"
- "Dwellings Around the World"
- "What Is Prejudice?"
- "The Plains Indians"
- "The Role of Women in American Society"
- "Causes of the Civil War"
- "The Bill of Rights"

Although some of these unit topics are more appropriate for upper-grade students (e.g., "Causes of the Civil War"), it is the actual subject matter that teachers include that determines for whom units are appropriate. For instance, units that address increasingly more complex aspects of the American family could be developed for primary-, intermediate-, or middle-grade students.

Computer-Based and Traditional Sources of Units

The ERIC Clearinghouse for Social Studies/Social Science Education

Increasingly, the Internet has become an important resource for social studies. In Chapter 11, which focuses on technology applications, we will catalog and consider the growing number of computer-based resources that are available to social studies teachers and how they can be accessed. In addition, we will examine how emerging technologies can facilitate one-on-one communication and sharing of curriculum resources between teachers at remote sites. Units also are available through the national educational clearinghouse: **The ERIC Clearinghouse for Social Studies/Social Science Education,** Indiana University, 2805 East 10th Street, Bloomington, IN 47408. School supply houses that specialize in distributing social studies materials produced by commercial publishers are also excellent sources—for example, Social Studies School Service, 10200 Jefferson Boulevard, P.O. Box 802, Culver City, CA 90232–0802. Professional organizations also have developed collections of units for different grade levels on a variety of topics. Units typically can be found in teacher resource centers and other professional libraries.

"Women of the American Revolution" is an example of a unit designed for grades 5 through 8; it is available from a professional organization, the National Center for History in the Schools (Pearson, 1991). The basic goal of the unit is to introduce students to the American Revolution by focusing on the conflict through the perspective of women. The unit consists of four lessons of varying length, with corresponding objectives as follows (Pearson, 1991):

Lesson One Objectives:
1. To learn the role colonial women played in the turmoil that preceded the revolution.
2. To understand some of the causes that led to the Revolution.
3. To practice interpreting documents that reflect various points of view.

Lesson 2 Objectives:
1. To understand that war affects whole societies, not just soldiers.
2. To consider some of the ways women participated in the war.
3. To experience how history is written.

Lesson 3 Objectives:
1. To learn the sense in which the Revolution was truly revolutionary and to understand its limitations.
2. To understand that many 18th-century women recognized and resented their lack of legal and political autonomy.
3. To consider why, despite women's contributions, they failed to achieve legal and political rights.

Lesson 4 Objectives:
1. To understand the effect of the Revolution on women's lives.
2. To consider the way that human events can have unintended consequences.

A portion of the text of Lesson 2 from the unit is shown in Figure 4.3.

Social studies textbooks also are organized into units. For example, one third-grade text was divided into five units that normally would be spread over the 36 weeks of the school year. The subject matter of each unit was organized into three to five subtopics or chapters. Each chapter, in turn, was organized into three to six related lessons. Resource materials, follow-up activities, and evaluation measures were provided in each unit.

Teachers themselves are one of the major developers of individual units. Many of these units are shared within a school or district and often are published in curriculum guides and professional journals such as *Social Studies and the Young Learner* and *Social Education*. Still others are made available through ERIC.

FIGURE 4.3   Lesson Two

Lesson Activities

1. Ask students what men did during the Revolution. If students know that many men were soldiers, ask them to speculate about who was doing the work normally done by men. Tell them they are going to read a document which will help confirm their suspicions.

2. Have students read **DOCUMENT D**, an excerpt from Sarah Frazier's *A Reminiscence*, a description of her grandmother's part in the war.

   a. Discuss the document's reliability and representativeness. The document was written long after the events described, raising doubts about its accuracy. Moreover, the existence of an iron works suggests that these were people of greater wealth than was typical for yeoman farmers.

   b. Besides taking over men's occupations this document suggests women were busy with a variety of other activities. Have students list the responsibilities women assumed during the Revolution. They should begin with information obtained in this document, but also have them brainstorm about the kind of support armies require.

   a. Remind them that this was a war fought on home soil. When armies moved into a region, homes became hospitals, barracks for soldiers, and warehouses for supplies and ammunition.

   b. The constant interaction between soldiers and civilians allowed many women to become spies.

   c. Women also provided moral support; they often travelled with armies, sharing in soldiers' hardships even as they cooked, cleaned, nursed and comforted the men.

   d. Sometimes wives accompanied their husbands into battle, loading guns and attending the wounded. Even in regions free of combat, women improvised the scarce staples and manufactured goods no longer being brought from England.

   e. Remind students of the story which began this unit; women organized and acted when hoarding was suspected. Have them consider the accuracy of this account. Reading it to them again may be useful.

      • *If the dialogue is invented, how can they be sure the whole story is not made up?*

FIGURE 4.3   *(Continued)*

- *When historians write, where does the record of the past end and the story of the past begin?*
- *Another way to put this question is to ask them how free should historians to be to interpret the past?*

The issue is extremely complex and students cannot be expected to do more than discuss the question. One of the reasons for raising the issue at all is for them to understand how, until quite recently, women could be almost completely excluded from accounts of the Revolution.

   f.   After students have finished this list, ask them to speculate about what would have been the patriots' chances for victory without women supplying the resources and support to continue the struggle.

HISTORICAL RESOURCE: DOCUMENT D

Sarah Frazier's *A Reminiscence*, an account of her grandmother's behavior during the Revolution

Mary Frazier did much to help Washington's army at Valley Forge. Sarah Frazier wrote the following account about her grandmother's actions during the winter of 1777–1778.*

. . . day after day collecting from neighbors and friends far and near, whatever they could spare for the comfort of the destitute soldiers, the blankets, and yarn, and half worn clothing thus obtained she brought to her own house, where they would be patched, and darned, and made wearable and comfortable, the stockings newly footed, or open ones knit, adding what clothing she could give of her own. She often sat up half the night, sometimes all, to get clothing ready. Then with it, and whatever could be obtained for food, she would have packed on her horse and set out on her cold lonely journey to the camp—which she went to repeatedly during the winter . . .

All the cloth and linen that my Grandfather wore during the war were spun at home, most of it by [my grandmother's] own hands. All the clothing except weaving. All the business of every kind, she attended to Farm, Iron Works, and domestic matters. In Summer as soon as it was light she had her horse saddled, rode over the farm and directed the men about their work, often rode down to the creek, where Sharpless' Iron Works are now, and was back at breakfast time to give her attention and toil to the children, servants, & household affairs.

*Reprinted from *Pennsylvania Magazine of History and Biography*, XLVI (1922), pp 55–56.

Source: From *Women of the American Revolution* (pp. 27–29) by J. Pearson, 1991, Los Angeles: University of California, National Center for History in the Schools. Copyright 1991 by National Center for History in the Schools. Reprinted by permission.

In creating their own units, teachers build on their special interests, expertise, or unusual experiences, such as travels. Teacher-created units often begin with a general set of ideas centered around some topics or questions that teachers regard as important and that fit within the general framework of their curriculum. From this base of ideas the other specific details such as goals, objectives, materials, and activities are fleshed out to give the unit shape and reality.

Resource Units and Teaching Units

resource units
teaching units

Units are sometimes classified as **resource units** and **teaching units.** Although the two types share many of the same elements, resource units generally are more extensive and detailed than teaching units. Also they often are designed as multipurpose collections of materials and lessons to be used eclectically by many different teachers for a variety of students. A resource unit typically would list more subtopics, objectives, teaching strategies and activities, resources, and evaluation procedures than an individual teacher needs to use for a topic. Drawing on a resource unit, a teacher can create a customized teaching unit tailored for a specific population of students and for a given length of time.

Creating Units

Student interests and experiences, as well as those of the teacher, can provide the impetus for units. Teachers can obtain such data informally by tracking the patterns of student subcultures. They also can keep abreast of issues within the community that the school embraces. A more systematic and focused approach is to use a structured survey or questionnaire to determine what students know and wish to learn (see the K-W-L technique in Chapter 10).

Building Units Around Issues and Problems.   One effective way to structure units is to base them on significant personal or public social issues and problems (Shaver, 1992). Engle and Ochoa (1988) advocated building units around a problem and a series of significant questions. For example, a third-grade unit dealing with environmental issues might be organized around questions such as the following:

> Is it more important for the government to help people keep their jobs or protect the environment and endangered species? What will happen and who will be affected if the government acts to protect the environment? To help people keep their jobs? What should individuals do if their beliefs are different from those of the government?

Using Concept Maps to Plan Units.   One way for the teacher to sketch out

concept map

the general structure of a unit is through the use of a **concept map** (Novak & Gowin, 1984), which is a listing and an ordering of all of the major concepts to be discussed within a unit. Related concepts are joined in the map, along with a brief statement that explains how they are linked. As I discuss further in Chapters 6 and 10, concept maps have a number of uses in teaching. Our focus in this section is on their application to *unit planning*.

Concept maps offer teachers a planning tool for thinking through all of the important topics they wish to include in a unit and also for identifying relationships among topics. Maps provide a comprehensive graphic representation of the unit. Novak and Gowin (1984) suggested that, in creating a map, teachers should focus on four to seven concepts that are central to the unit.

A partially completed sample concept map that represents one teacher's initial ideas for a unit is shown in Figure 4.4. As the unit evolves, more topics can be added to the key nodes of the map. For example, the teacher may list the cities to be used as case studies, along with the features of each city that will be highlighted.

Formats for Unit Planning

Teachers have a variety of unit **formats,** or ways of organizing and presenting the information in a unit, to choose from. A sample format for developing a unit plan is provided in Figure 4.5. The choice of a format to use in unit planning, however, is largely a matter of personal preference. Teachers should identify a format in an existing unit that they find easy to follow and adopt it.

formats

FIGURE 4.4

Concept map used to plan a unit

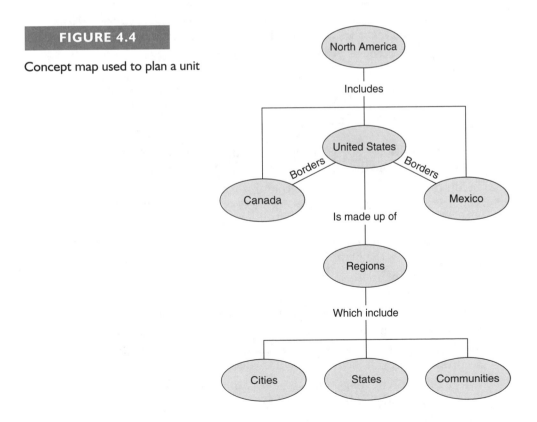

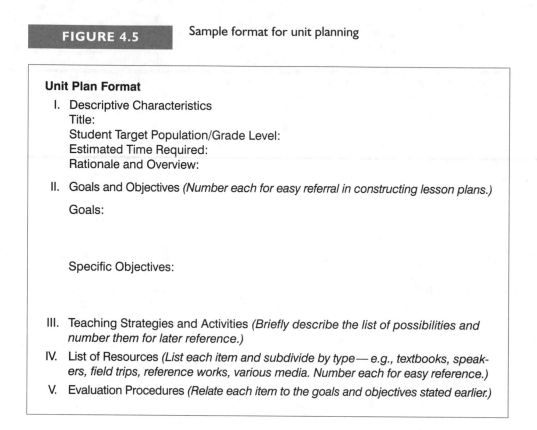

FIGURE 4.5   Sample format for unit planning

Unit Plan Format

I. Descriptive Characteristics
   Title:
   Student Target Population/Grade Level:
   Estimated Time Required:
   Rationale and Overview:

II. Goals and Objectives *(Number each for easy referral in constructing lesson plans.)*

   Goals:

   Specific Objectives:

III. Teaching Strategies and Activities *(Briefly describe the list of possibilities and number them for later reference.)*
IV. List of Resources *(List each item and subdivide by type — e.g., textbooks, speakers, field trips, reference works, various media. Number each for easy reference.)*
V. Evaluation Procedures *(Relate each item to the goals and objectives stated earlier.)*

In summary, the general process of creating a unit can be outlined as follows:

1. Develop an idea for a special topic of study and translate it into a brief, clear statement of your theme or problem focus. (Unit Title)

2. Break the big idea or theme for the unit into a set of more specific ideas and smaller subtopics or list of key questions you wish to address. (List of Topics)

3. Indicate for which group of students or grade levels the unit is intended and include them in the planning if possible. (Target Student Population)

4. Make an approximate determination of how much time can be spent on the unit. (Time Required)

5. Construct a brief overview of what the unit is to be about and why it is important and useful for the intended class to learn it. (Rationale)

6. Identify a goal or a set of basic goals that the unit will be designed to accomplish. (Goals)

7. Outline the specific objectives to be accomplished with the unit and arrange them in sequential order. (Objectives)

8. Identify and develop related significant teaching strategies and activities. (Teaching Strategies and Activities)

9. Identify, locate, and organize all of the individuals and instructional resources that are available and will be needed. (Resources)

10. Develop a plan to evaluate the effectiveness of the unit. (Evaluation Procedures)

Organizing Subject Matter into Lessons

lessons

As we have seen, one important element of teaching units is the provision for a series of interrelated **lessons.** Apart from units, teachers also fashion lessons to achieve discrete objectives that can be achieved over a short period of time. A lesson may last for a single class period or may extend over several days (e.g., Figure 4.3).

Lesson Plans

Lesson planning includes taking into account what has come *before* the lesson and what is to *follow* it, as well as what happens *during* it. It also requires careful attention to the conditions under which learning is to occur. Effective lesson planning demands an awareness of the prior knowledge and special needs of individual students within a class and requires teachers to give careful thought to the specific details of what is to be achieved. In addition, it involves consideration of how instructional activities can accomplish objectives in an interesting and meaningful way for a particular group of students. Above all, in planning lessons, the teacher should have an informed grasp of the subject matter under investigation. In Dewey's (1961) words:

> When engaged in the direct act of teaching, the instructor needs to have subject matter at his fingers' ends; his attention should be upon the attitude and response of the pupil. . . . the teacher should be occupied not with the subject matter itself but in its interaction with the pupils' present needs and capacities. (p. 183)

The Fundamental Elements of Lesson Planning.   Six fundamental elements to consider in developing a lesson plan structure and format are:

- Lesson title
- Goals and objectives
- Initiatory activity
- Teaching strategies
- Resources
- Transition\Assessment

To help illustrate how these elements operate within a lesson, for each item, I include an example with commentary that is adapted from a lesson plan developed by the National Geographic Society (1988, pp. 14–15).

1. *Lesson Title.* Giving each lesson a title communicates its focus. *Example:* "The Geography of Petroleum."

2. *Goals and Objectives.* The lesson should be linked with the larger instructional goals that the teacher has established. The objectives that the lesson is designed to achieve should be stated clearly and as specifically as possible. Although the lesson itself may not explicitly identify for students the goals and objectives it is to achieve, it should be related clearly to them in the prior planning of the lesson. *Example:* To use maps and graphs to identify the major areas of world petroleum production and consumption.

initiatory activity

3. *Initiatory Activity.* A lesson plan should begin with an **initiatory activity** that arouses curiosity, puzzles, or somehow focuses attention on what is to be learned. *Example:* Ask students to imagine an end to all international sales of petroleum tomorrow. What would be the impact on the United States? How would students' lives change? What would happen to countries that consume major amounts of petroleum but produce little or none? Use Japan as an example.

4. *Teaching Strategies.* Teaching strategies and activities refer generally to the set of procedures that teachers employ to achieve their instructional objectives. As we consider in the chapters that follow, different types of strategies are used for different objectives. Strategies incorporate questions, statements, directions, actions, and the sequence in which they are to occur. Strategies also deal with how the teacher plans to structure and present new subject matter and relate it to students' prior knowledge. They also indicate teacher and student roles in the lesson. *Example:* Direct students to examine maps in an atlas to identify major petroleum-producing countries. (See *Goode's World Atlas*, p. 48.) List their findings on the chalkboard. Have students shade and label these countries on their world outline maps.

5. *Resources.* Somewhere within the lesson for easy reference should be a list of the various resources that will be used during the lesson. The order in which the materials are to be used should be indicated clearly. Time required for the lesson, which is a resource, optionally may be included.

6. *Transition/Assessment.* Each lesson should include some transition to the next one. This shift may consist merely of a summary of the day's activities, with some indication of what is to follow and how the two lessons are related. It also might consist of some assessment of a phase of learning that has just been completed (see Chapter 13). Additionally, it might provide opportunities for students to apply, extend, or experiment with what they have learned. *Example:* Have students research the environmental implications (such as air pollution, global warming, oil spills) of the widespread use of petroleum as an energy source.

A lesson plan for kindergarten children that incorporates these six basic elements is shown in Figure 4.6.

FIGURE 4.6   Sample lesson plan format for kindergarten

CLOTHES TELL STORIES

Purpose of the Lesson

To demonstrate to the pupils that clothes may tell us something about those who are wearing them.

Expectations

Upon completion of this lesson, pupils should be able to:

Identify three uniforms and tell what people wear them.

Recognize and tell some information that uniforms suggest about the wearers.

Resources

Webstermasters, pp. 39, 40

drawing paper and crayons

magazines, newspapers, catalogues (optional)

children's clothing — see Evaluation (optional)

Strategies

Arousing Interest

Ask four pupils to stand in front of the class. Then tell the class: "Look at their clothes. How are their clothes alike?" (Wearing pants, sneakers, sweaters; colors.) Say: "Think about other clothes that you have, and tell why you are not wearing them today." As they tell you why, emphasize the fact that for every choice there is a reason. "Do you have special clothes you wear on special days?" Indicate to the class your clothes tell a story about you. Repeat comments made by two or three of the pupils to illustrate the point. For instance, "Arthur wore sneakers to school because they are good for playing and running at lunchtime. Mary is wearing a short-sleeve top because it is very warm today, and she wants to be as cool and as comfortable as possible." Then say: "I'm going to try to see if I can tell some things about you by looking at your clothes. I'll try to think of some things that have not been mentioned yet." By now, you know the pupils well and may have a lot of fun surprising the class with what you have to say. For example, "Margaret, you are wearing blue. Because you often wear blue clothes I think blue is one of your favorite colors."

Computer-Based and Traditional Sources of Lesson Plans

As with unit plans, an especially rich store of lesson plans for all grade levels and across a wide range of topics is available over the Internet, described in Chapter 11. A number of teachers, professional groups, and even commercial organizations have established World Wide Web pages that are accessible free around the clock and offer K–12 lesson plan collections and resources for developing lessons, such as maps that can be copied.

Houghton Mifflin, for example, offers an array of activities within its *Social Studies Center* [http://www.eduplace.com/s/indexlo.html]. The web home page is shown in Figure 4.7. Note that the home page includes links to other related

FIGURE 4.6   *(Continued)*

The Lesson

Distribute Webstermasters, pp. 39 and 40. Read the titles. Help the pupils identify each picture. Guide the pupils in recognizing the story the clothes in each picture tell about the person. Spend some time discussing each picture. This will help pupils to group pictures later.

As you discuss the pictures, ask: "Have you ever seen anyone dressed like this?" If pupils have, encourage them to tell about it. Ask: "Why is this person dressed this way? What does this clothing tell us? What do you think this person is doing? What do you think this person is about to do?"

Say: "Suppose you wanted to put some of the clothes these people are wearing in a group. Look at the pictures on both pages. Which pictures would you choose for a group? Circle the pictures that have the clothes you chose to group together."

Have pupils share their responses and tell why the pictures were chosen for the groups.

Ending the Lesson

Ask the pupils: "How are clothes on pages 39 and 40 alike? How are they different from each other?" Compare all the clothes on one page at a time.

Distribute drawing paper. Have the pupils draw pictures of clothes they wear that tell a story about them. Say: "It could be a bathing suit that tells you like to swim. It could be a cap that says you like baseball, but be sure it tells something about you. It could be your favorite clothes." Or, pupils may find and cut out magazine pictures of such clothes to paste on the page. At the bottom of the page, you may wish to write the pupil's comments about their pictures.

Transition/Assessment

Display pictures on a bulletin board of people wearing uniforms similar to those that pupils identified during the lessons. You may also use the Webstermasters pictures again or the pupils' drawings. Ask pupils to relate stories the clothes suggest about the people wearing them by telling why or for what occasions the clothes are being worn. Each pupil should be able to relate at least two "stories." On a second bulletin board, display children's bedclothes, children's playclothes, and children's party clothes. If you cannot get children's clothing, use pictures instead. Ask the pupils to identify the types of clothing displayed. Each pupil should identify two types.

social studies sites on the Internet, such as maps. Figure 4.7 also presents the list of outline maps that can be accessed. When you click on the "Activities" button on the home page, you will be offered a variety of resources, including the lesson plan in Figure 4.8 [http://www.eduplace.com/ss/citsub.html].

A sample from the extensive collection of lessons available electronically through ERIC appears in Figure 4.9. The lesson, authored by Lisa Knight, an elementary teacher, creatively explores issues related to the topic of supply and demand.

FIGURE 4.7   Social studies center

Welcome to the Social Studies Center!

Social Studies Fake Out!

Test your knowledge of history, geography, and other aspects of social studies by playing our interactive web game, Social Studies Fake Out! -- the social studies fact game.

We the People Internet Support

Check out the wealth of free materials we're developing to help you use the Internet with every unit of Houghton Mifflin's new social studies program, *We the People*.

Current Events in the Social Studies Classroom

Here's a new feature you can use to bring the real world right into your classroom. Every month we'll present a student investigation for grades 1-8 of a current news topic, including relevant Internet links and teaching suggestions.

The GeoNet Game

If you don't think geography is fun, you haven't played GeoNet, the geography game based on the National Geography Standards! Try your hand at this game and help save the world from threatening aliens. Can you earn enough points to become a GeoChampion? There's only one way to find out . . . .

Social Studies Project Watch

Are you sponsoring a project related to Social Studies? Would you like to find other classrooms to participate? Send your project description to projects@hmco.com.

Social Studies Links

Are you looking for Social Studies sites on the Internet? We've organized our links thematically to make it easier for you to find just what you're looking for. We update them regularly, so please be sure to check back often.

Social Studies Activities

Are you looking for something new to try with your class? Here are some activities that will enhance any social studies program. These activities are organized thematically and grouped by grade range. You can also search through our activity database to find classroom activities by grade level in any curriculum area.

Outline Maps

Looking for a map of the northern hemisphere to spruce up that final report? Want a political map of Asia for your students to use during the next unit? Then check out our great collection of outline maps now!

FIGURE 4.7 (Continued)

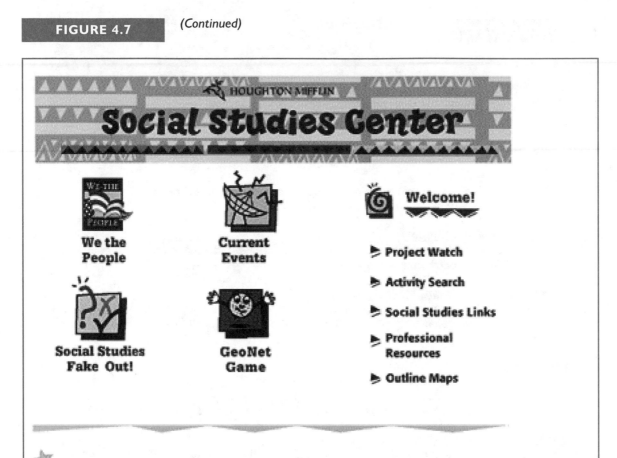

Have you ever wished you could influence the design of a Web site? This is your chance! We need your input to make Education Place the best site on the Web for teachers, parents, and students. Please take five minutes to complete our questionnaire and become a part of the Education Place development team.

Special Announcement: Attention Social Studies Educators! Houghton Mifflin's new social studies program, *We the People,* is sweeping the nation. To receive an overview brochure or to have a representative contact you, please send an e-mail to ss@hmco.com (please include your name, school, and mailing address). Check out our great *We the People* Internet resources too.

Current Events -- The United Nations is the only arena where the nations of the world come together to debate their problems. This year that organization has chosen a new leader, or Secretary General, Mr. Kofi Annan of Ghana. Find out about this important world leader in this month's Current Events by exploring the related teaching hints, links, and activities.

FIGURE 4.7   *(Continued)*

Online Outline Maps

Below is a selection of outline maps for use in the classroom or at home. Feel free to print or download any of these maps for your personal use in activities, reports, or stories.

- Africa: Political

- Africa: Political and Physical

- Asia and the South Pacific: Political

- Central America: Political

- Colonial America, 1776

- Eastern Hemisphere

- Europe: Political

- European Countries

- North America

- North America: Political

- Northern Asia: Political

- Northern Hemisphere

- South America: Political

- South and Central America: Political

- Southeast Asia: Political

- Southern Asia: Political

- Southern Hemisphere

- United States: Capitals

- United States: Climate

Source: From *Social Studies Center* by Houghton Mifflin, 1996 (Internet).

FIGURE 4.8   Sample of Internet resources available for planning lessons

City, Suburb, or Country

Cultures, Geography, Art

In this activity students make a picture web to describe a place. Students discuss the characteristics of life in the country, in a suburb, and in a city. Students compare and contrast general environmental differences, and explore their immediate environment.

You can use an Assessment Rubric to assess students' mastery of the objectives.

WHAT YOU NEED

- Paper
- Magazines
- Scissors
- Glue
- String

WHAT TO DO

1. Write "City" or "Suburb" or "Country" on the paper.

2. Find pictures of things from that place. Examples are:
   - kinds of jobs
   - animals
   - buildings

3. Glue pictures on the paper.

4. Connect the picture to the word with string.

Share Your Picture Web with Others!

- Describe the special things you find in a city, suburb, or country.
- Compare your home to the place described in the picture web.

Education Place   Site Index   Social Studies Center   SS Activity Index

Source: From *Social Studies Center* by Houghton Mifflin, 1996 (Internet).

FIGURE 4.9 Lesson plan

These lesson plans are the result of the work of the teachers who have attended the Columbia Education Center's Summer Workshop. CEC is a consortium of teachers from 14 western states dedicated to improving the quality of education in the rural, western, United States, and particularly the quality of math and science education. CEC uses Big Sky Telegraph as the hub of their telecommunications network that allows the participating teachers to stay in contact with their trainers and peers that they have met at the Workshops.

Title: Supply and Demand

Author: Lisa Knight, Meadow Glade Elementary, Battle Ground, WA

Grade Level: Appropriate for grades 4–7

Overview: This lesson allows for personal involvement in the concept of supply and demand, which helps the students see how it relates to their everyday life.

Objectives: Students will be able to:

1. Define the terms *supply* and *demand*.
2. Identify what happens when demand exceeds supply.
3. Identify what happens when supply exceeds demand.
4. Explain how supply and demand affect choices such as careers, types of cars made, etc.
5. Give recent examples of instances where demand exceeded supply and the results.
6. Explain how economic stability or affluence affects supply and demand.

Resources/materials:

Teacher materials: Tokens, prize for each student in class (it can be something as simple as chocolate kisses)

Student materials: Pencil, 3 index cards

Activities and Procedures:

1. Students will be given a box of tokens with at least two different colors in it and asked to select any number of them from 1 to a handful.
2. Place a value on the tokens. (Make certain this is done *after* students have already selected their tokens.)

FIGURE 4.9　　*(Continued)*

3. Pull out an object students would desire to win and let the students know that they will only receive an "A" on this lesson if they own this selected item of which you happen to have EXACTLY one. You will announce the bidding to be open at 10 and they may use their tokens to purchase the item.

4. Continue auction until a student has paid a high price for this item and received it. Then pull out a large supply of the very same item just sold while announcing that you do just happen to have a few more of these items and you're willing to open the bidding at 1. *Wait & watch reaction!*

5. Write *supply and demand* on board. Ask the individual who bought the over-priced item to define what these terms mean to him in light of the experience he just had, explain why he was motivated to pay such a high price for it, and let us know if he would have paid so much had he known there were enough items to go around.

6. Guide students in a discussion which covers all objectives. (I found an effective lead-in to objective #6 is to ask the following: "What if these tokens represented money, and this was all the money you had available for two months?")

Tying It All Together:

1. Ask students to think of three items in their desks and to secretly set a price for each one of them on an index card which is folded so that it can stand upright on the desks.

2. Instruct students to then take out the items and place them by the appropriate "price tag" on their desks.

3. Invite students to go "shopping" and check out all the prices in the "store."

4. Lead the students in the discussion which will naturally follow with questions such as:

   "Now that you know how other merchants priced their items, how will it affect your pricing of the same items?"

   "Were there some items that would be in high demand because of their low supply? How might that affect pricing?"

5. Students may want to stock their "shelves" differently after doing some comparison shopping and seeing the availability of certain items. You may then choose to give them another opportunity to price three items of their choice and discuss their changes and why they were made.

Source: From *Supply and Demand* (pp. 184–186) by L. Knight, 1994, Columbia Education Center (Internet).

Formats and Procedures for Lesson Planning

A quick review of lesson plans found in curricular guides, teachers' manuals for basal texts, and teachers' publications and periodicals will reveal great variety in formats. As with units, there are many different notions concerning what written lesson plans should include and which format should be used to construct them. Examples vary in structure, terminology, degree of detail, and the number of elements they include. Compare, for example, the three types of lesson plans presented in Figures 4.3, 4.6, and 4.10.

Similar to the process of adopting a format for unit planning, selecting a format for lesson planning is largely a matter of a teacher's professional judgment and/or school requirements. Some schools, for example, request that teachers employ a format and set of procedures that have been standardized in the school or district.

An example of a standardized approach to lesson planning that was adopted by a number of schools across the United States during the past decade is a 7-step plan developed and popularized by Madeleine Hunter (1984). Hunter's lesson plan design makes provisions for the following elements:

1. Establish the anticipatory set. (Get students' attention.)
2. Explain the objective of the lesson.
3. Provide instructional input.
4. Model the desired student behavior.
5. Check for understanding. (Get feedback.)
6. Provide for guided practice.
7. Provide for independent practice.

The issue of mandated lesson plan formats and procedures has become a controversial one among teachers and professional groups. Some of the reasons schools have given for instituting such policies are to establish minimal teaching standards and to expedite communication among teachers, supervisors, and administrators. For some teachers, however, such a requirement presents a serious constraint. They regard such formats as overly restrictive and inflexible, inappropriate for many types of significant learning activities, and, in general, an infringement on their professional prerogatives.

Balance in Instructional Planning

Another important issue that teachers need to address in planning is providing *balance* in the type of goals and objectives used in lessons and units. Such balance involves ensuring that the curriculum they develop addresses in some proportion each of the three dimensions of reflection, competence, and concern. Before reading further, reexamine the list of objectives that appeared earlier in the chapter and see whether you can identify which of the three dimensions each one represents.

Planning for Reflection, Competence, and Concern.   In Chapter 1, I suggested that the purpose of citizenship education is the development of the reflective, competent, and concerned citizen. The *reflective* citizen has knowledge of a body of concepts, facts, and generalizations concerning the organization, understanding, and development of individuals, groups, and societies. In addition, the reflective citizen is knowledgeable about the processes of hypothesis formation and testing, problem solving, and decision making.

The *competent* citizen has a repertoire of skills. These include social, research and analysis, chronology, and spatial skills.

The *concerned* citizen has an awareness of his or her rights and responsibilities, a sense of social consciousness, and a well-grounded framework for deciding what is right and wrong. In addition, the concerned citizen has learned how to identify and analyze issues and to suspend judgment concerning alternative beliefs, attitudes, values, customs, and cultures.

Further, I stated that the social studies curriculum should incorporate at each grade level some balance among lessons that seek to develop reflection, competence, and concern. Although individual lessons may not include objectives that address all three dimensions, each unit should include some balance that the teacher considers appropriate. Further, the year's program should contain a mix of objectives that reflect the curricular priorities the teacher has established. To illustrate, if a teacher has decided that the dimension of competence is the most important one to emphasize for the year and concern the least important, the distribution of objectives should reflect this fact; that is, over 33% of them should deal with competence and the smallest percentage with concern.

Both the units and the total curriculum can be analyzed for balance. Figure 4.10 shows a sample of objectives that were used to frame a first-grade unit. Notice that although all three dimensions are included in the example, one receives greater emphasis (the reflective dimension).

Developmental Considerations in Instructional Planning

Imagine a teacher lecturing to a first-grade class on the principle of supply and demand. Intuitively, we recognize that this technique is inappropriate because it emphasizes abstractions and symbols rather than sensory experiences.

In contrast, planning that is developmentally sensitive emphasizes concrete examples, includes multiple alternative strategies, and links children's prior knowledge to new information. Even very young children can grasp the essence of supply and demand through the medium of a game employing toys and candy, objects well grounded in their everyday experiences.

Examples of instructional techniques that are especially appropriate for elementary- and middle-grade students in social studies classes are:

role-playing	field trips
manipulatives	learning centers
constructing dioramas	collages

FIGURE 4.10	Sample of objectives to frame a first-grade unit

First-Grade Unit: Comparing Families

Sample Unit Objectives That Emphasize the Reflective Citizen Dimension

Students should be able to:

1. Identify at least four types of family groupings.
2. List two ways in which families are alike.
3. Identify at least one rule that families typically have.
4. State two ways in which family members satisfy each other's needs.

Sample Unit Objectives That Emphasize the Competent Citizen Dimension

1. Draw a picture that shows how people in a family help one another.
2. Help construct a class birthday graph showing the months of the birthdays of all the class members' families (e.g., see Chap. 7).
3. Demonstrate through a role-play enactment a solution to a typical conflict that might occur within a family.

Sample Unit Objectives That Emphasize the Concerned Citizen Dimension

1. Take a position on a moral dilemma involving an issue of whether a child should break a promise to a parent to help an injured pet.
2. Identify those family activities they most enjoy doing and tell why.

Source: From *Looking at Me: Teacher's Manual* (pp. 62–63) by C. Cherryholmes, G. Manson, and P. H. Martorella, 1979, New York: McGraw-Hill. Copyright 1979 by McGraw-Hill.

creating bulletin boards
games and simulations
constructing graphs, charts, and tables

visual media
models

Variety in Instructional Planning

Subsequent chapters offer a variety of instructional strategies, activities, and materials to engage students and to foster the exemplary social studies teaching we considered in Chapter 1. In Chapter 5 we examine how the types of questions and group activities we employ affect the quality of our instruction. I demonstrate how simulations and role-playing and puppetry techniques can be used effectively to achieve certain objectives. In Chapters 6, 7, and 8, I detail teaching strategies related to the three dimensions of reflection, competence, and concern.

In applying these strategies in their planning, teachers need to guard against over-reliance on any one approach, however successful it may be. They need to ensure that their lesson and unit plans incorporate variety, as well as qualitatively significant activities.

Drama and role-playing can be used to involve students in hands-on activities.

In Chapters 9 through 13, I suggest other criteria to consider for monitoring in planning. These include cultural and gender sensitivity, attention to special needs, degree of student engagement in the learning process, authentic assessments, and the inclusion of socially significant subject matter.

Allocation of Time in Planning

In recent years increasing attention has been paid to how instructional time in classrooms is used by teachers and by students. Time, like texts and other instructional materials, represents an important resource for social studies teachers to accomplish their objectives. In planning and executing lessons, teachers need to attend carefully to how time is distributed across various activities. A major issue is the extent to which significant goals and priorities receive the lion's share of attention in the curriculum.

Time is an instructional issue for teachers on both a daily and a long-term basis in the curriculum. Teachers should oversee whether time for social studies instruction is portioned out appropriately within individual units and across topics. As a teacher becomes more skilled in organizing schedules and resources and in planning lessons and units, more time will be available to focus on the actual instructional process and how it can be made more effective. Perhaps most important, there will be increased opportunities to focus on the needs, interests, and progress of individual students.

Premium Instructional Time.   Experienced teachers realize that not all time during the day is of equal value for instruction, and so they often try to ensure that "premium" time is used for especially important instructional objectives. The periods just before lunch and just before dismissal, for instance, are "poor" instructional time, while that shortly after arrival in the morning is "premium" time.

Scheduling Social Studies Instruction

Part of the planning process for an elementary teacher is to decide what each day's schedule of instruction will be. How much time is to be spent on each subject may be left to the individual teacher to decide, or the school district may establish general recommended guidelines for schedules. A typical school day begins around 8:45 and ends about 2:45. With an hour out for lunch, this leaves about 5 hours each day. Of the 5 hours, approximately one is likely to be taken up with recess, rest room breaks, announcements, preparation for lunch and leaving, settling in after various breaks, and other miscellaneous tasks that are noninstructional in nature. This leaves roughly 4 hours each day for instruction.

During the 4 hours, teachers have to schedule instruction in reading and language arts, mathematics, and science, as well as social studies. At some points during the week, room in the schedule probably has to be made for music, physical education, art, and possibly other subjects, such as foreign languages. Specialty teachers provide some of this instruction in many school districts, and classroom teachers often have to build their schedules around those of the specialists.

No one pattern for scheduling is best; it is important to be cognizant, however, that sufficient time is spent on social studies instruction and that an equal share of premium instructional time is allocated. Four alternative ways to approach scheduling are shown in Figure 4.11. The total time to be allotted each week varies with the grade level.

FIGURE 4.11   Alternative patterns for scheduling social studies instruction

Schedule 1:	Social Studies, Monday through Friday, 40 minutes each day
Schedule 2:	Social Studies, Monday, Wednesday, and Friday, 60–70 minutes each day
Schedule 3:	Social Studies, Monday through Friday, every other week, 80 minutes each day
Schedule 4:	Social Studies, sometime during Monday through Friday, complete at least five activities in the Social Studies Center

Some teachers prefer to set a basic fixed schedule for each day and to maintain most of the instructional slots throughout the week. Others prefer to construct the schedule to fit the time requirements of the lessons they have planned. Consider a lesson that involves a simulation game likely to take 60 minutes to complete and discuss. Rather than rush the lesson or divide it into two days, the teacher may modify the schedule to accommodate the increased time demand.

Some teachers prefer to study certain subjects in a concentrated fashion for a limited period of time. For example, instead of studying social studies for 40 minutes a day, 5 days a week, 36 weeks a year, a teacher may determine that, given the nature of the subject matter, it may be more desirable to spend 80 minutes daily for half of the school year.

Guidelines for Social Studies Program Development

Apart from guides for units and lessons, a number of guidelines for developing complete social studies *programs* at the state and local levels have been developed. Organizations such as the National Council for the Social Studies (NCSS) periodically issue general guidelines for curriculum planning that cover a range of issues and provide checklists of practical considerations and suggestions.

One illustration is the *NCSS Social Studies Curriculum Guidelines* (NCSS, 1990). It provides nine basic benchmarks for developing a social studies program. Each of the nine guidelines, in turn, has a related set of more specific subguidelines.

1. The social studies program should be related directly to the age, maturity, and concerns of students.
2. The social studies program should deal with the real social world.
3. The social studies program should draw from currently valid knowledge representative of human experience, culture, and beliefs.
4. Objectives should be thoughtfully selected and clearly stated in such a form as to provide direction to the program.
5. Learning activities should engage the student directly and actively in the learning process.
6. Strategies of instruction and learning activities should rely on a broad range of learning resources.
7. The social studies program must facilitate the organization of experience.
8. Evaluation should be useful, systematic, comprehensive, and valid for the objectives of the program.
9. Social studies education should receive vigorous support as a vital and responsible part of the school program.

A similar set of seven guidelines for program development were created by Engle and Ochoa (1988):

1. The curriculum should have a relatively small number of topics.

2. The topics selected should be those with the greatest potential for stimulating thought or controversy.

3. Students should be asked continually to make value judgments about factual claims and to generate hypotheses.

4. The social science disciplines should be treated as sources of information that can help answer questions, rather than truth to be learned.

5. Information from areas other than the social sciences, such as from the humanities, should be used.

6. The curriculum should use varied sources to study in depth a relatively small number of topics.

7. The curriculum should draw on students' experiences to help answer questions.

Group Activities

1. After consulting several sources, identify a format for a lesson plan that you prefer. Discuss the features of the format that you consider to be desirable and the reasons why.

2. For each of the primary-, intermediate-, and middle-grade levels, locate either a social studies resource unit or a teaching unit on any topic. Discuss what you consider to be the strengths and weaknesses of the units. What things would you add?

3. Consult the sample schedules for social studies instruction given in the chapter and construct the weekly schedule that you would prefer if you were teaching a second-grade class, a fourth-grade class, or a sixth-grade class. What is the rationale for your choice?

Individual Activities

1. Select a topic, a grade level, an objective, and a lesson plan format (either those within the chapter or another). Then develop a sample social studies lesson for one of the primary grades and one for the intermediate grades.

2. Using the Internet and the format included in this chapter, create your own unit. Identify any grade, K through 8, and any topic.

3. Consult the example of a partially completed concept map used for planning a teaching unit that appears in the chapter. Identify a grade level and a topic for a unit. Then create a concept map that incorporates all of the subjects you would include in the unit.

4. Consult Figure 4.7 and construct two additional objectives relating to the unit theme for each of the three dimensions.

References

Bloom, B. S. (Ed.). (1956). *Taxonomy of educational objectives, the classification of educational goals. Handbook I: The cognitive domain.* New York: David McKay.

Brophy, J. E., & Alleman, J. (1993). Elementary social studies should be driven by major social education goals. *Social Education, 57,* 27–32.

Cherryholmes, C., Manson, G., & Martorella, P. H. (1979). *Looking at me: Teacher's manual.* New York: McGraw-Hill.

Dewey, J. (1961). *Democracy and education.* New York: Macmillan.

Engle, S. H., & Ochoa, A. S. (1988). *Education for democratic citizenship.* New York: Teachers College Press.

Glatthorn, A. A. (1987). *Curriculum renewal.* Alexandria, VA: Association for Supervision and Curriculum Development.

Hunter, M. (1984). Knowing, teaching, and supervising. In P. Hosford (Ed.), *Using what we know about teaching* (pp. 169–192). Alexandria, VA: Association for Supervision and Curriculum Development.

Krathwohl, D., Bloom, B. S., & Masia, B. B. (1969). *Taxonomy of educational objectives, the classification of educational goals. Handbook II: The affective domain.* New York: David McKay.

McClain, J., et al. (1985). *China: A teaching unit for primary grades.* Cedar Falls: University of Northern Iowa, Malcom Price Laboratory School. (ERIC Document Reproduction Service No. ED 286804)

National Council for the Social Studies (NCSS). (1990). *Social studies curriculum planning resources.* Washington, DC: Author.

National Geographic Society. (1988). *Teaching geography: A model for action.* Washington, DC: Author.

Novak, J. D., & Gowin, D. B. (1984). *Learning how to learn.* Cambridge, UK: Cambridge University Press.

Pearson, J. (1991). *Women of the American Revolution.* Los Angeles: University of California, National Center for History in the Schools.

Shaver, J. P. (1992). Rationales for issues-centered social studies education. *The Social Studies, 83,* 95–99.

Chapter

Engaging Students in Learning Through Small Groups, Questions, Role-Playing, and Simulations

Grouping Students for Learning

Planning for Small-Group Work

Multipurpose Small-Group Techniques

Cooperative Learning Group Techniques

Cooperative Learning and Student Achievement

Using Structured Questions to Aid Learning

Patterns of Effective Questioning

Effective Use of Time

Selection of Questions

Effective Sequencing of Questions

The Taba Questioning Strategies

Engaging Students in Role-Playing and Simulations

The Nature of Role-Playing

Role-Playing and Puppetry

The Nature of Simulations

Guidelines for Developing and Conducting Simulations

Tamika, William, Jordan, and Clarice are clustered around a small table. They comprise a group known as The Write Stuff. The rest of their classmates are organized similarly into groups at other locations in the fourth-grade classroom.

Their teacher, Ms. Rivera, has spent the last 10 minutes discussing and illustrating different landforms and examples of where they occur throughout the world. For the next phase of the lesson, she asks each of the "experts" to leave their groups and to meet with other similar experts at designated locations. Each set of experts will be comparing answers to questions about different landforms. A cooperative learning activity is under way!

As the previous chapter revealed, in planning exciting and challenging social studies lessons and units, teachers have an assortment of effective tools at their disposal. In this chapter we consider three sets of instructional strategies that may be incorporated into all social studies lessons and activities, no matter what their objectives: small groups, structured questions, and role-playing enactments and simulations.

Each of the three chapters that follow, in turn, identifies other specific instructional strategies that focus on developing the three dimensions of the effective citizen: reflection, competence, and concern.

Grouping Students for Learning

Groups such as committees, teams, and social organizations play a major role in our society. In schools, placing students into groups for instructional purposes has a long history (Schmuck & Schmuck, 1983). Traditionally, teachers and administrators in the elementary and middle schools have assigned students of all ages to groups for a variety of cognitive and affective objectives. These include completing tasks efficiently, encouraging tolerance of diversity, and providing greater opportunities for in-depth discussions.

Structured group settings that include diversity also afford children an opportunity for social dialogues that can stimulate cognitive growth. They offer the promise of environments where youngsters can explore alternative perspectives, develop new insights, and modify prior knowledge. As Newman, Griffin, and Cole (1989) noted, "When people with different goals, roles, and resources interact, the differences in interpretation provide occasions for the construction of new knowledge" (p. 2).

Planning for Small-Group Work

Before organizing students into small groups, teachers need to consider a number of basic issues. These issues include making provisions for adequate space and sound control and for avoiding potential distractions. Teachers also should vary grouping techniques to prevent boredom. As a further critical consideration, they need to determine the optimal size of a group in relation to the objective of an activity.

Groups may be as small as two members or as large as the whole class. There is no magic number in determining the optimal size of a "small" group,

These children are helping each other learn key points from a chapter in their social studies text.

although five to seven students is a good general rule for many social studies activities. As we shall see, certain group techniques specify the number of students required and the procedures they must follow.

Members of a group also must be capable of assuming or experimenting with the *roles* they are to play within the group in order for the group to function effectively. A simple example is the role of *recorder* in a group, which requires some basic writing, organizing, and reading skills. All children need to practice and experiment with different types of groups and alternative roles within them.

In working with young children, it may be helpful first to provide them with models or case studies of different structured group activities. This may be done through such activities as viewing and discussing videotaped examples of effective groups at work.

Effective group activities also require as a prerequisite that students possess a number of basic social skills (see Chapter 7), including:

- listening
- taking turns
- working quietly
- sharing ideas
- asking for information and explanations
- accepting others' ideas
- sharing roles and responsibilities

Identifying Group Members.   Following are some of the many possible ways of identifying the members for a group:

- student self-selection
- random assignment
- assignment by backgrounds
- assignment by special abilities or skills
- assignment by behavioral characteristics

Aside from student self-selection, the remaining procedures involve some teacher decisions. The alternative procedures require the teacher to assess how certain student characteristics are related to the task and effective operation of the group. Although there is no one best way to identify group members, there are better ways for different objectives.

For instance, consider an activity in which the objective is to improve the level of multicultural understanding within a classroom. Assignment by general background to include a mix of racial or ethnic representatives within each group is likely to be a better choice than student self-selection of groups. Similarly, consider a class where a number of behavioral problems exist at the beginning of a school year. An important grouping consideration for some tasks may be to ensure that potentially disruptive students are not grouped together.

sociogram

Using Sociograms.   One way that teachers working with intermediate- and middle-grade students can gather systematic diagnostic data on their personal preferences for group mates is to construct a **sociogram** (see Fox, Luszki, & Schmuck, 1966). A sociogram is a diagram of the pattern of children's social choices among their classmates. Students first are asked to complete privately and in writing the answers to two questions: With which three children in this class would you most like to work? and With which three children in this class would you prefer not to work?

Tabulating Students' Preferences.   The students' responses then are collected and tabulated, as shown in Figure 5.1. Positive choices are given a +1, and negative choices a –1. For the class shown, the results indicate a number of popular

FIGURE 5.1   Tabulation of class preferences

Student number	1	2	3	4	5	6	7	8	9	10	11	12	13	14	15	16	17	18	19	20	21	22	23	24	25
1									−1							−1	+1	−1		+1		+1			
2															+1		−1	+1			−1	+1		−1	
3	+1			+1					−1				−1	−1								+1			
4			+1						−1						+1		−1	+1	−1						
5	+1								−1							−1	+1				−1	+1			
6					+1				−1						+1		−1	+1			−1				
7					−1							−1		−1	+1			+1				+1			
8			+1													−1	−1	+1			−1	+1			
9			+1						−1				−1			−1	+1					+1			
10			+1						−1						+1		−1	+1	−1						
11			+1	−1					−1	+1			−1									+1			
12	+1		+1						−1								−1	+1	−1						
13			+1						−1			+1		+1			−1				−1				
14	+1		+1						−1								−1		−1			+1			
15									−1						+1		−1				−1	+1			+1
16	−1			−1					−1						+1			+1				+1			
17	−1		+1								+1										−1				−1
18		−1	+1						−1						+1	−1						+1			
19									+1						−1	−1						+1		−1	+1
20			+1	+1											−1	−1		−1				+1			
21									−1	−1					+1		−1	+1				+1			
22			+1	−1					−1			−1			+1			+1							
23			+1						−1						+1					−1	−1	+1			
24		+1	+1									−1			−1							+1			−1
25	+1		+1						−1								−1	+1				−1			
Total +	5	1	15	2	1	0	0	0	3	0	1	1	0	12	0	0	14	0	0	1	0	17	0	0	2
Total −	2	1	0	3	1	0	0	18	1	0	3	0	4	2	3	17	0	6	0	4	5	1	0	2	2

children and a range of less popular students. The results also reveal a set of isolated students who attracted neither positive nor negative reactions. They show further that a few children, such as Student 16, were rejected by many classmates.

In several cases, feelings were reciprocated; that is, some students who preferred to work with someone else were, in turn, identified as a choice by that person. More complex patterns also emerged. For example, some students preferred not to be in the same group.

Summarizing Students' Preferences.   The data in Figure 5.1 may be summarized in a format similar to the one shown in Figure 5.2. To permit easy gender identification, different colors of pencils or pens should be used for boys and for girls. In the smallest circle (labeled A) were placed the numbers of all of the children who received *no* negative ratings and *more than* three positive ratings. In the outermost ring (labeled D) were placed the numbers of students who received *more than* three negative choices and *fewer than* two positive choices. Students who were not chosen at all were placed outside the circles.

Of the remaining students, those who received more positive choices than negative choices or an equal number were placed in Circle B. Those who received more negative ratings than positive ones were placed in Circle C.

With the results of the sociogram in hand, the teacher can begin working to modify undesirable patterns of interpersonal relationships through such strategies as giving isolated and rejected students recognition and planning responsibilities in classroom activities. The teacher also can use the students who are viewed as desirable associates as peer helpers and leaders in making group assignments.

FIGURE 5.2

Summary of tabulation data

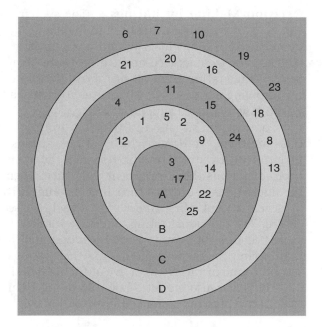

Multipurpose Small-Group Techniques

Aside from size and composition of the membership, there are other considerations in using small groups for social studies instruction. Certain group techniques are *multipurpose* in the sense that they have relatively flexible designs and are not tied to any particular set of objectives. Others have been designed to promote specific instructional objectives, such as raising achievement scores or improving interpersonal relationships. We first consider some multipurpose techniques and then a class known as cooperative learning techniques that have been designed for specific objectives.

Some of the many multipurpose group techniques that may be used effectively in social studies instruction are brainstorming, decision making by ratings, and composite reports.

Brainstorming.   Brainstorming is an effective technique when the objective of a group is to get as many different solutions to a problem as possible on the table for consideration (Osborn, 1963). The main ingredient for a brainstorming session is a solvable problem, such as, How can we make our school a safer and cleaner place?

A brainstorming session requires a leader to guide the discussion and a recorder to list on a large sheet of paper or chalkboard the possible solutions that the group members generate. The ground rules are that all ideas must be accepted and recorded without evaluation. After all ideas have been recorded quickly without comment, they can be discussed. As a final step, the group members can come to some agreement concerning which solutions are the most useful.

Decision Making by Ratings.   The system of decision making by ratings can be used with intermediate- and middle-grade students. It requires that various choices of individuals within a group be weighted and averaged through ratings. The technique commits a group to accept the decision that receives the best average rating from all members. It is an especially appropriate technique for resolving issues for which several attractive alternative actions exist, none of which have attracted support of a majority.

Consider the situation in which a group of seven students in a fifth-grade class are trying to decide which various actions their local government should take to reduce crime. Through research, the students identify and list five major types of actions the government may take. Then they individually rate each of the five actions in order of their first through fifth choices (see Figure 5.3).

Each student's first choice is given a 1, the second a 2, and so on, to the last choice. The individual ratings then are totaled; the action with the *lowest* total score becomes the group's choice. An optional final step in the rating technique is to permit the members to discuss their ratings further and then to conduct a second round of ratings to arrive at the final decision.

The figure also indicates how the rating technique can produce a *group* position that represents some compromise for everyone. In Figure 5.3 the group's

| **FIGURE 5.3** | Example of decision making by ratings |

Possible Actions Identified From Research	Issue: How Our Local Government Can Help Reduce Crime						
	Individual Ratings of Group Members						
	Julio	Khari	Ann	Bill	Justin	Lea	Hakim	Totals
Hire More Police	4	1	2	5	1	5	2	20
Put Police on Foot Patrols	1	5	1	4	3	2	5	21
Ban Hand Guns	2	4	4	3	5	3	1	22
Community Citizen Watch Groups	3	3	3	2	2	2	3	18
Longer Jail Terms for Criminals	5	2	5	1	4	4	4	25

selection through rating (Community Citizen Watch Groups) was *not* the first choice of any single member. Further, it was only the third choice of a majority of the members.

Composite Reports and Data Retrieval Charts.   A composite report is one that integrates, synthesizes, and summarizes all of the information that members of a group have collected on a subject. Rather than being asked to present a series of individual reports, often students in the intermediate grades are organized into groups to do research on a topic. The collective findings of the group then are presented to the class or the teacher in a single organized and systematic report. Some of the formats that have been used for composite reports are collages, dioramas, bulletin boards, and student-made films, filmstrips, and videotapes.

Where students have limited opportunities to meet together as a group to construct their reports, **data retrieval (or data) charts** may be an especially convenient and efficient form of composite report. Such charts require the group to have a *division of topics* among all members and a *set of common properties* that each member researches within a topic. A completed chart involving a group of three students, each studying a country, is shown in Figure 5.4.

The chart itself may be constructed on the chalkboard, craft paper, poster board, or a similar medium. It may be organized by the group as a whole or completed in separate modules or sections by individual members. Then, when the group assembles, the individual pieces can be spliced together to form the chart. Other applications of data retrieval charts are discussed in Chapters 6 and 10.

data retrieval charts

| FIGURE 5.4 | Data retrieval chart |

Status of Women			
Characteristics	**U.S.**	**Sweden**	**Bangladesh**
Life Expectancy	79 Years	81 Years	39 Years
Child Mortality Rate	1 in 91 dies before her 5th birthday	1 in 167 dies	1 in 5 dies
Teenage Marriages	Less than 1% already have married	8% already have married	69% already have married
Number of Children	Less than 2 children on average	1 or 2 children	5 or 6 children
College Enrollment (Ages 20–24)	59% of women are enrolled	37% are enrolled	Less than 2% are enrolled
Percentage of Paid Work Force	45% of paid work force	49% of paid work force	14% of paid work force
Life Span Compared to Males'	Live 7 years longer than men	Live 7 years longer than men	Live 2 years less than men

Cooperative Learning Group Techniques

cooperative
learning
techniques

One special class of small-group techniques designed to achieve both cognitive and affective objectives is called **cooperative (or collaborative) learning.** The term refers generally to grouping techniques in which students work toward some common learning goal in small heterogeneous groups of usually four or five students. Heterogeneity typically includes characteristics such as gender, race, ethnicity, and ability.

Slavin (1990) identified seven types of cooperative learning techniques. Some have specific, structured procedures such as those developed at Johns Hopkins by Slavin and his associates: Student Teams Achievement Divisions (STAD), Teams-Games-Tournaments (TGT), and Jigsaw II. Others, such as those developed by Johnson and Johnson (1984) and Sharan and Schachar (1988), have more flexible structures.

Advocates of cooperative learning techniques assert that they motivate students to do their best, to help one another, and to organize their thinking through dialogue and elaboration (Johnson & Johnson, 1984; Slavin, 1990; VanSickle, 1992). They also note that cooperative groups foster interdependence, individual accountability, and group processing of information, whereas traditional types do not.

Cooperative Learning and Student Achievement

With regard to the relationship of cooperative learning to academic achievement, Slavin (1990) concluded, "There is wide agreement among reviewers of the cooperative learning literature that cooperative methods can and usually do have a positive effect on student achievement" (p. 6). It is important to note, however, that Slavin's analyses of the existing research have revealed two essential conditions for cooperative learning techniques to be effective: (a) There must be a group goal that can result in some form of recognition (e.g., class newspaper, certificate, bulletin board, grades, rewards) and (b) success must depend on individual accountability (e.g., individual quiz scores are summed to produce a group score).

Cooperative Learning and Affective Outcomes.   In addition to achievement outcomes, researchers have discovered that cooperative learning techniques can promote positive intergroup relations, self-esteem, attendance, and positive attitudes toward school and the subjects being studied (Slavin, 1990, 1991). For example: "When students of different racial or ethnic backgrounds work together toward a common goal, they gain in liking and respect for one another. Cooperative learning also improves the social acceptance of mainstreamed academically handicapped students by their classmates" (Slavin, 1990, p. 54). In sum, it appears that cooperative learning techniques that meet the criteria outlined by Slavin can produce positive cognitive and affective outcomes.

One specific approach has had wide applicability to all types of social studies subject matter and can be used in grades 4 through 8. This cooperative learning technique, the **Jigsaw technique,** is especially effective with subject matter that has a high degree of factual detail.

Jigsaw
technique

The Jigsaw Technique.   Educators and psychologists working in the Austin, Texas, schools in the 1970s to improve relationships between Anglo, Hispanic, and black students devised a cooperative learning technique to reduce racial tensions (Aronson, Blaney, Stephan, Sikes, & Snapp, 1978). They called it *Jigsaw* because it resembled the structure of a jigsaw puzzle. The objective of the technique was to encourage children to cooperate, share, and work together effectively, and, in the process, begin to break down interpersonal barriers.

Jigsaw required students to work in small interracial groups and to share parts of a solution to a common challenge. The challenge generally was successful performance on a quiz or assignment given by the teacher. Each member of the group was given only some of the "pieces of a puzzle" (part of the social studies information that the quiz would address). No single member of the group was supplied with enough information to solve the problem alone. Only through sharing and relying on all of the others in the group could each member succeed. At the conclusion of the exercise, all of the group members took *individual* tests covering *all* of the collective subject matter that had been shared.

Aronson et al. (1978) offered a brief example of how they developed their technique:

> For example, in the first classroom we studied, the next lesson happened to be on Joseph Pulitzer. We wrote a six-paragraph biography of the man, such that each paragraph contained a major aspect of Pulitzer's life. . . . Next we cut up the biography into sections and gave each child in the learning group one paragraph. Thus every learning group had within it the entire life story of Joseph Pulitzer, but each child had no more than one sixth of the story and was dependent on all the others to complete the big picture. (p. 47)

After the completion of the experimental program that used Jigsaw, the investigators reported that, in integrated schools, Anglos learned equally well in both Jigsaw and competitive classes. However, blacks and Hispanics performed *better* in Jigsaw classes than in non-Jigsaw ones. Further, it was found that, at the conclusion of the study, students liked both groupmates and others in their class better than when the study began. In sum, Jigsaw produced both positive achievement and attitudinal outcomes (Aronson et al., 1978).

Variations of the Jigsaw Technique.   The original Jigsaw technique can be used for any social studies activity for which a body of subject matter can be divided easily into four or five pieces for individuals. For example, in studying about four families around the world, each child in a group might be given the information for one of the countries.

Often, however, this technique requires extra effort on the part of the teacher to reorganize or rewrite material. Some subject matter cannot be organized to stand alone without reference to other sections. In addition, the original Jigsaw was found by researchers to be not as effective as some alternative cooperative learning techniques.

One variation on the original Jigsaw that often is easier to implement in social studies instruction was developed at Johns Hopkins (Slavin, 1986). Called the **Jigsaw II technique,** it also can be used with any subject matter, including conventional textbook passages, with little or no modification. Further, it provides more structured group roles and places more emphasis on the achievement of group goals than the original Jigsaw. Other variations exist as well (see Mattingley & VanSickle, 1991).

Jigsaw II requires a group of four or five students selected in the following fashion: one high-ability student, one low-ability student, and two or three average-ability students. Further, to the extent possible, Jigsaw II requires that the makeup of the group reflect the ethnic and gender composition of the class as a whole.

Individual accountability in the Jigsaw techniques often is maintained by having each student take a quiz over all of the subject matter studied by the

Jigsaw II
technique

group. Procedures in Jigsaw II developed for calculating team scores from students' individual quiz scores require some analysis. Three key concepts are *base score*, *quiz score*, and *improvement points*.

A base score is one the teacher assigns at the beginning of a Jigsaw II activity, based on the student's social studies grade or some standardized test score. After a group has finished its Jigsaw II task, individuals typically take a quiz over the subject matter studied and receive a personal quiz score. Each student's new quiz score then is compared with his or her previous or base score. If merited, individuals earn "improvement points" for their group by comparing their quiz scores with their base scores and using the formula shown in Figure 5.5.

For example, consider a group of four students. Suppose Billy's base score was 70 and he received a 65 on a quiz. Following the scoring procedures shown, he would be awarded 10 improvement points. Tamara had a base score of 100, and her quiz score was the same. She would receive 30 improvement points. Sarah's base score was 85 and the quiz was 89; she earned 20 improvement points. Steve had a quiz score of 89, compared with a base score of 100; he received 0 improvement points.

The group's score consists of the *total of the improvement points of all members of the team*, not their raw scores. In this case, the group score was 60 (10 + 30 + 20 + 0). If some teams have four members and others have five, the score of the group with five is four-fifths of the total. In each new round of Jigsaw II, the prior quiz score becomes a new base score. For example, in the prior illustration, Sarah's new base score for the second round would be 89.

An Example of Jigsaw II Procedures.   The following example of an application for Jigsaw II involves a quiz and a basal text chapter that deals with branches of the government:

1. Select a chapter within the text and identify four basic topics, themes, or issues that the chapter encompasses.
2. Organize four- or five-member teams according to the group selection criteria given earlier (ability, ethnicity, gender). Then allow the groups to establish their identities and names (e.g., The Hot Shots, The Wizards).

FIGURE 5.5		

Scoring procedures for Jigsaw II

Source: Compiled from *Using Student Team Learning* (3rd ed.), by R. E. Slavin, 1986, Baltimore: Johns Hopkins University, Center for Social Organization of Schools.

Quiz Score	Improvement Points
More than 10 points below base score	0
10 points below to 1 point below base score	10
Base score to 10 points above base score	20
More than 10 points above base score	30
Perfect score (regardless of base score)	30

3. Distribute to each team a copy of an "expert sheet" that contains a list of the four topics, themes, or issues that have been identified as focusing on some important aspect of the chapter material (see example in Figure 5.6). Each topic should be presented in the form of a question.

4. Assign a topic on the expert sheet to each member of each team. Designate these individuals as "experts" on their topics. Where there are five team members, assign one of the topics to two members.

5. Have all students read the chapter selected in class or for homework, focusing on his or her topic from the expert sheet.

6. After students have read the chapter, allow experts from different teams who have the same topic to meet and discuss their topic. It may be helpful to provide a discussion sheet similar to the one shown in Figure 5.7 for each expert group.

7. Have the experts return to their teams after the expert group discussions are concluded. They should take turns teaching the information related to their topics to the other members.

8. After the teaching has concluded, have each student take an individual quiz covering all of the topics. All students are to answer all questions.

9. Calculate individual improvement points and report results as team scores (individual scores may be kept for grading purposes). Recognize publicly, through such forms as announcements, bulletin board listing, or a newsletter, the progress of the teams. Periodically remind students that team scores are based on improvement points.

10. Repeat the preceding steps for subsequent chapters within a unit or until a cluster of chapters has been studied. After each round of quizzes, recalculate the team scores based on individual improvement points and publicize the

---

FIGURE 5.6   Sample expert sheet for a Jigsaw II activity

Expert Sheet

"The Branches of the Federal Government"

Topics:

Expert I. What is the main function of the *legislative* branch of the federal government, and how does it differ from the other branches?

Expert II. What is the main function of the *judicial* branch of the federal government, and how does it differ from the other branches?

Expert III. What is the main function of the *executive* branch of the federal government, and how does it differ from the other branches?

Expert IV. How does a bill become a law at the national level?

FIGURE 5.7	Sample discussion sheet for a Jigsaw II activity

Discussion Sheet for Expert I Group

Topic: What is the main function of the legislative branch of the federal government, and how does it differ from the other branches?

Points to consider in your discussion:

1. What is Congress?
2. What is the House of Representatives?
3. What is the Senate?
4. How are senators and representatives chosen?
5. What powers does the legislative branch have?
6. How is the legislative branch different from the other two branches?
7. How is the legislative branch similar to the other two branches?
8. Why did the authors of the Constitution set up three branches of the government?

new team standings. At the conclusion, publicly recognize in some fashion the team with the highest score.

Jigsaw techniques are versatile. They lend themselves to a number of adaptations in social studies instruction. Slavin (1986), for example, suggested that teachers might have students conduct research on topics, rather than reference basal texts. Also, instead of using quizzes to ensure student accountability, teachers may assess through such forms as group essays, dioramas, skits, computer databases, or oral reports. For example, the composite report group technique discussed earlier and illustrated in Figure 5.4 could be modified and incorporated into a cooperative learning activity.

The STAD Technique.   Just as with Jigsaw II, in STAD, four or five students are assigned to teams that are mixed by performance, gender, and ethnicity. Subject matter can be presented through a variety of forms, including lectures, visual media, and text assignments. After the presentation, students work in their teams to master the subject matter. Typically, they are given aids such as study sheets, discussion guides, or outlines of the material. Although team members assist one another in learning the assigned material, students are tested individually on what they have learned. The procedures used to determine improvement points and to allocate awards are the same as with Jigsaw II.

The TGT Technique.   TGT is similar to STAD in all respects, except the testing component.

Cooperative learning activities allow students to see fellow classmates as resources and helpers, rather than as competitors.

TGT replaces the quizzes with weekly tournaments in which students compete with members of other teams to contribute points to their team scores. The competition takes place at three-person "tournament tables" against others with similar past records in the subject. A "bumping" procedure keeps the competition fair. The winner at each tournament table brings six points to his or her team, regardless of table; this means that low achievers (competing with other low achievers) and high achievers (competing with other high achievers) have *equal opportunities for success*. As in STAD, high-performing teams earn certificates or other forms of *team rewards*. (Slavin, 1987, p.13)

The Group Investigation Technique.   Another cooperative learning strategy that has wide applicability in social studies instruction in the intermediate and middle grades is the **Group Investigation Technique** (Sharan & Sharan, 1992). In comparison with Jigsaw techniques, the Group Investigation strategy is more open-ended and permits in-depth study of complex problems and issues. It affords groups considerable latitude in how they define and study a topic and report their findings. To achieve its ends, it requires students who already have learned to work effectively in groups.

> **Group Investigation Technique**

Leighton (1990) outlined six steps that group investigation involves:

1. Identification of topics and choices by teacher and students
2. Formation of learning teams based on interests
3. Investigation of topics selected with teacher assistance
4. Preparation of presentations for the class with teacher assistance
5. Presentations to the whole class
6. Evaluation of the work, based on predetermined criteria

An example of how the strategy might be implemented in a social studies class inquiring into the causes of the American Revolution was provided by Leighton (1990, p. 326):

> First, students would be divided into temporary brainstorming groups of three or four, each charged with generating a list of questions one might ask in relation to study of the Revolution. The whole class would compile a composite list of questions, which would be sorted into categories. Learning teams would include those who are particularly interested in investigating each category of questions. The teacher's role is to guide the formation of teams so that, to the extent possible, each team includes a fair sampling of students.
>
> The learning teams review the questions in their category and pull together those questions most amenable to the investigation. They set the goals for the work and divide the tasks among themselves. Then they begin to study the topic they have chosen. When their studies are complete, they present their findings to the class. A representative from each learning team is delegated to a central coordinating committee to ensure that team reports are presented in orderly fashion and work is equitably distributed within each team.
>
> Evaluation may be designed by the teacher alone or in collaboration with a representative student group. The content on which students are evaluated must reflect the priorities established by the original choice of inquiry topics and by the presentations themselves. Students may be assessed individually on the basis of either the sum of the whole class presentations or the particular material developed within each group.

Using Structured Questions to Aid Learning

How many questions does the typical elementary school teacher ask in an hour? Over a decade ago, researchers (Brown & Edmondson, 1984) discovered that teachers ask about two questions every *second*, or 100 to 200 per hour. These questions range from the type, Does everyone have his or her pencil out? to those such as, Why do we say Columbus discovered America, when someone was already here when he arrived?

In sum, evidence suggests that a great number of the communications between teacher and students consist of questions and answers. More often than not, teachers initiate the questions, read them from texts, or assign them in writing to students (Wilen & White, 1991). Questions are used extensively both in large- and small-group instruction, as well as with individual students.

What types of questions do teachers typically ask or assign to students? Borich (1996, p. 344) suggested that questions can be organized into seven general categories—those that

1. Provoke interest or gain attention
2. Assess the state of students' knowledge
3. Trigger recall of subject matter

4. Manage instruction
5. Encourage more-advanced levels of thinking
6. Redirect attention
7. Elicit feelings

Patterns of Effective Questioning

Just as with the use of grouping techniques, teachers have a number of decisions to make regarding the use of questions in instruction. Both the *type* and the *sequencing* of questions can affect significantly the level of interaction, thinking, and learning that results from instruction. Effective questioning techniques can focus attention on the important objectives of a lesson or an activity. They also can encourage students to participate in discussions and move thinking along in a systematic fashion.

In turn, questions that originate from students during instruction help identify areas that are unclear or were neglected during the teacher's planning. They also help students clarify their thinking and sharpen their verbal skills (Steinbrink, 1985). Encouraging students to generate questions, orally or in writing, should be an ongoing feature of social studies instruction.

Effective questioning requires that teachers employ types of questions matched to their instructional objectives. Some questions are particularly useful for stimulating discussions; others are helpful in determining what students have learned; and still others are powerful inducements to creative thinking, to suggest but a few of the ends to which questions can be directed.

Some techniques associated with effective questioning apply to all questions, such as effective *use of time*, *selection*, and *sequencing*. Teachers can draw on a store of tested principles and strategies in these areas (e.g., Wilen & White, 1991) for sharpening the questioning skills they use in social studies instruction.

Effective Use of Time

wait time

Ask a friend a question and time how long you have to wait before he or she begins to answer you. A critical element of effective questioning is **wait time,** the time between when a teacher asks a question and the point at which an answer is expected.

When wait time is short, teachers ask a question and expect an answer immediately. If one is not forthcoming, teachers tend to restate the question, rephrase it, ask a new one, or provide the answers themselves. When wait time is long, teachers ask the question and wait 3 seconds or longer for an answer. Tobin (1987) reported that most teachers in the studies of wait time maintained an average wait time of between 0.2 and 0.9 seconds.

Consider the implications for a class of young children—say, second grade—who must attend to and reflect on a question and coordinate their conclusion with their motor response of raising their hands, all in about a half-second! It is not surprising that many youngsters eventually decline to participate altogether in question-and-answer marathons in which they know they cannot compete successfully.

The Effects of Increasing Wait Time. The pioneering research of Rowe (1969) demonstrated the powerful effects of extending wait time. She found that if a teacher prolonged the average time waited after a question was asked to 5 seconds or longer, the length of students' responses increased. Conversely, she found that short wait time produced short answers.

Rowe also discovered that teachers who learned to use silence found that children who ordinarily said little began to start talking and to offer new ideas. Teachers themselves, as they extended their waiting time, also began to include more variety in their questions.

Other studies have shown that, depending on the type of questions used, extended wait time is associated with longer student responses and increased student-to-student interaction. Extended wait time also has been related to greater student achievement.

Tobin's (1987) analysis of the related research has suggested that teachers can learn to increase their wait time through feedback and analysis of their questioning patterns. He suggested that at least 3 seconds is an average threshold of wait time for teachers to attempt to establish. However, wait time will be less when questions require little reflection (e.g., Who was our first president?) and greater when questions require problem solving and weighing of alternatives (e.g., Why was Washington such a popular president?).

Selection of Questions

Another important consideration in effective questioning is selecting questions that are *clear, specific,* and *focused.* These expedite communication, probe for details, keep a discussion on target, and foster sustained critical thinking. They also encourage students to make comparisons, identify causal relationships, see linkages to their own lives, and establish factual claims.

Desirable Types of Questions. Examples of desirable types of questions are:

- Why do you agree with the candidate's position?
- What would happen if the world's supplies of oil and natural gas were used up?
- What were some major causes of the Civil War?
- What are some ways neighborhoods change over time?
- What are some ways cities, suburbs, and rural areas are alike and different?
- Suppose you were in Rosa Parks's place. What would you have done?
- What evidence do you have that auto emissions are bad for the environment?

Types of Questions to Avoid.   Teachers should be sensitive to the types of questions that generally are *ineffective* in social studies instruction. These types of questions include those that are *ambiguous, require only a yes-or-no answer,* or are *slanted.* Such questions limit or stifle thinking and often are a source of frustration and confusion for students. Examples of the types of questions to avoid are:

- What happened in the American Revolution?
- Was George Washington our first president?
- What makes our community the best in the state?
- Where do families live?
- How did Sojourner Truth live her life?
- What does our flag mean?
- What was the first Thanksgiving about?

Effective Sequencing of Questions

Another important questioning technique is learning to order questions in a sequence that stimulates the development of students' higher-level thinking. A logical sequence ensures a rationale for the order in which the questions are asked. It also affords students an opportunity to link information and to integrate prior and new knowledge.

question script   Sequencing is part of the process of developing a set, or *script*, of questions in advance of teaching a lesson. A **question script** is a basic set of questions that have been constructed, rehearsed, and logically sequenced prior to their use in a lesson or activity. *Rehearsal* refers to the process whereby a teacher reflects on exactly how the questions will be phrased and where in the lesson or activity they are to occur. The function of a script in instruction is to move students from more concrete to more abstract, lower to higher, levels of thinking.

The presence of a script ensures that several well thought out and carefully phrased questions will be used to guide students' thinking, as well as the development of a lesson or activity. Unlike spontaneous questions, which teachers develop as instruction unfolds, a script shapes a lesson. It encompasses a small number of questions, usually three to five, that relate to the subject matter under investigation. Scripts may be supplemented by other spontaneous questions that are needed during a lesson, such as clarification or summarization questions (e.g., What do you mean by "the crazy clothes"? or Could you sum up your idea in a single sentence?).

The Taxonomy of Educational Objectives.   An example of sequencing questions according to the levels of thinking they require is found in the *taxonomies of objectives* developed by Bloom and his associates. The most widely used taxonomy as a guide for framing questions is the one for the cognitive domain (Bloom, 1956), which identifies six levels of thinking, simple (knowledge) to complex (evaluation). The levels, along with an example of a question that is matched with them, are shown below.

Level of Thinking	Sample Question
Knowledge	Who was our first President?
Comprehension	Which month has the most birthdays? The next most? Which has the least? (From a chart of class birthdays)
Application	Using the mapping techniques we learned yesterday, how would you show someone to get to your home by car?
Analysis	What does each of the figures in the cartoon represent? What is the cartoonist trying to tell us?
Synthesis	From our study of cities, what things do you think are the most important to consider in building a new city and why?
Evaluation	What would happen if the sun suddenly died out?

Although it is desirable to have all students ultimately thinking at the highest level possible, most individuals need to move gradually from a lower to a higher level. Getting students to reach a higher level of thinking becomes a matter of asking questions that call for progressively more complex cognitive tasks and allowing sufficient time for reflection.

For example, suppose you and I have just viewed the film *Gone with the Wind* together. As we leave the theater, we begin to discuss the film. My initial question is, "Do you remember the names of all of the major characters?"

From that conversational opener, we progress to "Which parts did you enjoy the most? Why?" Toward the middle of the discussion, I inquire, "Did this film remind you of any others you have ever seen? In which ways?" We conclude our discussion by entertaining the final question, "What was the meaning of that film?"

Compare that sequence of questions with a second discussion. In this scenario, as you and I emerge from the film, I inquire, concerning this stirring 3-hour epic, "How would you sum up the meaning of the film in a sentence?"

In the first case, the sequence of questions has helped me organize my thoughts in a way that prepares me for the final complex question. The very same type of question that occurs at the *beginning* of the second discussion, however, is likely to be difficult to tackle at first. Furthermore, even if I could respond to it at the outset, my answer is likely to be less thoughtful and complete than if I had the opportunity to order and build my thinking on a foundation of more concrete and specific details.

Similarly, in unstructured classroom questioning, it is important to engage students in discussions at the appropriate level of questioning. This fit sometimes requires trial and error, where a teacher discovers that he or she needs to lower the level of questions after drawing a blank from students. Consider the following exchange in which the teacher, Ms. Carpenter, drops back to a lower level after her students fail to respond to the initial question. Later she begins to work her way back to the original question.

Ms. Carpenter:	What was the importance of the Wright brothers' invention?
Class:	(Silence)
Ms. Carpenter:	In what ways do we and other people use airplanes and other aircraft?
Sally:	For trips and wars.
Rupert:	To spy on other countries.
Steve:	I think planes carry the mail.
Evangelene:	There's a helicopter that looks at traffic and helps people in accidents.
Ms. Carpenter:	(After 5 minutes of discussion) How would our lives be different if we didn't have airplanes and other aircraft?

The Taba Questioning Strategies

Taba questioning strategies

Some educators have devised questioning scripts that are designed to stimulate specific types of cognitive outcomes. Taba (1969) and her associates, for example, developed a series of scripts, based on their research, that can be applied to all topics within the social studies curriculum across all grade levels. Two of the strategies that incorporate their scripts are considered here.

Both strategies include a set of core questions to be asked in the sequence indicated. Each strategy also is constructed to achieve a specific set of instructional objectives. The first is designed to fulfill one of three objectives: (a) Diagnose what students know and do not know about a topic prior to studying it, (b) identify what they have learned as a result of studying a topic or experiencing an event, and (c) encourage all students in the class to participate in a discussion of a topic.

This strategy uses a basic three-question script consisting of an *opening* question, a *grouping* question, and a *labeling* question as follows:

Example	**Function of Question**
Opening Question	
What comes to mind when you hear the word *freedom?*	Calls for recollections of information. Allows all students to participate in the discussion on an equal footing.
What did you see in the film?	
What do you think of when you hear the name *George Washington?*	

Grouping Question

Look over our list of items.	Requires students to organize
Could any be grouped together?	information on the basis of simi-
Why did you group them in that way?	larities and differences they perceive and to provide a rationale for their classification.
Could any things on the board be grouped together?	
Why did you put those items together?	

Labeling Question

Let's look at group A. Can you think of a one- or two-word label or name for it?	To summarize and further refine thinking.

Besides the three scripted questions, throughout the discussion supplemental questions and statements such as the following types would be used as needed:

Clarifying Question.   *Example:* What sort of strange clothing? Can you give an example of what you mean by "poor"?

Refocusing Statement/Question.   *Example:* Let me repeat the original question. Remember what I asked?

Summarizing Question.   *Example:* How could we put that in this space on the board? Could you put that in a single sentence?

In implementing the Taba strategy, the teacher records all students' responses on the board or a chart without evaluation. Similarly, class members are not permitted to challenge other students' responses. Students' comments are listed verbatim or with minor modifications. When comments are lengthy, students are asked to summarize them. The teacher should accept any rationale that a student provides for grouping items together.

The second Taba strategy has a single objective: Students will be able to summarize and interpret data and then draw conclusions and generalizations based on the data (Taba, 1969). This strategy, like the first, employs a basic script of three questions: an *opening* question, an *interpretive* question, and a *capstone* question as follows:

Example	Function of Question
Opening Question	
What did you see on the trip?	Calls for recollection of information.
What did we learn about the Russians?	Allows all students to participate in the discussion on an equal footing.
Interpretive Question	
What differences did you notice between the two countries?	Gets students to draw relationships between data being considered, to compare and contrast information.
How did Roosevelt feel about the issue that was different from how Hoover felt?	
Capstone Question	
What conclusion could we draw from our investigation?	Asks student to form a conclusion, a summary, or a generalization.
From our study, what can you say about families?	

Throughout the discussion, as needed, the second Taba strategy uses supplemental questions and statements similar to the following:

Mapping-the-Field Question.   *Examples:* Have we left out anything? Did we miss any points?

Focusing Question.   *Examples:* What types of clothing did they wear? How many people actually were affected?

Substantiating Question.   *Example:* What did you see in the film that leads you to believe that? Why do you say that?

role-playing techniques

simulation techniques

Engaging Students in Role-Playing and Simulations

We turn now to the final class of instructional techniques that can be applied across social studies topics: *role-playing* and *simulations*. Although they can be used for many types of objectives, **role-playing** and **simulation techniques** are especially useful tools for examining abstract issues. They also facilitate consideration of affective matters that entail beliefs, attitudes, values, and moral choices. They aid by allowing students to "take on a role," step outside their usual perspective on issues, and explore alternatives.

Often in social studies classes, we find it necessary to engage students in subject matter that is potentially complex or emotion laden. For example, we

Role playing can be a useful tool for examining abstract issues.

may wish to have children understand how supply and demand affect the market price of goods in a capitalist economy. Or we might need to have our students develop more sensitivity to cultural diversity.

The Nature of Role-Playing

Successful role-playing activities require advance planning and careful attention to the details of how the steps are to unfold. Teachers need to be prepared for the honest emotions that may emerge when students become immersed in a role. Beyond the dramatic enactment of the role-playing itself also lie the important stages of setting up, discussing, and internalizing the insights gained during the enactments (Shaftel & Shaftel, 1982).

Role-playing activities can be broken into five stages:

1. Initiation and direction
2. Describing the scenario
3. Assigning roles
4. Enactment
5. Debriefing

Initiation and Direction. Every role-playing activity begins with some *problem* that the class or teacher has identified. Until students become accustomed to role-playing procedures, teachers should choose topics that are not controversial or sensitive. Once students are comfortable with the technique, they can move on to more urgent concerns.

Before moving on to the enactment, the class should be "warmed up" for dramatic activity. Simple pantomime scenes or one-sentence scenarios (e.g., you have just dropped your lunch tray) for the students to act out can serve this purpose. Once the class is psychologically prepared, the role-play itself can actually be set up.

Describing the Scenario.   The problem to be discussed should have some clear relevance to a social issue. The actual problem episode that is to trigger the role-playing may be presented orally, pictorially, or in writing. A simple story problem may be some variation of an incident such as the following: Gina pushes Tyrone out of the line in the cafeteria because he is teasing her. Ms. Wharton sees Gina and rushes up to the students.

Assigning Roles.   Role assignment needs to be approached cautiously to avoid both the appearance of any possible typecasting and the inclusion of any reluctant actors. Using volunteers or drawing by lots eliminates the suggestion of typecasting, but it has the disadvantage of possibly involving students who cannot function effectively in the roles to be assigned.

Often it may be desirable to select students who are most likely to give the greatest validity to the roles identified. This strategy ensures that the problem-solution alternatives will be presented effectively. In either event, assignment requires sensitivity and some experimentation to ensure a productive enactment.

Once assigned, all participants, as well as the rest of the class members (the audience), should be briefed on each of the roles. In most cases this can be an oral briefing. However, role-profile cards such as the one shown in Figure 5.8 may be supplied and referred to during the role-play if necessary.

The students in the audience have roles too, albeit temporarily passive ones. At the conclusion of the enactment, they can be asked to assess whether the roles assigned appeared to be enacted genuinely and to suggest alternative ways of playing the roles. They also may be asked to focus on a specific actor and identify vicariously with him or her.

Enactment.   A briefing with the characters individually before the role-play event begins can establish how they plan to enact their roles. Although enact-

FIGURE 5.8   Sample role-profile card

Tamika: Everyone in the class seems to like you. You are considered to be the smartest one in the class. Most children like to have you on their team when choosing up sides for games. You enjoy school and the work you do there.

ments may be modified during the actual event, rehearsal helps students clarify their roles.

It is important to remind students that during the enactment they should use the names of the characters. This procedure reinforces the fact that individual class members themselves are not the objects of analysis. Similarly, it often is necessary to remind players to *stay in role*—that is, deal with events as their characters actually might. Some children have a tendency, in humorous or anxiety-producing situations, to stop the role-play enactment and to respond as an observer. Gentle prodding to them and to the audience participants who may become noisy or distracting early in the role-play activity helps establish the ground rules.

Debriefing.   The debriefing phase is a crucial and integral part of role-playing. It requires the greatest attention and guidance on the teacher's part to ensure productive and meaningful results. The debriefing period should immediately follow the enactment. The characters should be allowed to share any feelings they had while they were playing their roles and possibly to entertain questions from the audience. At some point an exploration of alternative ways of handling the characters' roles should occur. If participants are willing, they can be asked to reenact the event in different ways, possibly switching roles.

The debriefing session may take many forms, depending on the issue, the maturity of the group, and its experience with role-playing. At some point the issue embedded in the role-play event should be abstracted and clearly addressed so that attention shifts to real experiences, individuals, and places. The teacher then can help students draw parallels between the role-play enactment and real events.

Role-Playing and Puppetry

One of the interesting ways to introduce even very young children to role-playing techniques is through the use of puppets. They can be used by the teacher to reenact and dramatize historical events and social issues and to demonstrate social phenomena, such as customs and rules. Because puppets are perceived by children as toys, often they can be used to encourage very shy or reticent students to participate in role-playing. Children of all ages and even adults usually enjoy working with puppets.

Sources of Puppets.   Many companies sell a variety of commercial puppets for use in school activities. Simple paper-plates-on-a-stick and finger, mitten, and mitt puppets, such as those shown in Figure 5.9, are inexpensive and easy to create.

Scenarios for Role-Playing with Puppets.   Figure 5.10 illustrates an activity in which puppets might be used to engage primary-level students in a discussion concerning the effects of name-calling. Following are other examples of

FIGURE 5.9   Types of teacher- and student-made puppets

Paper-Plate Rod Puppets and Masks

Materials

Paper plate; skewer or cardboard tube for rod control; paper features.

Procedure

Tape rod control onto back of paper plate. Children can make their own features or use those provided by the teacher to glue onto the plate. By cutting out eye holes, puppets can be converted into masks.

Policeperson

Mitt Puppets

Materials

Two pieces of 8 by 9-inch paper bag; mural paper or fabric; trim.

Procedure

Make a master pattern on lightweight cardboard of mitt puppet for children to trace on desired materials; cut out.

Run a thin line of glue around border edges of one body piece, but leave bottom edge unglued.

Lay second body piece over glued edge of bottom piece; press flat and dry thoroughly. (Pieces may also be stapled or sewn together.)

Create features and costumes with crayons, marker pens, scrap fabric and trims.

Farmer

Paper Bag Puppets (Flap Mouth)

Materials

Small or medium sized paper bag; paper features; assorted fabric scraps.

Procedure

Children may make their own features for paper bag puppets or cut out and color the basic features supplied by the teacher.

Provide assorted scrap fabric and coloring medium to decorate the bags; the bag surfaces lend themselves well to gluing and painting activities.

To operate, place fingers inside flap of bag as shown; move up and down.

Hand position

Pilgrim

Source: From *Puppetry and Early Childhood Education* (pp. 162, 165, 168) by T. Hunt and N. Renfro, 1982, Austin, TX: Nancy Renfro Studios, Inc. P.O. Box 164226, Austin, TX 78716, 1-800-933-5512. Reprinted by permission.

FIGURE 5.10   An activity in which puppets might be used

Activity 43: "Name Calling"

Use hand puppets to dramatize a story such as the following.

Puppet #1   (Speaking to Puppet #3) Oh, good. Time for recess. Let's play tag.

Puppet #2   Can I play?

Puppet #3   Go away ugly (or fatso, shorty, weirdo, carrot head), we don't want you to play!

Puppet #2   (Moves away with head down.)

Discussion

How would you feel if you were Puppet #2?

Why do you think Puppet #3 treated Puppet #2 that way?

What would you do if you were Puppet #2?

What could Puppet #1 do to make Puppet #2 feel better? (Have students act out a positive ending.)

What could Puppet #3 do to make Puppet #2 feel better? (Have students act out Puppet #3 apologizing.)

Draw attention to the following points:

    This kind of behavior hurts.

    People come in all different sizes and shapes.

    It is prejudice not to play with someone because of the way he or she looks.

Source: From *Teacher, They Called Me a _____!* (p. 32) by D. Byrnes, 1987, New York: Anti-Defamation League of B'nai B'rith.

problem scenarios for role-playing by children using puppets. Students also can be encouraged to suggest incidents that could be used.

    1.   Suzanne and Bruce always want to sit in the chair closest to the television set. The scene starts with Suzanne and Bruce fighting over who gets to sit in the chair.

    2.   Timmy has just turned 7 years old, and he thinks he should get an allowance to spend as he pleases. His father thinks that Timmy is too young for an allowance and that he would just spend it on silly things such as bubble gum cards. His mother thinks an allowance would be all right but should be saved for college. Timmy doesn't agree with either parent. The scene begins with Timmy's parents telling him how they feel.

The Nature of Simulations

Closely related to role-playing is simulation. Often called *simulation games,* instructional simulations are activities designed to provide lifelike problem-solving experiences in the form of a game. They provide a representation of some phenomenon, event, or issue that actually exists or existed in the real world. These characteristics distinguish a simulation from a simple game, such as Bingo or baseball, in which there are rules and some goal but no representation of real social events. Simulations appear in many forms, including board games and computer programs.

A major asset of simulations is that they enable many students to relate easily to and become highly interested in a problem they might not otherwise take very seriously. Furthermore, simulations often allow students to assume more control over their own learning and to be less dependent on the teacher.

Both a strength and a limitation of simulations is that they permit study of a *simplified* representation of some reality. All simulations limit the number of variables they present to players; otherwise they would be too complicated. In this respect, simulations make the study of a problem easier to understand, but they also distort it somewhat.

In a simulation of Congress, for example, not all of the actual considerations that weigh on lawmakers in their deliberations could be included and weighed. Similarly, the activity shown in Figure 5.11 deals only with a small number of issues related to the complex world refugee crisis. This basic board game simulation allows even younger children to experience some of the many difficulties that refugees encounter as they seek asylum in a new nation.

Sources of Simulations.   Teachers have access to a variety of commercial simulations (Horn & Cleaves, 1980; Muir, 1980, 1996; Schug & Kepner, 1984). The majority of these have been designed for secondary students, but some have been developed for use with young students. The majority of simulations for social studies instruction fall into two broad categories: *computerized* formats for one person or a small group and *noncomputerized* formats for small groups that employ board games or role-play activities. The emergence of personal computers, with their capacity for handling many variables quickly, has provided opportunities for an assortment of complex simulations. These simulations often allow students to more closely approximate real events than noncomputerized media. In Chapter 11 we consider some examples of computerized simulations.

Examples of *noncomputerized* simulations, with a brief explanation of each, are:

- *Balance of Power* (Simulates four imaginary nations trying to keep peace)
- *Equality* (Provides an ethnic group activity in an imaginary city)
- *Hunger on Spaceship Earth* (Examines world hunger problems)
- *Mini-Society* (Generates a working economic system in the classroom)
- *Powderhorn* (Analyzes how power is manipulated by groups)
- *Rafá, Rafá* (Analyzes cultural differences between groups)
- *Seal Hunt* (Illustrates how cooperative behavior can be essential to survival)

Guidelines for Developing and Conducting Simulations

Teachers also may create their own simulations. An example of a simulation designed for a fifth-grade class is shown in Figure 5.12. It deals with the issue of environmental pollution in the fictitious community of Pleasantville. The simulation contains all of the detailed material to be given to the students. It may be modified easily to tailor the situation to local community conditions.

Comprehensive guides for constructing an effective simulation are available to assist teachers in developing their own simulations (e.g., Greenblat, 1987). Typically, they suggest a series of basic steps similar to the following:

1. Define the problem or issue that the simulation is to represent.
2. State the objectives of the simulation as narrowly and clearly as possible.
3. Specify the actors or parts that are to be played.
4. Spell out in some detail the roles that the players are to assume or what they are to achieve.
5. Indicate the resources and the constraints or rules that exist for the players.
6. Specify clearly the decision-making mechanisms or how the simulation is to operate.
7. Develop a trial version of the simulation and field-test it.
8. On the basis of the field test, modify the simulation and retest it until all "bugs" have been eliminated.

To employ simulations effectively in instruction, one can follow the same set of guidelines suggested earlier for role-playing. Again, the *debriefing* period is a critical and integral phase of a simulation activity. In establishing a time frame for the use of simulations, a teacher must set aside a sufficient block of time to discuss students' insights and reactions. It is important in this discussion period also to relate the simulated events to ones within students' experiences.

Group Activities

1. Find a class at grade levels 4 through 8 in which the teacher will let you develop a sociogram. Explain the purpose of the activity and indicate the nature of the questions you will ask students. Indicate the grade level and size of the class. Complete the sociogram by using the procedures discussed in the text and analyze the results. Share the findings with the teacher and compare your analyses. At the end, summarize the data as shown in the chapter; then discuss your experiences and results.

2. Work in triads. Follow the procedures for developing the activity that are outlined in the chapter. Select a chapter from the class basal social studies text and design a cooperative learning activity. After the activity is com-

FIGURE 5.11   Sample simulation activity

Take Refuge!

Materials: A die
Gameboard
Rules of the game
2 to 4 players

Cut out the playing pieces along the dotted lines. Fold each along the solid line; glue the bottom to a square of lightweight cardboard to form a stand.

To make the gameboard and parts more durable, mount them with rubber cement on cardboard, then cover each with clear plastic adhesive paper. Before you cover them, add color with felt tip markers.

After you play the game, answer these questions:

1) How many good things happened to you as you played this game?

2) Did you find this game frustrating? Why or why not?

3) How would you feel if the things that happened in this game happened to you in real life?

Rules of the Game

Each player chooses a token and throws the die. The highest number starts by putting his or her token on square 1. Other players follow accordingly. Whenever a player lands on a shaded square, he or she must follow the instructions for that square.

The first player to reach square 58 is the winner. But to reach that square, you must throw the exact number needed to land on 58. If you throw a number higher than what you need, move to 58 and continue the count by moving backwards. When you reach 58, you have become accepted as a refugee.

3. You forgot your passport! Return to 1.

6. Miss a turn while you look for food.

9. You sprain your ankle on a rugged path. Wait here until all the others have passed you.

11. A fallen tree blocks your path. Miss a turn while you go around it.

14. A wild animal chases you back to 12.

16. You discover a shortcut. Go to 20.

19. You're lost. Return to 17.

22. A scary noise awakens you. Run to safety at 21.

26. Your brother has fallen behind. Find him at 23.

28. A border patrol is looking for you. Hide in 27.

32. You're stuck in a barbed wire fence. Miss one turn.

34. The police arrest you and send you back to your country. Return to 1.

38. You are placed in a transit camp. Miss 2 turns.

40. You are so hungry, you take corn from a field. The farmer chases you back to 39.

44. A heavy storm comes. Take shelter in 42.

48. Miss a turn waiting for a boat to take you across the river.

51. Bad winds slow you down. On your next turn, move forward only 1 space.

53. You left your passport on the other side of the river. Go back to 50.

57. You get a fever. Miss 2 turns.

FIGURE 5.11 (Continued)

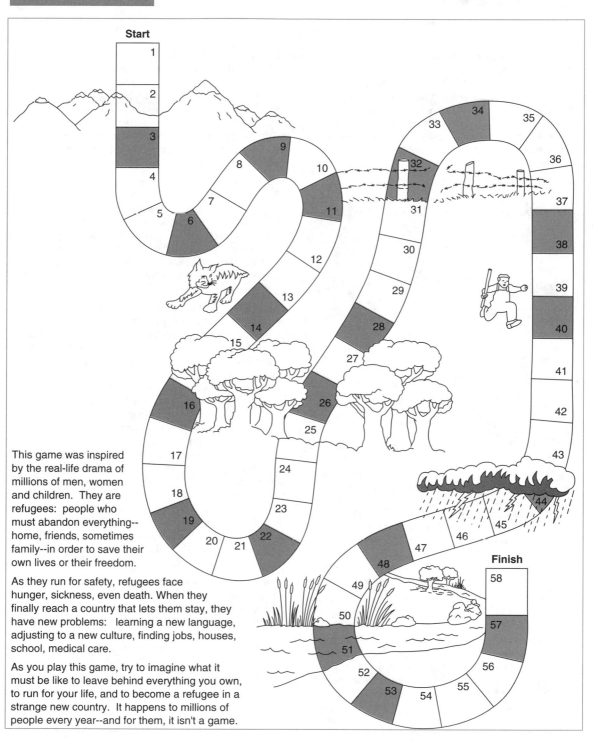

Start

1
2
3
4
5
6
7
8
9
10
11
12
13
14
15
16
17
18
19
20
21
22
23
24
25
26
27
28
29
30
31
32
33
34
35
36
37
38
39
40
41
42
43
44
45
46
47
48
49
50
51
52
53
54
55
56
57
58

Finish

This game was inspired by the real-life drama of millions of men, women and children. They are refugees: people who must abandon everything--home, friends, sometimes family--in order to save their own lives or their freedom.

As they run for safety, refugees face hunger, sickness, even death. When they finally reach a country that lets them stay, they have new problems: learning a new language, adjusting to a new culture, finding jobs, houses, school, medical care.

As you play this game, try to imagine what it must be like to leave behind everything you own, to run for your life, and to become a refugee in a strange new country. It happens to millions of people every year--and for them, it isn't a game.

FIGURE 5.12   Example of a teacher-made simulation

Pollution

Pleasantville can be described as a rather average small city with a population of just over 50,000. A glance at the map of the city shows that Pleasantville has some general characteristics in common with most other cities of its size in that we find homes, businesses, and some industries located in the city. Pleasantville has other characteristics common to most cities, which do not show on the map, such as schools, social organizations, and a city government.

Map of Pleasantville

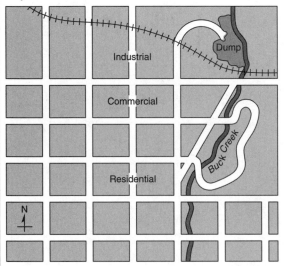

Another characteristic Pleasantville has in common with many other cities is that it has a problem about which its citizens are concerned. The problem is that of how to dispose of all the trash, garbage, and junk produced by the people, businesses, and industries in the city. In the past the residents neither knew nor cared what happened to their refuse once the garbage truck picked it up. The residents of Pleasantville have become more aware of the problem of solid waste disposal, however, as they have begun to notice rubbish and junk accumulating in vacant lots, on the stream banks, and along the roadsides at the edge of the city.

The problem of environmental pollution has arisen partly because Pleasantville has grown in size over the past few years and there is more and more refuse to dispose of. This has resulted in more work for the Department of Sanitation. Another result has been that more trash is being hauled to the city dump, which at present is nearly filled to capacity.

Many residents of Pleasantville have noticed that the major contributor to the unsightly trash piles in vacant lots and to the filling of the dump has been the "immortal" container, that is, the pop-top aluminum can and the nonreturnable, nonreusable bottle. Cans and bottles can be found nearly everywhere--along the railroad tracks, in the park, and along the stream banks. They may even be found in front yards after someone has carelessly tossed a can or bottle from a car window.

Hoping to help solve the problem, the local Conservation Club has organized a "Clean Environment" campaign. Through the urging of Conservation Club members and other concerned residents, local ordinances have been posted threatening fines and possible arrest for the illegal dumping of "immortal" containers and other junk. The cans and bottles keep sprouting, however, and parts of the local environment have become disgraceful eyesores.

This pollution of the environment has become a daily and often heated topic of discussion in Pleasantville. One of the most controversial issues arising as a result of the "Clean Environment" campaign concerns a locally owned industry--the Kool-Kola Bottling Company. Kool-Kola is bottled in pop-top aluminum cans and nonreturnable bottles. Many of these containers end up along the roadsides and in vacant lots. Members of the Conservation Club have asked representatives of the Kool-Kola Company to help solve this problem by marketing Kool-Kola in either returnable or easily disposed-of containers. The Kool-Kola Company hesitantly agreed to try the first alternative for a limited time period. However, when the local grocers stated that they were not willing to sell soft drinks in returnable containers because of the extra handling costs involved, the Kool-Kola Company withdrew its offer. Presently the Conservation Club is attempting to arouse public support for a boycott of Kool-Kola if the company continues to market it in nonreturnable containers.

As a result of the gradual filling of the dump and the unsightly buildup of trash along the streets, stream, and tracks, several local groups have decided that they should consider more drastic actions toward the solution of the problem. The question they hope to answer is: "What steps do we take to rid ourselves of the cans and bottles that are cluttering up Pleasantville's environment?"

Source: From "Simulation and Inquiry Models Applied to the Study of Environmental Problems" by J. B. Kracht and P. H. Martorella, 1970, *Journal of Geography, 69,* pp. 273–278.

FIGURE 5.12   (Continued)

Procedures for Simulation. The simulation experience is to provide for the resolution of a specific aspect of the solid-waste problems in Pleasantville, that of dealing with nonreturnable soft-drink containers. Interest groups that will have a voice in the decision-making process leading to the resolution of the problem are (1) the Pleasantville Conservation Club, (2) local grocers, (3) the Kool-Kola Bottling Company, (4) the Department of Sanitation, (5) the City Council, and (6) the local electorate. The teacher should provide for the selection of individuals to play specified roles. The authors recommend that three pupils represent each of the first four groups, seven pupils represent the City Council members, and the rest of the class represent the local electorate.

Phase I
The authors suggest the following sequence for the simulation:
1. Present the class with the Pleasantville case study.
2. Identify the various actors and select people to fill the roles, explaining that they are to resolve the problem in the best way possible by acting out the roles assigned to them.
3. Explain that the representatives of the Conservation Club, grocers, Kool-Kola Company, and Department of Sanitation are to arrive at one or two alternative solutions to the solid-waste problem in Pleasantville that reflect basic concerns of their particular group (note the list of concerns following no. 4 below).
4. Allow time for the interest groups to caucus.

A. Concerns of the Conservation Club
1. General cleanliness of the environment.
2. Elimination of nonreturnable, immortal containers.
3. Elimination of pollution caused by the present city dump.
4. Elimination of the pest problem.

B. Concerns of the Local Grocers
1. Satisfaction of consumer demand.
2. Maximize profits.
3. Minimize handling costs.

C. Concerns of the Kool-Kola Company
1. Satisfaction of consumer demand.
2. Satisfaction of dealer demand.
3. Maximize profits.
4. Minimize costs.

D. Concerns of the Department of Sanitation
1. Satisfaction of the maximum number of constituents.
2. Avoid the conversion of solid-waste pollution to other forms of pollution.

3. Speed of disposal.
4. Cost of disposal.
5. Aesthetic considerations.

Phase II
1. Once the groups have arrived at their alternative solutions to the problem, the solutions may be presented to a public meeting of the City Council. After the presentations by the concerned groups and discussion by the council members, the meeting should be opened for discussion of the issues by the electorate.
2. Following the discussion the City Council should select, modify, or formulate three solutions that will be submitted to the electorate in a referendum.

Phase III
1. Before the actual voting takes place, individual members of the electorate may wish to try to persuade others to accept a particular point of view.
2. The final decision is made when the voting takes place.

Evaluation
After the pupils have simulated the resolution of the environmental problem, the teacher should not hesitate to encourage student evaluation. This evaluation may take two forms. First, the final solution to the problem might be considered. Questions such as the following may be asked:

1. Was the solution relevant to the problem?
2. What will be the consequences of the solution?
3. Will the solution create new problems?

Second, the simulation experience itself may be evaluated:

1. Was the simulation experience realistic and accurate?
2. In what ways can the simulation be changed or improved?
3. Did the simulation provide for meaningful interaction of all participants?
4. Can simulation experiences provide for the interaction of other actors in the resolution of related environmental problems?

pleted, discuss some of the important issues that surfaced. Note what you would do differently.

3. Work in a group of four or five and select a film that is appropriate for use in a primary social studies class. View it and individually develop a brief questioning script consisting of four or five questions. Sequence the questions from simple to complex ones. In your group, compare the different scripts and the rationale for them. Repeat the process with a film for an intermediate-grade class.

4. Arrange to observe a teacher in an elementary school during a social studies lesson. In one column on a sheet of paper list verbatim all of the questions the teacher asks during the class. Also note the teacher's wait time after each question. In an adjacent column write how the students responded. After you leave the school, analyze your data in relation to the discussion of questioning in the chapter.

5. Arrange with a local teacher to work with a class in grades 4 through 8. Work in dyads and field-test either the refugee or environmental simulation games in the chapter. Follow the procedures outlined in the chapter. For the simulation *Take Refuge!* you will need to organize the class into groups and to make multiple copies of the game. After you have debriefed the game with the class, discuss your experiences and results.

Individual Activities

1. Identify a class of students in grades 1 through 8 and a topic for a social studies lesson. Develop a set of key questions for the lesson, applying the Taba strategy that employs an opening-grouping-labeling question sequence. Also develop a small set of supplemental questions (e.g., a clarification question) that you anticipate will be needed during the discussion. Lead a discussion by using the script. If possible, audio- or videotape the session and analyze the outcome.

2. Repeat the activity above with the following changes: Identify a class from grades 4 through 8 and develop a set of questions applying the second Taba strategy.

3. Construct one each of the paper-plate/rod, mitt, and paper bag puppets suitable for use in a primary-grade social studies class.

References

Aronson, E., Blaney, N., Stephan, C., Sikes, J., & Snapp, M. (1978). *The Jigsaw classroom.* Beverly Hills, CA: Sage.

Bloom, B. S. (Ed.). (1956). *Taxonomy of educational objectives, the classification of educational goals. Handbook I: The cognitive domain.* New York: David McKay.

Borich, G. D. (1996). *Effective teaching methods* (3rd ed.). Upper Saddle River, NJ: Merrill/Prentice Hall.

Brown, G., & Edmondson, R. (1984). Asking questions. In E. Wragg (Ed.), *Classroom teaching skills* (pp. 97–120). New York: Nichols.

Byrnes, D. (1987). *Teacher, they called me a ____!* New York: Anti-Defamation League of B'nai B'rith.

Fox, R., Luszki, M. B., & Schmuck, R. (1966). *Diagnosing classroom learning environments.* Chicago: SRA.

Greenblat, C. S. (1987). *Designing games and simulations.* Beverly Hills, CA: Sage.

Holy Childhood Association. (no date). *Take refuge!* Washington, DC: Author.

Horn, R. E., & Cleaves, A. (Eds.). (1980). *The guide to simulation games for education and training* (4th ed.). Beverly Hills, CA: Sage.

Hunt, T., & Renfro, N. (1982). *Puppetry and early childhood education.* Austin, TX: Nancy Renfro Studios.

Johnson, R. T., & Johnson, D. W. (Eds.). (1984). *Structuring cooperative learning: Lesson plans for teachers.* New Brighton, MN: Interaction.

Kracht, J. B., & Martorella, P. H. (1970). Simulation and inquiry models applied to the study of environmental problems. *Journal of Geography, 69,* 273–278.

Leighton, M. S. (1990). Cooperative learning. In J. Cooper (Ed.), *Classroom teaching skills* (4th ed., pp. 307-335). Lexington, MA: D. C. Heath.

Mattingley, R. M., & VanSickle, R. L. (1991). Cooperative learning and achievement in social studies. *Social Education, 55,* 392–395.

Muir, S. P. (1980). Simulation games for elementary social studies. *Social Education, 44,* 35–39.

Muir, S. P. (1996). Simulations for elementary and primary school social studies: An annotated bibliography. *Simulation and Gaming, 27,* 41.

Newman, D., Griffin, P., & Cole, M. (1989). *The construction zone: Working for cognitive change in school.* New York: Cambridge University Press.

Osborn, A. (1963). *Applied imagination* (3rd ed.). New York: Scribner.

Rowe, M. B. (1969). Science, soul and sanctions. *Science and Children, 6,* 11–13.

Schmuck, R. A., & Schmuck, P. (1983). *Group processes in the classroom* (4th ed.). Dubuque, IA: W. C. Brown.

Schug, M. C., & Kepner, H. S., Jr. (1984). Computer simulations in the social studies. *Social Education, 75,* 211–215.

Shaftel, F. R., & Shaftel, G. (1982). *Role-playing for social values.* Upper Saddle River, NJ: Prentice-Hall.

Sharan, S., & Schachar, C. (1988). *Language and learning in the cooperative classroom.* New York: Springer.

Sharan, Y., & Sharan, S. (1992). What do we want to study? How should we go about it?: Group investigation in the cooperative social studies classroom. In R. J. Stahl (Ed.), *Cooperative learning in social studies: A handbook for teachers* (pp. 257–276). Menlo Park, CA: Addison-Wesley.

Slavin, R. E. (1986). *Using student team learning* (3rd ed.). Baltimore, MD: Johns Hopkins University, Center for Social Organization of Schools.

Slavin, R. E. (1987). *Cooperative learning student teams* (2nd ed.). Washington, DC: National Education Association.

Slavin, R. E. (1990). *Cooperative learning: Theory, research, and practice.* Upper Saddle River, NJ: Prentice Hall.

Slavin, R. E. (1991). Synthesis of research on cooperative learning. *Educational Leadership, 48,* 71–82.

Steinbrink, J. E. (1985). The social studies learner as questioner. *The Social Studies, 76,* 38–40.

Taba, H. (1969). *Teaching strategies and cognitive functioning in elementary school children* (Cooperative research project 2404). Washington, DC: U.S. Office of Education.

Tobin, K. (1987). The role of wait time in higher cognitive level learning. *Review of Educational Research, 57,* 69–95.

VanSickle, R. L. (1992). Cooperative learning, properly implemented works: Evidence from research in classrooms. In R. J. Stahl & R. L. VanSickle (Eds.), *Cooperative learning in the social studies classroom: An invitation to social study* (pp. 16–20). Washington, DC: National Council for the Social Studies.

Wilen, W. W., & White, J. J. (1991). Interaction and discourse in social studies classrooms. In J. P. Shaver (Ed.), *Handbook of research on social studies teaching and learning* (pp. 483–495). New York: Macmillan.

Chapter

Aiding Children in Developing and Applying Concepts, Generalizations, and Hypotheses

Concepts in the Social Studies Curriculum

Personal and Public Dimensions of Concepts

Misconceptions and Stereotypes

Concepts in Social Studies Texts and Materials

The Process of Learning a New Concept

Sources of Difficulty in Concept Learning

Instructional Strategies for Concept Learning

Concept Analyses

Assessing Concept Learning

Instructional Model for Teaching Concepts

Discovery and Expository Approaches in Teaching Concepts

Concept Hierarchies

Concept Teaching Materials and Activities

Facts, Generalizations, and Hypotheses in the Social Studies Curriculum

The Nature of Facts

The Nature of Generalizations

The Nature of Hypotheses

Instructional Strategies for Developing Generalizations

Expository and Discovery Approaches for Teaching Generalizations

Using Data Retrieval Charts

The Reflective Citizen and Problem Solving

Uses of the Term *Problem* in Instruction

Instructional Strategies for Problem Solving

Problem Springboards

Let us peek in on a third-grade geography lesson. Over the span of a 30-minute session, students encounter a jumble of information. Some aspects are factual and some hypothetical. The knowledge children construct from the experience may be fragmented or systematically encoded and linked in a holistic pattern.

Later, as we analyze the lesson, we note that the students' related prior knowledge initially was dotted with misinformation. In the course of the lesson, they also referenced a number of concepts. Some were familiar but one, desert, was new. After *examining several maps, consulting Encarta (a multimedia encyclopedia), and collecting facts from several trade books dealing with landforms, the children also begin to develop a generalization about deserts.*

What are concepts, facts, and generalizations? What role do they play in the development of the reflective, competent, and concerned citizen?

To function effectively and to advance, a democratic society requires reflective citizens who have a well-grounded body of concepts, facts, and generalizations concerning human behavior, their nation, and the world. In applying such knowledge to civic affairs, citizens must be able to develop and test hypotheses and to engage in problem solving by using factual data and well-formed concepts. These reflective abilities are acquired cumulatively; they begin early in the home, become more formalized with the onset of kindergarten and schooling, and may develop throughout life.

schemata

*In an earlier chapter, it was noted that individuals organized knowledge into structures known as **schemata**. The elements of these schemata include a complex, interrelated web or network of concepts, facts, generalizations, and hypotheses. We now consider teaching strategies and learning environments designed to provide students with subject matter and experiences that stimulate the development of such knowledge structures.*

Concepts in the Social Studies Curriculum

concept

All learning, thinking, and action involve **concepts.** They broaden and enrich our lives and make it possible for us to communicate easily with others. Because individuals share many similar concepts, they can exchange information rapidly and efficiently without any need for explaining in detail each item discussed. Similarly, when a communication breakdown occurs, it often is because one of the parties lacks the necessary concepts embedded in the conversation. Not infrequently, this breakdown happens in social studies textbooks when the author assumes certain knowledge that the student does not actually have.

Concepts are hooks on which we can hang new information. When we encounter new subject matter that does not appear to fit on any existing conceptual hook, we may broaden our idea of what some existing hook can hold or may create a new one. These conceptual hangers allow us to tidy up our knowledge structure. They also make it easier to learn and remember information.

In their simplest form, concepts may be regarded as categories into which we group phenomena within our experience. Concepts allow us to sort out large numbers of people, objects, and events into categories such as cars, plants, nations, and heroes. As phenomena are sorted into concept categories, we discern their basic or distinguishing characteristics. We may check these characteristics against our memories of past examples or prototypes that represent our notion of a typical case of the concept.

Personal and Public Dimensions of Concepts

Concepts, however, are more than just categories. They also have **personal** and **public dimensions** because the categories into which we sort our experiences contain all of the personal associations we have accumulated in relation to the concept. As an illustration, an individual's concept of *money* encompasses more than a mental file drawer that includes checks, bank drafts, currency, and credit cards. The concept also is attached to our economic goals, our perceptions of financial issues, and many other personal associations with money that make each person's concept unique.

Considerable evidence demonstrates that culture generally plays a large role in shaping this personal pattern of associations (see, e.g., Cole & Scribner, 1974; Hunt & Banaji, 1988; Whorf, 1956). Some investigators also have argued that language, specifically, is an important influence.

In contrast to the set of unique personal associations that each of our concepts incorporates, some defining properties are shared in common: the public aspects of concepts. They are the characteristics that distinguish one concept from another and permit easy exchanges of information and experiences. These shared features of concepts mean that although a professional banker and I, for example, have had different levels of experiences with *money*, we can communicate easily with one another concerning the fundamental aspects of the concept.

personal dimensions (of a concept)

public dimensions (of a concept)

Misconceptions and Stereotypes

Much of the formal learning of concepts in schools often consists of correcting **misconceptions**—incorrect or incomplete concepts—as well as forming new ones. Many students, for example, have the misconception that all deserts are hot places. When students focus on the *noncritical* properties of concepts and assume they appear in all examples of the concept, they often develop *stereotypes*. As an illustration, on the basis of a limited range of experiences with Americans classified as *Italians*, a little boy may have developed the stereotype that Italians are "people who have dark hair, use their hands when talking, and like spaghetti." From his limited and isolated experiences with some members of the ethnic group, the child has overgeneralized to all Italians.

misconception

Concepts in Social Studies Texts and Materials

By the time they finish school, students will have encountered the names of thousands of concepts in their social studies classes and textbooks and their daily life experiences. A sample list of some that are found commonly in elementary social studies programs, materials, and texts are shown here. Only a fraction of items such as these actually will be learned as concepts and become more than a familiar word (Martorella, 1971).

city	ocean	mountain	community
nation	colony	boundary	freedom
river	family	North	culture
democracy	war	peace	waste
revolution	map	holiday	assembly line
island	suburbs	earth	shelter
power	prejudice	supply	nationality
poverty	scarcity	money	transportation
equator	desert	conflict	neighborhood

The typical basal text includes a great many concepts; some it attempts to teach the students, and many it assumes they already know. If the concepts in texts and instructional materials are to be more than words for students, they must be taught prior to or concurrently with lessons that assume their understanding.

Often texts and reading materials for young children are heavily loaded with abstract concepts, which then are explained with other abstract concepts. Consider the concepts in an example from a basal social studies text for the second grade. Alongside a picture of a globe with an equator drawn around it, this statement appears: "The globe also shows the equator. The equator is an imaginary line. It goes all around the globe."

The Process of Learning a New Concept

It would be difficult for you to recall vividly the processes that were involved in learning many of the concepts you already possess. To recapture this sensation, I will ask you to learn two new concepts. In doing so, I will be placing you in the shoes of a student who frequently is confronted with the same type of cognitive task in social studies classes. As you engage in the learning process, reflect on your strategies, successes, mistakes, and feelings about the process.

Consider the two concept instruction frames in Figure 6.1 and Figure 6.2 and then answer the questions they pose. When you think you have learned the concept, compare your responses with the Answer Key at the end of this chapter.

The experiences associated with attempting to learn these new concepts should have sensitized you to some of the problems that students experience. Difficulties often begin with trying to remember (and spell correctly) what appear as strange names. Your experience also may suggest how students sometimes have thoughtful reasons for wrong answers. Most importantly, the exercise should have revealed how *learner problems are often due to the nature of the instruction provided, rather than to student inadequacies.*

Sources of Difficulty in Concept Learning

The exercise also should have confirmed that different levels of difficulty are associated with demonstrating learning of a concept. Recall that I asked you to

FIGURE 6.1 The concept of *Squarp*

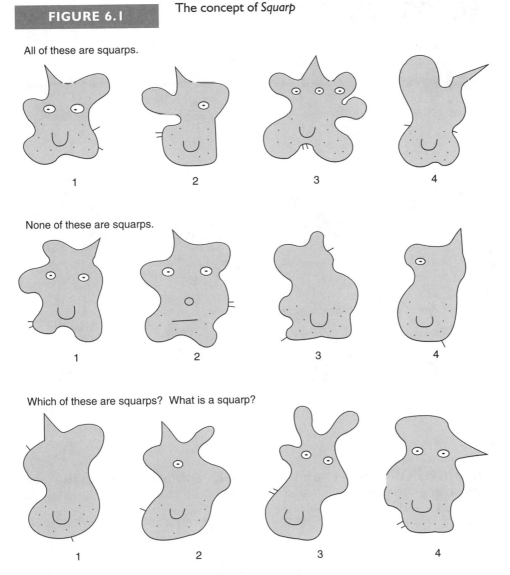

All of these are squarps.

1 2 3 4

None of these are squarps.

1 2 3 4

Which of these are squarps? What is a squarp?

1 2 3 4

state the **concept rule** (or definition) for each of the two concepts, as well as to *identify* examples. Stating the concept rule in your own words or even selecting a correct definition among incorrect ones is a different and more difficult task from identifying examples from nonexamples.

concept rule

The two examples in the exercise were designed to represent different types of problems associated with concept learning. Two types of concepts, *disjunctive* and *conjunctive*, were included (Bruner, Goodnow, & Austin, 1962). Zrapples represented disjunctive concepts; squarps represented conjunctive concepts.

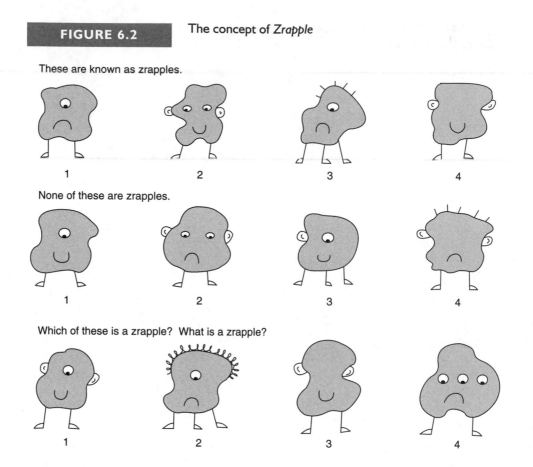

| FIGURE 6.2 | The concept of *Zrapple* |

These are known as zrapples.

1   2   3   4

None of these are zrapples.

1   2   3   4

Which of these is a zrapple? What is a zrapple?

1   2   3   4

Disjunctive, Conjunctive, and Relational Concepts. **Disjunctive concepts** such as zrapples have *two or more* sets of alternative characteristics that define them, rather than a single one. In social studies *citizen* is such a concept. Citizens of the United States are those who *either* are born in the country *or* fulfill some test of citizenship *or* are born in another country of parents who are citizens of the United States.

The other concept, *squarp*, which is conjunctive, is the least complex type to learn. A **conjunctive concept** has a single, fixed set of characteristics that define the concept. All of the many different examples of squarps share the same essential set of characteristics. An example of a conjunctive social studies concept is *globe*. A globe is a round object that has a map of the earth drawn on it.

You were not asked to learn the most complex type, a **relational concept.** Unlike the other two types, relational concepts have no single fixed set of characteristics. Rather, they can be defined *only by comparison to or in relationship with other objects or events. Justice, far, prosperous, greed, fair,* and *near* are examples of relational concepts in social studies. One cannot tell, for instance,

disjunctive concept

conjunctive concept

relational concept

whether a person, place, or thing is "near," only whether it is near something else, and then only by using some criterion to make a judgment of nearness. Philadelphia may or may not be considered to be near Baltimore. It depends on whether the context of analysis deals with city blocks or planets.

Concrete and Abstract Concepts. A further source of difficulty associated with learning concepts is their degree of concreteness or abstractness. *Concreteness* refers to what we can perceive directly through one of the five senses. *Abstractness* refers to what we cannot directly perceive through our senses.

In practice the line between what is concrete and what is abstract seldom is drawn so clearly. Consider the list of social studies concepts presented earlier. Some clearly cannot be directly perceived, such as *freedom*; others clearly can, such as *map*. However, many concepts—community and family, for example— lie somewhere between being concrete or being abstract. Aspects of community and family are visible, such as people, but other important characteristics, the relationships of individuals to one another, for example, are abstract. So too with many other concepts similar to zrapple and squarp.

Instructional Strategies for Concept Learning

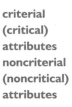

Among all of the concepts that we learn, only some are appropriate to teach formally in schools. Many concepts, such as *pencil*, *flag*, and hundreds of other common ones generally are learned informally by students. Others are too complex to teach directly.

Teaching concepts begins with a teacher's identification of a list of significant concepts appropriate for teaching in the social studies program. A simple rule of thumb might be to teach at least one new important concept each time a unit is introduced. After identifying the concepts, the teacher then can analyze each one in preparation for selecting materials and teaching strategies.

Concept Analyses

A concept analysis involves identifying (a) the *name* most commonly associated with the concept, (b) a simplified *rule* or definition that specifies clearly what the concept is, (c) the **criterial attributes** that make up the defining characteristics of the concept, and (d) some **noncriterial attributes** that are characteristics often associated with the concept but nevertheless nonessential.

An analysis also involves selecting or creating some different **examples** of the concept, including a **best example** or clearest case of the concept, and some related **nonexamples** of the concept. These provide contrast by showing what the concept is not.

Statements of the criterial attributes and definitions of concepts can be found in general dictionaries, specialized dictionaries such as the *Dictionary of Political Science*, and textbooks. Identifying the noncriterial attributes of concepts

criterial (critical) attributes
noncriterial (noncritical) attributes

best example (of a concept)
concept example
concept nonexample

requires some reflection because they take many forms. As noted in the example of the little boy and Italians, noncriterial attributes appear in examples of virtually any concept. As a result their presence often misleads students into believing they are essential features of the concept.

Because of the diversity of concepts, no specific number of examples is required to teach a concept. The set of examples provided, however, should represent adequately the range of cases that appear in common usage. For example, in teaching the concept of *transportation*, the set of examples should include land, sea, and air, motorized and nonmotorized, and large-scale and small-scale cases, as shown later in this chapter.

Nonexamples are most helpful to a learner if they are related closely to the concept being learned in one or more respects. For example, in teaching the concept of *island*, it is helpful to use nonexamples such as isthmus and peninsula and then to point out how they differ from island.

Consider how a typical concept analysis might proceed by using the concept of *island*:

- Concept name. Which name is associated most commonly with the concept? (*Illustration:* island)

- Concept definition. What is a clear and simplified definition that describes the essence of the concept? (*Illustration:* An island is a body of land surrounded by water.)

- Criterial attributes. What are the distinct, essential characteristics that make up the concept? (*Illustration:* land, water, surrounding)

- Sample noncriterial attributes. What are some nonessential characteristics that often are present in cases of the concept? (*Illustration:* habitation, tropical climate, vegetation)

- Best example. What is the best or clearest example of the concept? (*Illustration:* aerial photo of a body of land showing vegetation and water surrounding the land)

- Other concept examples. What are some other interesting, different, and learner-relevant examples of the concept? (*Illustration:* islands with people, islands with no vegetation, islands in different bodies of water, islands in very cold climates)

- Concept nonexamples. What are some contrasting cases of what the concept is *not* that will help highlight its significant features? (*Illustration:* peninsula—a body of land that has water on only three sides)

Assessing Concept Learning

Concept learning can be assessed at several levels. The most basic level requires students to select an example of the concept from a set of cases that includes nonexamples. For example, a teacher asks a student to identify an example of an *atlas* from a collection of different types of reference books or to point to an instance of an island on a map. Further levels of testing include:

- Identifying the criterial attributes of the concept (*Illustration:* from a list of characteristics, select water, land, and surrounding as those criterial for island)
- Identifying the noncriterial attributes of the island (*Illustration:* from a list of characteristics, select climate, size, and vegetation as those noncriterial for island)
- Identifying the concept rule (*Illustration:* from a list of choices, select the correct definition of island)
- Stating the concept rule (*Illustration:* correctly answer the question, What is an island?)
- Relating the concepts to other concepts (*Illustration:* correctly answer the question, How are islands and peninsulas similar and different?)
- Locating or creating new examples of the concept (*Illustration:* using an atlas, locate five new instances of island)

The discussion in Chapter 13 includes a complete example of an assessment item for concept learning.

Instructional Model for Teaching Concepts

Research concerning how individuals learn concepts has provided a sophisticated, empirically based set of instructional guidelines for aiding students in learning concepts (Howard, 1987; Martorella, 1991; Tennyson & Cocchiarella, 1986). From the extensive body of research on concept learning, we can abstract a basic instructional model that consists of eight steps as follows:

1. Identify the set of examples and nonexamples you plan to use and place them in some logical order for presentation. Include at least one example that best or most clearly illustrates an ideal type of the concept.
2. Include in the materials or oral instructions a set of cues, directions, questions, and student activities that draws students' attention to the criterial attributes and to the similarities and differences in the examples and nonexamples used.
3. Direct students to compare all illustrations with the best example and provide feedback on the adequacy of their comparisons.
4. If criterial attributes cannot be identified clearly or are ambiguous, focus attention on the salient features of the best example.
5. Where a clear definition of a concept exists, elicit or state it at some point in the instruction in terms that are meaningful to the students.
6. Through discussion, place the concept in context with other related concepts that are part of the students' prior knowledge.

7. Assess concept mastery at a minimal level—namely, whether students can discriminate correctly between new examples and nonexamples.

8. Assess concept mastery at a more advanced level; for example, ask students to generate new exemplars or to apply the concept to new situations.

Discovery and Expository Approaches in Teaching Concepts

discovery instructional strategy

expository instructional strategy

In implementing the instructional model for teaching concepts, teachers may elect to use a **discovery instructional strategy.** Students engaging in learning concepts through discovery approaches try to determine which attributes are criterial to the concept and to infer its rule. The teacher in discovery approaches serves as a resource and a guide.

An alternative is to use an **expository instructional strategy,** wherein the teacher makes explicit the defining elements of the concept, including the criterial attributes and the concept rule. With expository approaches, the teacher provides relevant data to students in the most direct way possible (Borich, 1992).

Effective discovery and expository teaching strategies both try to stimulate student curiosity and involvement. They both also use thought-provoking questions and are sensitive to the individual differences among students.

Let us consider how a teacher, Mr. Comer, might teach the concept of *globe* to a second-grade class, illustrating first the discovery and then the expository approach. In both cases, he initially completes an analysis of the concept (see

Teaching strategies should stimulate and engage students.

Figure 6.3). Then he consults and applies the eight-step instructional model for teaching concepts.

Mr. Comer's discovery lesson might unfold as follows. As a way to *focus attention on the best example*, he asks, "Which of you boys and girls has ever seen one of these (illustrating best example of globe) before?"

To *identify the concept name*, Mr. Comer asks, "What do we call this?" If no one knows, he states, "This is called a globe."

As a way to *identify the concept's criterial attributes and to relate it to students' prior knowledge*, the teacher asks a series of questions: "What does the shape of the globe remind you of? How would you describe the shape to someone? What is this drawing called (pointing to map on globe)? Have you ever seen anything like this drawing of the earth before (pointing to map)? How is this map like others you have seen? In which ways is it different?"

As he introduces each new case, Mr. Comer guides the students to *identify noncriterial attributes that appear in concept examples*: "Notice the things that are different in all of the examples (pointing out size, colors, materials). These are not important differences. Globes often come in different sizes. They also have different colors and are made of many different materials."

Following this step, the teacher *presents additional examples and nonexamples*: He introduces the sets that are outlined in Figure 6.3. He also engages the students in a discussion related to the criterial and noncriterial attributes of globes. In each case, students are asked questions such as: "How is this (example) similar to the first one (best example)? How is this (nonexample) different from the first one? Is this (new example) also a globe? Why is this (new nonexample) not a globe?"

To get the students to *verbalize the concept definition*, Mr. Comer follows these procedures: "Let's try to list on the chalkboard all of the things we can say about all globes. Who can complete the sentence I have just written on the

| FIGURE 6.3 | A teacher's analysis of the concept of *Globe* |

Concept Name: Globe

Concept Definition: A round object that has a map of the earth drawn on it.

Criterial Attributes: Roundness, map, earth, drawn on

Sample Noncriterial Attributes: Size, colors, composition

Best Example: Relief globe showing countries and major cities

Other Concept Examples: Transparent globes, inflatable globes, relief globes, globes showing cities, globes made of different materials, globes of different colors, globes of different sizes

Concept Nonexamples: Maps of the earth, maps of a place on the earth, round objects, drawings on round objects

board, 'Globes are _____ .'?" If students do not verbalize the concept rule, the teacher holds up a globe and states and writes on the chalkboard: "A globe is a round object that has a map of the earth drawn on it."

As a way to *assess learning at minimal level*, Mr. Comer instructs the students to identify new examples of a globe: "Here is a set of pictures of some objects. As I call your name, come up and point to the examples of the globes. The rest of the class can see whether they agree with the choices."

To *assess learning at a more advanced level*, the teacher gives the following directions: "Take out your social studies books. Turn to page 38 and wait until everyone is ready. Now examine the map on page 38. Who can tell me one of the ways the map is like a globe?" After students have responded to this question, Mr. Comer asks, "Who can tell me the ways the map is different from a globe?"

Had Mr. Comer used an expository approach, he would have included the same elements as a discovery approach, but he would have attempted to achieve his objectives more directly and explicitly. Wherever possible, he would have called the students' attention to information he regarded as important, rather than expect them to detect patterns on their own.

For example, he would have pointed out the criterial features of the best example for the students, perhaps by writing them on the chalkboard and referring to them as each new example was introduced. At some point early in the lesson, Mr. Comer also would have written the concept rule on the chalkboard or directed students to a functional definition in the text or reference materials.

Further, as the lesson developed, he would have directed attention to the absence of one or more of the criterial attributes in the nonexamples. Through feedback and practice opportunities, he would ensure that all students demonstrated an understanding of the criterial attributes and rule of the concept. Assessment of concept learning would proceed in the same fashion as with a discovery approach.

With either a discovery or expository approach, the instructional model for teaching concepts is applicable to a wide range of social studies concepts. Some concepts, however, are complex to teach because they are difficult to analyze and define in a clear and unambiguous way that covers all examples of the concept. As an illustration, the attributes of concepts such as *ethnic group*, *community*, *third-world nation*, and *revolution* are not easily identified. The reason is that, in each case, examples of the concepts resemble each other but do not possess the same characteristics in common (Wittgenstein, 1953).

To illustrate, let us briefly analyze the concept of *community*, which typically is introduced in the primary grades. When we begin to examine examples of communities that are drawn from varied socioeconomic, religious, ethnic, and spatial contexts, we discover they share "resemblances" that allow us to categorize them all as communities. However, we also find that not all communities have characteristics in common that would permit us to fit them all under one definition.

For such concepts, teachers need to be flexible in implementing Steps 2, 4, and 5 of the instructional model for teaching concepts. They especially need to engage students more in the exploration of the range of variations within examples than in seeking out common attributes. Their ultimate goal should be to assist students in constructing their own models of the concept.

Concept Hierarchies

Often it is helpful for both the teaching and learning of concepts to order a series of concepts into a **concept hierarchy** (see Novak & Gowin, 1984). Organizing concepts in this way for students at some point in instruction helps relate new concepts to prior knowledge and facilitates remembering information.

concept hierarchy

Developing hierarchies of concepts initially involves placing them in context in an organized way through identifying the most all-encompassing of the concepts in a set. Then the concepts are related to one another in a logical sequence through a diagram. The diagram may include brief phrases that link the concepts.

Consider the following set of concepts: *harbor, valley, lake, gulf, ocean, plateau, water body, mountain, landmass, isthmus, river, delta,* and *peninsula.* In Figure 6.4 these concepts are organized in a logical hierarchical sequence according to their relationship to one another (see also Kleg, 1986, 1987; Martorella, 1994).

Concept Teaching Materials and Activities

In a number of ways, teachers can create special materials or activities related to concept development. These include the use of *concept minitexts, student concept folders,* and *concept bulletin boards.*

Concept Minitexts.   A *minitext* is a short, self-instructional text designed by a teacher to teach a single concept to a specified student group. It may be used at any grade level where children are able to read. Minitexts include *all* of the

| FIGURE 6.4 | A concept hierarchy |

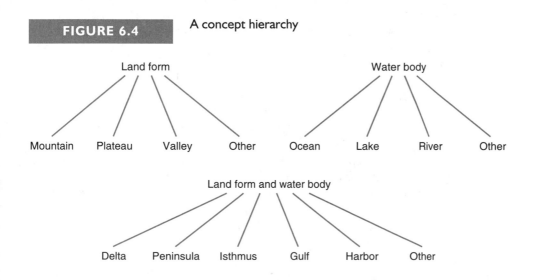

instruction a child will require to learn a new concept, including an assessment at the end.

They may use pictures from magazines, photos, drawings, and the like, as well as narrative material, integrated into an interesting format. For interest appeal and durability, they usually have an attractive cover and are sturdily constructed. Sample pages from a minitext designed to teach the concept of *family* to a young child are shown in Figure 6.5.

To construct a minitext requires the completion of a concept analysis and the application of the eight-step instructional model for teaching concepts. Unlike informational texts and other books, the purpose of a minitext is to teach *one* important concept effectively. The criterion for a successful minitext is whether a student for whom it is designed is able to learn the target concept as a result of using the minitext.

Concept Folders.   An ongoing activity in which both the teacher and the students can participate is the creation of classroom *concept folders*. One concept (e.g., *family, map, pollution, prejudice, poverty*) is identified for each folder. The number of concept folders to be created for a classroom is flexible. Concept folders may be tied in to units and used to provide in-depth information on key subjects. They also may be included in learning centers (see Chapter 12).

The teacher and the students first identify and clarify the criterial attributes and the rule of the concept for each folder and examine some examples and nonexamples. Then they begin to collect data related to the concepts in the folders, which are kept in the classroom. A time limit is set for collecting items.

Data may be in the form of pictures, cases, articles, photographs, slides, or observations. For primary children, the teacher needs to provide examples of the types of materials they may collect in the folders. Containers such as file folders, shoe boxes, and large envelopes can be used to store the data. All items the children contribute to the folders should include their names for returns.

After the stated period of time, students in small groups can examine and discuss the contents of each folder. They also may create a display. The teacher may wish to add more structure to the activity by providing a set of discussion questions or, alternatively, to lead the discussions.

Concept Bulletin Boards.   A bulletin board, prepared either by the teacher or by the students, can be used to highlight examples and nonexamples of a concept. As with concept folders, bulletin boards can contain pictorial or written materials.

Examples and nonexamples of concepts should be placed close to each other and labeled appropriately. After the initial bulletin board is developed, students can be encouraged to look for further examples and similar nonexamples and add to the display. An outline of a bulletin board display for *transportation* follows.

FIGURE 6.5 Section of a minitext to teach the concept of *Family*

Look at this word:

family

Do you know what it means? Do you have a family? Mostly everyone we know has a family, but sometimes they are different. My family is my mother and father, my brother and sister, and me. Maybe your family has no sisters and 3 brothers. Families come in all sizes and colors but they have many things that are the same.

A family is a group of 2 or more people. It can have 2 people or 50 people. One person is not a family.

The people in a family must live together for at least part of the time. When you get older and move out of your house, you will still be in the family because you have lived with them for at least part of the time.

The last thing to know about a family is that the people must be related by blood, marriage, or adoption. You are related to your grandparents, parents, aunts, uncles, cousins, and brothers and sisters by blood. When a man and a woman get married, they are a family. When a child is adopted by a family, he or she becomes part of that family.

Source: From *Family Minitext* by R. Husik, (n.d.), Philadelphia: Temple University, Department of Elementary Education

These Are Transportation		These Are Not Transportation

(Attach pictures of the following items under the appropriate headings.)

Bus full of people		Room full of people
Subway	Jet airplane	Kite
Train	Golf cart	Ferris wheel
Ships	Submarine	Fish in water
Raft	Rocket	Swimming pool
Escalator	Truck	Carton
Glider	Bicycle	Stationary exercise bicycle
Blimp	Balloon	Cloud
Elevator	Car	Carousel
Tricycle	Monorail	Park bench
Motorcycle	Horse	Cat
Rickshaw	Wagon	Chair
Stagecoach	Canoe	Rocking horse
Oxen and cart	Tractor	Windmill
Helicopter	Dog sled	Arrow being shot
Moving sidewalk	Wheelchair	Toy train

As a follow-up activity, students may be asked to group and label the set of examples. For example, a child might sort the items into three categories that he or she labeled "air machines," "land machines," and "water machines." Children in small groups also can be asked to compare and explain their categories.

Facts, Generalizations, and Hypotheses in the Social Studies Curriculum

In what ways are facts, generalizations, and hypotheses distinguished from concepts? As we have seen, concepts are the building blocks of knowledge. They are part of every fact and generalization that we know. If our concepts are ill formed or incomplete, so will the ideas we build from them be improperly shaped. When we think, make a decision, or act, we draw on a network of schemata that includes interwoven concepts, facts, generalizations, and hypotheses—the major elements of reflection.

The Nature of Facts

fact

Citizens are bombarded daily with facts and assertions that appear to be facts. Facts appear in many forms and relate to trivial, as well as significant, matters. A **fact** is a statement about concepts that is *true* or verifiable for a particular case on the basis of the best evidence available. From a concept cluster that includes *island,* *ocean, group,* and *state,* the fact statement arises: "A group of islands located in the Pacific Ocean makes up one of our states." Other examples of facts are:

- Our Congress consists of the House of Representatives and the Senate.
- Franklin Roosevelt served more terms than any other President.
- The state with the largest population is California.
- Tallahassee is south of Peoria.
- When our Constitution was adopted, women were denied the right to vote.
- In our country, Christmas is celebrated on December 25.

Often an assertion is accepted as a fact by an individual even though it may not be supported by evidence or may be considered by most people to be false. Many people accept as a fact, for example, that Columbus was the first European to reach America, even though considerable evidence to the contrary exists. Other assertions are accepted as facts on the basis of the best evidence available at one point, only to be proven false later. The *fact* that the sun revolved about the earth was only grudgingly discarded by the world as false in favor of the newly verified *fact* that the moving body was actually the earth.

In our society facts are valued. Individuals often go to great lengths, spending much time and even money to get them. People who have knowledge of facts or have access to such knowledge often have considerable power and status; witness heads of countries, inventors, and columnists.

Learning Facts in Meaningful Contexts.   All students need to have experiences in locating, identifying, organizing, and verifying significant facts. The facts they are asked to remember also should have functional meaning. A student can learn two lists of 50 pairs of names—one with capitals and states and the other with nonsense words—in the same way. Neither list has any real immediate functional value beyond gaining recognition or success, unless some meaningful context is provided.

Facts learned outside of some meaningful context are often quickly forgotten, long before they can be put to any functional use. More importantly, they are not integrated into students' schemata of previously acquired knowledge. This last point is illustrated by the child who had memorized all of the names of American presidents in the correct order but who cannot give the names of any three presidents who served during the last half of the 20th century.

Teaching students techniques for more efficiently retrieving meaningful facts from memory is a worthy instructional objective. Citizens frequently need to remember a great number of names, places, events, dates, and general descriptive information in order to clarify and link new knowledge in functionally meaningful ways. In Chapter 10 we consider some of the general techniques that are useful for helping students comprehend, remember, and access factual data acquired in social studies instruction.

The Nature of Generalizations

generalization   From an instructional perspective, a **generalization** is a statement about concepts that is true or verified for all cases on the basis of the best evidence available. Generalizations are similar to facts in that they also are true statements about relationships between or among concepts. Generalizations, however, summarize and organize a great deal of information obtained from analyses of many sets of facts. The summary results in a single, wide-reaching assertion that applies to the past, present, and even future. In contrast, facts assert claims about specific instances.

To illustrate, compare the following fact and related generalization.

Fact:

- New Orleans typically is warmer in the winter than Milwaukee.

Generalization:

- Climate varies from place to place.

Unlike facts, generalizations also have the capacity to *predict* when they appear in the form of "If . . . then" statements. For example: "*If* there is a national election, *then* the turnout of white-collar, professional, and business people likely will be greater than that of semiskilled and unskilled workers." The statement makes a prediction that "If one set of conditions is present (national election), a second set of consequences will follow (a pattern of voter turnout)."

As students engage in examining and analyzing data for patterns and then summarizing their conclusions, they progress toward deriving generalizations. For instance, after children have examined and compared pictures of various families from many countries, socioeconomic settings, and racial groups, they have an information base for developing a generalization. They now can be guided to find an organizing principle for bringing order to their experiences under a generalization such as Families everywhere take many different forms.

Other examples of social studies generalizations that children could formulate after analyzing and summarizing data are as follows (adapted from Harcourt Brace Jovanovich, 1990):

- Events happen in sequence.
- A community's activities are unique and are affected by natural resources, landforms, and climate.
- Communities change over time.
- Each person is a member of different groups.
- All places have a past: neighborhoods, communities, and countries all have histories.
- The environment can affect how people live.
- As a society becomes more complex, so does its government.

The Nature of Hypotheses

Unlike a fact or a generalization, which is a verified truth statement, a **hypothe-**   hypothesis
sis is an untested idea or guess that seeks to explain some phenomenon. The
process of forming a hypothesis begins when we make some attempt to resolve or
answer questions such as Why do people in different places often wear different
types of clothes? Why do we say the Pledge of Allegiance every day in school?
What are the causes of poverty? Why does the government subsidize the tobacco
industry at the same time that it requires health warnings on cigarette packs?

The hypotheses we propose in order to answer questions such as these may
be sophisticated and informed, or they may be naive and poorly grounded. In
either case, hypotheses, once formed, then are *tested* through the gathering and
comparing of evidence that supports or refutes them. When a hypothesis
appears to "hold up" or to be true after extensive evidence has been gathered, it
can be regarded tentatively as either a fact or a generalization. Which of these
two it will be depends on whether it applies to a *particular* case (fact) or to *all*
cases (generalization) within some universe. Not infrequently in the social sciences, as a result of future tests in the context of new evidence, an original
hypothesis may be revised or even discarded. Figure 6.6 presents a summary of
the differences among concepts, facts, generalizations, and hypotheses.

Some hypotheses can never be verified or refuted because all of the necessary evidence is impossible to obtain. Speculations about what might have happened had certain events in history been altered fall into this category—for
example, the hypothesis: The United States would not be a major world power
if Jefferson had not approved the Louisiana Purchase.

Students engaged in the development and testing of hypotheses need practice and assistance at each grade level, including help with generating plausible
hypotheses to explain and answer simple but interesting problems and questions, as well as assistance with gathering and comparing data to test them.

Children in the primary grades can begin their experiences through practice
in developing basic hypotheses for fundamental issues such as Why do people

FIGURE 6.6	The nature of concepts, facts, generalizations, and hypotheses

Concepts	Categories into which we group people, objects, and events
Facts	Statements about concepts that are true or verified for a particular case on the basis of the best evidence available
Generalizations	Statements about concepts that are true or verified for all cases on the basis of the best evidence available
Hypotheses	Untested ideas or guesses that seek to explain some phenomena

around the world have different houses? Students in the intermediate and middle grades can go beyond the school into the community to do fieldwork that tests their hypotheses (see Chapter 2). For example, intermediate- and middle-grade students might develop and conduct a survey to test the hypothesis: People in our neighborhood will recycle trash if encouraged to do so.

As they progress in developing and testing hypotheses, children can be introduced gradually to the concept of *multiple causality*, which is crucial to analysis of many issues in the social studies. Understanding multiple causality requires that students recognize and accept that more than one hypothesis may be correct; often several causes explain or account for an event. This last statement relates to events rooted in history (e.g., What caused the Civil War?), as well as to everyday social phenomena (e.g., What causes conflicts in families?).

Instructional Strategies for Developing Generalizations

As in teaching concepts, strategies for aiding students in the development and testing of generalizations may employ either *expository* or *discovery* approaches. The two approaches differ chiefly in the degree to which they place the responsibility on students to identify relationships among cases and to derive the actual generalization. Both approaches involve students in thinking, doing, and learning. Both also guide students in understanding the necessary relationships among items. To provide variety, instruction should include some mix of both approaches.

Expository and Discovery Approaches for Teaching Generalizations

Expository approaches may take many forms, ranging from simply calling attention to statements in texts and helping students find supporting evidence, to having students themselves offer generalizations that the class tests.

The basic steps in an expository approach might be summarized as follows:

1. State, write, or call attention to some generalization that is the learning objective for the lesson.
2. Review major concepts that are part of the generalization.
3. Provide instructions, questions, cases, relevant materials, and assistance to illustrate and verify the generalization.
4. Have students identify, find, or create new cases of the generalization.

As an example, consider a fourth-grade class in which the objective is to have the students understand the generalization: The environment influences the type of shelter that people have. Ms. Olski, the teacher, begins the lesson by first writing the generalization on the chalkboard.

Next she reviews the major concepts in the generalization: *environment*, *influences*, and *shelter*. This is done by asking the class to refer to the text glossary. She then summarizes the meanings on the board.

Once the concepts have been clarified, the class is divided into five groups, each of which is given one of the following questions to answer.

- What are the parts of your home?
- What are the different types of shelters that people in this area have?
- How are these different shelters constructed?
- What different kinds of weather conditions do we have in this area?
- What are some things that all shelters in this area have?

After discussion, each group shares its conclusions with the class. Then Ms. Olski outlines their major points on the board, under the headings *Area*, *Type of Shelter*, and *Type of Environment*.

At this point the teacher introduces pictures of many types of shelters in use around the world, including houseboats, caves, tree houses, yurts, thatched huts, stilt houses over water, and solar houses. Along with each type, she provides a short explanation concerning its construction and the environments in which such shelters are found. Each example of shelter also is summarized under the three headings on the board.

The class is redirected to the generalization written on the board at the outset of the class. The teacher then leads a brief question-and-answer session covering the relationship of the various examples to the generalization.

As a following step, Ms. Olski asks each of the five groups to identify some new cases of shelters. She also asks each group to consider how the environment in which the various shelters are found has influenced the design.

The children are encouraged to use the library, as well as to consult the trade books available in the classroom. At the conclusion of its research, each group shares its findings with the entire class, adding its information to the three categories on the board. Ms. Olski then summarizes the findings and relates them to the generalization.

Had Ms. Olski used a discovery approach, the procedures would have contained many of the same elements. The chief difference would have been that she initially would not have revealed the generalization. As we saw in the example of the discovery approach used to teach a concept, the role of the teacher is to structure the introduction and analysis of materials and procedures in such a way that students themselves will infer or discover a generalization from their investigations.

Instead of stating the generalization at the outset by writing it on the board, Ms. Olski would begin by reviewing the significant concepts embedded in the generalization. Most of the remainder of the session would proceed as in the expository approach.

Toward the end of this discussion, the students would be asked to sum up what they had learned about shelters and environment. After raising some focused questions about the reasons for similarities and differences in the shelters the class had examined, Ms. Olski might ask: "How could we put in one sentence what we have learned about the relationship of environment to people's shelters all over the world?"

Using Data Retrieval Charts

data retrieval chart

In using either discovery or expository strategies to teach generalizations, **data retrieval (or data) charts**, accompanied by focus questions to process the data, are useful media. Such charts consist of rows and columns of categories and cells of related data (see Chapter 5). For intermediate-grade children, cells usually contain written information. However, charts can include pictures and three-dimensional objects for use with primary-grade children. Data charts are particularly appropriate for group projects (see Chapter 5). Tasks can be divided easily, with each member taking responsibility for providing either a row or a column of data.

To provide the structure for the chart, a teacher first needs to identify the generalization to be taught. From this comes the categories of items that will be used for the rows and columns of the chart.

Let us examine an example of how a basic generalization can serve to shape the structure of a chart that primary children will use. The generalization to be developed with the chart is: Lifestyles change over time. The cells of information in the chart will contain a mixture of pictures and written data.

In addition to determining the generalization to be developed to construct the shell of the chart, we need to identify what the two sets of categories, our row and column indicators, will be. In examining the generalization, we can see that we will require data on some *representative lifestyles* and some *time periods*. Let us say that we assign the data on lifestyles to columns and that we pick five aspects of lifestyles: clothing, automobiles, houses, toys, and children's entertainment.

To the rows we assign three indicators of time periods: today, when our parents were children, and when our grandparents were children. Our chart shell, as shown in Figure 6.7, is now complete. It remains for the teacher and the students to fill in the cells with pictures, drawings, and narrative. The teacher, for example, could begin by partially completing a chart to model for students how data are to be recorded in the cells

After the cells have been filled with information, some further structure is required to analyze, compare, and summarize the material. One procedure for systematically processing the data obtained for each family is to begin by comparing the information by rows (e.g., What was life like when your grandparents were children?) or by focusing on contrasts (e.g., How did life when your grandparents were children differ from life today?).

If a discovery approach were used, the teacher would have students complete the chart and process the questions. Then students would be encouraged to

FIGURE 6.7	Data retrieval chart shell

Lifestyles Change Over Time					
Time Periods	Style of Clothing	Types of Automobiles	Style of Houses	Children's Toys	Children's Entertainment
Today					
When Parents Were Children					
When Grandparents Were Children					

try to summarize all of the data in a single sentence, as a way to infer the generalization concerning lifestyles.

With an expository approach, the teacher would begin by stating the generalization or by writing it on the chalkboard. After the cells were filled with information and the data were analyzed, the teacher would direct the students' attention to how they supported the generalization.

The Reflective Citizen and Problem Solving

The terms *inquiry*, *critical thinking*, *the scientific method*, **reflective thinking**, and *problem solving* all have been used at one time or another to refer to the process by which individuals find solutions to problems through reflection. In the process of problem solving, students engage in activating prior schemata that include related concepts, facts, generalizations, and hypotheses. They also integrate new subject matter into meaningful knowledge structures.

reflective thinking

Problem solving thus is a way to better organize and interrelate existing knowledge, as well as to acquire new information. The elements of reflection are not learned as isolated bits of information but as part of a pattern of psychologically meaningful knowledge. Students do not first learn facts, for example, and *then* engage in problem solving. They use knowledge already acquired and add new elements, such as facts, concepts, and generalizations, *as* they engage in problem solving.

Most discussions of reflective thinking or problem solving derive from the work and writings of the American philosopher and educator John Dewey. His ideas on reflective thinking are laid out in detail in two books, *How We Think* (Dewey, 1933) and *Democracy and Education* (Dewey, 1916). In these works, especially the first, Dewey developed clearly the nature of a problem and its relationship to reflective thinking. His ideas have been applied to the teaching of social studies by a number of prominent social studies educators, including Griffin (1992), Engle (1976), and Hunt and Metcalf (1968).

Uses of the Term *Problem* in Instruction

problem

The term **problem,** as it occurs in discussions of problem solving, generally is used in three ways. It refers to *personal* problems that individuals experience, such as how to become more popular, get along with others, or cope when you lose your job. The term also is used to refer to significant *social* problems faced by our society or the world. These might be such issues as poverty, inequality of opportunity, crime, and unemployment. (In Chapters 8 and 9, we consider in detail the treatment of social problems in the curriculum.) A third usage relates to the condition wherein individuals find a new situation problematical or experience a *psychological* state of doubt. The classic example of this usage was provided by Dewey, who cited the case of an individual who comes to a fork in a road and has no sign to serve as a guide concerning how to proceed.

Instructional Strategies for Problem Solving

problem-
solving
instructional
approach

Problem-solving instructional approaches may be based on one or more meanings of the term *problem*. The broadest application of problem solving, however, involves the third meaning of *problem*, creating a state of psychological doubt. It allows the teacher to use any subject matter in a problem-solving approach.

A psychological problem is created when the teacher succeeds in structuring, displaying, and sequencing subject matter in a special way. It is not the subject matter itself, but the way it is presented that makes it psychologically problematical. The power of the approach derives from the natural tendency of individuals to be highly motivated to relieve the cognitive discomfort they experience. They attempt to do this either by solving the problem or by finding explanations to account for it.

Any subject matter can be used for problem solving in this sense. The only requirement is that a teacher be able to frame it so as to pose and then help resolve an interesting and intriguing question. Not every topic, however, lends itself easily to the development of problem-solving strategies, because it is often difficult to create a sharp, relevant problem focus for all students. Given individual differences among students, all members of a class may not experience the problem with the same level of intensity or even perceive that a problem exists.

cognitive
disequilibrium

Problem-solving strategies require that teachers create **cognitive disequilibrium** in students. This is a state wherein a student perceives that something

Strategies that encourage students to search for information
to solve problems also help
them develop and apply
research skills.

is peculiar, frustrating, irritating, puzzling, disturbing, contrary to what is
expected, or incongruous. Disequilibrium is induced to cause students to attend
to the subject matter being taught, regardless of its topical content or their relative degree of interest in it. Students are asked to resolve the basic issue that
puzzles them: Why is this so? or How can this be? or What is the cause of this?

FIGURE 6.8	General problem-solving instructional model

1. Structure some aspect of the subject matter students are to learn to create a puzzle, dilemma, discrepancy, or doubt.

2. Have the students internalize the problem by asking them to verbalize it. Clarify the problem if necessary.

3. Solicit some hypotheses from the students that might explain or account for the problem. Clarify terminology where necessary, and allow sufficient time for student reflection.

4. Assist students in testing the validity of the hypotheses generated and in examining the implications of the results. Where necessary, assist in providing reference materials, background information relevant to the subject matter, and keeping students on the topic.

5. Aid students in deciding on a tentative conclusion that seems to be the most plausible explanation for the problem, based on the best evidence available at the time. Stress the tentative nature of the conclusion, because future studies and further evidence may lead to a different conclusion.

Source: Adapted from *How We Think* by J. Dewey, 1933, Boston: D. C. Heath.

A basic five-step model for this type of problem solving, adapted from Dewey (1933), is presented in Figure 6.8. It outlines the basic sequence of activities that a teacher should follow in engaging students in problem solving.

An example of how the problem-solving model actually operates, with movement back and forth between the steps, is given in Figure 6.9. It presents a teacher's summary of a class session involving a group of 10- and 11-year-old children that lasted 90 minutes. The general subject matter under consideration was political elections and political institutions. Because the lesson occurred in February a few days before Abraham Lincoln's birthday, the teacher used Lincoln as the springboard for developing the initial problem focus.

Problem Springboards

problem springboard

In the lesson just analyzed, two brief quotations from the same individual served as the **problem springboard.** A *problem springboard* is an initial activity in a lesson that presents puzzling or intriguing data. Springboards can take many forms: charts, tables, graphs, pictures, cartoons, drawings, maps, recordings, films, videotapes, field trips, and observations, as well as different types of print materials.

One of the teacher's major roles in creating problem-solving activities is to ascertain what is likely to appear problematical to students in the context of the subject matter to be studied. Unless a teacher has organized material in a way that arouses students' initial curiosity concerning the problem, they are not likely to attend to the problem. If students do not perceive any psychological problem that requires a solution, no real problem solving will occur.

The general problem-solving instructional model outlined in Figure 6.8 provides only a basic road map. Dewey himself suggested that problem solving, as it occurs in natural settings, does not always follow through steps in a set order. In solving problems, individuals often "jump ahead," temporarily skipping steps, and at other times they return to a step already passed. He cautioned:

> The five phases . . . of thought that we have noted do not follow one another in a set order. On the contrary, each step in genuine thinking does something to perfect the formation of a suggestion and promote its change into a leading idea or directive hypothesis. It does something to promote the location and definition of the problem. Each improvement in the idea leads to new observations that yield facts or data and help the mind judge more accurately the relevancy of facts already at hand. The elaboration of the hypothesis does not wait until the problem has been defined and an adequate hypothesis has been arrived at; it may come at any intermediate time. (Dewey, 1933, p. 115)

More than the form of the subject matter, it is how and when the teacher introduces it, as well as the questions, comments, and cues he or she uses, that determine whether a psychological problem is created for students. As students express surprise or disbelief, look perplexed, or shake their heads, for example, they offer signs that a teacher has succeeded.

FIGURE 6.9 Summary of a problem-solving activity involving a class of fifth- and sixth-grade students

Initially the students were asked to respond to the question, "What comes to mind when you think of Abraham Lincoln?" The function of this question was to settle the class, review their prior associations with Lincoln, and alert them to the problematic episode that was forthcoming. After approximately 10 minutes of free exploration without challenges, the class was told that the teacher wished to share a problem with them.

"Listen to these two statements made by Abraham Lincoln, and then tell me if you can see what my problem is. The first statement, let's call it A, is taken from the works of Abraham Lincoln":

Statement A

Let us discard all this quibbling about this man and the other man, this race, and that race and the other race being inferior, and therefore they must be placed in an inferior position. Let us discard all these things, and unite as one people throughout this land, until we shall once more stand up declaring that all men are created equal.[a]

"Is there anything in this statement that seems odd or out of order?" The students thought not, and so we proceeded to the second statement, B. "Listen to this second statement, let's call it B, also taken from the works of Lincoln":

Statement B

I will say, then, that I am not, nor ever have been, in favor of bringing about in any way the social and political equality of the white and black races: that I am not, nor ever have been, in favor of making voters or jurors of negroes, nor of qualifying them to hold office, nor to intermarry with white people....

And inasmuch as they cannot so live, while they do remain together there must be the position of superior and inferior, and I as much as any other man am in favor of having the superior position assigned to the white race.[b]

"Do you notice anything wrong now? What is the problem here?" At this point, students were given some time to reflect upon the statements, verbalize the discrepancy in various ways, and generally to clarify the specific problematic issue. After the problem was restated in several ways, the statements were both repeated to the class.

To implement the third step of the model, the question was raised, "How do you account for these two statements, both made by Lincoln?" The students had many immediate hypotheses, which were clarified and recorded on the board. Four basic hypotheses were suggested as follows:

1. He changed his mind.
2. He was speaking to different groups with each of the statements, and he told each group what he thought they wanted to hear.
3. One statement was what he thought to himself (e.g., as in a diary), and the other one was the one he told people.
4. He was misunderstood (i.e., his words were taken out of context).

After exhausting the many responses, some of which were simply variations on the same theme, the point was emphasized that several possibilities existed concerning our guesses (hypotheses). Only *one* might be correct, *several* answers might be true, or *none* of our explanations might be correct.

FIGURE 6.9   *(Continued)*

"What kind of information," the students were asked, "would we need to have in order to check out our guesses and see if they might be correct?" Responses were clarified and listed on the board under the label "Initial Facts Needed." They fell into four categories: (1) when the statements were made, (2) to whom they were made, (3) what the rest of the statements (context) were like, and (4) where they were made.

At this point several possibilities were open to the teacher: (1) have the students themselves initiate a search for relevant facts, either individually or in groups; (2) ask certain students to volunteer or appoint volunteers to research the facts; or (3) provide certain facts for the students to test the hypotheses. The third option was exercised due to time and other constraints and to focus attention on the testing rather than on the data-gathering process. In effect the teacher acted as a research resource for the students. Such a role is both legitimate and often efficient, depending on the objectives of a lesson. The amount and sequencing of factual information provided by the teacher, however, are important variables.

Consider the procedures employed by the teacher. With respect to the first fact needed, the students were informed that statement A was made on July 10, 1858, and that statement B was made on September 18, 1858. These dates were read aloud and then written on the board. The class expressed surprise.

"What do these facts do to any of our guesses?" the class was asked. The students suggested that the facts eliminated the first hypothesis. After soliciting their rationale, the teacher qualified their conclusion with the observation that "Lincoln *might* have changed his mind on this point in just two months, but it was a short period of time for such an important issue."

As to the second fact required, the students were briefly instructed on how the quotes and their sources could be authenticated. "In this case," they were told, "we are placing some faith in the reliability of the historian who gave us the information that it is correct." It was noted that we often have to do this but that sometimes the historian proves to be in error, as later research reveals. In indicating that our best immediate evidence was that the statements were *not* taken out of context, it was also indicated that the statements were parts of speeches.

While the teacher had no information concerning to whom the speeches were made, the class was told that statement A was made in Chicago while statement B was given in Charleston. These facts were written on the board alongside the respective dates:

Statement A: July 10, 1858, Chicago.

Statement B: September 18, 1858, Charleston.

These new facts were greeted with "oohs" and "aahs."

Again the question was raised, "What do these facts do to our guesses?" The students suggested that the third and fourth hypotheses were rejected and the second was strengthened. When pressed for an explanation of how hypothesis 2 was strengthened by the facts, they indicated that the audience for statement A was Northern while that for B was Southern. When pressed for further clarification of this point, they indicated that the Chicago group, being Northern, would be *against* slavery while the Charleston group, being Southern, would favor it.

Psychologically speaking, the class was ready to stop at this point. It had struggled with a problem and had reached what appeared to be an obvious conclusion supported by facts. Many of the children were smiling with some satisfaction, and all the hands had gone down.

FIGURE 6.9 *(Continued)*

The problem was regenerated quickly, however, with the following sequence of instructions: "By the way, what was Lincoln's purpose in making speeches in 1858?" Some were not sure; most said he was running for President. In a 2–3-minute lecture, the group was briefed concerning Lincoln's remote presidential possibilities in 1858, the conditions that made his nomination actually possible, and how presidents campaigned and were elected in that period. This new information clearly presented some confusion within the class.

Someone then contributed a vague recollection of the Lincoln-Douglas debates and suggested that the statements might have been part of them. No one knew the context of the debates. This information was provided for the class and followed by the question, "In what state did Lincoln's Senate campaign take place?" After some discussion this question was resolved in favor of Illinois.

Then the students were asked, "What would Lincoln be doing campaigning in the *South* for a Senate seat in Illinois?" This question caused considerable consternation and generated a great deal of discussion but was never answered to anyone's satisfaction. I then added two bits of new information to the facts already listed on the board:

Statement A: July 10, 1858, Chicago, *Illinois*

Statement B: September 18, 1858, Charleston, *Illinois.*

Amid the noisy reactions, the teacher raised in succession the issues of why the class had seemed so sure of its earlier conclusion, how the new facts affected their list of hypotheses, and how Lincoln could make such contradictory public statements in the same state. They acknowledged that their stereotypes of Northern and Southern behavior colored their interpretation of the earlier facts, that they now required more facts, and that communication systems in 1858 were much different than those we have today.

A wall map of the United States was used to illustrate the next set of facts. Chicago was located and the general characteristics of its population in 1858 noted. Similarly the city of Charleston, in the southern part of Illinois, was identified on the map. From this discussion it emerged that Illinois in Lincoln's day, much like today, represented sharp divisions in political opinion in the northern and southern sections. The location of Charleston, Illinois, suggested the possible kinship with the proslavery stands of the bordering Southern states as well as physical separation from Chicago.

The students had renewed confidence in hypothesis 2, after their momentary loss of faith. The final challenge to their tentative conclusion took the form of the question, "How did senators get elected in those days?" No one knew. It was explained that people didn't get to vote for senators until the twentieth century, about the same time that women were given the right to vote. This explanation was followed by the question, "What would Lincoln be doing *campaigning* for the Senate?" A final brief explanation sufficed: Lincoln campaigned for state legislators pledged to vote for him as senator if they were elected to the state legislature.

[a]Quoted in Richard Hofstadter, *The American Political Tradition* (New York: Alfred A. Knopf, 1948), p. 116.

[b]Ibid.

case studies

Case Studies as Problem Springboards.   **Case studies** are brief sets of data that present a single idea, issue, or event in some detail. Case studies attempt to present in-depth coverage of a narrow topic. Further, through concrete materials, they seek to make vivid some general or abstract issue in the context of a problem.

Case studies may be presented through many media: transparencies, teacher-made sheets, records, video- and audiocassettes, films, and various print materials. Four basic types of case studies are (Newmann with Oliver, 1970):

1. *Stories and Vignettes.*   These are dramatized accounts of either authentic or fictitious events.
2. *Journalistic Historical Events.*   These include original newspaper accounts, recordings, or video records of historical events, eyewitness accounts, and the like.
3. *Research Reports.*   These include materials such as the results of studies, statistical tables, and census reports that have been organized and summarized.
4. *Documents.*   This category includes a range of items such as speeches, diaries, laws, and records.

For the primary grades, case studies that emphasize dramatized stories and concrete elements such as artifacts and pictures are particularly effective. For instance, in conjunction with a lesson concerning the local community, a long-time resident might be invited to bring photos to class and relate the changes the area had undergone since he or she was a child.

For the intermediate and middle grades, a case might be constructed around a taped interview with a logger and a set of photos showing the effects of deforestation. This case could be used to launch a unit on how to manage our natural resources.

Answer Key: Concept Learning Exercise

In Figure 6.1, numbers 1 and 4 are *squarps*. Squarps are figures that have a smile (upturned mouth), freckles, two extended whiskers, and a point on the head.

In Figure 6.2, numbers 2 and 3 are *zrapples*. Zrapples are figures that have *either* one eye and a frown (downturned mouth) *or* two ears and a smile (upturned mouth).

Group Activities

1. Select a basal social studies textbook for any grade 3 through 8. Identify the text title, the grade level, the author and publisher, and the copyright date. List all of the concepts that are included in 10 pages of the text, beginning

with the first page of a chapter. For this exercise include only those concepts that are nouns or adjectives. After you have collected the data, discuss these questions: Which concepts appear with the most frequency? Which do you consider to be the most difficult? The least difficult?

2. Select a social studies concept that typically is taught in grades 4 through 6. Using the information in this text, create a minitext to teach the concept. After the minitext has been revised and completed, field-test it with a student for whom it was designed and who has not yet learned the concept. Compare your minitexts and your field-test results. What changes would you make on the basis of your experiences?

3. Refer to Chapter 2 for this activity. Identify two generalizations from each of the social sciences, other than those found in this textbook. As references you may wish to consult introductory textbooks and specialized reference works. Select only generalizations suitable for developing social studies lessons. Compare your lists and discuss any problems you had in identifying appropriate generalizations.

4. Select one of the four types of case studies described in the text. Identify a class or group, grades 3 through 8, with whom you would use the material and develop a case study on any subject appropriate for that audience. Discuss specifically how you would use the case as a springboard to a problem-solving activity.

Individual Activities

1. Develop a strategy to teach a social studies concept to a second-grade student. Use the eight-step instructional model and the concept analysis form provided in the chapter. You may use either a discovery or an expository approach.

2. Repeat the procedures from the previous activity, except substitute a sixth-grade student.

3. Select one of the generalizations identified in the previous activity and a grade level 3 through 8. Develop a lesson plan to teach the generalization by using either a basic expository or discovery strategy.

References

Borich, G. (1996). *Effective teaching methods* (3rd ed.). Upper Saddle River, NJ: Merrill/ Prentice Hall.

Bruner, J. S., Goodnow, J., & Austin, G. A. (1962). *A study of thinking.* New York: Science Editions.

Cole, M., & Scribner, S. (1974). *Culture and thought.* New York: John Wiley.

Dewey, J. (1916). *Democracy and education.* New York: Macmillan.

Dewey, J. (1933). *How we think.* Boston: D. C. Heath.

Engle, S. H. (1976). Exploring the meaning of the social studies. In P. H. Martorella (Ed.), *Social studies strategies: Theory into practice* (pp. 232–245). New York: Harper & Row.

Griffin, A. F. (1992). *A philosophical approach to the subject matter preparation of teachers of history.* Dubuque, IA: Kendall/Hunt.

Harcourt Brace Jovanovich. (1990). *Harcourt Brace Jovanovich social studies scope and sequence.* Orlando, FL: Author.

Hofstadter, R. (1948). *The American political tradition.* New York: Knopf.

Howard, R. W. (1987). *Concepts and schemata: An introduction.* Philadelphia: Cassell.

Hunt, E. B., & Banaji, M. R. (1988). The Whorfian hypothesis revisited: A cognitive science view of linguistic and cultural effects on thought. In J. W. Berry, S. H. Irvine, & E. B. Hunt (Eds.), *Indigenous cognition: Functioning in context* (pp. 57–84). Boston: Martinus Nijhoff.

Hunt, E. B., & Metcalf, L. E. (1968). *Teaching high school social studies: Problems in reflective thinking and social understanding* (2nd ed.). New York: Harper & Row.

Husik, R. (no date). *Family minitext.* Philadelphia: Temple University, Department of Elementary Education.

Kleg, M. (1986). Teaching about terrorism: A conceptual approach. *Social Science Record, 24,* 31–39.

Kleg, M. (1987). Genocide: A concept action model. *Social Science Record, 24,* 68–73.

Martorella, P. H. (1971). *Concept learning in the social studies: Models for structuring curriculum.* Scranton, PA: INTEXT.

Martorella, P. H. (1991). Knowledge and concept development in social studies. In J. B. Shaver (Ed.), *Handbook of research on social studies teaching and learning* (pp. 370–384). New York: Macmillan.

Martorella, P. H. (1994). Concept learning and higher-order thinking. In J. M. Cooper (Ed.), *Classroom teaching skills* (5th ed.). Lexington, MA: D. C. Heath.

Newmann, F. M., with Oliver, D. W. (1970). *Clarifying public controversy: An approach to teaching social studies.* Boston: Little, Brown.

Novak, J., & Gowin, D. B. (1984). *Learning how to learn.* Cambridge, UK: Cambridge University Press.

Tennyson, R. D., & Cocchiarella, M. J. (1986). An empirically based instructional design theory for teaching concepts. *Review of Educational Research, 56,* 40–71.

Whorf, B. (1956). *Language, thought and reality.* Cambridge, UK: Cambridge University Press.

Wittgenstein, L. (1953). *Philosophical investigations.* New York: Macmillan.

Chapter **7**

Aiding Students in Developing Effective Citizenship Competencies

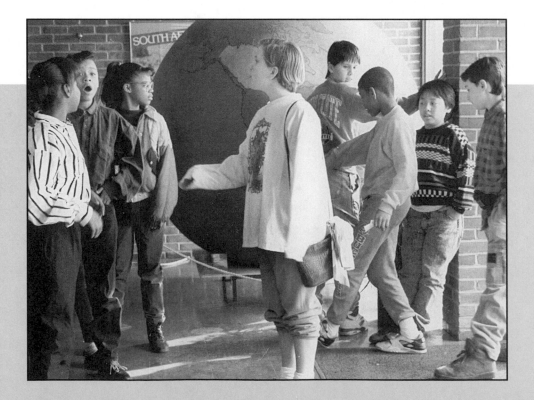

The Nature of Citizenship Skills

Social Skills

Research and Analysis Skills

Chronology Skills

Spatial Skills

During the first unit of the year, our work as a class focused on writing a book about the classroom and the school. Different activities involved surveying the school population for basic demographic information, for example, age and ethnic groups, drawing maps of the classroom, interviewing teachers, and writing autobiographies."

"Three weeks of the unit were spent working with maps. By the end of the year, I hope that my [third-grade] students will be able to interpret and use maps in meaningful ways. Rather than show them a map and teach them how to use scale and key, I decided to start our work on maps by having students construct a map of the classroom." (Wilson, 1990, p. 7)

Children, such as the third-graders in the example above, acquire and use skills most effectively in the context of solving meaningful problems and performing tasks they regard as interesting, functional, or important. Skills facilitate knowledge construction by enabling us to locate, analyze, validate, and apply information efficiently. Effective social studies instruction encourages students to both develop and use skills. It *also provides guidelines for when and why it is appropriate to employ the skills (Brophy, 1992).*

The Nature of Citizenship Skills

Citizens require a repertoire of competencies (skills) to function effectively in our complex society. Numerous lists of skills have been advanced for development throughout the social studies curriculum. For example, all basal social studies textbook programs provide enumerations of the various skills that are embedded in the materials. Typically, such lists sequence the skills in the order they are to be taught, K through 12. They also suggest the relative degrees of emphasis each type of skill should receive (Jarolimek & Parker, 1993).

Skills Lists for the Social Studies Curriculum, K–12

One such comprehensive set of skills, shown in Figure 7.1, was produced by the National Council for the Social Studies' Task Force on Scope and Sequence (Task Force on Scope and Sequence, 1989). It provides a detailed inventory of the diverse competencies that students are to develop within their social studies programs.

The list includes three major categories of skills and a number of subcategories. It also suggests the degree of emphasis that each type of skill should receive at different grade levels. This and other similar lists can serve as references for identifying skills to emphasize in planning lessons and units.

In the remainder of the chapter, we consider ways in which social studies programs across the elementary and middle grades can nurture the development and application of skills in the context of lessons and units. We focus on a sample of the skills outlined in Figure 7.1 that are organized under four categories of competencies central to effective citizenship: *social skills*, *research and analysis skills*, *chronology skills*, and *spatial skills*. Skills related specifically to technology applications are discussed in Chapter 11.

Social Skills

Whether at home, at school, on the job, or at a party, having good relationships with others, or "getting along," requires social skills. They are the glue that binds groups and society as a whole together harmoniously and productively. In whatever we hope to accomplish cooperatively with other individuals, social skills are instrumental in achieving our goals.

If our social environment is rich in positive models and experiences as we mature, we continuously acquire and integrate sets of valuable social skills. Once mastered, such skills often are applied to settings different from the ones in which they were learned. In this fashion, over time, many people manage to assimilate naturally the basic social competencies necessary to navigate successfully through life.

FIGURE 7.1

Essential skills for social studies

Suggested strength of instructional effort: ▬▬ Minimum or none ▬▬ Some ▬▬ Major ▬▬ Intense

I. Skills related to acquiring information

A. Reading skills

K–3 4–6 7–9 10–12

1. Comprehension

- Read to get literal meaning
- Use chapter and section headings, topic sentences, and summary sentences to select main ideas
- Differentiate main and subordinate ideas
- Select passages that are pertinent to the topic studied
- Interpret what is read by drawing inferences
- Detect cause and effect relationships
- Distinguish between the fact and opinion; recognize propaganda
- Recognize author bias
- Use picture clues and picture captions to aid comprehension
- Use literature to enrich meaning
- Read for a variety of purposes: critically, analytically, to predict outcomes, to answer a question, to form an opinion, to skim for facts
- Read various forms of printed material: books, magazines, newspapers, directories, schedules, journals

2. Vocabulary

- Use usual word attack skills: sight recognition, phonetic analysis, structural analysis
- Use context clues to gain meaning
- Use appropriate sources to gain meaning of essential terms and vocabulary: glossary, dictionary, text, word lists
- Recognize and understand an increasing number of social studies terms

3. Rate of reading

- Adjust speed of reading to suit purpose
- Adjust rate of reading to difficulty of the material

B. Study skills

K–3 4–6 7–9 10–12

1. Find information

- Use various parts of a book (index, table of contents, etc.)
- Use key words, letters on volumes, index, and cross references to find information
- Evaluate sources of information—print, visual, electronic
- Use appropriate source of information
- Use the community as a resource

2. Arrange information in usable forms

- Make outline of topic
- Prepare summaries
- Make timelines
- Take notes
- Keep records
- Use italics, marginal notes, and footnotes
- Listen for information
- Follow directions
- Write reports and research papers
- Prepare a bibliography

C. Reference and information-search skills

1. The library

- Use card catalog to locate books
- Use *Reader's Guide to Periodical Literature* and other indexes
- Use COMCATS (Computer Catalog Service)
- Use public library telephone information service

2. Special references

- Almanacs
- Encyclopedias
- Dictionary
- Indexes
- Government publications
- Microfiche
- Periodicals

FIGURE 7.1 *(Continued)*

Suggested strength of instructional effort: —— Minimum or none ▬ Some ▬ Major ▬ Intense

K–3 4–6 7–9 10–12

K–3	4–6	7–9	10–12	Skill
Some	Some	Major	Intense	News sources: newspapers, news magazines, TV, radio, videotapes, artifacts

3. Maps, globes, graphics
   Use map- and globe-reading skills

K–3	4–6	7–9	10–12	Skill
Min	Major	Major	Some	Orient a map and note directions
Min	Major	Major	Some	Locate places on map and globe
Min	Some	Major	Major	Use scale and compute distances
Min	Some	Major	Intense	Interpret map symbols and visualize what they mean
Min	Some	Major	Major	Compare maps and make inferences
Min	Some	Major	Major	Express relative location
Min	Some	Major	Major	Interpret graphs
Min	Some	Major	Major	Detect bias in visual material
Min	Some	Major	Major	Interpret social and political messages of cartoons
Min	Some	Major	Major	Interpret history through artifacts

4. Community resources

K–3	4–6	7–9	10–12	Skill
Min	Some	Major	Major	Use sources of information in the community
Min	Some	Major	Major	Conduct interviews of individuals in the community
Min	Some	Major	Major	Use community newspapers

D. Technical skills unique to electronic devices

1. Computer

K–3	4–6	7–9	10–12	Skill
Min	Some	Major	Major	Operate a computer using prepared instructional or reference programs
Min	Some	Major	Major	Operate a computer to enter and retrieve information gathered from a variety of sources

2. Telephone and television information networks

K–3	4–6	7–9	10–12	Skill
Min	Some	Major	Some	Ability to access information through networks

II. Skills related to organizing and using information
A. Thinking skills

1. Classify information

K–3	4–6	7–9	10–12	Skill
Min	Some	Major	Major	Identify relevant factual material
Min	Some	Major	Major	Sense relationship between items of factual information

K–3 4–6 7–9 10–12

K–3	4–6	7–9	10–12	Skill
Some	Some	Major	Major	Group data in categories according to appropriate criteria
Some	Some	Major	Major	Place in proper sequence: (1) order of occurrence (2) order of importance
Some	Some	Major	Major	Place data in tabular form: charts, graphs, illustrations

2. Interpret information

K–3	4–6	7–9	10–12	Skill
Min	Some	Major	Intense	State relationships between categories of information
Min	Some	Major	Intense	Note cause and effect relationships
Min	Some	Major	Intense	Draw inferences from factual material
Min	Some	Major	Intense	Predict likely outcomes based on factual information
Min	Some	Major	Major	Recognize the value dimension of interpreting factual material
Min	Some	Major	Major	Recognize instances in which more than one interpretation of factual material is valid

3. Analyze information

K–3	4–6	7–9	10–12	Skill
Min	Some	Major	Major	Form a simple organization of key ideas related to a topic
Min	Some	Major	Major	Separate a topic into major components according to appropriate criteria
Min	Some	Major	Major	Examine critically relationships between and among elements of a topic
Min	Some	Major	Intense	Detect bias in data presented in various forms: graphics, tabular, visual, print
	Some	Major	Intense	Compare and contrast credibility of differing accounts of the same event

4. Summarize information

K–3	4–6	7–9	10–12	Skill
Min	Some	Major	Major	Extract significant ideas from supporting, illustrative details
Min	Some	Major	Major	Combine critical concepts into a statement of conclusions based on information
Min	Some	Major	Major	Restate major ideas of a complex topic in concise form

FIGURE 7.1   *(Continued)*

Suggested strength of instructional effort: —— Minimum or none ━━ Some ▣▣ Major ▦▦ Intense

K–3 4–6 7–9 10–12

Form opinion based on critical examination of relevant information

State hypotheses for further study

5. Synthesize information

Propose a new plan of operation, create a new system, or devise a futuristic scheme based on available information

Reinterpret events in terms of what *might* have happened, and show the likely effects on subsequent events

Present visually (chart, graph, diagram, model, etc.) information extracted from print

Prepare a research paper that requires a creative solution to a problem

Communicate orally and in writing

6. Evaluate information

Determine whether or not the information is pertinent to the topic

Estimate the adequacy of the information

Test the validity of the information, using such criteria as source, objectivity, technical correctness, currency

B. Decision-making skills

Identify a situation in which a decision is required

Secure needed factual information relevant to making the decision

Recognize the values implicit in the situation and the issues that flow from them

Identify alternative courses of action and predict likely consequences of each

Make decision based on the data obtained

Take action to implement the decison

C. Metacognitive skills

K–3 4–6 7–9 10–12

Select an appropriate strategy to solve a problem

Self-monitor one's thinking process

III. Skills related to interpersonal relationships and social participation

A. Personal skills

Express personal convictions

Communicate own beliefs, feelings, and convictions

Adjust own behavior to fit the dynamics of various groups and situations

Recognize the mutual relationship between human beings in satisfying one another's needs

B. Group interaction skills

Contribute to the development of a supportive climate in groups

Participate in making rules and guidelines for group life

Serve as a leader or follower

Assist in setting goals for the group

Participate in delegating duties, organizing, planning, making decisions, and taking action in a group setting

Participate in persuading, compromising, debating, and negotiating in the resolution of conflicts and differences

C. Social and political participation skills

Keep informed on issues that affect society

Identify situations in which social action is required

Work individually or with others to decide on a appropriate course of action

Work to influence those in positions of social power to strive for extensions of freedom, social justice, and human rights

Accept and fulfill social responsibilities associated with citizenship in a free society

Source:© National Council for the Social Studies. Used by permission.

Socially Competent Children

We regard as *socially competent* those individuals who have acquired the necessary skills to work and communicate effectively with a variety of people in different situations. As teachers can testify, children appear at the school door for the first time with varying levels of proficiency in social skills. Social competency often is learned, at least in part, informally and naturally through family training and peer imitation. Children, for example, usually learn not to interrupt a conversation when another is speaking or how to listen as well as to talk.

One study concluded that, among other behaviors, the socially competent 6-year-old can

- get and maintain the attention of adults in socially acceptable ways
- use adults as resources in socially acceptable ways
- express both affection and hostility to adults
- both lead and follow peers, compete with them, and express both affection and hostility to them

Conflict Resolution Skills

Arguably, one of the most important skills that socially competent citizens in a democratic society have is the ability to resolve conflicts in a nonviolent and socially acceptable manner. Conflicts surround us. In all regions of our nation, children of every age and from every socioeconomic stratum are exposed to conflict in a variety of forms. Nightly on television they can view episodes of conflict between parents and among other adults, between ethnic groups or countries, among politicians, and between neighborhood gangs. The alarming national statistics on child abuse and gang deaths also suggest that many students often experience violent conflict firsthand and are themselves the victims of conflict and misplaced aggression.

Strategies for Resolving Conflicts.   Many of children's personal conflicts deal with access to desired concrete objects (e.g., candy, toys), rather than with abstractions (e.g., different points of view). Classroom activities that encourage children to experiment with alternative ways of resolving conflicts can help prepare them to cope with the larger conflicts that reside within our society. These techniques include helping them understand the sources of disagreements and confrontations and work out constructive solutions to their own conflicts.

Approaches to teaching conflict resolution skills should communicate to children that the presence of some levels of conflict is a normal, everyday occurrence in a complex, interdependent society and world. Conflicts arise when the goals of individuals or groups clash. The resolution of conflict can be destructive (e.g., a fight, a battle) or constructive (e.g., a compromise, a treaty).

A number of practical programs, guidelines, and strategies exist for aiding teachers in addressing conflict resolution (Carruthers et al., 1996). For example,

Young citizens need to learn how to resolve conflicts in non-violent and mutually agreeable ways.

Scherer (1992) outlined 10 basic negotiating skills that teachers can help children develop. These are shown in Figure 7.2. Another example of an excellent resource is Byrnes's (1987) little book, *Teacher, They Called Me a _____!* It includes items for both primary- and intermediate-grade children, and many of them involve conflict themes.

FIGURE 7.2	Basic negotiating skills

- Check whether you understand the other person correctly and whether he or she understands you.
- Tell the other person what you think: don't try to read another's mind or tell others what you think they think.
- Talk about needs, feelings, and interests, instead of restating opposing positions.
- Recognize negotiable conflicts and avoid non-negotiable ones.
- Know how you tend to deal with most conflicts and recognize others' styles.
- Put yourself in the other's shoes.

- Understand how anger affects your ability to handle conflict and learn how to avoid violence even when you're angry.
- Reframe the issues; talk about them in other ways to find more common ground between yourself and the other person.
- Criticize what people say, rather than who or what they are.
- Seek win-win solutions, not compromises; find solutions where all parties get what they need, rather than solutions where all get some of what they need.

Source: From "Solving Conflicts—Not Just for Children" by M. Scherer, 1992, *Educational Leadership, 50,* p. 17.

Educators for Social Responsibility (23 Garden Street, Cambridge, MA 02138) has developed a variety of innovative materials and programs for elementary- and middle-grade students. These include the following:

- (Grades Preschool–3): D. E. Levin, *Teaching Young Children in Violent Times: Building a Peaceable Classroom*
- (Grades K–6): W. J. Kreidler, *Elementary Perspectives: Teaching Concepts of Peace and Conflict*
- (Grades K–6): W. J. Kreidler, *Creative Conflict Resolution: More Than 200 Activities for Keeping Peace in the Classroom, K–6*

In Figure 7.3, Kreidler (1990) offers an example of a concrete strategy for introducing primary-grade children to conflict resolution issues. The objective of his activity is to show how conflicts can escalate and what can be done to defuse them.

| **FIGURE 7.3** | An example of a concrete strategy on conflict resolution |

CONFLICT ESCALATES
Grade levels: (K-2) 3-6

Objectives:
To introduce the concept of conflict escalating. To identify behaviors that cause conflict to escalate.

Instructions:
1. Introduce the term "escalate," relating it to "escalator." Explain that when a conflict gets worse, people say it escalates.

2. Draw an escalator on the board as follows:

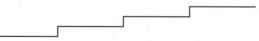

3. Read the following Conflict Escalator Story aloud once. Then read it a second time and ask the class to signal you each time the conflict goes up another step on the escalator. Each time they identify an escalation, write it on the escalator. Continue until you have reached the top of the escalator.

4. Review each step on the escalator and ask the class: What do you think the person was feeling at this step on the escalator? Write their responses under the appropriate escalator step. (There may be more than one feeling at each step.)

Discussion Questions: What happens to feelings as conflicts escalate? What makes conflicts escalate? When you are in a conflict, what puts you on the escalator? How can you get on to the down escalator? (Or: How can you de-escalate conflicts?)

CONFLICT ESCALATOR STORY
A Hatful of Trouble

Tyrone wanted a new ball cap, but couldn't get one. Shanda came to school wearing a new Red Sox cap and Tyrone told her it looked stupid.

Shanda said, "Not as stupid as that old one you wear."

Tyrone grabbed Shanda's cap and put it on his head. Shanda tried to grab it back, and it fell on the floor. Tyrone stepped on it to keep Shanda from picking it up and left a big footprint on the cap.

Shanda was furious. "You jerk! You're going to buy me a new cap!" she yelled. Then she grabbed Tyrone's shirt. When he tried to get away from her, his shirt ripped.

"You're going to buy me a new shirt," he yelled.

Source: From "Beyond 'He started it!' Empowering Elementary Children Through Conflict Resolution" by W. J. Kreidler, 1990, *Forum: The Newsletter of Educators for Social Responsibility, 90,* pp. 3, 5. Reprinted with permission from Educators for Social Responsibility.

Other activities that address conflict themes involve the use of the following, adapted from Anderson and Henner (1972):

1. *Open-ended sentences* for completion or to initiate a paragraph, such as "One reason that countries have wars is _____ ."

2. *Tense situations* or scenarios in which the class is given a question or premise to consider involving a conflict. Students then are asked to role-play the characters in the scene. For example, they enact an incident in which a group of youngsters unjustly accused of breaking windows tries to figure out how to make the guilty people confess.

3. *No-conflict settings* that demonstrate the positive, as well as the negative, possibilities of conflict. Students may be asked to react to scenarios similar to the following: What would football and basketball be like if there were no conflicts in the games?

4. *Fighting words* that include cases illustrating how individuals often insert into an argument provocative words they know will anger another. Students could be asked to consider words, phrases, or actions that they and others use to provoke family members or friends. They also may be asked to identify the occasions on which the words or actions might be used and the responses they produce.

Role-playing, puppetry, and simulations are especially effective instructional tools for developing conflict resolution skills. Under the protection of roles or the disguise of puppets, children have an opportunity to explore and test different solutions. These techniques are discussed in detail in Chapter 5.

Research and Analysis Skills

Research and analysis skills are interrelated and often inseparable in applications. *Research* can be viewed as the process of finding information in response to some question. It includes the identification, gathering, and recording of data. *Analysis*, however, involves the process of examining, verifying, and comparing data to arrive at some conclusion. Often such skills are labeled **critical thinking skills** because they incorporate elements that are essential for informed thought.

critical thinking skills

The ability to select appropriate information, record it accurately, and organize it in some accessible fashion constitutes one of the social scientist's most important collection of skills. It also is a vital competency for the effective citizen; we all, on occasion, need to have a complete and correct account of some event and to secure this information in a form that can be accessed easily.

Three subcategories of research and analysis skills that all citizens require and that we examine in more detail are *identifying and using reference sources*, *interpreting and comparing data*, and *processing information from pictures*.

Identifying and Using Reference Sources

One issue in using reference sources effectively is identifying just what a "reference" might be. Virtually anything or anyone may serve as a reference for a particular question or problem. For example, if we are trying to decide whether a film is worth seeing, we may either call a friend who has seen it for an opinion or locate a recent review of the film in a newspaper or magazine.

The telephone book and the Yellow Pages are examples of reference sources that most individuals have around their homes and use frequently. Similarly, when we wish to discover the meaning or correct spelling of a word, we typically consult a dictionary.

Because the range of reference materials available in their homes is often limited, students should be encouraged to go beyond them. This advancement involves learning about the nature and use of specialized reference works typically found in libraries (usually in the Reference Materials section). Where computer-based references are used (see Chapter 11), technology skills also are required.

The notion that many sources can and should be considered as appropriate reference possibilities is an important one for students to learn. Similarly, they should understand the basic criterion for judging the value of a reference work: How useful and authoritative is it for solving a problem or answering a question?

Sample Reference Works for Social Studies.   A sample of the numerous reference works that both teachers and students have found to be useful in the social studies follows:

- *Album of American History.*   This multivolume history of the United States is composed of pictures arranged chronologically.

- *Dictionary of American Biography.*   This is a multivolume source of information on deceased Americans who have made some significant contribution to American life. Included are politicians, artists, musicians, writers, scientists, educators, and many other types.

- *Dictionary of American History.*   This multivolume work is arranged alphabetically and includes articles on a variety of historical topics, some famous and some not so well known.

- *Discoverers: An Encyclopedia of Explorers and Explorations.*   This single volume includes details on a number of individuals who were pioneers in their time, along with their exploits.

- *Goode's World Atlas.*   This is an authoritative and comprehensive atlas of the world.

- *The Illustrated History of the World and Its People.*   In 30 volumes a wealth of information is presented on the geography, people, history, arts, culture, and literature of individual countries of the world. Also covered are such topics as foods, religions, dress, holidays, festivals, customs, and educational systems of the countries, as well as many other aspects.

- *Statesman's Yearbook.* A succinct thumbnail sketch of each country is provided in one volume.

- *The Story of America: A National Geographic Picture Atlas.* An extensive collection of visual, spatial, and narrative data on each of the states.

- *The Timetables of History.* In a chronologically organized single volume, a wide variety of important dates are included, covering seven major categories of American life.

- *Worldmark Encyclopedia of the Nations.* This multivolume guide to nations is arranged alphabetically by country and provides basic information on each country's social, political, historical, economic, and geographical features.

Encyclopedias as References. To promote a well-balanced understanding of individuals or groups, teachers should alert students to the limitations of encyclopedias. Because of their attempt to be comprehensive, encyclopedias are severely constrained in the amount of space they can devote to any single topic. No matter how authoritatively and carefully any topic has been researched and written, an encyclopedia entry must omit a great deal of material. This limitation applies to both print and electronic encyclopedias.

Consider, for example, if you were asked to sum up your life in an essay that someone will use to learn about you. The restrictions are that the essay must be no more than 250 words, all of the information must be accurate and objective, the reading level must be no higher than the fourth grade, and you must include everything anyone would need to know. The reader will have no other information about you. If you feel at all uncomfortable about having to record your life's history under these limiting conditions, keep in mind that entire groups and nations are often described in encyclopedias under the same constraints.

Activities for Introducing Reference Materials. One way to introduce reference materials in a meaningful context is to create interesting, puzzling, or intriguing questions for students that require them to use such sources. The difficulty of the questions may be varied for different age and ability groups by providing more or fewer clues. The actual reference resources to be used in answering the questions may be made available within the classroom. As alternatives, students may be given a list of helpful reference materials or just be allowed to use the school library to identify resources on their own.

Two types of activities that can be used to introduce reference materials in the context of solving interesting problems are a *problem sheet* and a *task card*.

Problem Sheet. Consider the activity in Figure 7.4 for intermediate- or middle-grade students.

The **problem sheet** could have contained additional information that would **problem sheet** make the solution somewhat easier. For example, the following data can be inserted into the paragraphs of the original description to give students more

FIGURE 7.4   Sample problem sheet

Problem Sheet

Directions

You are to discover the identity of Country Z, a real country, described below. Use any reference sources that you wish. The ones that have been identified for you may be especially helpful. After you have discovered which country it is, list all of the references you consulted. Then tell whether each of the references helped you learn the identity of the country and in what way.

Data on Country Z

Country Z covers an area of about 900,000 square miles and has approximately 25,000,000 people. Arabic is the official language of the country. However, many people also speak French, because the country once was controlled by France.

Country Z is bordered on the north by the sea and by desert areas in other parts of the country. The nation lies north of the equator, and its coastal areas have a warm temperate climate. There are plateaus and mountains but no major lakes.

Major agricultural products include wheat, oranges, watermelons, and olives. Livestock consists of horses, cattle, sheep, goats, and camels. Country Z also has many fisheries. Two of its major exports are natural gas and oil.

Follow-up Activity

Which reference sources did you use to determine the identity?

Which sources were useful and in what way?

clues. These additions make it easier to limit the list of countries that could match the description.

1. The country has approximately 20 people per square mile.
2. Life expectancy is about 62 years.
3. Approximately half of the people live in urban areas.
4. The name of the capital begins with the same letter as the name of the country.
5. The country shares a border with seven other countries.

Country Z is, in fact, Algeria, officially known as the People's Democratic Republic of Algeria. Any similar set of data that presents a puzzle or problem—whether it deals with a country, a city, an event, or an individual—can satisfy the same objective. The aim is to have students discover the functional value of reference sources through an interesting and challenging activity.

Task Card.   Even a basic set of questions listed on a card can be used to introduce reference materials in an interesting way. A **task card** can be used espe-

task card

cially effectively in learning centers where young children are working indepen-dently of the teacher (Chapter 12). The sample task card in Figure 7.5 contains a set of questions, all of which can be answered by consulting the appropriate book from the list of 10 reference sources provided earlier.

Interpreting and Comparing Data

A key aspect of research and analysis is interpreting and comparing data accu-rately and meaningfully. This skill requires paying careful attention to what is heard, seen, felt, and even tasted or smelled. Data are encountered through all of our senses. We may process these data firsthand through personal encounters, such as attending a concert or a meeting, and also indirectly, as when we read a book that describes a person, place, or event.

Comprehensive Skills Programs.   Comprehensive programs that promote children's reasoning abilities are available for youngsters across all ages and devel-

FIGURE 7.5	Sample task card

Task Card

Directions

The set of questions below can be answered by using the reference books identi-fied earlier. All of these books are in the library. Find the reference book that answers each of the questions and then write the answers on a separate sheet of paper.

1. Who was the founder of the Girl Scouts of America?
2. What are some of the customs and dress of the people of Chad?
3. What are the main functions of the Federal Reserve Board?
4. How does the per-capita income of Saudi Arabia compare with that of other countries in the Middle East?
5. Locate a picture of a Model T Ford. When did it appear, and what was unusual about it?
6. What do you consider to have been the most important contribution of Charles Ives?
7. What are the major industries in Algeria?
8. What are some of the major events that happened in the year your mother (or your father) was born?
9. Locate Butte in the index for the state of Montana. What major park is south-east of it?
10. Locate and copy a recipe from a foreign country.

opmental abilities. They also cover a wide variety of skills. One such program, *Philosophy for Children*, which was developed by the Institute for the Advancement of Philosophy for Children (1987), includes materials for elementary, middle, and secondary grades. Skills that the program attempts to develop include:

- Classifying and categorizing
- Defining terms
- Drawing inferences from premises
- Finding underlying assumptions
- Formulating causal explanations
- Searching for informal fallacies
- Predicting consequences
- Working with contradictions
- Identifying and using criteria

Cultural Filters in Interpreting and Comparing Data.   Effectively processing and interpreting data requires a recognition that each of us also filters what we experience through lenses that are shaped by our experiences and culture. These lenses are considered in more detail in Chapters 9 and 12, but they merit brief attention here as well.

We are all familiar with the phenomenon that different individuals processing the same data often focus on different aspects and, as a result, report different accounts of what was experienced. Five people from a rural area, for example, who visit the same section of the Bowery in New York for the same length of time may come away with different accounts of what each observed. One may focus on the despair in the faces of the derelicts encountered. Another may talk about the noise and the traffic. Still another may emphasize the drab visual landscape, the scattered debris on the sidewalks and streets, and the decaying areas. A fourth may remember the melange of smells that seemed offensive but distinct. The last member may have little clear recollection of any of the above aspects, but instead vividly recall with some detail the assortment of little shops and vendors.

Each of the accounts may be a reasonably accurate report of what one person actually experienced, but they are clearly different. Further, each single observation offers only a limited view. Taken as a whole, however, the set of perspectives may present a more adequate account of the Bowery than any single report.

Interpreting and Comparing Written Materials.   In our citizen roles, we often must process and interpret information from such sources as texts and books, articles, charts, graphs, tables, and pictures. In the social studies, it is especially important that students early on begin to develop the skills to interpret and compare carefully a variety of written materials reflecting different perspectives, including those of text authors. As competent citizens, students must be able to distinguish fact from opinion, bias from objectivity, reality from fiction, and extraneous from essential information. They also must be able to differentiate neutral from emotion-laden terms and to consider what is excluded from, as well as included in, written material.

The acquisition of such skills is a complex process that occurs slowly over time for children. Further, stage theorists argue that the process is related, at least in part, to the developmental level of the students (Cole & Cole, 1989). Written material, in particular, often presents students with special problems in making interpretations and comparisons, frequently because they have difficulties with reading in general (see Chapter 10).

Interpreting and Comparing Charts, Graphs, and Tables.   In our society much of the information we share with one another is communicated through charts, graphs, and tables. Each edition of a local paper carries numerous examples of each. They abound in newspapers and periodicals such as the *New York Times, USA Today, Time, Newsweek,* and *U.S. News and World Report,* as well as student editions of newspapers. They also appear in televised newscasts.

Citizens, journalists, newscasters, and social scientists alike use charts, graphs, and tables to summarize information or to simplify communication. For example, if demographers wish to cut through reams of statistical data and detailed narrative to represent one dimension of population distribution, they may use a table such as that shown in Table 7.1. For other purposes, a graph may be more appropriate (see, for example, Figure 7.6).

For students, however, extracting facts, generalizations, and hypotheses from charts, graphs, and tables is frequently a difficult task. This is particularly the case when the chart, graph, or table contains many details and quantitative data.

Charts, graphs, and tables, when accompanied by probing questions and teacher-guided analysis, can serve as springboards to reflective thinking within lessons and units. For example, consider Mr. Hernandez, who wishes to have his fourth-grade students develop and test generalizations about population patterns. He initially might engage them in an analysis of the census data pre-

TABLE 7.1	Reservation	Population
Ten largest American Indian reservations (population in thousands), 1990	Navajo, AZ–NM–UT	143.4
	Pine Ridge, NE–SD	11.2
	Fort Apache, AZ	9.8
	Gila River, AZ	9.1
Source: From *1990 Census Profile* (p. 6) by U.S. Department of Commerce, Bureau of the Census, 1991, Washington, DC: Author.	Papago, AZ	8.5
	Rosebud, SD	8.0
	San Carlos, AZ	7.1
	Zuni Pueblo, AZ–NM	7.1
	Hopi, AZ	7.1
	Blackfeet, MT	7.0

FIGURE 7.6

A graph on population distribution

Source: From *1990 Census Profile* (p. 3) by U.S. Department of Commerce, Bureau of the Census, 1991, Washington, DC: Author.

Ten states with the highest percentage black: 1990
(Rank in 1980 in parentheses)

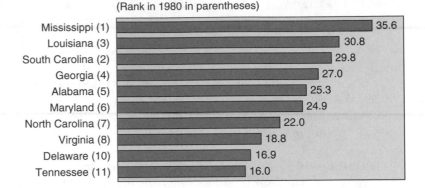

Mississippi (1)	35.6
Louisiana (3)	30.8
South Carolina (2)	29.8
Georgia (4)	27.0
Alabama (5)	25.3
Maryland (6)	24.9
North Carolina (7)	22.0
Virginia (8)	18.8
Delaware (10)	16.9
Tennessee (11)	16.0

Ten states with the largest black population: 1990
(In thousands. Rank in 1980 in parentheses)

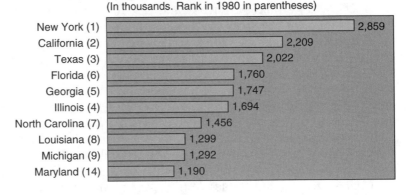

New York (1)	2,859
California (2)	2,209
Texas (3)	2,022
Florida (6)	1,760
Georgia (5)	1,747
Illinois (4)	1,694
North Carolina (7)	1,456
Louisiana (8)	1,299
Michigan (9)	1,292
Maryland (14)	1,190

sented in Figure 7.6. Referring to a large wall map of the United States, he then could ask the class members to place red stickers on the states that had the highest percentage of black populations in the most recent census. This could be followed by an analysis of the pattern that emerged and a request for hypotheses to account for it. Students could test their hypotheses by collecting information on the states from reference works such as almanacs.

Beyond assistance in skillfully interpreting the data of others, students also need guidance in representing their own analyses in the form of charts, graphs, and tables. They need first to gain competency in handling small, simple sets of data, rather than to be overwhelmed at the outset. Teachers can help provide natural experiences by incorporating charts, graphs, and tables into all of their lessons and current affairs discussions to help explain a point, answer a question, or frame a problem.

Even young children may be introduced to the use and interpretation of these forms of data through basic, concrete examples and activities. For example, a graph similar to the one shown in Figure 7.7 might be constructed in a first-grade classroom by using colored paper rectangles organized on a bulletin board.

FIGURE 7.7

Birthday graph

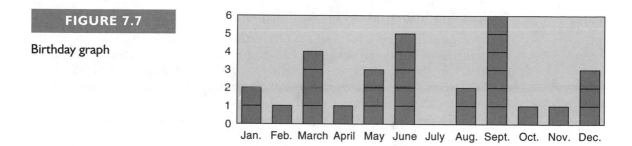

In the graphing activity, children are asked to name the months of the year, and these are recorded along the bottom of the graph. Each child identifies or is given the month of his or her birthday and a paper rectangle. Children then paste the pieces at the base of the graph, above the appropriate month. A different colored piece should be used for each month. After the children are finished, the units for each month may be counted and listed at the left of the graph. The class then can interpret and compare the data in the graph.

If the activity is done at the beginning of the year, the teacher can make a record of the original chart. As new students join the class, the chart can be modified. As a follow-up activity, the children can identify which months increased and by what amount.

Children in the intermediate and middle grades may experiment with computer tools to help them represent data in the form of charts, graphs, and tables. An example is the pie chart in Figure 7.8. It was completed by a sixth-grade student using a basic computer software graphing program called Data Plot (see Chapter 11).

FIGURE 7.8

Percentage of time spent in various activities this past Saturday and Sunday by members of our group

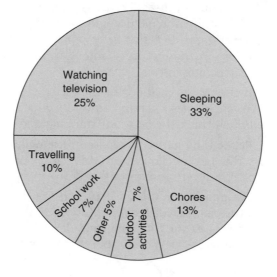

Processing Information From Pictures

Pictures also represent a form of data that must be processed in order to extract meaning from them (see Chapter 10). Some of the most interesting teaching materials in the social studies are pictures or pictorial print materials. Visual materials can enrich and enliven instruction. Research data also suggest that imagery facilitates learning (Somer, 1978; Wittrock, 1986; Wittrock & Goldberg, 1975). For primary-grade children especially, pictorial materials are excellent ways to present social studies subject matter.

Types of Pictures.   Teachers use many types of pictures in teaching. Five types common to social studies instruction are *informational pictures*, *tell-a-story pictures*, *open-ended pictures*, *expressive pictures*, and *political cartoons.*

informational pictures

tell-a-story pictures

open-ended pictures

Many pictures, such as one showing a mountain or the Washington Monument, appear to be self-explanatory and **informational.** Some, such as Figure 7.9, help students see relationships or **tell a story.** Others are more **open-ended,** permitting different viewers to read varied interpretations of what is being communicated. These types of pictures can serve as springboards for discussion of issues.

Still other photos are **expressive;** they portray human emotions or arouse them in the viewer. Shots of starving people, war-ravaged areas, and little children are examples of expressive pictures. An additional type of picture, often containing a caption, makes a social or political statement and is typically characterized as a *political cartoon.*

expressive pictures

Strategies for Analyzing Open-Ended and Expressive Pictures.   The following steps are suggested for the discussion of open-ended and expressive pictures.

1.   Encourage the children to make inferences about what is happening through such questions as, "What is happening in this picture?" Allow the children time to study the picture and to think about it. Encourage expansion on short answers and diversity in responses by such questions as, "Do you see anything else in the picture?" and "Can anyone else tell me what he or she thinks is happening in this picture?"

2.   If people are included in the picture, focus on their feelings and intentions. Ask such questions as, "How do you think the person is feeling?" and "What do you think the person is thinking about?"

3.   Relate the picture to events in the children's lives. Raise such questions as "Does this remind you of anything in your own lives? or "Does this make you think of anyone you know?"

4.   Summarize or draw closure on the discussion. If a problem was suggested in the picture, elicit some solutions and discuss the pros and cons of each. Such questions as the following may be helpful: "How could we label this picture?" "What was this picture about?" "What will happen now?"

FIGURE 7.9

Using pictures to show relationships

Source: From *Looking at Me: Webstermaster Activity Sheets* (p. 43) by P. H. Martorella, L. Martelli, and A. Graham, 1983, New York: McGraw-Hill. Copyright 1983 by McGraw-Hill Book Company.

Things Change.

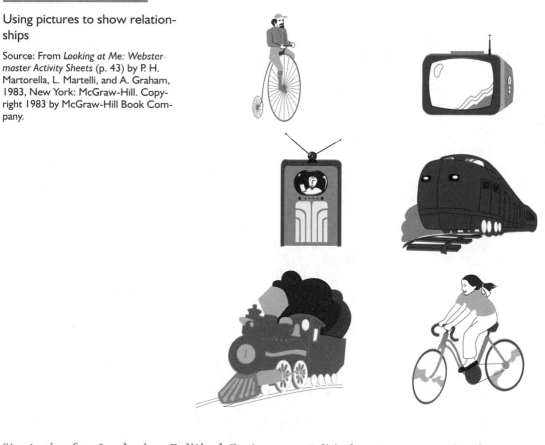

Strategies for Analyzing Political Cartoons.   Political cartoons are a visual form that can be especially effective for dramatizing an issue in social studies instruction. However, they often are difficult for children or even adults to process. This difficulty results from the fact that they frequently have complex concepts embedded, require considerable prior knowledge, and employ visual metaphors.

Young children can be introduced to simple cartoons that are literal as a way to acquaint them with the medium (Steinbrink & Bliss, 1988). Older children can be assisted in acquiring strategies for dismantling cartoons. Questions that teachers can use with students in processing cartoons are similar to those recommended for open-ended and expressive pictures:

1. What do you see in the picture?
2. What does each of the figures, items, logos, and symbols in the picture stand for?

3. What issue is represented in the picture?

4. What do you think the cartoonist thought about each of the figures in the picture?

5. What would be an appropriate caption for the cartoon? (If a caption exists, cover it with tape.)

Chronology Skills

Much of what we typically do both in daily living and in social studies classes involves *chronology*, some understanding of how people, places, objects, and events are oriented in time. As adults we are comfortable with related time concepts such as *a long time ago*, *recently*, *in the past*, and *infinity*. For young children, however, time and temporal concepts are often difficult to grasp. Elkind (1978, p. 108) observed, "To the young child there is little difference between 'later,' 'in a few minutes,' or 'next week,' which are all understood primarily as 'not now.' . . . only late into middle childhood does he begin to appreciate years and dates" (see also Downey & Levstik, 1991; Muir, 1990). Vukelich and Thornton (1990) concluded that only during the ages of 9 to 11 do the time understandings required to comprehend history develop significantly.

From a very young child's perspective, a basic concept of *time* involves an understanding of which items came first and which came last. It also includes a sense of what typically happens as the result of the passage of units we call seconds, minutes, hours, days, weeks, months, or years. Further, it encompasses a familiarity with basic vocabulary inherent in chronology discussions.

For older students, the concept evolves to include an understanding of the interrelationship of events and individuals over a temporal period. It also encompasses a sense of what is meant by a unit such as a century. Eventually it includes an understanding of the abstractness and arbitrariness of all units of time, whether they be measured in nanoseconds (billionths of a second), eons, or some new standard.

Activities Using Time Lines

Activities that require students to arrange and view people, places, objects, and events as occurring in sequence—such as time lines—help establish the perspective of chronology. Allowing children to arrange a series of pictures of events, such as those shown in Figure 7.10, in the correct temporal order works toward the same objective.

Time lines provide a simple system for listing, ordering, and comparing events over some period. They function as a summary statement of a series of events. In addition, they can represent a schema of how an individual has organized data into a meaningful chronological pattern.

FIGURE 7.10

Series of six events to be arranged in correct chronological order

Source: From *Looking at Me: Webstermaster Activity Sheets* (p. 41) by P. H. Martorella, L. Martelli, and A. Graham, 1983, New York: McGraw-Hill. Copyright 1983 by McGraw-Hill Book Company.

Any unit of time, ranging from a day to centuries, may be used in a time line. Similarly, any context or theme may be the basis for a time line—for instance, What I did today in the order I did it. Two illustrations of time lines with differing degrees of detail are shown in Figures 7.11 and 7.12.

Time lines may be organized horizontally or vertically. They also may be three-dimensional. For instance, a clothes-hanger mobile can be used to organize drawings, pictures, artifacts, or art work that visually symbolize items such as forms of transportation, inventions, and changing lifestyles from different time periods. Similarly, lengths of yarn and objects or pictures can be used. An example of this last approach for constructing a three-dimensional time line activity is presented in Figure 7.13.

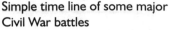

FIGURE 7.11

Simple time line of some major
Civil War battles

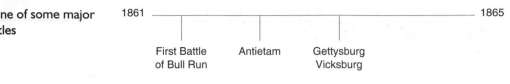

Some major battles of the Civil War

1861 ————————————————————— 1865

First Battle   Antietam   Gettysburg
of Bull Run   Vicksburg

FIGURE 7.12   The Lumbee Indians: Searching for justice, searching for identity

		American Revolution			Post–		
1587–1590	1700s	1776–1783	1835	1860s	Reconstruction	1954	1950s–1980s
Theory: coastal Indians mixed with members of "Lost Colony" to form Lumbees.	Theory: Lumbees formed from a mixture of tribes wiped out by disease and war.	Participated in American Revolution and received land for service.	Lost many rights under 1835 North Carolina constitution.	Abuse of Lumbees led to "Lowry War."	Attempts to place Lumbees in black society. Establishment of separate schools.	Legal end to segregation.	Lumbees gained more legal power and now seek national recognition.

Source: From *Tar Heel Junior Historian* (p. 23) by Tar Heel Junior Historian Association, 1989, Raleigh, NC:
Author. Copyright 1989 by Tar Heel Junior Historian Association.

Other Chronology Activities

Some of the other ways students can be helped to grasp concepts related to time
are *time visits, identification with some figure in the past,* and *developing imaginary
dialogues between famous historical figures.*

Time visits require students to pick some time in the past and then to compare conditions that once existed with those in their own lives. For example,
students might be asked to examine the similarities in and differences between
their lives and those of children of the colonial period.

To identify with a historical character, a student must try to imagine the
world of the past that the historical character experienced. Creating a make-
believe diary that the character might have authored is one way of building
such identification. A student might be asked to pick any special day during the
period under study and to write a page in a diary telling what the day was like.
The diary could record items such as what the individual would observe and
record and what would seem important and interesting.

| FIGURE 7.13 | Example of a time line activity |

Lifeline Time Line Activity

Materials List. The materials required for this activity are:

Roll of transparent tape for each group
Large box of crayons for each group
Pile of 3" × 5" blank cards for each group
Pile of colored construction paper for each group
Felt-tipped colored pens for each group
6' piece of string or yarn for each child
Pair of scissors for each child
Pencil or pen for each child

Procedures. The following procedures are suggested:

Organize the children arbitrarily into groups of five in an area where they will have lots of room to spread out with their materials. A floor area may be a good place. Give directions such as these: "Each of you hold up your piece of string (or yarn) like this." (Demonstrate by stretching out your arms with one end of the string in the left hand and the other in your right.) "This is your lifeline. One end is the beginning, and the other is the end of your life. You are to put on your lifeline all of the things you can think of that have been or are important in your life. You can draw pictures of the important things or cut out things that show them." (If the children are old enough, they also may be encouraged to write on the pieces.) "After you decide on the important things and make them, put them on your lifeline with tape or in some other way. Put the *first* important thing that ever happened to you *first* on the lifeline." (And so on.) *"You may include anything you like and show it in any way you like.* Use and share any of the materials you have in your group."

Once each child is started, try to refrain from helping too much to avoid structuring children's responses. As they complete their lifelines, children should be paired off to share them, describing and explaining each event. After each pair finishes, create a new pair until each child has finished and has had an opportunity to share with at least two others. Finally, after the children hang their lifelines around the room or on lines strung up, let them move about to examine those they have not seen.

Source: Adapted from *Man: A Course of Study (MACOS)* by Education Development Center, 1968, Cambridge, MA: Author. Copyright 1968 by Education Development Center.

To create an imaginary dialogue between individuals, students must incorporate actual historical data and real figures from different time periods, such as George Washington and Abraham Lincoln. Through the imaginary dialogues, the students attempt to create a plausible discussion that might have taken place between the personalities. In this way they compare and contrast both different periods and individuals.

Spatial Skills

In an increasingly interdependent nation and world, citizens have greater need than ever before for skills that can better orient them in space. Competent citizens must be able to locate themselves and others spatially in order to travel, exchange ideas, and access artifacts. Spatial skills most often appear in social studies in the discipline of geography, but they are distributed throughout all areas of the social sciences. Identifying political boundaries, the locations of cities, landmarks, and landmasses, and determining the relationship of one object in space to another are all part of spatial understanding.

The Impact of Spatial Perspectives

As citizens we also need to become aware of how our spatial perspectives and vocabularies influence many of our social, political, and economic perspectives. Whether we view something as far away, densely populated, large, hot, barren, or growing, for example, may impact on whether we decide to visit a region, seek a job there, or change our residence.

Even the language we use in describing an area can skew our perspective. Collins (no date) noted, for example, "Terms we select to describe other nations—and the present state of their social, economic, political development—influence students' perception of those nations." As an illustration, for years Africa was characterized by teachers and texts as "the dark continent," thus creating a host of negative associations. Further, unlike most other regions of the world, the continent, rather than the nations within it, was studied as a whole. This practice created the misperception of a high degree of uniformity among all Africans.

Maps and Globes as Spatial Tools

The most common ways individuals in our society use to orient themselves and to answer related spatial questions are through the application of existing maps and the creation of new ones. To a lesser extent, individuals consult globes to answer questions.

Initially, maps and globes are difficult to understand when children first encounter them in the primary grades (Muir, 1985). A *globe* is a model of the earth; *maps* are models or representations of portions of a globe. More simply stated, maps are representations of some object or place on the earth as seen from a bird's-eye view.

To a child, maps and globes do not look at all like what they represent. Elements such as "imaginary lines," which do not exist in reality but are clearly visible on maps and globes, are confusing. Concepts that are entwined in spatial skills, such as *boundary lines, earth, latitude, longitude,* and *equator,* have no concrete referents in the real world. Moreover, many of the maps and globes used in classrooms contain far more information than the average elementary student can understand or use.

Map and Globe Distortions.   Children should be sensitized to the relevant distortion and measurement issues associated with different projections. In representing regions on the earth, maps and globes do so with varying degrees of distortion. Since the first maps, nations often have deliberately distorted, for political purposes, the maps they used. They have done this, for example, by extending or reshaping boundaries and rerouting rivers, as suits their interpretation of historical claims. Apart from those deliberate distortions, all projections of areas on the earth's surface are functionally distorted in some ways because of the problem of translating a curved surface onto a flat one.

The National Geographical Society, in 1989, adopted the **Robinson projection** (see Figure 7.14) as one that produced the least distortion for most nonspecialized map applications. It is compared with the traditional **Van der Grinten projection** shown in Figure 7.15, which the society had used since 1922 for most of its world maps.

Notice the differences in the sizes and shapes of Greenland and the United States shown in each of the projections. Because of its location on the earth, in seven different projections the shape and size of Greenland will be different in each of them. Even in the Robinson projection shown, Greenland is still 60% larger than it should be. In the Van der Grinten projection, it is 554% larger.

Robinson
projection
Van der
Grinten
projection

Integrating Maps and Globes Into All Social Studies Instruction

Jarolimek and Parker (1993, p. 174) suggested that maps can furnish eight basic types of information:

FIGURE 7.14   A Robinson projection

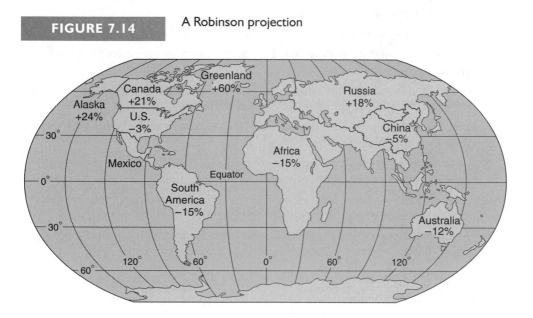

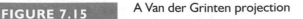

FIGURE 7.15   A Van der Grinten projection

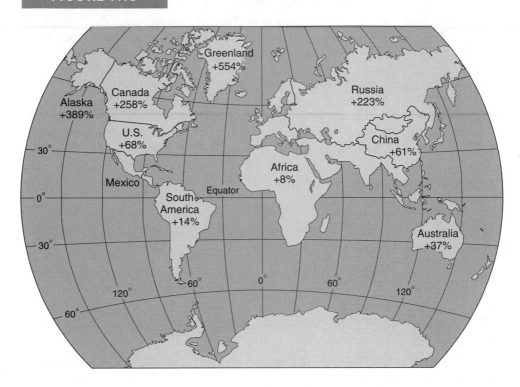

1. *Land and water forms*—continents, oceans, bays, peninsulas, islands, straits
2. *Relief features*—plains, mountains, rivers, deserts, plateaus, swamps, valleys
3. *Direction and distance*—cardinal directions, distance in miles or kilometers and relative distance, scale
4. *Social data*—population density, size of communities, location of major cities, relationship of social data to other factors
5. *Economic information*—industrial and agricultural production, soil fertility, trade factors, location of industries
6. *Political information*—political divisions, boundaries, capitals, territorial possessions, types of government, political parties
7. *Scientific information*—locations of discoveries, ocean currents, location of mineral and ore deposits, geological formations, air movements
8. *Human factors*—cities, canals, railroads, highways, coaxial and fiber-optic cables, telephone lines, bridges, dams, nuclear power plants

Ideally, maps and globes should be an integral part of all social studies instruction. A natural and functional way to integrate the use of maps and globes into social studies is to use them to help answer questions that the teacher or the students generate while studying a subject (e.g., Why does it get colder as you travel south in Australia?).

As they learn about people in other parts of the nation or the world, students should locate where they live on a map or a globe. They also should discover early on that one type of map or globe can answer some spatial questions, whereas other types will be needed for different questions.

Examples of different types of maps that answer various questions are shown in Figures 7.16 and 7.17. The two maps answer questions concerning (a) the use of a scale to determine distance between two cities in a region and (b) the location of certain natural resources. Maps also can help provide answers to questions such as Where are concentrations of minorities and ethnic groups in the United States? Where are the most promising areas to locate new major league baseball franchises? Where are the ski runs and chairlifts located at a ski resort?

Introducing Maps and Globes

Because maps and globes are the primary tools for teaching spatial skills, it is important that children be properly introduced to them. The initial stages of instruction in map and globe usage should concentrate on those aspects for which immediate concrete referents are available. These include developing and using maps of the child's immediate environment, such as the school, classroom, and home and the areas bordering each.

FIGURE 7.16

Map showing distance between two cities

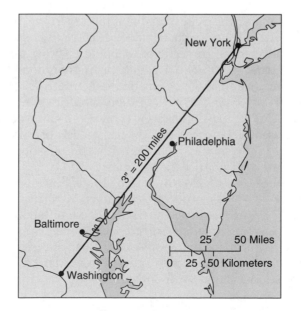

| FIGURE 7.17 | United States: Natural resources |

Key:

Oil

Fish

Forests

Source: From *City, Town and Country*, T. E. Workbook by Joan Schreiber, et al. Copyright © 1983 by Scott, Foresman and Company. Reprinted by permission.

body maps

In the primary grades, children can begin to map the most immediately concrete objects they know—themselves—through the use of **body maps.** These are outlines of the children's bodies drawn on large sheets of paper. An example of this type of activity appears in Figure 7.18.

After students have had experiences in creating body maps, they can transfer the general principle of mapping to other familiar concrete objects found in their classroom, school, home, or neighborhood (see Figure 7.19). In addition to commercially produced spatial tools, materials such as toys and blocks may be used in mapping activities for building cities and the like.

Unlike maps, globes give children a three-dimensional model of our planet. In essence, a globe is like the toy models of cars and dolls with which students are already familiar. Through the use of globes, children can see the relationships between all of the landmasses and bodies of water on the earth. They also can begin to develop a sense of the relative distances between major points on the earth. When students have access to a *relief globe*, they can even feel elevated areas of the earth such as the Rocky Mountains.

Several useful sets of guidelines and strategies for introducing children to the use of maps and globes are available. Seefeldt (1989) laid out guidelines for what children require in order to make effective use of maps. She argued they must understand the following:

FIGURE 7.18

Mapping activity for young children

MAKING A BODY MAP

General objectives

Observe an outline description of self—one general and basic way to identify personal characteristics. Observe how outlines can provide only a limited description of something; other data are required for a more complete and accurate description. Introduce a basic notion of a map.

Materials

Large sheets of paper for each member of the class or a large roll of paper approximately 4 feet wide.

Commentary

A body map provides a concrete representation of one aspect of self for a child. It is used here to build on the earlier discussion of physical vs. behavioral dimensions of self. The child is led to discover simple mapping and its limitations, namely that it omits many characteristics of an item. He or she experiences the utility of being able to describe something through only an outline map of it, and also the loss of detail when we look no further than the shape of an item.

Suggested procedures/questions

Introduce the activity by a comment such as, "We are going to make body maps today. We are going to discover one way of looking at ourselves." Be sure that a large area on the floor has been cleared or that a large flat section of a wall is available. You may have children lie on the floor or stand against the wall to be traced by you. If you feel that some of the children can do the job capably, let them help you later. In either event, be sure to tape down the corners of the section of paper with which you are working. One suggested strategy is to do four students at a time. If you wish, you can have the children hold hands and create a series of linked maps. As you complete a map, write the name of the child in the foot.

Because this sequence of activities will take several days, you may wish to stop at this point. The next steps are to have the children cut out their maps and hang them around the room or on a string clothesline. After the children have done this, have them discuss the following types of questions: "In what ways are all of the maps alike?" "In what ways are the maps different?" "What kinds of things about each of us do the maps show?" "What kinds of things about each of us do the maps leave out?"

At a later point you may wish to have the children add characteristics to their maps through coloring or painting. In concluding this activity, take some time to discuss the point emphasized under the second objective.

FIGURE 7.19   Sample map of concrete, familiar objects

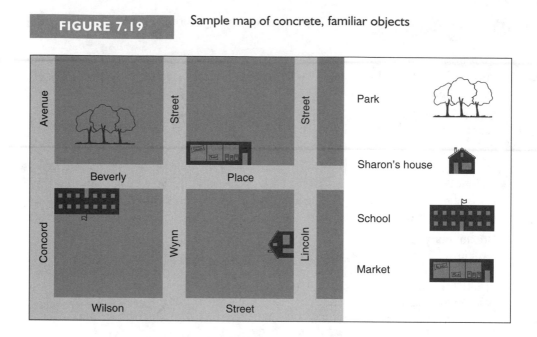

1. *Representation.* To fully understand maps, children must be able to understand that a map represents something else—a place.
2. *Symbolization.* A map, itself a symbol for a place, uses other symbols. Colors symbolize land and water, lines symbolize roads and railroad tracks, and other symbols are used for houses, churches, or schools.
3. *Perspective.* The concept that a map pictures a place as if you were looking at it from above is often difficult for young children to grasp. You must foster their understanding of a "bird's-eye view."
4. *Scale.* Maps reduce the size of an actual place. Children can be introduced to the idea that a map is like the original place, except it is much smaller. Making maps small makes it easier for people to think about the place and to hold the map. (pp. 172–173)

Bartz (1971) recommended that a child's first map of the United States should be special. It should be created in the form of a huge jigsaw puzzle with large, thick pieces. This is so a child could hold it, walk on it, and observe it from different perspectives.

Bartz suggested further that maps used with children should meet the three basic criteria of *simplicity, visibility,* and *usefulness of information.* Maps for instruction with children should (a) contain only as much information as is needed, (b) be easily seen and examined, and (c) include information that children can apply in some way to their daily lives. The George F. Cram Company has developed such a map, the *U.S. Discovery Floor Map,* which measures 64" × 52" (800-227-4199). It is a map of the U.S. that is placed on the floor and can be walked on.

Large maps allow children to engage in hands-on activities.

In a different vein, Louie (1993, p. 17) suggested that teachers consider using children's literature as a vehicle for furthering the development of spatial skills. She offered examples of skills and representative works of children's literature that could be used to foster the skills at different grade levels. Some examples are:

- K–2 *Skill:* Recognizes and uses symbols to represent things. *Literature: My Camera: At the Aquarium*, by Janet Perry Marshall (Boston: Little, Brown, 1989). ISBN 0-316-54713-1.
- 3–4 *Skill:* Uses distance, direction, scale, and symbols. *Literature: Roxaboxen*, by Alice McLerran, illustrated by Barbara Conney (New York: Lothrop, Lee & Shepard, 1991). ISBN 0-688-07592-4.

Key Spatial Concepts

As children begin to explore different types of maps and globes, they may be introduced to other key spatial concepts. These include *place location*, *map symbols*, *scale*, and *cardinal directions*.

Place Location.   One of the most common uses of maps for citizens is to locate places. We often draw or consult maps to explain or determine where a

place location

place is located. Not infrequently, we supplement our maps with verbal directions about *relative* locations: "You can't miss it, it's right behind the K Mart."

In the intermediate grades, children can be given concrete experiences with *grids*. Some types of maps, such as those used for travel, frequently help us locate places by use of grids comprised of letters and numbers. The system devised for locating any place on the earth's surface employs special grids called *parallels of latitude* (east-west lines) and *meridians of longitude* (north-south lines). These typically are found on both maps and globes and often are introduced to students as *imaginary lines*.

Children can be introduced to the grid system of locating items by making the classroom itself a living map. To do this, the teacher should organize a grid by attaching sheets of letters to two of the opposing walls and numbers to the other two at exactly 2-foot intervals.

The grid-system activity can begin as a game, with the teacher providing general directions to find coins that are hidden in different places (e.g., "The penny is somewhere in the classroom"). Further clues can be more specific (e.g., "It is in front of my desk." "Look near the art center"). After the children locate the coin through these procedures, the teacher can introduce the grid system as a more efficient procedure to locate items.

To simulate lines, strings may be stretched across the floor, corresponding to each set of letters and numbers. The game then can be replayed with students covering their eyes while the teacher hides different items at various locations. The teacher proceeds to ask students to find the hidden items, this time using grid-coordinate directions (e.g., "The coin is located at B4").

Students can experiment with the grid system by themselves giving coordinates to locate other items within the classroom. As a concluding activity, the teacher can ask students whether they still could locate items by using grids if the strings were removed. The strings then are detached, and the students can test their hypothesis. At this point it is appropriate to introduce the concept of *imaginary lines* and to relate them to the longitude and latitude lines on the globe (see Figure 7.20).

Map Symbols.   One of the prerequisites for using any map properly is some understanding of the language used, or how to "read" a map. **Map symbols** can assist us in comprehending the information in a map; in addition, standard sym-

map symbols

Latitude and longitude lines on a globe

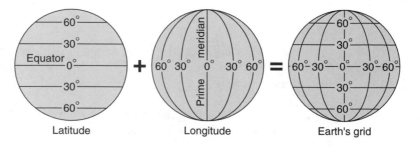

Latitude   Longitude   Earth's grid

FIGURE 7.21

Map symbols

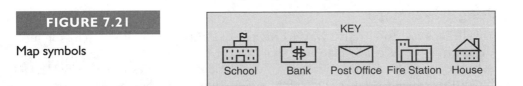

bols, such as those used for railroad tracks, enlarge children's spatial vocabulary. Once students understand the basic concept of a symbol, they can be introduced to those that are commonly used on maps, including the symbolic use of colors (e.g., blue to represent water) and boundary lines. Figure 7.21 illustrates some typical symbols used on simple maps.

Scale. The concept of *scale* (see Figure 7.22) is an important but complex element in map and globe communication. It requires students to understand proportional relationships between two items and to entertain notions of relative size (e.g., 150,000 square miles) and distance (e.g., 7,000 miles), which are well beyond their experience. Scale also is related closely to the concept of *symbol* in maps and globes.   scale

Scale emerges in the primary grades in discussions of the concepts of *larger* and *smaller* and in comparisons of toys and models. In the later grades, it is represented in the use of distance scales on maps. The inches-to-mile or centimeters-to-kilometers scale commonly found on road maps are examples.

Cardinal Directions. Part of the language of spatial communications generally is the use of **cardinal directions:** north, south, east, and west. Cardinal directions (points of the compass) often are confusing to both students and teachers.   cardinal directions

Teachers can use some basic strategies to help students gradually acquire these difficult concepts. These strategies include frequent use of natural landmarks and classroom locations as reference points and scavenger-hunt games in which students follow directional clues (e.g., "Go to the north side of the school building for your next instructions").

In teaching about cardinal directions, teachers must be careful that the students do not come to regard labeled points as *absolute* cardinal points. Some students, for example, will infer, mistakenly, that north, east, west, and south are *specific points* in space, rather than directions (e.g., believe that north is "up").

FIGURE 7.22   Scale

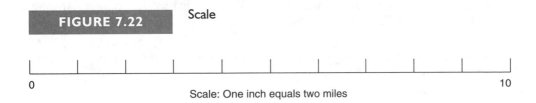

Using Travel Maps

Travel maps are an effective way to engage students in spatial problem solving. A class may be asked to plan and chart a trip to a distant city. As part of the task, they may be asked to indicate routes, landmarks, cities to be visited, relative distances, and the like. Different groups may work on the same trips and then compare their itineraries.

For older children, travel maps provide an opportunity to deepen their realization that maps have real and important functional purposes. Using a collection of travel maps from different cities, states, provinces, counties, and countries is likely to heighten student interest. This strategy also increases awareness of how travel maps around the world use many of the same conventions (e.g., symbols, scale, cardinal directions). A travel map of Venice, Italy, for example, although it has foreign names, has basically the same features as a travel map of San Francisco.

Sources of Travel Maps.   Although road maps are sold in book and map stores, they also are available free from some sources. Tourist bureaus of many states distribute free state maps. Address an inquiry to this bureau at the address of the state capital in which you are interested. Some foreign consulates and embassies may provide road maps of the country and of each major city within the country. Addresses for writing these agencies are generally available in reference works such as *The New York Times Almanac*.

Group Activities

1. Locate five political cartoons. In your group discuss how each might be used as a springboard for discussion in an intermediate-grade class.

2. Select a topic and create a problem sheet for a fourth-grade class. Use a real country, city, or person as the subject. Also create a list of clues, similar to those in the text, that could be used to help the students identify the subject. Try out the problem sheet with the members of the group and discuss possible modifications.

3. Select a group of five students from any grade between 3 and 8 and complete with them the lifeline activity described in the text. Identify the grade level and briefly describe and evaluate the results of the activity. Include copies of the students' lifelines with your report.

4. Examine the chart of social studies skills provided in the chapter. Among the list of skills, which do you consider to be the most important to develop? Which skills would you add to the list, and why?

5. Locate two multimedia encyclopedias such as *Encarta*. Compare their features with those of a traditional print encyclopedia.

Individual Activities

1. Identify five social studies reference works similar to the ones listed in the chapter and suitable for students in grades 4 through 8 to use. After each source write a brief description of the type of material that is referenced and a sample question that the book could answer. Then create a task card, as described in the chapter, that would require the use of the references.

2. Develop a collection of different types of maps (either originals or copies) that could be used with children. To locate them, consult newspapers and periodicals, as well as reference works. For each map, list the types of questions that the map answers.

3. Examine a collection of different maps and identify the map symbols they employ. From them, construct two posters, one for grades 1 through 4 and one for grades 5 through 8, that include an assortment of map symbols. Alongside each symbol, place the name of the object that the symbol represents.

4. Develop a collection of different types of tables, charts, and graphs that deal with issues suitable for discussion with children in grades 4 through 8. To locate the materials, consult newspapers and periodicals, as well as library reference works. For each table, chart, and graph, list the types of questions it could answer. Also indicate how each item might be used as a springboard for discussion with students.

5. Develop an activity for engaging children from grades 1 through 3 in mapping some spatial area within their immediate environment. Field test the activity with a group of five students for whom it is appropriate. Indicate the school and grade level of the students, provide copies of their maps, and describe and evaluate the results.

6. Locate an open-ended or expressive picture and develop a lesson around it for children in the primary grades. Consult the discussion guidelines in the chapter.

References

Anderson, J. L., & Henner, M. (1972). *Focus on self-development: Involvement.* Chicago: Science Research Associates.

Bartz, B. (1971). Maps in the classroom. In J. M. Ball, J. E. Steinbrink, & J. P. Stoltman (Eds.), *The social sciences and geographic education: A reader.* New York: John Wiley.

Brophy, J. (1992). Probing the subtleties of subject-matter teaching. *Educational Leadership, 49,* 4–8.

Byrnes, D. (1987). *Teacher, they called me a ____!* New York: Anti-Defamation League of B'nai B'rith.

Carruthers, W. L., Carruthers, B. J. B., Day-Vines, N. L., Bostwick, D., & Watson, D. C. (1996). Conflict resolution as curriculum: A definition, description, and process for integration in core curricula. *The School Counselor, 43*, 345–373.

Cole, M., & Cole, S. R. (1989). *The development of children*. New York: Scientific American.

Collins, H. T. (no date). What's in a name? *Resource pack: Project LINKS.* Unpublished manuscript, George Washington University, Washington, DC.

Downey, M. T., & Levstik, L. (1991). Teaching and learning history. In J. P. Shaver (Ed.), *Handbook of research on social studies teaching and learning* (pp. 400–410). New York: Macmillan.

Education Development Center. (1968). *Man: A course of study (MACOS)*. Cambridge, MA: Author.

Elkind, D. (1978). *A sympathetic understanding of the child: Birth to sixteen* (2nd ed.). Boston: Allyn & Bacon.

Institute for the Advancement of Philosophy for Children. (1987). *Philosophy for children*. Upper Montclair, NJ: Montclair State College, Institute for the Advancement of Philosophy for Children.

Jarolimek, J., & Parker, W. C. (1993). *Social studies in elementary education* (9th ed.). New York: Macmillan.

Kreidler, W. J. (1990). Beyond "He started it!" Empowering elementary children through conflict resolution. *Forum: The Newsletter of Educators for Social Responsibility, 90*, 3, 5.

Louie, B. Y. (1993). Using literature to teach location. *Social Studies and the Young Learner, 5*, 17–18, 22.

Martorella, P. H., Martelli, L., & Graham, A. (1983). *Looking at me: Webstermaster activity sheets*. New York: McGraw-Hill.

Muir, S. P. (1985). Understanding and improving students' map reading skills. *Elementary School Journal, 86*, 207–215.

Muir, S. P. (1990). Time concepts of elementary school children. *Social Education, 54*, 215–218.

Scherer, M. (1992). Solving conflicts—Not just for children. *Educational Leadership, 50*, 14–15, 17–18.

Schreiber, J., et al. (1983). *City, town and country: Teacher's edition—Workbook*. Glenview, IL: Scott, Foresman.

Seefeldt, C. (1997). *Social studies for the preschool-primary child* (5th ed.). Upper Saddle River, NJ: Merrill/Prentice Hall.

Somer, R. (1978). *The mind's eye*. New York: Dell.

Steinbrink, J. E., & Bliss, D. (1988). Using political cartoons to teach thinking skills. *The Social Studies, 79*, 217–220.

Tar Heel Junior Historian Association. (1989). *Teacher's supplement: North Carolina's coastal plain—Tar Heel Junior Historian*. Raleigh, NC: Author.

Task Force on Scope and Sequence. (1989). In search of a scope and sequence for social studies. *Social Education, 53*, 376—387.

U.S. Department of Commerce, Bureau of the Census. (1991, June). *1990 census profile*. Washington, DC: Author.

Vukelich, R., & Thornton, S. J. (1990). Children's understanding of historical time: Implications for instruction. *Childhood Education, 67*, 22–25.

Wilson, S. (1990). *Mastodons, maps, and Michigan: Exploring uncharted territory while teaching elementary school social studies*. East Lansing: Michigan State University, Center for the Learning and Teaching of Elementary Subjects, Institute for Research on Teaching. (ERIC Document Reproduction Service No. ED 328 470)

Wittrock, M. C. (1986). Students' thought processes. In M. C. Wittrock (Ed.), *Handbook of research on teaching* (3rd ed.), pp. 297–314. New York: Macmillan.

Wittrock, M. C., & Goldberg, S. G. (1975). Imagery and meaningfulness in free recall: Word attributes and instructional sets. *Journal of General Psychology, 92,* 137–151.

Chapter **8**

Aiding Students in Developing and Acting on Social Concern

Engle (1977) wrote, "A good citizen has many facts at his command, but more, he has arrived at some tenable conclusions about public and social affairs. He has achieved a store of sound and socially responsible beliefs and convictions. His beliefs and convictions are sound and responsible because he has had the opportunity to test them against facts and values" (p. 2).

Individuals of the type Engle described we characterize as concerned citizens. These citizens are cognizant of and responsive in an informed manner to the larger social world around them. The scope of their concern extends beyond local and personal issues to those at the regional, national, and international levels that affect the destinies of all humankind.

Concerned citizens establish personal priorities and make ethical decisions concerning issues they care about (see Benninga, 1991). In addition, they can make and keep commitments. Making a commitment involves identifying those social issues *that we personally plan to do something about. It is a decision to go beyond extending our knowledge of a subject; it involves acting on our conclusions.*

When we fulfill a commitment to do something we have decided is important, we become social actors. Action may take many forms, depending on our age, talents, and resources. For example, simply doing what we have concluded is "the right thing" can be a form of action. As we progress from awareness to action, we become increasingly efficacious.

Social Concern and Citizenship Education

I argued in earlier chapters that the three dimensions of reflection, competence, and concern characterize the effective citizen. Reflection and competence alone, without concern, are incomplete. To many Americans, it is obvious that among our citizens are some who are highly reflective and competent—witness embezzlers, slumlords, drug lords, and tax evaders—but who lack a basic grounding in social concern. In carrying out our citizenship roles, the dimension of concern provides a focus for the exercise of reflection and competence.

It also heightens awareness that we are members of a pluralistic democratic society and an increasingly interdependent world where sensitivity for the welfare of others and our planet arguably should become the norm. It reflects further the assumption that if our nation is to prosper and survive, the knowledge and skills we possess must be guided by our feelings and concern for others and the common social good, as well as our personal needs and aspirations.

The Morally Mature Citizen

During the past decade, educators, parents, and civic groups have expressed alarm over the lack of social concern evidenced by many youngsters in our society. In addressing this issue, the Association for Supervision and Curriculum Development (ASCD) developed a set of standards for what it labeled the
morally mature person
morally mature person. The ASCD standards, summarized in Figure 8.1, can be viewed as a general description of the ideal concerned citizen.

Elementary schools present an excellent educational environment for developing concerned citizens. Because they are relatively small and often closely knit social units, all phases of the school's policies and programs, including the social studies curriculum, can make a contribution toward this dimension of citizenship education.

In this chapter we examine illustrative areas in which teachers may contribute to the development of concerned citizens. In addition, we consider some of the basic issues that arise from related classroom activities. As we shall see, analysis of matters of social concern may involve one or more of the instructional strategies we examined in earlier chapters.

The Dimensions of Social Concern

In a pluralistic society, citizens frequently are called on to view issues from others' perspectives and to identify and resolve value conflicts. To make and act on social choices and commitments, concerned citizens need well-grounded systems of *beliefs*, *attitudes*, and *values*. And, because an important aspect of citizenship is deciding what are the right and the wrong things to do in a situation, individuals also need to develop a sound *ethical framework*.

FIGURE 8.1 The morally mature person

What kind of human being do we want to emerge from our efforts at moral education? What are the characteristics of the morally mature person?

A moment's reflection tells us that moral maturity is more than just knowing what is right. The world is full of people who know what is right but set moral considerations aside when they find it expedient to do so. To be moral means to *value* morality, to take moral obligations seriously. It means to be able to judge what is right but also to care deeply about doing it—and to posses the will, competence, and habits needed to translate moral judgement and feeling into effective moral action.

We submit that the morally mature person has six major characteristics, which are derived from universal moral and democratic principles. These characteristics offer schools and communities a context for discourse about school programs and moral behavior.

The morally mature person habitually:

1. *Respects human dignity,* which includes
   - showing regard for the worth and rights of all persons,
   - avoiding deception and dishonesty,
   - promoting human equality,
   - respecting freedom of conscience,
   - working with people of different views, and
   - refraining from prejudiced actions.

2. *Cares about the welfare of others,* which includes
   - recognizing interdependence among people,
   - caring for one's country,
   - seeking social justice,
   - taking pleasure in helping others, and
   - working to help others reach moral maturity.

3. *Integrates individual interests and social responsibilities,* which includes
   - becoming involved in community life,

FIGURE 8.1   *(Continued)*

- doing a fair share of community work,
- displaying self-regarding and other-regarding moral virtues—self-control, diligence, fairness, kindness, honesty, civility—in everyday life,
- fulfilling commitments, and
- developing self-esteem through relationships with others.

4. *Demonstrates integrity,* which includes
   - practicing diligence,
   - taking stands for moral principles,
   - displaying moral courage,
   - knowing when to compromise and when to confront, and
   - accepting responsibility for one's choices.

5. *Reflects on moral choices,* which includes
   - recognizing the moral issues involved in a situation,
   - applying moral principles (such as the Golden Rule) when making moral judgments,
   - thinking about the consequences of decisions, and
   - seeking to be informed about important moral issues in society and the world.

6. *Seeks peaceful resolution of conflict,* which includes
   - striving for the fair resolution of personal and social conflicts,
   - avoiding physical and verbal aggression,
   - listening carefully to others,
   - encouraging others to communicate, and
   - working for peace.

In general, then, the morally mature person understands moral principles and accepts responsibility for applying them.

Source: From "Moral Education in the Life of the School" by ASCD Panel on Moral Education, 1988, *Educational Leadership, 45,* p. 5. Reprinted with permission of the Association for Supervision and Curriculum Development. Copyright 1988 by ASCD. All rights reserved.

Each of us holds to some set of beliefs, attitudes, and values, all of which are related. Often people who have similar sets band together and become allies in common causes or interests. On the basis of shared beliefs, attitudes, and values, they join such organizations as social clubs, political parties, and religions, to name but a few. People also become friends for similar reasons.

By the same token, different beliefs, attitudes, and values can sharply divide us. Throughout history, such violent behavior as wars, inquisitions, riots, and holocausts have resulted from the inability of nations, groups, and individuals to tolerate differences in others. In less extreme cases, the failure to understand or consider objectively the implications of differences in the beliefs, attitudes, and values of others can breed suspicion, fear, and hatred. In the case of nations, it can make the majority of citizens insensitive to the rights of minorities. It also can increase tension and engender hatred among groups, reduce social, economic, and political intercourse, and hasten the outbreak of hostilities and atrocities.

The Nature of Beliefs

A **belief** may be defined as any assertion an individual makes that he or she   **beliefs**
regards as true (Rokeach, 1968). We each hold thousands of beliefs, some important and some trivial, some objectively verifiable and some not. A belief may not be verifiable or even true. It is necessary only that person think, feel, or act as if his or her assertions are factually correct for them to be beliefs.

Examples of beliefs that some individuals hold are:

- Extraterrestrial beings exist.
- Mozart was Italian.
- Studying Latin improves your English.
- Garlic repels vampires.

The sum total of all of the things we believe may be regarded as a *belief system*. Throughout our lives our belief systems typically undergo many changes as evidence gives us reason to cast aside old ones and acquire new ones. If our belief system is receptive to change, it can be called *open*. Those systems that resist change may be characterized as *closed*.

The Nature of Attitudes

Attitudes are closely related to beliefs. They are clusters of related beliefs that   **attitudes**
express our likes and dislikes, general feelings, and opinions about some individual, group, object, or event (Rokeach, 1968). We can have attitudes toward all sorts of people and entities—Japanese, Jews, peace, scuba diving, the environment, beers—or even toward nonexistent entities, such as elves and centaurs. Beliefs and attitudes are derived from many sources, including relatives and friends, the mass media, and different experiences (Triandis, 1971).

The Nature of Values

For more than a decade, a vast body of educational literature has developed dealing with the subject labeled at different times as *values*, *valuing*, and *values clarification*. Not surprisingly, many definitions and applications of the term have come into use as a result. We consider **values** to be the standards or criteria we   **values** use in making judgments about whether something is positive or negative, good or bad, pleasing or displeasing (Shaver & Strong, 1976). The standard we have, for example, for determining whether an individual's conduct toward us is good or bad may derive, in part, from our value of *helpfulness*.

We all share a number of basic or core values. According to Rokeach (1968), they include the following:

Independence	Freedom	Wisdom	True friendship
Courageousness	Salvation	Pleasure	Broad-mindedness
Social recognition	Self-respect	Honesty	Responsibility
Cleanliness	Happiness	Cheerfulness	
Helpfulness	Equality	Mature love	

The Nature of Value Judgments

**value
judgments**

In contrast to the values themselves are the actual assertions or claims we make, based on the values: our **value judgments**. Value judgments are ratings of people, objects, or events that reflect values.

Value judgments, which may be positive or negative, apply our value standards to some individual, group, event, or item. From the values of honesty, equality, and wisdom that we hold, for example, we make value judgments when we say, write, or think statements such as "Tom is an honest person," "Gay teachers are entitled to the same rights as heterosexual ones," "America needs more public libraries."

Often more than one value drives a value judgment. Thus our values of wisdom and equality may lead us to the judgment: All poor children should receive a free college education paid by the federal government. Value judgments are expressions or applications of our values and are closely related to our beliefs and attitudes. Figure 8.2 presents a summary of the contrasts among beliefs, attitudes, values, and value judgments.

FIGURE 8.2	The nature of beliefs, attitudes, values, and value judgments

Beliefs	Any assertions individuals make that they regard as true
Attitudes	Clusters of related beliefs that express our likes, dislikes, general feelings, and opinions about some individual, group, object, or event
Values	The standards or criteria we use in making judgments about whether something is positive or negative, good or bad, pleasing or displeasing
Value Judgments	Ratings of people, objects, or events that reflect values

Instructional Strategies for Examining Beliefs, Attitudes, and Values

In practice, authors of teaching strategies, texts, and other materials dealing with social concern often combine objectives relating to beliefs, attitudes, values, and ethical concerns. Because these all are interrelated, a teaching strategy that focuses on one invariably has some impact on the others. For example, a lesson dealing with *beliefs* about minorities may affect the importance we attach to the *value* of equality.

Strategies for Analyzing Attitudes

The most fundamental beliefs and attitudes that elementary students wrestle with—those related to *self*—are referred to as **self-concepts.** Each of us forms our self-concept, in large measure, by filtering what we perceive as the attitudes and reactions of other individuals toward us. The teacher who tells a little girl, "You certainly do a fine job when you are given an assignment," contributes to the child's attitude toward her self as a responsible, conscientious person. At the same time, she has to balance the teacher's view with that of her angry parent who remarks: "Can't you ever do what you are told?"

self-concepts

Self-Concept Activities.   Activities that encourage students to reflect on their views toward self can be used to introduce the examination of attitudes and values. There are many ways to help children take stock of their positive qualities and share with the teacher areas of special concern. Activities, however, should safeguard the rights of students and their parents to privacy. Teachers also should recognize the limitations of their professional training in dealing with children who have histories of serious emotional problems. For some children, extended probing self-analysis can be traumatic and requires special professional supervision and counseling.

Given these caveats, let us consider three types of self-concept activities that are appropriate if handled as described: *sentence completions*, *self statements*, and *fantasy exercises*.

Sentence Completions.   One way to encourage students to verbalize and discuss aspects of self is through the use of simple open-ended sentences. These allow children freedom to express their views without fear of sanctions. Older children may be asked to write out the responses; younger ones and nonreaders may be asked to respond orally. In either case, time should be provided for students to listen to each others' views, as well as to state their own.

Here are some examples of open-ended sentences:

1. The person I am most like is _____ .
2. The person I would most like to be is _____ .

One concrete way for young children to express these views toward self is by constructing self-portraits as this first-grade girl did.

3. Some of the things that make me happy are _____ .

4. Some of the things that make me angry are _____ .

5. Besides being an American, I am _____ .

Self Statements.   Similar to the preceding activity, self statements involve the completion of open-ended sentences. All of the students in a class respond anonymously on blank cards to a single sentence, which the teacher writes on the chalkboard: "I like myself because _____ ." Each student then completes the sentence on his or her card and turns the card over without showing or telling anyone else what was written.

After the students have finished, all cards should be collected face down, shuffled, and then read aloud to the class *without comments or requests for clarification*. A variation is for the teacher to type all of the students' responses on a single sheet of paper, which is then publicly displayed. This activity may be repeated a number of times during the year.

Fantasy Exercises.   Through fantasy, children often are able to express beliefs and attitudes they otherwise might find difficult to discuss. It also can serve as a highly effective vehicle for gaining insights about our attitudes toward self and others. An example of the use of fantasy is the activity in Figure 8.3. Fantasy animals serve as the vehicles for expressing attitudes and emotions. The activity offers a playful, concrete, and indirect way for children in the intermediate and middle grades to express their views.

Attitude Inventories.   One of the ways children can systematically examine, compare, and discuss attitudes toward objects other than themselves is through the use of **attitude inventories**. Depending on the topic and the capabilities of the students, they may be able to organize their own surveys and collect and analyze the results.

attitude inventories

An activity that can be done with primary-grade children who cannot write relates to their attitudes toward school. It requires the use of an *evaluation thermometer* similar to the one shown in Figure 8.4. Each day, a child records his or her feelings about daily activities by shading in the thermometer.

Another technique for surveying attitudes is the **semantic differential** (Osgood, Suci, & Tannenbaum, 1957), which can be used with students in the intermediate and middle grades. The technique measures the attitudes of an individual or group toward any object, individual, place, or event. It also can be used as one aspect of evaluation to assess the effects of a unit of instruction. This type of application is discussed in Chapter 13.

semantic differential

| **FIGURE 8.3** | Animal fantasy activity |

Give each child three sheets of blank paper. Ask each child to place in the lower right-hand corner of one sheet his or her first name. For the second sheet, instruct the children to place the first name of someone they love or like very much in the same location. (At this point, you may wish to establish the ground rule that class members cannot be used for this exercise.) Repeat the process for the third sheet, using as the object someone disliked very much. (Repeat the ground rule, if used.)

After the class is finished, ask everyone to do two things. First, draw an *animal* to represent each of the three people whose names were written on the sheets. Crayons, pencils, or colored pens may be used, but emphasize that this is not a drawing exercise. The children should not be concerned if their "animals" do not much resemble the real ones. Second, instruct the children to write on each sheet one or two words that best describe the animal.

After everyone is finished, the results should be shared in some systematic fashion. Comparisons should begin with each category (i.e., "self" first, "loved one" next, and so on). The drawings, as well as the adjectives, should be shared. Students should be encouraged to discuss their feelings about the exercise experience and their own personal discoveries.

FIGURE 8.4

Evaluation thermometer

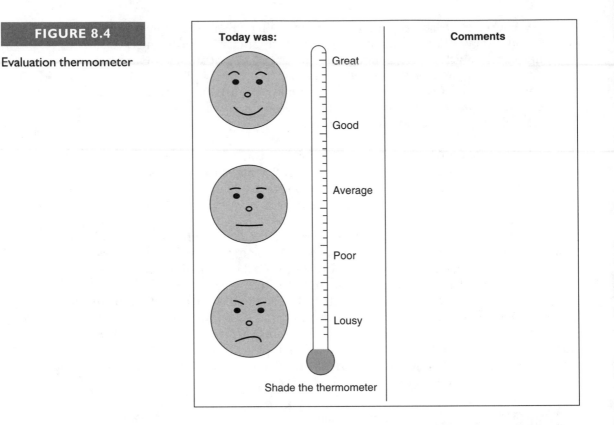

Constructing Attitude Inventories.   An inventory is constructed by first identifying some attitude object. This may include objects such as persons, groups,
places, or things (e.g., Malcolm X, refugees, City Park, nuclear power plants). The
name of the attitude object also may be replaced with a picture of it. Objects should
be chosen after consideration of the levels of knowledge, maturity, and interests of
the students and the nature of the scope and sequence of the curriculum.

Along with the object, pairs of adjectives are selected that express oppo-
sites—for example, happy-sad, rich-poor, good-bad (see Figure 8.5). Any set of
adjectives that make sense in relationship to the attitude object being analyzed
may be used.

No set number of pairs must be used, but no fewer than 5 and no more
than 10 is a suggested rule of thumb. The name of the topic is placed at the top
of the sheet, followed by the set of adjective pairs placed at the opposite ends of
a continuum that allows seven rating options. Each student is given a copy of
the inventory and completes his or her ratings, as illustrated in Figure 8.5.

Scoring a Completed Attitude Inventory.   Each point on the continuum in
Figure 8.5 is assigned a number from 1 to 7, with the space next to the positive

FIGURE 8.5   A student's completed attitude inventory

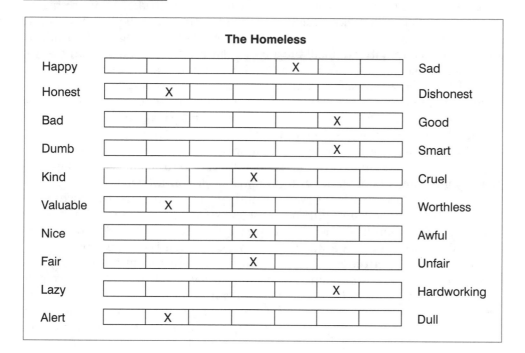

adjective (for example, "Nice") being assigned the number 7. The space next to the opposing negative adjective, "Awful," is assigned the number 1. The spaces in between are numbered accordingly.

After the children have completed the inventory, it is possible to measure whether each individual's attitudes toward the object are generally positive or negative. The student who completed the inventory in Figure 8.5 had a score of 51, which indicates a positive attitude toward the homeless. Because the inventory has 10 pairs, the highest possible score is 70, which would indicate an extremely positive attitude; the lowest possible score, 10, would indicate an extremely negative attitude. A score of 40 would suggest a moderate view.

A composite score representing the overall attitude of the class also can be obtained. This is done by summing all of the individual scores and then dividing the total by the number of respondents. Class scores then can be compared with those of other classes within a school.

Strategies for Analyzing Values

Because values are more enduring than beliefs and attitudes, they are highly resistant to change (Rokeach, 1968). In dealing with values, both in the formal and the informal curricula of the schools, educators often swing to either of two extremes. They may try to inculcate a particular set of values that seem reasonable, inoffensive, or sanctioned by the local community and society at large; for example, respect, responsibility, trustworthiness, caring, justice and fairness, and civic virtue and citizenship (Cohen, 1995). Or they may promote the point of view that all values are relative, that one set of standards for making judgments about whether something is good or bad is as acceptable as another.

Neither is a tenable position for dealing with values in public schools. As suggested in earlier chapters, our democratic and pluralistic society supports many competing sets of values as legitimate. Value conflicts abound in our society and in our personal lives. We frequently must choose between virtue and pleasure, being honest and hurting someone's feelings, obeying a law or our conscience, and countless other competing values. Citizens also must make ethical choices when they take a stand for one set of standards over another.

To function as effective citizens within our constitutional framework, students must recognize that value conflicts are unavoidable and seldom occur in the form of clear choices between good and evil, right and wrong. Rather, they frequently surface as choices between two desirable ends (e.g., Should I help charity A or B?) or two undesirable ones (e.g., Should I vote for rascal A or B?).

Like individuals and groups, nations also must resolve value conflicts and make hard choices based on the best evidence and well-grounded ethical principles. No nation could long endure without a system for judging the relative importance of competing values in a given situation. Among other things, officials of nations must make value judgments about waging wars or negotiating for peace, choosing among allies, and allocating national resources.

We provide students with an insight into this process of making tough choices by guiding them through a rational analysis of both the values they hold and the bases for them. This examination includes comparing their existing values and priorities with competing sets. It also involves examining the implications of the judgments we make, based on our values. In addition, it encompasses attending to the discrepancies between what we assert as values and the values that are reflected in the decisions we make and the actions we take.

Establishing Value Hierarchies and Comparing Values.   Which values do you espouse? Which value is the most important to you? Which is the least important? Developing value hierarchies, determining what is a higher and a lower priority in our system of values, makes us reflect on what is important to us in life. When we compare our value preferences with those of others, we also gain a broader perspective on issues.

In the intermediate and middle grades, value hierarchies can be approached directly by providing children with a list of value terms and discussing their meanings. This procedure can be followed by asking them to organize a set of values in some order from most to least important and engaging them in a discussion of the reasons for their choices.

Consider, for example, the following set of values: wisdom, freedom, national security, material comforts, equality, family security, salvation. Given that all of these are regarded as important, which do you regard as the most important values? Record your preference and then arrange the remaining values in the order of your choice. Compare your choices with those of a classmate.

Another way in which the principle of assigning value hierarchies may be made more concrete is through a **value decision sheet** similar to the one shown in Figure 8.6, which is designed for a sixth-grade class. It calls for students to translate their value hierarchies into decisions about which things are more important than others.

value decision sheet

A *value decision sheet* presents a realistic situation and then calls for a decision about priorities in actions. Each action reflects a value; for example, in Figure 8.6 the value of *equality* is represented by the statement: All people should be treated equally.

Truly internalizing and comparing the values of others requires us to put ourselves in their shoes, to see and experience life as they do. Children's literature is one of the important vehicles teachers can use to introduce students to differing value systems and significant value issues. This technique is described in more detail in Chapter 10.

FIGURE 8.6   A value decision sheet

Building a New City

A new community is being planned. Everything in the community is new. All of the decisions about how the community will be built must be planned carefully: where the people will live, where they will shop, work, go to school, practice their religion, and have fun.

Below are some things the planners will have to think about. Put a 1 in front of the thing that you believe is the most important one for the planners to think about. Put a 2 in front of the next most important thing. Continue until you have numbered all of the items from 1 to 7.

_____ People should be free to buy or build a house any place they like.

_____ Lots of churches and temples should be built.

_____ There should be plenty of schools, libraries, and colleges so that everyone can learn.

_____ There should be a large police department.

_____ People should have lots of things to do that they really enjoy.

_____ All people should be treated equally.

_____ There should be jobs for everyone who wants them.

FIGURE 8.7   Sample role-play activity

PACKING YOUR SUITCASE

Adaptation for young children

Part 1

Read children this version of the scenario, which simplifies the details and stresses the perspective of a refugee child:

"A war is going on in your country. Your parents feel your family is in danger living at home. They decide to escape to another country where you could be safer. At supper one night they tell you that your whole family will leave first thing in the morning. After supper you are to pack the things you will take with you in a backpack or suitcase that you will carry yourself. You can only take five kinds of things. Pack your bag with the things you would want to take with you."

Ask the children to go home and actually pack a little bag with the things they would want to take or to make a list of those things.

Part 2

Have the children share their lists or bags and discuss how they made their choices.

    a. What did they take and why?

    b. What did they have to leave behind and why?

    c. What was the hardest thing to leave behind?

Part 3

Encourage the children to express how they might feel if they really had to pack and leave home. Explain the purpose of this experience to the children: to help them understand the feelings of refugees who must really face this experience.

Source: From *Uprooted: Refugees and the United States* by D. M. Donahue and N. Flowers, no date, Palo Alto, CA: Educators' Network, Amnesty International USA.

Role-playing and simulations also are excellent techniques for helping children better understand the frames of reference and values of others (see Chapter 5). The role-play enactment described in Figure 8.7, for example, tries to develop empathy for the plight of refugees who are uprooted and forced to flee their homes, often on a moment's notice.

Instructional Strategies for Promoting Ethical Growth

The analyses of our beliefs, attitudes, and values eventually intersect with basic ethical issues. Ethical decisions deal with questions such as What is proper? What is just? What is the fair thing to do? Determining the right course of action, when competing choices are available, is often difficult or painful. It also often involves more than looking to tradition or to what immediately benefits us personally.

Moral Dilemmas

Consider the discovery in 1990 of a mutant gene that makes some families highly prone to one form of cancer. As a consequence, it now is possible to identify, through a test, family members who are almost certain to develop the cancer during their lifetime. Carriers have a 50% chance of developing the cancer by age 30 and a 90% chance by age 60.

moral dilemmas

At the same time, nothing medically can be done to treat those who have the gene. No one can tell where or when in the body it will appear, and nothing can be done to prevent its occurrence. Given these conditions, should doctors be allowed to test for the defective gene for anyone who requests it? Would such types of genetic testing be a proper part of a requirement for a job application? For volunteers to the armed forces? For insurance purposes?

Our body of ethical principles guides us in answering basic moral questions such as these as they recur throughout our lives. In turn, the network of beliefs, attitudes, and values that undergird our ethical framework is pressed into action whenever we confront a basic dilemma concerning what is right.

Initially many of us derive our moral codes from our parents or parent surrogates. They point the way to what is right and wrong behavior. In some form they reward us when we respond correctly and rebuke us when we err. As children we learn early on a host of moral dos and don'ts in this fashion.

If an individual never progresses beyond this stage of imitation and repetition of behavioral patterns as responses to moral issues, his or her ethical framework does not mature. Morality for such an individual is largely a matter of imitating patterns of responses that were learned long ago and that have been refined and reinforced over the years.

In those cases where individuals develop without clear guidelines, however, they may face life without an ethical compass to guide their decisions. They are likely to skip from situation to situation, doing what seems prudent at the time. What is right becomes a matter of what is expedient. Each moral decision bears little relationship to the last one or to the next one. If nothing happens to change the behavior of such individuals, they remain ethically rootless.

The Moral Development Theories of Jean Piaget and Lawrence Kohlberg

Kohlberg and his associates developed, refined, and tested a theory of **moral development** that drew from Piaget's earlier work (Kohlberg, 1976). One aspect of Piaget's developmental research dealt with the ways individuals reason about matters of right and wrong. As they mature, Piaget argued, children begin to understand that the needs of others must be taken into account in making moral judgments.

moral development

He discovered that children, over time, exhibit qualitatively different types of moral reasoning. For instance, young children are prone to pay attention to what an authority figure, such as a parent, says to determine what is the right or the wrong thing to do in a situation. As they grow older, however, children are more likely to take into account the principles of reciprocity and cooperativeness in making a moral decision (Piaget, 1965).

Kohlberg's Stages of Moral Development.   In building on Piaget's research, Kohlberg identified six closely related **stages of moral development,** which are summarized in Figure 8.8.

stages of
moral
development

Kohlberg contended that individuals proceed from stage to stage, with each stage building on the preceding one. No stage may be skipped, and progression through the stages is not inevitable, he maintained; moral development may be retarded at any stage. Attaining higher levels of moral reasoning requires increasing capability in logical reasoning and perspective taking.

Onset of Stages of Moral Development.   Kohlberg's theory postulates that, as a rule of thumb, the probabilities are that children in the primary grades would be at Stages 1 and 2 and that those in the intermediate grades would be at Stages 2 and 3. Most middle-grade students would be at Stage 3, with some at

FIGURE 8.8   Kohlberg's stages of moral development

	Stage	What Is Right
Stage 1	Heteronomous Morality	To avoid breaking rules; be obedient for its own sake; avoid harm to persons and property
Stage 2	Instrumental Purpose, Exchange	To follow rules when in your interest; do what is fair
Stage 3	Mutual Expectations, Interpersonal Conformity	To measure up to expectations of those you respect; observe the Golden Rule.
Stage 4	Social System, Conscience	To observe the law and rules; contribute to society.
Stage 5	Social Contract	To observe the social contract; evidence respect for core values such as life and liberty.
Stage 6	Universal Ethical Principles	To uphold universal ethical principles: justice, equality of human rights, and respect for individual human dignity.

Source: Adapted from "The Cognitive-Developmental Approach to Moral Education" by L. Kohlberg, 1976, in *Social Studies Strategies: Theory Into Practice* edited by P. H. Martorella, pp. 127–142. Copyright 1976 by L. Kohlberg.

Stage 2 and a few at Stage 4. Most secondary students would be at Stages 3 and 4. Kohlberg maintained that the majority of individuals, both youngsters and adults, typically never advance beyond the third or fourth stages of development.

The Role of Moral Dilemmas in Moral Development. Moral development, according to Kohlberg's theory, is stimulated through confrontations and dialogue concerning moral dilemmas (Kohlberg, 1976). The dilemmas consist of episodes involving matters of right and wrong in which only two courses of action are available. An individual must take a position on one side of the argument or the other, offer reasons for the choice, and entertain the competing position and alternative rationale.

Kohlberg's sample dilemmas were based on traditional ethical issues drawn from moral philosophy. They centered around such matters as fairness, equity, honesty, obedience, observance of laws, and property rights. Each dilemma briefly and clearly framed a simple issue that called for a direct categorical answer.

Neither of the two possible positions regarding a dilemma is considered to be morally preferable or indicates a more advanced stage of moral reasoning. Rather, it is the *type* or *quality* of reasoning that individuals use to defend their positions that indicates which dominant stage of moral development has been reached.

For example, consider the situation where two small children are asked whether it is right to take a dollar from the billfold of a rich man if he is out of the room and cannot see the child taking the money. One child says no, because a promise was made to a parent never to take anything that belonged to someone else. The other child says yes, because the rich man will never know and no punishment will result. Both children reflect only Stage 1 reasoning, as described in Figure 8.8. Neither child reasons beyond the point of obeying an authority or avoiding punishment.

Kohlberg's Critics. Kohlberg's theories have attracted a broad range of criticisms (e.g., Gibbs, 1977; Kurtines & Grief, 1974; Noddings, 1984). Some of the major complaints concern whether his studies truly apply across all cultural groups and both genders. Gilligan (1982), for example, challenged whether males and females have similar moral perspectives.

Other critics have raised serious questions about whether reasoning relating to dilemmas posed in classroom exercises is indicative of how individuals would respond to real moral crises. Still others have challenged the validity of the stages themselves. Cole and Cole (1989) captured the essence of this vein of criticism:

> Despite its comprehensiveness and its ability to inspire research, Kohlberg's theory of moral development has had a somewhat stormy history. . . . Although several studies have confirmed that children progress through Kohlberg's stages of moral reasoning in the predicted order . . . others have failed to support the idea that Kohlberg's stages follow each other in an invariant sequence from lower to higher. Instead of a steady progression upward, subjects sometimes regress in their development or seem to skip a stage. (p. 578)

Alternative Strategies for Moral Education in Public Schools

Between two extreme positions—supporting the modeling of authority figures and encouraging rootlessness—lies an alternative role in moral education for public schools in a pluralistic democracy. This approach rejects the notion that students should be indoctrinated to respond to moral questions with prescribed or consensus answers (see Lickona, 1991). It also rejects the position that students should be taught that one moral course of action is as good as another.

An appropriate moral education program for schools is one that is compatible with the goals of a democratic society (see Doyle, 1997; Kohn, 1997). Such a program engages children in the consideration of realistic moral issues and then provides them with opportunities for dialogue in groups under the guidance of the teacher. In describing such an approach, Damon (1988) observed, "In such groups, the teacher poses the problem and guides the discussion, but the children are encouraged by the peer dialogue to express their own views and to listen to each others' feedback" (pp. 150–151).

Examining Moral Dilemmas in Social Studies.   As noted in the discussion of Kohlberg's views, dilemmas offer a practical and stimulating strategy for initiating moral discourse in social studies classes. Moral dilemmas have always intersected with dramatic and significant events in history. Consider the moral predicament of Herbert Hoover.

As president, he was caught in a terrible dilemma: He believed earnestly that it would be a bad policy for the federal government to give direct help to needy people. Doing so, he believed, would ruin their character and ultimately establish the precedent that they should look to their government for solutions to their problems instead of solving them themselves. At the same time, he saw that the old ways of government were not working, or at least not quickly enough to help many people. All around him he saw the economy collapsing and the poor being crushed.

What should he do? Should he radically change the role of the federal government and intervene to directly help millions of individuals? By his standards, this action would corrupt the character of the people. It also would violate his principles concerning the appropriate role of the government in citizens' lives.

Or should he stick to his guns and let the economic problems run their course? This strategy would preserve for the long run the system that, by his standards, had always served the country well. However, it also would prolong the short-term, acute misery of most Americans. Moreover, it might turn the nation against democracy and capitalism.

We all know which horn of the dilemma Hoover seized. Historians and politicians subsequently have debated for decades the appropriateness of his moral decision.

Although history and current affairs are filled with actual instances of moral dilemmas, fictitious cases are also suitable for framing important moral issues. Consider a moral dilemma that little Willie Doit faces: He once broke his arm while climbing a high wall, and his mother and father made him promise never again to climb in high places without their permission. One day, on his way home from school, Willie sees a small boy who somehow has climbed a tall tree. The little boy is crying because he now is frightened of the height and is too scared to come down.

No one else is in sight. Willie is sure the little boy is going to fall to the pavement because he is so scared. If no one helps the little boy right away, he may be injured seriously. What should Willie do? Should he obey his parents or help the little boy?

Guidelines for Constructing Moral Dilemmas.   Teaching strategies that capitalize on students' natural interest in fundamental issues of right and wrong, like the two presented, focus on competing moral choices. Such approaches help students of all ages develop an ethical framework grounded in reason by engaging them in analyzing, discussing, and taking a stand on realistic dilemmas.

Construction of a moral dilemma includes the following considerations:

1.   The issue should be appropriate for the students' age and interests and should be related to subjects they are studying (e.g., considering, in a unit on laws, whether it is ever appropriate to break a law).

2.   The issue presented should offer students only two basic choices for a decision: Should A or B be done?

3.   Both choices for the dilemma should be likely to attract some support within the class. (If there is no difference of opinion at the outset, it will be difficult to generate discussion.)

4.   The dilemma must involve an issue of what is a just or fair course of action. Right or wrong in the case of a dilemma does not mean factually correct or incorrect.

5.   All of the material used in presenting the dilemma, whether written, oral, or visual, should be succinct and clear. The focus should be clearly on the dilemma and the decisions that are required.

An example of both a dilemma and the related probe questions for use with intermediate-grade students is provided in Figure 8.9.

Guidelines for Presenting and Discussing Moral Dilemmas.   For the presentation and discussion of a dilemma, the following procedures are suggested:

1.   Present the dilemma to students in the form of a handout statement, an oral reading, a role-play scenario, or other media format.

2.   Organize the students into discussion groups and allow them to take a position with respect to the issue raised in the dilemma. Be sure that, in each group, both positions on the issue are represented at the outset.

| FIGURE 8.9 | Moral dilemma activity |

Gladys has waited all week to go to the movies. On Saturday, her parents give her some money so that she can see a special movie in town that will be there only one day. When Gladys gets to the movie theatre, there is already a long line with many children waiting to buy tickets. Gladys takes a place at the end of the line.

All of the sudden, a big wind blows the money out of Gladys's hand. Gladys leaves the line to pick up her money. When she gets back, there are lots more people in line and a new girl named Mary has taken her place. Gladys tells Mary that she had that place and asks Mary to let her back in line. If Mary does not let Gladys in line, Gladys will have to go to the end of the line and there may not be enough tickets left and she won't get a chance to see the movie.

1. Should Mary let Gladys back into the line?
2. Why do you think that is what Mary should do?

Probe Questions:

3. Does it make a difference if Mary doesn't know why Gladys left the line?
4. How does Mary know whether or not Gladys is telling the truth?
5. Why is telling the truth important?
6. Gladys comes back and tells Mary that she left the line to chase after her ticket money which the wind blew out of her hand. Would you let Gladys in line if you were Mary? Why?
7. If Mary is Gladys's friend, should that make a difference? Why?
8. Suppose that instead of the wind blowing the money out of Gladys's hand, Gladys decided to leave the line to get an ice-cream cone. If that is what happened, should Mary let Gladys in line when she comes back?
9. What's the difference between leaving the line to get some ice cream and leaving the line to chase some money?

Source: From *Moral Judgment Interview* by L. Kohlberg, (no date), Cambridge, MA: Harvard University.

3. Use a series of probe questions to follow up the dilemma. When it appears that there is convergence on one point of view, raise questions that force consideration of the other. Act as a devil's advocate to argue whatever position is currently not popular.

4. Keep the focus on the dilemma. It is important to keep students' attention on the issue they are trying to decide. If necessary, arbitrarily eliminate options that might draw students off the hard choice to be made.

5. Encourage the students to try to put themselves in the shoes of all characters in the dilemma.

Social Issues as a Curricular Focus

social issues

As the earlier example of President Hoover's economic dilemma illustrated, engaging students in an analysis of beliefs, attitudes, values, and ethical concerns often intersects with **social issues.** The term often is used loosely in the social studies to apply to any topic that has social implications, addresses social problems, or is controversial (see Olner, 1976). From an instructional perspective, we consider a social issue to be any matter in dispute that affects a sizable group of people and is solvable.

Once a matter is resolved to the satisfaction of most of those involved, the issue ceases to exist. These are somewhat subjective and general criteria for identifying social issues. They leave teachers with wide latitude to select topics for discussion and analysis that are appropriate for the age level and background of their students.

Social issues often are expressed most clearly in the form of questions. Examples are:

- How can we make our neighborhood a safer place to live?
- Should citizens be allowed to choose the school their children will attend?
- How can we rid our neighborhood of crime?
- Where should we locate a new prison?
- How can we provide adequate shelter for all citizens?
- Should murderers be given the death penalty?
- How can we prevent nuclear destruction?
- How can governmental policies more adequately provide equal opportunities for all Americans in such areas as jobs, housing, schooling, and legal justice?

Even young children can be introduced to social issues. Engle and Ochoa (1988) argued that, in grades three and above, in each year children should study in-depth one major social problem. They stated:

> The purpose of the study of social problems is threefold. The first reason is to give young citizens an understanding about major compelling social problems, such as the worldwide environmental crisis. . . .
>
> A second reason . . . is to give students experience in dealing with such problems much as intelligent adults are expected to deal with them. . . .
>
> A third and closely related reason for studying a major social problem each year, rather than at the end of the social studies program, is that such study will emphasize the relevance of other work under progress in the social studies. (p. 142)

Social Issues and Controversy

Teachers should be alerted that the examination of social issues frequently generates controversy in an open society. Johnson and Johnson (1988) defined *con-*

troversy in academic contexts as "conflict that exists when one student's ideas, information, conclusions, theories, and opinions are incompatible with those of another and the two seek to reach an agreement" (p. 59). Controversy is a normal part of life in a democracy. In our society the rights and privileges we share as citizens provide us with the tools to debate or resolve, peacefully and constructively, controversial issues.

The opportunities for controversy result naturally through the normal exercise of our rights and responsibilities. We need not seek them out. Acts as simple as renting our house to whomever we wish or even contracting certain diseases can involve us in controversy.

Students need to accept controversy as a dimension of democracy, rather than always seek to avoid it. Young citizens should be exposed to it early in social studies classes in a form that takes into account their level of maturity and experiences (McBee, 1996). They also should recognize that there are likely to be times in every responsible citizen's life, regardless of age, when he or she creates or is embroiled in controversy.

Guidelines for Handling Discussions of Controversial Issues

A number of guidelines and positions pertain to the treatment of controversial issues in social studies classes (Cox, 1977; Kelly, 1986). The National Council for the Social Studies (NCSS) produced a comprehensive position statement and set of guidelines to aid teachers in handling controversy (NCSS, 1967); included are recommendations that teachers:

Protect the right of students to express and defend opinions without penalty.

Establish with students the ground rules for the study of issues.

Promote the fair representation of different points of view.

Insure that activities do not adversely reflect upon any individual or group because of race, creed, sex, or ethnic origin.

Teach students *how* to think, not *what* to think.

Adhere to written policy concerning academic freedom established by the Board of Education.

Give students full and fair consideration when they take issue with teaching strategies, materials, requirements or evaluation practices.

Exemplify objectivity, demonstrate respect for minority opinion, and recognize the function of dissent. (NCSS, 1967, p. 2)

Teacher Positions on Controversial Issues.   Invariably, at some point in the discussion of controversial issues, students wish to know what the teacher thinks. For a teacher to suggest that he or she had no opinion is silly or dishonest and is likely to puzzle students. If it is important for them to form a position on the issue, why hasn't the teacher done so?

Teachers have several options when such a question arises. They may state their positions at that point or suggest that they have a tentative position but would like to hear all of the students' arguments before making a final decision. Alternatively, they may indicate that they have a position but would rather not state it until the discussion is finished and students have made their own decisions. When teachers really have no opinion because of the nature of the issue, they also should share this fact and the reasons why.

It is important for students to understand that, in a controversy, the positions of those in authority, including that of the teacher, are not necessarily the best or the correct ones. Moreover, in many controversies authority figures (and often "authorities" on the subject of the controversy) take competing positions. The most prudent course for all citizens is to seek out all points of view, to consider the facts, to come to a tentative conclusion, and to keep an open mind to new arguments.

Academic Freedom in the Classroom

In dealing with social issues that may engender controversy, social studies teachers require a high degree of **academic freedom**. "A teacher's academic freedom," the NCSS noted, "is his/her right and responsibility to study, investigate, present, interpret, and discuss all the relevant facts and ideas in the field of his/her professional competence" (NCSS, 1967).

academic freedom

Challenges to Academic Freedom.   Challenges to academic freedom occur when individuals seek to constrain the free and open airing of different points of view in the classroom. This threat arises when either discussions or the use of instructional materials that a teacher considers relevant to the study of an area are curtailed. Basic types of threats to academic freedom in the social studies classroom include:

1. Teacher self-censorship because of fear of criticism or reprisals
2. Prohibitions against using certain individuals or groups as resource persons in the classroom
3. Prohibitions against the study of certain topics, areas, or individuals
4. Selection, alteration, or exclusion of curricular materials in ways that impede free and open inquiry in the classroom

Handling Complaints Concerning Social Studies Materials.   Challenges to a teacher's right to use certain materials, such as a particular trade book, in social studies classes are common threats to academic freedom. When criticisms or challenges surface, it is important for a teacher to distinguish between those that are based on misinformation and those that are attacks on academic freedom. A school or a district should have in place a policy or set of procedures for handling complaints that requires individuals to document the specific details of allegations. All social studies teachers should have a copy.

One element of the school's set of procedures should be a form that those airing complaints are asked to complete and file formally. A sample form, shown in Figure 8.10, has been developed by the NCSS (NCSS, 1967). Contact the NCSS for further information and assistance (<http://www.ncss.org>).

Filing a formal complaint puts an individual or group on record with respect to the specific nature of the complaint, its perceived degree of seriousness, and the desired action. It also forces the critic to actually examine the alleged offensive material, rather than rely on secondhand accounts.

Group Activities

1. Find a case that was decided before the Supreme Court in the past five years that involved First Amendment rights. Discuss the ways in which the case extended or limited personal freedoms.

2. How much freedom do you think a teacher in the elementary grades should have regarding social studies lessons and materials? In the middle grades?

3. In your own community, identify five significant social issues that you believe a concerned citizen should examine and/or become involved in. Develop a rationale for why you think these issues are especially important. Discuss your conclusions.

4. Select some area in which attitudes might be analyzed in an elementary- or middle-grade class. Use one of the topics listed in the chapter or one of your own choosing. Develop an attitude inventory related to the topic you have selected that is appropriate for children in grades 4 through 8. Then identify a class to field test the inventory. Discuss the results and any changes you would make, based on your experiences.

Individual Activities

1. Using the criteria found in the chapter, construct a moral dilemma suitable for use with primary-grade students. Then develop related discussion questions for each.

2. Repeat the previous activity, except create a dilemma suitable for middle-grade students.

3. Construct a value decision sheet, similar to the example in the chapter, for an intermediate-grade class.

4. Select one of the lists of values identified in the chapter and identify a group of fifth-grade students. Explain to the group each of the values and then ask each of the students to arrange the values in order of importance. Ask the students to share their lists and their reasons. Record and evaluate your findings.

| FIGURE 8.10 | Suggested model of a complaint form |

Request for Reconsideration of Social Studies Materials

Type of material (book, film, pamphlet, etc.):

_____

Title of material: _____

Author (if known): _____

Publisher: _____

Date of publication: _____

Request initiated by (name, address, phone number):

_____

_____

_____

Do you have a child in the school concerned? ☐ Yes ☐ No

Complainant represents:

_____ (self)

_____ (organization—name)

_____ (other group—identify)

1. To what in the material do you object? (Please be specific. Cite words, pages, and nature of content.)

2. Why do you object to this material?

3. Are you acquainted with the range of materials being used in the school system on this general topic?

4. Do you approve of presenting a diversity of points of view in the classroom?

5. What would you like your school to do about this material?

   (a) Do not expose or assign it to my child.

   (b) Withdraw it from all students as well as my child.

   (c) Send it back to the appropriate school department for reevaluation.

Signature of Complainant_____

Date: _____

Source: *From Academic Freedom: A Policy Statement* (p. 1) by National Council for the Social Studies, 1967, Washington, DC: Author. © National Council for the Social Studies. Used with permission.

References

ASCD Panel on Moral Education. (1988). Moral education in the life of the school. *Educational Leadership, 45*, 4–8.

Benninga, J. (Ed.). (1991). *Moral, character, and civic education in the elementary school.* New York: Teachers College Press.

Cohen, P. (Spring, 1995). The content of their character. *ASCD Curriculum Update,* 1–8.

Cole, M., & Cole, S. R. (1989). *The development of children.* New York: Scientific American Books.

Cox, C. B. (1977). *The censorship game and how to play it* (Bulletin 50). Washington, DC: National Council for the Social Studies.

Damon, W. (1988). *The moral child.* New York: Free Press.

Donahue, D. M., & Flowers, N. (no date). *Uprooted: Refugees and the United States.* Palo Alto, CA: Educators' Network, Amnesty International USA.

Doyle, D. P. (1997). Education and character: A conservative view. *Phi Delta Kappan, 78,* 440–443.

Engle, S. H. (1977). Comments of Shirley H. Engle. In R. D. Barr, J. L. Barth, & S. S. Shermis (Eds.), *Defining the social studies* (Bulletin 51, pp. 103–105). Washington, DC: National Council for the Social Studies.

Engle, S. H., & Ochoa, A. S. (1988). *Education for democratic citizenship: Decision making in the social studies.* New York: Teachers College Press.

Gibbs, J. (1977). Kohlberg's stages of moral development: A constructive critique. *Harvard Educational Review, 47,* 43–61.

Gilligan, C. (1982). *In a different voice.* Cambridge, MA: Harvard University Press.

Johnson, D. W., & Johnson, R. T. (1988). Critical thinking through structured controversy. *Educational Leadership, 45,* 58–64.

Kelly, T. E. (1986). Discussing controversial issues: Four perspectives on the teacher's role. *Theory and Research in Social Education, 14,* 113–138.

Kohlberg, L. (1976). The cognitive-developmental approach to moral education. In P. H. Martorella (Ed.), *Social studies strategies: Theory into practice* (pp. 127–142). New York: Harper & Row.

Kohlberg, L. et al. (no date). *Moral judgment interview.* Unpublished manuscript, Harvard University, Cambridge, MA.

Kohn, A. (1997). How not to teach values: A critical look at character education. *Phi Delta Kappan, 78,* 429–439.

Kurtines, W., & Grief, E. B. (1974). The development of moral thought: Review and evaluation of Kohlberg's approach. *Psychological Bulletin, 81,* 453–470.

Lickona, T. (1991). *Education for character.* New York: Bantam.

McBee, R. H. (1996). Can controversial topics be taught in the early grades? *Social Education, 60,* 38–41.

National Council for the Social Studies (NCSS). (1967). *Academic freedom: A policy statement.* Washington, DC: Author.

Noddings, N. (1984). *Caring: A feminine approach to ethics and moral education.* Berkeley: University of California Press.

Olner, P. M. (1976). *Teaching elementary social studies.* New York: Harcourt Brace Jovanovich.

Osgood, C. E., Suci, G. J., & Tannenbaum, P. H. (1957). *The measurement of meaning.* Urbana: University of Illinois Press.

Piaget, J. (1965). *The moral judgment of the child* (M. Gabain, Trans.). New York: Free Press.

Rokeach, M. (1968). *Beliefs, attitudes and values: A theory of organization and change.* San Francisco: Jossey-Bass.

Shaver, J. P., & Strong. W. (1976). *Facing value decisions: Rationale-building for teachers.* Belmont, CA: Wadsworth.

Triandis, H. C. (1971). *Attitude and attitude change.* New York: John Wiley.

Chapter

Preparing Children to Live in a Global and Culturally Diverse World

Suddenly *we have to make calls all over the globe—from Croatia to Burma to Haiti—with no safe ideological compass to guide us. We have yet to formulate a clear and reliable answer to a pressing international question: What should be the principles that guide us in intervention abroad—and how can they combine the realism needed for a newly unstable world with the idealism that Americans demand of their statecraft?" (Fukuyama, 1992, p. 24)*

In the preceding quote, writing in the wake of communism's collapse, Fukuyama summarized some of the challenges that face Americans in the post–cold war era. What role should our nation play in the world? In the 21st century, what will be the relationship of the United States to the rest of the world? To what extent is our national identity sacrificed as we become globally interdependent? Will heightened global awareness foster cooperation or breed divisiveness? Will our cultural diversity enrich us or fragment us into competing ethnic enclaves?

The reflective, competent, and concerned citizen of the 21st century increasingly will be confronted with such questions. In answering, citizens will be forced to bal-

ance immediate national interests with those of the world as a whole. As members of an interconnected world, they also must be sensitive to the cultural differences that exist among nations.

Balancing National and Global Concerns

Appeals to citizens to advance our national interests often invoke themes that emphasize *patriotism* (support for your country) and *nationalism* (placing interests of your country above others). In contrast, advocates for a global perspective challenge us to consider "the greatest good for the greatest number" or the concerns of the world as a whole, including those of our nation.

One of the positive aspects of patriotism and nationalism is the creation of a sense of community, of belonging to a larger enterprise and sharing in a collective tradition. We identify with our nation's victories and defeats, pride and shame in such events as the Olympic games, wars, explorations in space, and concern for the environment. Patriotism and nationalism also can be a cohesive force that binds citizens together. These forces can encourage people to work cooperatively, to contribute to the next generation's welfare, and, if necessary, to be willing to sacrifice their lives for the common good.

Extreme patriotism and nationalism, however, can lead to the oppression of dissident minorities and hatred and distrust of other nations. These forces can create barriers to greater understanding across cultures and reduce the opportunities for people to work together to achieve common goals. They also can create an exaggerated sense of superiority, as occurred in Nazi Germany. And, in an era when an increasing number of nations possess both nuclear weapons and unstable political leadership, excessive patriotism and nationalism can threaten the very existence of the world.

In addition to constructively channeled patriotism and nationalism, a heightened level of global awareness in an increasingly interdependent and shrinking world is essential (Anderson, 1991; Tye & Tye, 1992). Potentially, the benefits of increasing global linkages are enormous, including vast economic, cultural, and environmental gains. At the same time, global awareness should reveal our national stake in helping alleviate conditions that require the attention of all nations of the world.

Ramler (1991) stated:

Now, at the edge of the 21st century, all the countries of the world are interconnected in virtually every aspect of life. World markets have been developed [that] offer consumer goods, labor, technology, and energy. The global economy irrevocably ties the economic health of the U.S. to events abroad. Thus, the U.S. must continually redefine its position within the context of global development.

Today the flow of ideas, information, and services is linked globally; and these linkages reach each household and every person. The flow includes the arts, the sciences, sports, medicine, tourism, and entertainment, as well as such unfortunate phenomena as drug traffic, disease, and environmental damage. (p. 44)

Global Education in an Interconnected World

Global concern involves both an understanding of the nature and interdependence of other nations and an interest in their welfare. It also means a willingness to identify and make important decisions that may improve the lot of the world at the expense of an immediate national interest. **Global education,** in turn, refers to the process of engendering global concern in our citizens.

global education

> Global education refers to efforts to cultivate in young people a perspective of the world that emphasizes the interconnections among cultures, species, and the planet. The purpose of global education is to develop in youth the knowledge, skills, and attitudes needed to live effectively in a world possessing limited natural resources and characterized by ethnic diversity, cultural pluralism, and increasing interdependence. (NCSS, 1981, p. 1)

Angell and Avery (1992) emphasized the importance of tying world issues to events and objects within children's immediate environment in global education. One way this can be accomplished is for children to discover linkages between their community and the rest of the world.

Chartock (1991) provided a comprehensive model for how connections can be implemented at any grade level (see Figure 9.1). Chartock identified seven types of links that students and teachers can explore (e.g., ethnic restaurants). To help identify the linkages, students are encouraged to use community members as resources.

Some social studies educators have urged that the entire social studies curriculum adopt a global focus. For example, Kniep (1989) proposed such a program developed around the five themes of *interdependence, change, culture, scarcity,* and *conflict,* and the four categories of persistent problems: *environmental concerns, human rights, peace and security,* and *national/international development.* His ideas are discussed in more detail in Chapter 3.

Peace Education.   A number of organizations have promoted the theme of world peace as a focus for global education. These include Peace Links, Educators for Social Responsibility, the Center for Teaching Peace, the International Center for Cooperation and Conflict Resolution, and the United States Institute of Peace. The concerns of these organizations include teaching children about the ways that wars, violent acts, and general conflicts are initiated and how they can be avoided and controlled. These organizations also seek to acquaint students with the threat of potential nuclear destruction, the effects of warfare, and alternative strategies for maintaining peace and stability throughout the world.

FIGURE 9.1

Local links to developing countries and the world

Are you aware of the links to other countries that exist in your own community? Next to each question, try to identify by name a link in your community that might be useful to your students in their search for knowledge about developing countries and the world. Have your students fill out this questionnaire, too. The individuals identified could be guest speakers or subjects of interviews.

| *Nature of the Link* | *Name* |

A. Community/Family Links

    1. Immigrants living in your town/city?

    2. Family members (related to your students) who come from another country?

    3. People who are familiar with immigrant groups that settled in your area?

    4. Veterans of military service?

B. Education/Recreational Links

    1. Faculty in schools/colleges in your area who come from another country?

    2. Students who come from another country?

    3. Students/faculty who have traveled to other countries?

    4. Teams that have players from other countries?

    5. Teams that have traveled to other countries to play?

    6. Peace Corps returnees?

C. Environmental Links

    1. Experts who can discuss global/local environmental problems such as pollution or acid rain?

D. Business/Trade/Industrial Links

    1. Small businesses that import goods (gift shops, for example)?

FIGURE 9.1 *(Continued)*

Nature of the Link	Name

2. Large businesses that import/export goods (factories, for example)?

3. Banks?

4. Ethnic restaurants?

5. Rotary Club exchanges?

E. Religious/Social Links

1. World religions in your community?

2. Church/synagogue organizations with links to other countries?

3. Festivals that celebrate origins?

4. Organizations attempting to solve local problems related to hunger, homeless-ness, and refugee placement?

F. Medical Links

1. Hospitals with doctors/nurses from other countries?

2. Experts on global diseases (AIDS, for example)?

3. Experts on good/bad drugs coming in and going out of this country?

4. Experts familiar with population issues?

G. Cultural Links

1. Visiting artists/performers in your com-munity?

2. Museums with exhibits from other countries?

3. Plays/films from other countries?

4. Musical groups from other countries?

5. Sister City visitors?

Some agencies also produce curriculum materials for the elementary and middle grades. An example of a program to use in teaching elementary children how to seek and appreciate the utility of peaceful resolutions of conflict is *Teaching Students to Be Peacemakers* (Johnson & Johnson, 1991). The program involves 30 days of training, 30 minutes each day, to teach students negotiating and mediating skills. After the training, students have an opportunity to actually apply their skills to dealing with conflict situations in the classroom or on the playground.

As an illustration, each day two students serve as mediators. They adjudicate a fair solution to conflicts that students cannot resolve themselves. Students also have the opportunity to consider how their learning can be generalized to conflicts outside the school, including those among nations.

Some other materials and programs that have been developed for peace education, along with their sources, are listed here:

- J. McGinnis and K. McGinnis, *Education for Peace and Justice: A Manual for Teachers*, 4 vols. St. Louis, MO: The Institute for Peace and Justice, 2747 Rutger Street, St. Louis, MO 63104.

- S. Judson, Ed., *A Manual on Nonviolence and Children.* Philadelphia: New Society Publishers, 4722 Baltimore Avenue, Philadelphia, PA 19143.

- D. Woollcombe, *Peace Child: A Study Guide for Schools.* Washington, DC: The Peace Child Foundation, P. O. Box 33168, Washington, DC 20033.

- G. C. Abrams and F. C. Schmidt, *Peace Is in Our Hands.* Philadelphia: Jane Addams Peace Association, 1213 Race Street, Philadelphia, PA 19107.

- Educators for Social Responsibility, *Perspectives: A Teaching Guide to Concepts of Peace.* Cambridge, MA: Educators for Social Responsibility, 23 Garden Street, Cambridge, MA 02138.

Multicultural Education

Each day's wave of current events reinforces our awareness that our globally interdependent world is a melange of people of different colors, religions, languages, and customs. Our own nation is a microcosm of this diversity. Learning about these patterns of humanity and their social, political, and economic implications is the essence of **multicultural education.** "Multiculturalism is based on the idea of 'multiple perspectives'——that there is more than one way to view and understand an event, an idea, or an era" (Singer, 1994, p. 286).

multicultural education

Multicultural education has special significance for our nation because of our rich mix of racial and ethnic groups. In addition, multicultural education intersects with the major themes in our history and our abiding national commitment to equity in the treatment of citizens.

In the past half-century, the move for equity for all racial and ethnic groups in our society received a dramatic impetus from the civil rights struggles of the

1950s and 1960s and the attendant legislation and judicial rulings that they spawned. The wave of moral indignation and political restructuring generated by the succession of historic, often tragic, events that came to be known as the civil rights movement forced the nation to attack the roots of racism.

What began as a series of concrete, dramatic steps by a few brave individuals on behalf of fundamental justice for blacks, by the decade of the 1980s had blossomed into an international outcry on behalf of people and groups everywhere who suffered oppression or injustice at the hands of those in power. In the United States this outcry included an introspective analysis of the treatment of ethnic groups that had suffered dramatically, consistently, and extensively from racism, such as Native Americans, Hispanic Americans, Latino Americans, and Asian Americans, as well as African Americans.

The outcry also forced an examination of our treatment of ethnic and religious minorities in general. By the close of the decade, American ideals were globalized into a passion for social justice for all human beings and an increasing sensitivity for the rights of minorities across the world. Apartheid in South Africa and the treatment of Palestinians in the Middle East, for example, became hotly debated political issues in our nation. The amorphous mass of displaced Americans, the homeless, and the homeless of the world, upwards of 16 million refugees who have neither home nor country, became part of the American political agenda.

In the 1990s, in the wake of the dissolution of the Soviet Union, the reorganization of Eastern Europe, ethnic violence throughout the world, and the end of the cold war, came a renewed pragmatic urgency to our efforts for multicultural understanding. There also are increasing global political and economic reasons for our schools to emphasize multicultural education. As Sobol (1990) underscored: "We live in a small and multicultural world. If we wish to communicate effectively with the majority of the world's people—who are not white and who don't speak English—we must know more about how they see the world, how they make sense of experience, why they behave as they do" (p. 28).

Consider the cross-cultural transaction reported by Gollnick and Chinn (1994, pp. 342–343), involving a fourth-grade teacher and her class and religious dietary attitudes. How would you handle the incident and the related discussion? In thousands of classes daily across the United States, similar encounters and opportunities for multicultural education occur.

Religious Dietary Attitudes

Allison Beller is a fourth-grade teacher in a suburban school district. The community is primarily middle class. The children come from diverse ethnic and religious backgrounds. Part of her curriculum includes some basic lessons in cooking. Today's lesson involves the preparation of hamburgers. Beller is aware that one of the children is a vegetarian and that two others do not eat red meat. She has prepared burgers with ground turkey for two students and substituted what she felt was an appropriate alternative for the vegetarian child.

Beller is stunned, therefore, when the vegetarian child states before the class that eating hamburger is wrong and sinful. "My daddy says that hamburgers come from the cows that are killed and it is wrong to kill cows or anything else. He says that if you eat the hamburgers, you are as bad as the people who killed the cow."

The other children in the class are also shocked at the accusation and sit in their places speechless.

Sensitizing students to the rich American tradition of cultural pluralism and its implications is a fundamental part of the process of multicultural education. As Bennett (1986) observed:

> A basic assumption of multicultural education is that different ethnic groups can retain much of their original culture if they so choose, and can be multicultural at the same time. In other words, it is believed that people can learn about multiple ways of perceiving, behaving, and evaluating so that they can conform to those aspects of the macroculture that are necessary for societal well-being, without eroding acceptance of their original ethnicity. It is assumed that ethnic traditions and beliefs can be preserved under conditions of intercultural contact that will reduce myths and stereotypes associated with previously unknown groups. These are big assumptions. (p. 56)

Banks (1984) has contended that, in its role of supporting cultural pluralism and promoting multicultural education, the school should "help students to break out of their cultural enclaves and to broaden their cultural perspectives. Students need to learn that there are cultural and ethnic alternatives within our society that they can freely embrace" (p. 9). He observed further: "The major

Our classrooms reflect the diversity of our nation.

goal of multicultural education is to change the total educational environment so that it promotes a respect for the wide range of cultural groups and enables all cultural groups to experience equal educational opportunity" (p. 23).

What multicultural education advocates have proposed requires an ongoing commitment on the part of all teachers and schools, as well as key actors—such as parents—in the social environment beyond the school. Many skills associated with multicultural education are developed slowly over time. Some, such as perspective taking, are acquired only when students reach the appropriate developmental stage. And all are affected by the training received in the home and experiences outside of the school.

Even preschoolers learn from their home and neighborhood environment to imitate and promote attitudes of tolerance and intolerance, appreciation and rejection of individuals and groups that are culturally different (Byrnes, 1987; King, 1990). Byrnes (1988) has warned that, for example, in some families: "Children may be told that people belonging to certain minority groups will kidnap them or hurt them if they aren't careful. Some children are scolded or even beaten if they play with children of different races, religions, or socioeconomic status" (p. 268).

Emerging Issues in Multicultural Education

Is there such a thing as "an American culture"? To some extent, we all share in an amorphous cultural framework that makes us "American" (Spindler & Spindler, 1990). In addition, we have potential points of cultural reference, should we care to use them, that allow us to distinguish ourselves from the larger cultural American framework. We may choose to identify with one or more subcultures that are distinguished by distinctive ways of acting, thinking, and feeling (Kleg, 1993).

Cultural groups that are identified by ethnicity (e.g., *ethnic groups)* view themselves as belonging together and gaining identification by virtue of their ancestry, real or imagined, and common customs, traditions, or experiences, such as language, history, religion, or nationality. Individuals often use the terms *cultural* or *ethnic* interchangeably in referring to themselves and others. Because many of the groups in our nation prize those distinguishing characteristics that give rise to their individuality, we regard our nation as being **culturally pluralistic,** or *multicultural.*

cultural pluralism

The key issue in multicultural education for many is: How can we celebrate the richness and uniqueness of our diversity and the multiple perspectives that differing groups offer, while at the same time stress the common bonds that unite and strengthen our nation politically, economically, and socially? The impassioned debate that continues over this issue touches on many areas (Banks, 1991; Bullard, 1992; Martel, 1992; Ogbu, 1992; Ravitch, 1992), and the fallout has implications for how the textbooks, instructional materials, and curricula in schools will be shaped in the future.

The debate includes disagreements over such matters as the language that is used to label groups, the factual accuracy of the existing alternative historical perspectives (e.g., Eurocentric vs. Afrocentric), whose perspectives should be represented, and which perspective should be the dominant or mainstream one. The debate also has taken on a note of urgency. As Banks (1992, p. 33) noted, "People of color, women, and other marginalized groups are demanding that their voices, visions, and perspectives be included in the curriculum."

Multicultural Perspectives in Instruction

Addressing the issues of perspectives is crucial to multicultural understanding and, in fact, to an informed analysis of all social data. For example, in his seminal text, *Red, White, and Black: The Peoples of Early America*, Nash (1982) argued that:

> [T]o cure the historical amnesia that has blotted out so much of our past we must reexamine American history as the interactions of many peoples from a wide range of cultural backgrounds over a period of many centuries. . . . Africans were not merely enslaved. Indians were not merely driven from the land. . . .
>
> To break through the notions of Indians and Africans being kneaded like dough according to the whims of invading European societies, we must abandon the notion of "civilized" and "primitive" people. . . .
>
> Africans, Indians, and Europeans all had developed [cultures] that functioned successfully in their respective environments. None thought of themselves as inferior people. (pp. 2–3)

Similar to Nash, Benitez (1994) had advocated that teachers employ an "alternative perspectives approach" in teaching history. "With this approach," she wrote,

> the teacher presents historical events from alternative, i.e., non-male, non-Judaeo-Christian, or non-Northwestern European, perspectives. . . . The following are examples using this approach:
>
> - **Pre-colonial.** Discuss the concept of discovery with the students. Point out that Asians immigrated via Alaska and that more than 500 native cultures thrived before the Europeans landed in North America.
> - **Colonial.** Point out that the Spanish colonized more than one-third of the present United States, including Florida, Louisiana, Texas, New Mexico, Arizona, and California, and that some Spanish settlements preceded British settlements by almost a century. . . .
> - **Seventeenth century through today.** Review the history of European settlements in North America from the perspective of the mainland American Indian. Ask students to write about or discuss how they would feel as an American Indian at several different historical junctures and vis-à-vis different groups of Europeans, taking into account the changing perceptions American Indians had of the white newcomers. Then ask students to write an essay entitled "The Invasion from the East" from the perspective of an American Indian. (p. 143)

Merryfield and Remy (1995) have emphasized the importance of involving students in firsthand experiences with people from different cultures as a way to gain insights into their perspectives. Samples of the strategies the authors advocate are:

Students practice active listening by interviewing people from another culture.

Example: Students interview a Vietnamese immigrant about his perspectives on refugees and political asylum.

Students work cooperatively with people from another culture toward common goals.

Example: Students work with employees from a local Honda plant to develop a video on "cross-cultural understanding and economic cooperation." . . .

Students are immersed in another culture.

Example: Students raise money and plan a study tour to visit rainforests in Costa Rica. (Source: Merryfield & Remy, 1995)

Naylor and Smith (1993) suggested that "holidays offer excellent opportunities for increasing children's understanding and appreciation of cultural diversity." The authors suggest several activities, such as the one in Figure 9.2, that are appropriate for primary- and intermediate-grade children.

Henderson (1992) offered an apt illustration of how Ms. Smiley, a middle-grade teacher, reflectively brought a multicultural education perspective to her planning and development of a social studies lesson (see Figure 9.3).

In a similar vein, Banks (1993) has suggested that in social studies classes multicultural education might be advanced by including five different perspectives that represent different sources of information (see Figure 9.4). Each perspective offers students a different insight from which to construct a more informed grasp of an historical event. Chapter 4 includes an illustration of how these five perspectives could be incorporated into a unit dealing with the Westward Movement.

In another example, in Figure 9.5, we have a lesson that offers primary children an insight into Navajo cultural perspectives.

FIGURE 9.2

Learning about holiday symbols and traditions in the primary grades

Source: From "Holidays, Cultural Diversity, and the Public Culture" by D. T. Naylor and B. D. Smith, 1993, *Social Studies and the Young Learner, 6*, pp. S3–S4.

Holiday Symbols and Traditions

Symbols and traditions provide recognition, meaning, and common experiences for holidays. Children are often familiar with symbols and traditions associated with commonly celebrated holidays. This familiarity can lead to an exploration of the nature and role of symbols and traditions and the variations in holiday symbols and traditions associated with groups within and across nations.

Suggested Activities:

1. A *card-matching exercise for primary children.* Put the name of a holiday on one card and symbols associated with it on one or more other cards. Then have children match the holidays and their symbols. Examples include: Easter—cross, colored eggs, rabbit; Thanksgiving—turkey, Pilgrim's hat.

Sample multicultural lesson

Source: From *Reflective Teaching: Becoming an Inquiring Educator* (p. 7) by J. G. Henderson, 1992, New York: Macmillan.

As she [Ms. Smiley] plans her unit on Columbus, she looks for materials that help her critically examine the topic. She reads Kirkpatrick Sale's *The Conquest of Paradise: Christopher Columbus and the Columbian Legacy* . . . [New York, Knopf, 1990], which questions Columbus' motives and ecological values. Based on this examination, she decides to include activities that will broaden her students' multicultural perspectives. She shows students a segment of an old cowboy movie in which Native Americans are portrayed as savages. Then she asks students to list adjectives that express how they feel about Native Americans. While teaching the unit, Ms. Smiley will present information from the Native American as well as the European point of view. When the students have completed the unit, she will ask them to make another list of adjectives expressing how they feel about Native Americans. She will analyze and discuss any differences between the two lists with her students.

FIGURE 9.4   A multiperspective approach to multicultural education

Perspective	Source of Information
Personal/Cultural	Students' personal and cultural experiences
Popular	Mass media, pop culture, and films
Mainstream Academic	Research from mainstream scholars
Transformative Academic	Research that challenges mainstream findings and/or methodologies
School	Information in school texts and related media

Source: From "The Canon Debate, Knowledge Construction, and Multicultural Education" by J. Banks, June-July 1993, *Educational Researcher*, pp. 4–14.

FIGURE 9.5   Focus on Native Americans

Lesson Plan

TEACHING ABOUT NATIVE AMERICANS: A SAMPLE LESSON PLAN

Grade Level: Primary to Intermediate (Grades 3 and 4)

Basic Concepts: Culture and diversity

Organizing Generalization: An individual's culture strongly influences his or her behavior and values.

Culture Area: Southwest Region

Time Period: Post-European Contact to 1990

Background:

In the study of the Navajo, students have learned about such things as traditional hogans, sheep herding, and artwork, including weaving. They have also studied the physical beliefs of the Navajo. The wonderful story of *Annie and the Old One* (Miles 1971) will help link these cultural elements to the real world of the Navajo children and Navajo values, behavior, and way of life.

Objectives:

Knowledge (Content): Students will

1. state in their own words why they believe Annie acted as she did. Their discussion should reflect an awareness of her love for her grandmother, her reluctance to face her grandmother's impending death, her developing understanding of the Navajo belief in the circle of life, and her subsequent change in behavior;

2. relate Annie's family and feelings for them to their own families and experiences; and

3. discuss the relationship between values and behavior, and give some examples from their own lives.

Skills: Students will

1. practice making inferences—"Why was the weaving stick important to Annie and her grandmother?"

Values (Organic): Students will

1. gain understanding and appreciation of another culture's beliefs regarding death; and

2. begin to understand that behavior, including their own, is related to values and that their way of life (culture) helps to determine their values and their behavior.

Activities:

1. Read aloud *Annie and the Old One* (Miles 1971).

2. Class discussion:

   a. "Annie's Navajo world was good" (3). What do we already know about Annie's Navajo world? Answers are likely to be related to environment,

FIGURE 9.5 (Continued)

family, and ways of life. Illustrations in the book are excellent and will help students understand the relationship between the environment and way of life. Solicit ideas about what Navajo people believe is important. The story gives examples of the importance of some items (weaving stick, sheep, etc.), people, and basic belief systems.

b. Give some examples of how Annie was trying to keep her mother from finishing the rug.

c. Why was Annie trying to keep her mother from finishing the rug? Discuss the following statements:

- "My children, when the new rug is taken from the loom, I will go to Mother Earth."

- "Your grandmother is one of those who lives in harmony with all nature—with earth, coyote, birds in the sky. They know more than many will ever learn. Those Old Ones know."

d. Navajo people believe in the circle of life. Discuss the following statements:

- "The sun comes up from the edge of earth in the morning. It returns to the edge of earth in the evening. Earth, from which good things come for the living creatures on it. Earth, to which all creatures finally go."

- "The sun rose but it also set." "The cactus did not bloom forever." "She would always be a part of the earth, just as her grandmother had always been, just as her grandmother would always be, always and forever."

e. What does this mean, ". . . Annie was breathless with the wonder of it"?

f. How did Annie's behavior change? Why?

g. Can you think of any beliefs that you and your family have that help you decide how to act? The teacher should record these ideas on a chart or chalkboard.

h. Encourage students to summarize, in their own words, the relationship between culture, values, and behavior.

EXTENSION

Depending on the focus and length of the unit of study, the teacher might want to extend this lesson to helping students understand the behavior of Native American people in other historical periods.

Evaluation:

Students will be able to state the generalization in their own words.

Materials and Resources:

Miles, M. *Annie and the Old One*. Boston, Mass.: Little, Brown and Company, 1971.

Navajo rug, model of a Navajo loom, and weaving stick, if possible.

Source: From "Teaching About Native Americans: A Sample Lesson" by K. D. Harvey, L. D. Harjo, and J. K. Jackson, 1990, *Teaching About Native Americans* (Bulletin 84), p. 7. Washington, DC: National Council for the Social Sciences. © 1990 National Council for the Social Sciences. Used with permission.

Designing Strategies for Multicultural Education

Experiences that effective multicultural education programs might provide for students include:

1. Learning how and where to obtain objective, accurate information about diverse cultural groups
2. Identifying and examining positive accounts of diverse cultural groups or individuals
3. Learning tolerance for diversity through experimentation in the school and classroom with alternative customs and practices
4. Encountering, where possible, firsthand positive experiences with diverse cultural groups
5. Developing empathic behavior (trying to put yourself in the shoes of a person from a different cultural group) through role-playing and simulations
6. Practicing using "perspective glasses"—that is, looking at an event, historical period, or issue through the perspective of another cultural group or gender
7. Improving the self-esteem of all students
8. Identifying and analyzing cultural stereotypes
9. Identifying concrete cases of discrimination and prejudice taken from children's daily lives

These nine types of experiences all aim to heighten students' awareness of the diversity among us, while respecting their own cultural anchors.

Guidelines for Selecting Appropriate Curriculum Materials for Multicultural Education

As they observe and participate in the evolving debates concerning the most appropriate forms of multicultural education, teachers should consider several general propositions. These may prove helpful in identifying and examining subject matter and working with students:

1. All historical accounts are only selective representations of an event, and they reflect the background or perspective of the recorder.
2. Obtaining a variety of perspectives on an event often extends our understanding of it. Each perspective may provide information the others missed or dismissed as unimportant. Depending on our objective and the issue, one perspective also may be more helpful than another.
3. Often multiple perspectives of an event are directly contradictory. In that event, we must judge which is the most informed or reliable.

4. For many issues, we may not have access to all of the different perspectives that exist. For others, the perspectives we would like to have do not exist or have not been discovered.

5. Regardless of which perspectives are obtained and whether they are shared in oral or written form, we should hold them to the standards of the best available scholarship.

To aid in the selection of multicultural curriculum materials, a number of detailed guidelines are available. As an example, Etlin (1988) provided a basic five-point checklist for teachers to consider in assessing the appropriateness of multicultural materials.

1. Does the text or other items [instructional material] give proportionate coverage to our country's different ethnic groups?
2. Does it present them in the variety of roles and situations that all our country's people deal with, rather than limit them to one or two stereotypical contexts?
3. Does it present stories and historical incidents from the point of view of the people concerned, whatever their ethnic group, rather than that of the traditional single-culture U.S. society?
4. Does it use language that recognizes the dignity of the groups involved, not using demeaning slang terms? Does it avoid using dialect unless it's presented respectfully and serves a necessary purpose?
5. If it's fiction or a reader, does the story line avoid distributing power and competence on the basis of ethnic group stereotypes? (p. 11)

The National Council for the Social Studies (NCSS) also has published a more extensive set of guidelines for multicultural education: *Curriculum Guidelines for Multicultural Education* (NCSS, 1992). The document provides 23 categories of guidelines for evaluating a school's program, along with a rating form. The NCSS guidelines also develop a rationale for multicultural education.

Resources for Multicultural Education

A fine assortment of instructional materials is available to aid teachers in dealing with multicultural issues. For example, Byrnes (1988) identified three plays that can help sensitize elementary students to prejudice and discrimination:

● *Escape to Freedom: A Play About Young Frederick Douglass* (Davis, 1978)
● *Maria Theresa* (Atkinson, 1979)
● *Don't Ride the Bus on Monday: The Rosa Parks Story* (Meriwether, 1973)

The references at the end of the chapter also include a number of books that contain lists of student materials, organizations that provide resources, and reference materials and periodicals for teachers. Many organizations, including the NCSS, provide collections of written materials and media, which are updated periodically. The NCSS, for example, each year in the April/May issue of *Social Education* publishes a list of notable children's trade books that includes a selection of works with multicultural themes. *Instructor* magazine similarly periodically publishes reviews of related children's books.

Examples of materials and organizations that provide resources for multicultural education follow:

Instructional Materials

Building Ethnic Collections: An Annotated Guide for
*   School Media Centers and Public Libraries*
Libraries Unlimited
P.O. Box 263
Littleton, CO 80160

Ethnic American Minorities: A Guide to Media and Materials
R. R. Bowker
P.O. Box 1807
Ann Arbor, MI 48106

Materials and Resources for Teaching Ethnic Studies:
*   An Annotated Bibliography*
Social Science Education Consortium
855 Broadway
Boulder, CO 80302

Our Family, Our Friends, Our World: An Annotated Guide to Significant
*   Multicultural Books for Children and Teenagers*
R. R. Bowker
121 Chanlon Road
New Providence, NJ 07974

Multicultural Perspectives in Music Education
Music Educators National Conference
1902 Association Drive
Reston, VA 22091

Organizations

Afro-Am Educational Materials
809 Wabash Avenue
Chicago, IL 60605

The Anti-Defamation League of B'nai B'rith
823 United Nations Plaza
New York, NY 10017

Asia Society
469 Union Avenue
Westbury, NY 11590

Asian/Pacific American Heritage Council
Box 11036
Alexandria, VA 22312

Council for Indian Education
517 Rim Rock Road
P.O. Box 31215
Billings, MT 59107

Council on Interracial Books for Children
1841 Broadway
New York, NY 10023

Stanford Program on International and Cross-Cultural Education
Littlefield Center, Room 14
Stanford University
Stanford, CA 94305-5013

National Council of La Raza
1725 Eye Street, N.W.
Washington, DC 20006

Gender Issues and Sex-Role Stereotypes

Multicultural education embraces the analysis of gender issues (King, 1990). As a reflection of the broader social ferment concerning equity for all groups within our society, discrimination on the basis of gender has come under increasing attack. **Sex-role stereotypes** are one aspect of gender issues. Such stereotyping includes attributing roles, behaviors, and aspirations to individuals or groups solely on the basis of gender.

sex-role stereotypes

Discrimination based on gender may surface in any number of ways in school contexts. It may occur, for example, through teachers' patterns of activity assignments, group placements, content of compliments and criticisms, and types of behavior tolerated. Examples range from the treatment of females in textbooks and curriculum materials (e.g., women are absent from historical periods or have stereotyped roles), to differential treatment of males and females in the classroom (e.g., girls are asked to bake the cookies for the party, and the boys to set up the tables), to erroneous assumptions about attitudes and cognitive abilities (e.g., girls are assumed to be more emotional than boys), to institutional practices that appear to favor one gender over another (e.g., males are favored over females for administrative positions).

Probably one of the most effective ways for teachers to combat any sex-role stereotyping that occurs in instructional materials, textbooks, and the mass media is to challenge it directly. Teachers first can sensitize students to its presence and then examine analytically factual bases and counterexamples. This approach can have the residual effect of alerting students to stereotypes of all varieties, including those that are racial, ethnic, or political.

Another strategy is to provide students with curriculum materials that reflect the perspectives, contributions, and achievements of women. A case in point is *The Gentle Tamers*, by Dee Brown (1981), which contains firsthand accounts of women who helped build the West. Included are stories from the accounts of Elizabeth Custer, Carry Nation, Virginia Reed, and Josephine Meeker.

Women's Perspectives in History

As a special effort to redress the relative absence of women and their contributions and perspectives in written history, the field of women's history has developed (see sample activity in Figure 9.6). Underscoring the neglect of women in the history of our nation, the Congress, in declaring March Women's History Month, wrote:

> American women of every race, class, and ethnic background helped found the Nation in countless recorded and unrecorded ways as servants, slaves, nurses, nuns, homemakers, industrial workers, teachers, reformers, soldiers, and pioneers; and . . . served as early leaders in the forefront of every major progressive social change movement, not only to secure their own right of suffrage and equal opportunity, but also in the abolitionist movement, the emancipation movement, the industrial labor union movement, and the modern civil rights movement; and . . . despite these contributions, the role of American women in history has been consistently overlooked and undervalued in the body of American history.

The National Women's History Project (P.O. Box 3716, 77838 Bell Road, Windsor, CA 95492-8515) and the Upper Midwest Women's History Center (6300 Walker Street, St. Louis Park, MN 55416) are examples of attempts to expand the focus of traditional history. These two organizations provide a woman's perspective on historical events, as well as information concerning the vital roles that women have played in history. Both projects have produced an array of curriculum materials for K through 12 social studies classes. These include biographies, videos, posters units, photographs, and reference books. An example of one set of materials published by the Upper Midwest Center for elementary students is shown in Figure 9.7.

Social Consciousness and Social Action

A frequent result of children's increased awareness of global and multicultural issues is a developing sense of **social consciousness,** an awareness that citizens have both a right and a responsibility to identify and redress some social needs—in short, to help build a better world.

**social
consciousness**

FIGURE 9.6   Focus on women's history

Women's History in the "Attic Trunk"

The old attic trunk has always been a source of fascination to those who discover it and the treasures it holds. The attic trunk can be explored in the classroom, too. It is a particularly useful method to introduce students to women's history of a particular era. An attic trunk from the decade of the twenties, for example, can be easily assembled to form hypotheses about the changing status of women in that decade.

The "attic trunk" for the twenties that I have constructed is a sturdy cardboard box with a hinged top covered with woodgrain-design contact paper. Although some items that I included are of general interest about the era, others relate specifically to women. The trunk is recognizable as a woman's possession. It contains original artifacts, women's accessories, and photocopies of other items, including historical documents that pertain to issues directly affecting women of the decade. Among the items and documents that I have been able to find or borrow are the following:

- High school and college yearbooks, 1923–1929
- Photocopies of John Held "flapper" drawings
- A fringed, satin flapper dress (a costume that I had made)
- Actual photographs from the era (my family's, which included family scenes, such as my grandparents and their three small children posed by the family car)
- Photocopies of magazine advertising, with emphasis on those ads directed toward women, from Blue Moon silk stockings to electrical appliances to automobiles to cigarettes and cosmetics
- An actual dress, purse, and other accessories from the period, borrowed from another teacher
- *Good Housekeeping,* April 1920, article supporting the Sheppard Towner Maternity Bill
- Principles of the National Birth Control League
- Editorial cartoons protesting restrictions on birth control
- Declaration of Principles of the National Women's Party, 1922
- Copy of the 1922 proposed ERA
- *Good Housekeeping,* September 1925, containing articles debating labor laws for women
- Any popular magazine article debating ERA in the twenties

Other teachers need not limit themselves to these examples.

Source: From "Women's History in the 'Attic Trunk'" by L. J. Barnes, 1988, in *Teaching American History: New Directions,* edited by M. T. Downey, p. 18. © National Council for the Social Studies. Used with permission.

| FIGURE 9.7 | Curriculum materials for students |

A Social History Describes Six United States Women

Curriculum Packet for K–8

By Sheila C. Robertson, Kathleen A. O'Brien, and K. G. Woods

Complete units on six non-famous real American women from the 19th and 20th centuries. Written on several reading comprehension levels, the unit includes six posters, concept definitions, biographies, historical lessons, and time lines.

Mary Longley Riggs

Worked among the Dakotas as educator and missionary. Mother of eight.

Mathilda Tolksdorf Shillock

German emigrant—wife, mother, homemaker, letter writer, and musician.

Caroline Seabury

Massachusetts native who taught in Mississippi before the Civil War. Kept a diary of her impressions of slavery and experiences during the Civil War.

Theresa Ericksen

Norwegian emigrant who served as a military nurse during the Spanish American War, Philippine Insurrection, and World War I.

Linda James Benitt

Farmer, public health official, member of the New Deal's Agricultural Adjustment Administration (AAA).

Ethyl Ray Nance

Woman of color who joined the Harlem Renaissance in New York, nursed an ailing mother, experienced discrimination, became a policewoman, and worked with the NAACP.

Source: From *Upper Midwest Women's History Center Collection, 1993* (p. 10) by Upper Midwest Women's History Center, 1993, St. Louis Park, MN: Author. Copyright 1993 by Upper Midwest Women's History Center. Reprinted by permission.

Social consciousness may be directed toward whatever can be changed easily and that will have minimal impact on society. It also can be focused on whatever requires complex changes and whose alterations will have far-reaching consequences. Ultimately social consciousness also breeds social responsibility.

Citizens of any age exhibit consciousness of social issues when they decide that something in their society requires redress. Social consciousness can be developed early in children. Berman (1990) suggested that teachers begin to engage young children in discussions about their relationship to society by first having them construct drawings representing how they view these relationships. A kindergarten child, for example, who draws a picture of the school playground showing litter and graffiti displays one level of social consciousness.

In a democracy each citizen is relatively free to identify the social issues he or she wishes to address. In developing concerned citizens, teachers have the responsibility to encourage youngsters of all ages to identify areas of social need and the corresponding strategies for change. This encouragement requires giving children "the opportunity to contribute to the lives of others and to the improvement of the world around them" (Berman, 1990, p. 78).

The general message a child should derive from activities that encourage social consciousness is: For a society to prosper and improve, citizens must in some way give, as well as receive; "Through citizenship, we receive a number of privileges as our birthright. At the same time, we also inherit the reciprocal responsibility to make some continuing contribution to our society."

Social Service Projects

**social service
projects**

An illustration of what an individual school can do to promote social consciousness and responsibility is a project implemented by the Ravenscroft School in Raleigh, North Carolina. Ravenscroft School has made social service part of the required curriculum.

Each month, students in the middle grades engage in social service activities such as recycling, making sandwiches for a local soup kitchen, visiting the elderly, collecting toys and clothes for the needy, and spending time with disabled students from other schools. Teachers then build on the experiences and reflections of students and encourage them to do follow-up research on such subjects as the causes of poverty.

Other schools and consortia of schools across the United States are engaged in similar curricular efforts to encourage the development of social responsibility (Lewis, 1991). In 1992 Maryland, the first state to make community service a requirement for graduation, passed a law that requires all students in the middle and high school grades to perform 75 hours of service in their communities.

Examples of social action projects that teachers and elementary youngsters have developed follow:

- A middle-school group formed a club to help the elderly in their neighborhood.
- A group of fourth graders collected food and clothing for hurricane victims.
- A sixth-grade class painted a mural on the wall of an abandoned house to cover up graffiti.
- First-grade students put on a play for a group in a nursing home.
- An elementary school helped raise funds for a family in distress.
- A primary class volunteered to clean up a littered area in the neighborhood.
- Individual students in a middle school visited shut-ins who wanted company.

Current Affairs

Engaging students in significant current affairs discussions invariably involves some aspects of global education, multicultural education, or social consciousness. By guiding students through an analysis and interpretation of the "news" as reported by the media, teachers can use current events as vehicles to address significant curricular objectives.

Our children live in a society that is inundated with current affairs information through the popular media, especially television. No matter where one lives in the United States (or elsewhere in the world, for that matter), it is possible to access televised news throughout the day by cable, satellite, or antenna reception. The various print media similarly afford us multiple opportunities to learn about current affairs.

Introducing Young Children to Current Affairs

"But they're too young to be exposed to all that stuff." Sound familiar? Some have argued that young children should be sheltered from, or at least not alerted to, many of the unpleasant events that often dominate the news. If such a position ever were tenable, the growth of television and a highly mobile society has made it impossible to hold. From their earliest years, American children have had the rest of the world, including outer space, brought to their cribs. In one evening they can encounter poverty, violence, murder, intolerance, injustice, hatred, deception, and dishonesty, to name but a few ills in the world that a typical evening of television-watching may present.

As teachers we cannot and should not try to shield children from the real world that they must confront as citizens. Rather, we should try to help them make some sense of the often frightening and confusing social phenomena around them as soon as they enter school. Involving children in current affairs also is part of preparing them to be effective citizens. For example, Passe (1988) concluded that children's study of current affairs will make them more likely as adults to be inquisitive about social issues.

Strategies for Analyzing Current Affairs

It's Friday. Time for current events!

Too often it happens that a certain day—usually the first or last of the week—is set aside in classrooms for "current events." When this practice occurs, students gain the impression that contemporary affairs are not an ongoing, vital part of everyday life. Rather, they are viewed as just another special subject—like art and music—scheduled into the curriculum once a week.

When current affairs have special significance for the local community, the nation, or the world, they also should be allowed to take precedence over the regularly scheduled subject matter. As an example, on the day after presidential elections, children ought to discuss, at their level of understanding, what occurred and the implications.

Contemporary affairs at the local, national, and international levels should be incorporated naturally into the social studies curriculum throughout the year. Children should be encouraged on an ongoing basis to bring to class or place on a special "living bulletin board" (one that grows as the class feeds it) pictures of and articles about events that especially interest or puzzle them. Similarly, as each new unit or lesson is introduced, a teacher may encourage the class to identify materials or share information from the news that relates to the subject matter under study. If a teacher does not live in the community where he or she teaches, it is important to read a local paper regularly in order to identify what the significant events and issues are at that level.

Primary-grade children studying about the characteristics and dynamics of families could be introduced to small contemporary case studies and picture stories that reflect current problems and lifestyles. Seefeldt (1989) recommended that young children's introduction to the examination of current affairs might begin by their seeing themselves as makers of news. This introduction could be accomplished by creating news stories based on their own experiences. She suggested that teachers begin by writing a short story on the board and reading it to the class. The students then would be encouraged to dictate an account of an event from their own experience.

> The experience of contributing to the news story and of sharing news items and events helps children understand the concept of news. Many young children, when first introduced to news, believe that to have news they must first have something new, like a new car, toy, or shoes, to contribute. As events or items of interest that have happened or will occur are shared, children develop an awareness of the concept of news. Many kindergarten children will begin to (a) pick out words they know from the story on the board, (b) speculate about what the news may be for the day, (c) offer additional news for the teacher to include on the board, or (d) ask the teacher to read it to them before sharing time.
>
> Show-and-tell, characterized by restless children who are waiting for their turns, can become a dismal failure with young children who do not have the ability to sit and listen as each child takes a turn. Nor does every child have something important or interesting to share every day. Rather than conducting show-and-tell, you can have a news-sharing session. Children can be encouraged to share personal news or news items they have found in the local paper or in newsmagazines, thus reinforcing the concept of news events. (Seefeldt, 1989, pp. 220–221)

With children in the intermediate grades, a teacher periodically may stimulate an analysis of contemporary affairs by action-oriented activities. An example is a simulated newscast: The class is divided into "news desks." These might be the local, state, national, and international desks. Students can be assigned to one of the four desks and asked to prepare the evening's report of events at these levels. After brainstorming what the news is at their desk, each of the groups can select a newscaster to report the news. After the newscast, the results can be discussed by the whole class for inaccuracies, interrelationships, and omissions—much as they might analyze real newscasts.

Using Newspapers and Print Materials

Two major sources of print materials for learning about contemporary affairs are newspapers and periodicals. Many of the print materials available at the "adult" level actually are written at a very low reading level and contain a number of instructive visual and chart materials. Their intelligent use, however, requires some understanding of how newspapers select, construct, often bias and distort, and feature stories (Kirman, 1992). We consider these and other issues related to print materials in more detail in Chapter 10.

Many newspapers and periodicals feature local or "colorful" news at the expense of national and international affairs. Among the major exceptions are the *New York Times* and the *Washington Post*, which are sold throughout the United States in most major metropolitan areas and are excellent sources of information for social studies teachers.

Student Versions of Newspapers and Periodicals.   Some publishers produce versions of weekly newspapers and periodicals adapted especially for elementary- and middle-grade students. Although they include materials that attempt to be both objective and interesting, they have some of the same limitations as other print materials.

Two examples of the more popular student newspapers are *Weekly Reader* and *Junior Scholastic*. Examples of periodicals are *COBBLESTONE* and *FACES*.

Effective use of newspapers requires an understanding of the type of information they contain and how news is represented within them.

Using Technology in Teaching Current Affairs

Computer and shortwave technologies also make it possible for students to enrich current affairs activities by linking resources and individuals in other countries to create an electronic global classroom (Kurshan, 1991). Global Learning Corporation, for example, markets a program called WorldClassroom, which combines social studies and science projects that students in different countries share via computers and modems. AT&T's The Learning Network has a similar structure. In Chapter 11 we consider in more detail some applications of this and other computer-based technologies to global education.

Using simpler technologies, some schools have integrated the use of short-wave radios into the social studies curriculum. For example, students at the Fisher Elementary School in Redford, Michigan, tuned into broadcasts in English from such countries as Australia, the Vatican, England, and Switzerland and correlated the information they obtained with geographic instruction. Because world-band radio reception is better in the evenings, students were permitted to sign out radios for home use.

Television networks also have created special news programs for schools. Turner Broadcasting System, producer of *CNN Newsroom*; The Discovery Channel, producer of *Assignment: Discovery*; and Whittle Communications, producer of *Channel One*, now provide news programs that may be taped free of charge under certain conditions.

For example, *CNN Newsroom* is a 15-minute, commercial-free program available daily over cable at no charge to schools. The program airs each weekday at 3:45 A.M. Eastern time over the CNN cable network. Teachers can record the program on their VCRs and use it later that morning or anytime they choose.

Each edition of the program begins with a news segment that covers the day's top stories. In addition, programs include topical features or "desks" as follows:

- *Futures Desk:* A forecast of emerging trends in the world.
- *International Desk:* An investigation of international news and events around the world.
- *Business Desk:* An explanation of finances, economics, and the world of work.
- *Science Desk:* A focus on latest developments in science and technology.
- *Editor's Desk:* An in-depth analysis of the week's biggest stories.

Guidelines for Developing Current Affairs Activities

Following are some general guidelines for developing current affairs activities. They include criteria for designing activities that can make a contribution to young citizens' understanding and use of current affairs information.

Current affairs activities should:

1. Develop a broad framework for viewing and linking contemporary affairs, from the local, to the regional, to the state, to the national, to the international level.
2. Demonstrate the links between the events that swirl about us and our lives.
3. Assess the factual dimensions of contemporary affairs from those that are opinions and biases.
4. Identify issues among general accounts of events.
5. Illustrate what is meant by a "point of view" concerning an issue.
6. Encourage students to take positions on issues of concern and to identify courses of action they plan to take.
7. Illustrate examples of controversies and constructive ways to resolve them.
8. Distinguish between trivial and significant news.
9. Develop a functional concept of *news.*
10. Identify alternative sources of information for contemporary affairs and some ways to gauge the relative merits of each.
11. Develop the principle that all citizens can and should be participants in events, as well as concerned spectators.
12. Support and demonstrate the general principle that contemporary affairs are an ongoing, vital part of daily life and the social studies curriculum.

Group Activities

1. Refer to the discussion of the *CNN Newsroom* in the chapter. Arrange to tape and critique an edition of the special free news program for students. Discuss what you consider to be the strengths and limitations of the newscast.

2. Focusing on the world scene, identify five significant issues that you believe a concerned citizen should examine or become involved in. Provide a rationale for why you think these issues are important. Discuss your conclusions.

3. Consider how your hometown community or some segment of it is linked with other nations. How is it dependent on other countries? How are they dependent on your community? Make a list of all goods, services, human exchanges, and the like that come into your community from the rest of the world. Then construct a similar list showing the resources going from the community to the rest of the world. Compare your results.

4. Consult your local reference librarian to obtain the addresses of the publishers of the student newspapers and periodicals listed in the chapter. Write to each and request a sample copy. When you receive the copies, analyze their strengths and weaknesses. Discuss your conclusions.

5. Locate a cartoon, letter to the editor, or article from the local paper that you think reflects racial, ethnic, or gender bias. Identify what you view as the bias and explain why.

Individual Activities

1. Write to the various organizations noted in the chapter that distribute teaching materials relating to gender issues, peace education, and multicultural education. Ask each to forward a list of its current curriculum materials and books.

2. Create three lists of possible activities similar to those described in the chapter that would encourage social consciousness in children. Develop one list of five or more activities for grades K through 2, one for grades 3 through 5, and another for grades 6 through 8. Give each activity a title and describe specifically how students would undertake it. Indicate the preparation and follow-up discussions that should accompany each activity.

3. Identify four developing countries and create a research folder for each. Collect and organize pictures, articles, and materials that may be used as background by a teacher or as subject matter by students. For each country, begin your search for material by contacting the appropriate embassy and some international agencies.

4. Identify a collection of children's books that have as their objective promoting multicultural understanding. Organize the books into two basic levels—primary and intermediate grades. List the author, title, publisher, and copyright date of each book. Alongside each work, indicate in a sentence or two the aspect of multicultural understanding that the book is designed to further.

5. Access the Internet and visit the WWW site of The Global School Net Foundation (<URL:http://www.gsn.org>). What resources are available through the site? Which most interested you?

References

Anderson, L. (1991). A rationale for global education. In K. Tye (Ed.), *Global education: From thought to action* (pp. 13–34). Alexandria, VA: Association for Supervision and Curriculum Development.

Angell, A. V., & Avery, P. G. (1992). Examining global issues in the elementary classroom. *The Social Studies, 83,* 113–117.

Atkinson, M. (1979). *Maria Theresa.* Carrboro, NC: Lollipop Power.

Banks, J. (1984). *Teaching strategies for ethnic studies* (3rd ed.). Boston: Allyn & Bacon.

Banks, J. (1991). Multicultural literacy and curriculum reform. *Educational Horizons, 69,* 135–140.

Banks, J. (1992). Multicultural education: For freedom's sake. *Educational Leadership, 49*, 32–36.

Banks, J. (1993, June–July). The canon debate, knowledge construction, and multicultural education. *Educational Researcher*, 4–14.

Barnes, L. J. (1988). Women's history in the "attic trunk." In M. T. Downey (Ed.), *Teaching American history: New directions* (pp. 18–19). Washington, DC: National Council for the Social Studies.

Benitez, H. (1994). Globalization of United States history: Six strategies. *Social Education, 59*, 142–144.

Bennett, C. I. (1986). *Comprehensive multicultural education: Theory and practice.* Boston: Allyn & Bacon.

Berman, S. (1990). Educating for social responsibility. *Educational Leadership, 48*, 75–80.

Brown, D. (1981). *The gentle tamers: Women of the old wild west.* Lincoln: University of Nebraska Press.

Bullard, S. (1992). Sorting through the multicultural rhetoric. *Educational Leadership, 49*, 4–7.

Byrnes, D. A. (1987). *Teacher, they called me a _____!* New York: Anti-Defamation League of B'nai B'rith.

Byrnes, D. A. (1988). Children and prejudice. *Social Education, 52*, 267–271.

Chartock, R. K. (1991). Identifying local links to the world. *Educational Leadership, 49*, 50–52.

Davis, O. (1978). *Escape to freedom: A play about young Frederick Douglass.* New York: Viking.

Etlin, M. (1988, May/June). To teach them all is to know them all. *NEA Today*, pp. 10–11.

Fukuyama, F. (1992, August 17 & 24). The beginning of foreign policy. *New Republic*, pp. 24–25, 28, 30, 32.

Gollnick, D. M., & Chinn, P. C. (1994). *Multicultural education in a pluralistic society* (4th ed.). Upper Saddle River, NJ: Merrill/Prentice Hall.

Harvey, K. D., Harjo, L. D., & Jackson, J. K. (1990). Teaching about Native Americans: A sample lesson. In *Teaching about Native Americans* (Bulletin 84, p. 7). Washington, DC: National Council for the Social Studies.

Henderson, J. G. (1992). *Reflective teaching: Becoming an inquiring educator.* New York: Macmillan.

Johnson, D. W., & Johnson, R. (1991). *Teaching students to be peacemakers.* Edina, MN: Interaction.

King, E. W. (1990). *Teaching ethnic and gender awareness.* Dubuque, IA: Kendall/Hunt.

Kirman, J. M. (1992). Using newspapers to study media bias. *Social Education, 56*, 47–51.

Kleg, M. (1993). *Racism and hate prejudice.* Albany: State University of New York Press.

Kniep, W. M. (1989). Social studies within a global education. *Social Education, 53*, 399–403.

Kurshan, B. (1991). Creating the global classroom for the 21st century. *Educational Technology, 31*, 47–50.

Lewis, B. (1991). *The kid's guide to social action.* Minneapolis: Free Spirit.

Martel, E. (1992). How valid are the Portland Baseline Essays? *Educational Leadership, 49*, 20–23.

Meriwether, L. (1973). *Don't ride the bus on Monday: The Rosa Parks story.* Englewood Cliffs, NJ: Prentice-Hall.

Merryfield, M. M., & Remy, R. C. (1995). *Teaching about international conflict and peace.* Albany, NY: SUNY Press.

Nash, G. (1982). *Red, white, and black: The peoples of early America.* Englewood Cliffs, NJ: Prentice Hall.

National Council for the Social Studies (NCSS). (1981). *Global education.* Washington, DC: Author.

National Council for the Social Studies (NCSS). (1992). Curriculum guidelines for multi-cultural education. *Social Education, 56,* 274–293.

Naylor, D. T., & Smith, B. D. (1993). Holidays, cultural diversity, and the public culture. *Social Studies and the Young Learner, 6,* S1.

Ogbu, J. U. (1992). Understanding cultural diversity and learning. *Educational Researcher, 21,* 5–14.

Passe, J. (1988). Developing current events awareness in children. *Social Education, 52,* 531–533.

Ramler, S. (1991). Global education for the 21st century. *Educational Leadership, 49,* 44–46.

Ravitch, D. (1992). A culture in common. *Educational Leadership, 49,* 8–11.

Seefeldt, C. (1989). *Social studies for the preschool/primary child* (3rd ed.). Upper Saddle River, NJ: Merrill/Prentice Hall.

Sobol, T. (1990). Understanding diversity. *Educational Leadership, 47,* 27–30.

Spindler, G., & Spindler, L. (1990). *The American cultural dialogue and its transmission.* Philadelphia: Falmer.

Tye, B. B., & Tye, K. A. (1992). *Global education: A study of school change.* Albany: State University of New York Press.

Upper Midwest Women's History Center. (1993). *Upper Midwest Women's History Center Collection, 1993.* St. Louis Park, MN: Author.

Comprehending, Communicating, and Remembering Subject Matter

Comprehending Social Studies Subject Matter
Building on Existing Knowledge in Reading
Strategies for Improving Reading Comprehension
The Reading-Social Studies Connection

Reading and Social Studies Text Materials
Reading Children's Literature
Reading Newspapers and Periodicals
Integrated Curriculum
Visual Literacy
Metaphors and Other Figures of Speech

Communicating Social Studies Subject Matter
Listening and Speaking
Integrating Writing Into the Social Studies Curriculum
Word Processing Tools in Writing

Remembering Social Studies Subject Matter
First-Letter Technique
Keyword Technique
Imagery Technique

As we have considered in earlier chapters, effective social studies instruction incorporates many elements of planning. It includes strategies for organizing and presenting subject matter in a way that achieves the teacher's goals and objectives. It also encompasses provisions for aiding students in comprehending, communicating, and remembering the social studies subject matter they encounter.

Comprehending Social Studies Subject Matter

Contemporary perspectives on reading underscore the fact that readers are not passive receivers of information from printed materials. Rather, they interact with text and construct meaning from it. This may or may not be the same meaning the author intended.

comprehension   **Comprehension,** as reading educators use the term, is a complex act representing a number of cognitive and affective processes, including recognizing words and relating them to previously learned information and making inferences. What readers actually comprehend from a passage of text "depends upon their knowledge, motives, beliefs, and personal experiences" (Camperell & Knight, 1991, p. 569).

It should be noted also that the subject matter of social studies often deals with places and cultural practices that students may never have encountered. In addition, the field draws heavily on abstract, rather than concrete, associations. Social studies also embraces subject matter that includes many specialized concepts and complex visual and tabular data.

Building on Existing Knowledge in Reading

Regardless of their ages or abilities, students' existing knowledge *(prior knowledge)* is a critical variable in reading comprehension: "All readers, both novices and experts, use their existing knowledge and a range of cues from the text and the situational context in which the reading occurs to build, or construct, a model of meaning from the text" (Dole, Duffy, Roehler, & Pearson, 1991, p. 241). Often this knowledge base is incomplete, or students fail to relate it to the information in the text. The existing knowledge may be inaccurate or at variance with texts, in which case students are likely to ignore or reject the new information.

Strategies for Improving Reading Comprehension

Beyond their existing knowledge, students bring strategies of varying levels of effectiveness to the reading process that are used to construct meaning from text. Dole et al. (1991) summarized five powerful strategies, supported by cognitively based research, that students can use to improve their comprehension of any texts, including social studies materials:

- Determining importance
- Summarizing information
- Drawing inferences
- Generating questions
- Monitoring comprehension

Determining importance refers primarily to the strategy of being able to assess which items in the text the author considers important. This strategy may include understanding the structure of the text, as well as how to look for clues to what is important.

The strategy of *summarizing information* relates to the ability to select what is significant, synthesize data, and then represent passages of text, either orally or in writing.

Drawing inferences involves being able to integrate prior knowledge with the information given in text to draw conclusions (e.g., inferring the character is male on reading "the Catholic priest blessed the little girl").

The strategy of *generating questions* in this context refers to students generating their own questions about text.

Comprehension monitoring consists of students' being aware of how much they understand about text and how to remedy omissions or confusion.

The Reading–Social Studies Connection

Helping students comprehend social studies subject matter typically involves aiding them in reading textbooks, newspapers, periodicals, and trade books. Approaches that incorporate well-grounded instructional strategies in reading and social studies can advance teachers' goals for both areas. Five techniques that meet these criteria are the *K–W–L technique, discussion webs, concept (or semantic) maps, graphic organizers,* and *data retrieval charts.*

The K–W–L Technique.   The **K–W–L technique** (Carr & Ogle, 1987; Ogle, 1986) is a basic way to (a) initiate study of a unit by motivating students and activating their prior knowledge and (b) assess what they have learned after the unit is concluded. Consider a unit of study on Native Americans. At the outset of the unit, a sheet similar to the one shown in Figure 10.1 is given to each stu-

K–W–L technique

| **FIGURE 10.1** | Illustration of the K-W-L technique |

K-W-L Chart
Native Americans

K (What we know about Native Americans.)	W (What we want to know.)	L (What we learned.)

dent or group (see Young & Marek-Schroer, 1992). After brainstorming, a cumulative list of known items is compiled. The process then is repeated for the items students wish to know about Native Americans. At that point the teacher also may include additional questions that the text analysis will address.

In the following stage, students consult the list of items in the W column. They also confirm or refute the accuracy of the items in the K column. As a final step, the students list in the L column what they have learned from their readings. Alternatively, the teacher may use some of the different forms of assessment discussed in Chapter 13 to determine what students have learned.

discussion webs

Discussion Webs.   A **discussion web** (Duthie, 1986) may be used to help students organize arguments or evidence from text. It is suitable for issues or questions that are not resolved or for which there are balanced pro and con arguments.

An example of a discussion web is given in Figure 10.2. As shown, a web begins with a teacher question related to materials that students have read. The format that follows is flexible, but students, individually or in small groups, need to locate information that supports both sets of answers; for example, under the "No" column, a student writes "Toys are different." After completing the web, students discuss the findings and then take an individual position on the issue (e.g., "Overall, today life is not that different").

concept (or semantic) mapping

Concept Maps.   **Concept (or semantic) mapping** is a flexible technique that has several applications in social studies instruction, including aiding students' comprehension (see also Chapters 4 and 6). The technique encourages students to organize categories of concepts and to identify relationships among them.

The concept mapping technique has many variations (e.g., Novak & Gowin, 1984). Basically it begins with the teacher or students identifying a series of major concepts in a narrative (e.g., a chapter), including one that is the central concept. These concepts then are organized and linked through a diagram that illustrates logical connections.

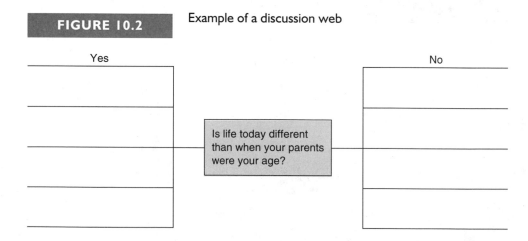

| **FIGURE 10.2** | Example of a discussion web |

The organization of the concepts typically is hierarchical (e.g., see Figure 6.4 in Chapter 6), but certain applications omit this condition. In some way, however, the central or overarching concept should be identified, either by assigning it the largest circle or by placing it at the top or the center of the page. In one variation, the teacher creates a partial map that shows some of the concepts and linkages to demonstrate relationships and model the technique, and then the students are asked to complete the map.

Figure 10.3 is a sample application of this approach, a concept map made by a sixth-grade student characterized as a low achiever (Novak & Gowin, 1984, p. 41). The map represents the student's organization of information after reading a textbook chapter. The teacher supplied the concepts of *feudalism, kings, guilds,* and *church* shown in the figure, and the student then completed the map.

A variation on the concept mapping technique that can be used to process information from reading materials employs sheets of paper and 3" × 5" cards. Their purpose is to help students discover relationships among concepts.

Each student receives a set of sheets and cards. On each sheet of paper, the teacher places the name of one hierarchical concept. For example, a teacher might give each student three sheets with the respective headings: Landform, Water Body, and Landform and Water Body. Each student also is given a collection of cards that have the names of the major concepts from a reading passage, such as a chapter. As an illustration, each card might have the name of one of the following concepts:

| **FIGURE 10.3** | A concept map for history prepared by a previously low-achieving student in sixth grade |

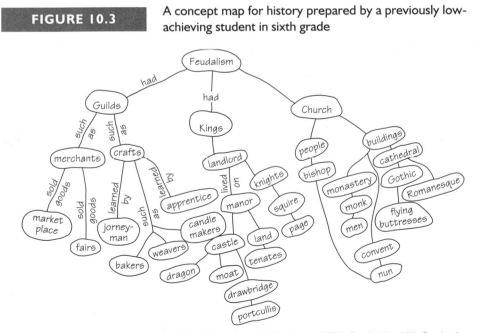

Source: From *Learning How to Learn* (p. 41) by J. Novak and D. B. Gowin, 1984, Cambridge, UK: Cambridge University Press. Copyright 1984 by Cambridge University Press. Reprinted with permission.

Mountain	Plateau	Valley	Ocean
Tributary	River	Delta	Gulf
Isthmus	Peninsula	Harbor	Hill
Mountain range	Island	Plain	Mesa

As a next step, students are asked to place each sheet at the top of their desks. Finally they are to place each of the concept cards under the appropriate sheet.

graphic organizer

Graphic Organizers.   A **graphic organizer,** similar to a concept map, is a representation of the relationships among major themes in a reading passage. Graphic organizers, which occur in many forms, can be used by students before studying material as a way to discern how the teacher or author has structured information. Alternatively, they can be used at the end of a session to serve as a summary.

Typically, graphic organizers appear as hierarchical diagrams similar to the one shown in Figure 10.4. In developing the graphic organizer to introduce the structure of the federal government, the teacher first identified major concepts in a segment of the student's textbook chapter. These are presented below.

branches of the government	legislative branch
House of Representatives	judicial branch
Supreme Court	executive branch
president	cabinet
vice president	federal courts
Senate	

The teacher constructed the diagram shown to represent the linkages between and among the concepts. Then students were asked to add other related concepts that appeared within the chapter. For example, they might have added the names of specific positions under "cabinet" and those of key committees under the "Senate" and the "House."

In Figure 10.5, Wood (1988) provides an excellent illustration of how a graphic organizer can be incorporated into a group activity that develops the social

FIGURE 10.4

Graphic organizer

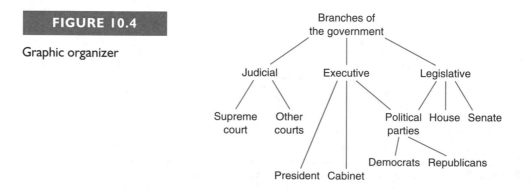

FIGURE 10.5   Interactive reading guide (social studies—intermediate level)

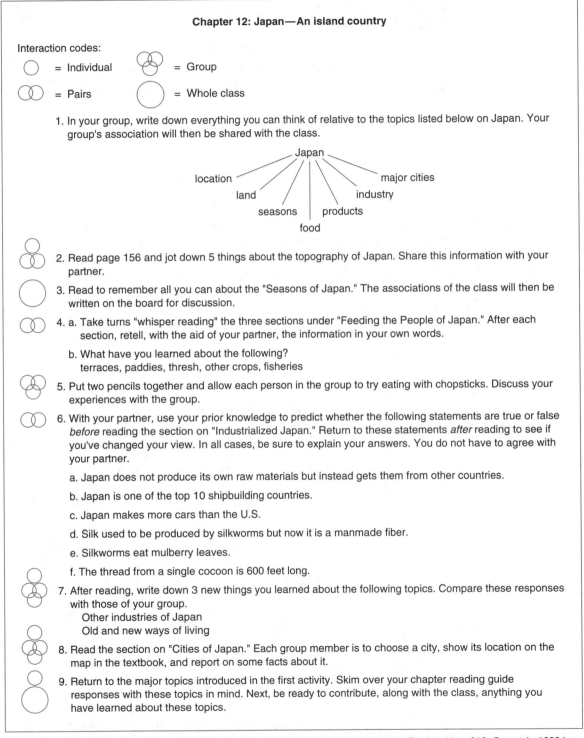

Chapter 12: Japan—An island country

Interaction codes:

◯ = Individual   ◉ = Group

◎ = Pairs   ◯ = Whole class

1. In your group, write down everything you can think of relative to the topics listed below on Japan. Your group's association will then be shared with the class.

Japan
location   land   seasons   food   products   industry   major cities

2. Read page 156 and jot down 5 things about the topography of Japan. Share this information with your partner.

3. Read to remember all you can about the "Seasons of Japan." The associations of the class will then be written on the board for discussion.

4. a. Take turns "whisper reading" the three sections under "Feeding the People of Japan." After each section, retell, with the aid of your partner, the information in your own words.

   b. What have you learned about the following?
   terraces, paddies, thresh, other crops, fisheries

5. Put two pencils together and allow each person in the group to try eating with chopsticks. Discuss your experiences with the group.

6. With your partner, use your prior knowledge to predict whether the following statements are true or false *before* reading the section on "Industrialized Japan." Return to these statements *after* reading to see if you've changed your view. In all cases, be sure to explain your answers. You do not have to agree with your partner.

   a. Japan does not produce its own raw materials but instead gets them from other countries.

   b. Japan is one of the top 10 shipbuilding countries.

   c. Japan makes more cars than the U.S.

   d. Silk used to be produced by silkworms but now it is a manmade fiber.

   e. Silkworms eat mulberry leaves.

   f. The thread from a single cocoon is 600 feet long.

7. After reading, write down 3 new things you learned about the following topics. Compare these responses with those of your group.
   Other industries of Japan
   Old and new ways of living

8. Read the section on "Cities of Japan." Each group member is to choose a city, show its location on the map in the textbook, and report on some facts about it.

9. Return to the major topics introduced in the first activity. Skim over your chapter reading guide responses with these topics in mind. Next, be ready to contribute, along with the class, anything you have learned about these topics.

FIGURE 10.6	Sample data retrieval chart

Cities	Climate	Population	Environmental Problems
Mexico City			
Toronto			
Los Angeles			

studies–reading connection. The activity includes a variety of techniques that help students comprehend text information and relate it to their prior knowledge.

data retrieval chart

Data Retrieval Charts.   Data retrieval charts, which we considered in Chapter 6, allow teachers and students to organize data from written text in a way that highlights important relationships. The format they employ offers comparisons and analyses not included in typical text discussions. The data retrieval chart shown in Figure 10.6 illustrates how a teacher can help students organize information in a social studies textbook chapter.

Reading and Social Studies Text Materials

An extensive body of research verifies the limitations of existing social studies text materials from a variety of perspectives (e.g., Armbruster & Gudbrandsen, 1986; Beck & McKeown, 1988, 1991; Siler, 1986–87). From a cognitive perspective, for example, one major criticism of social studies textbooks—especially history texts—is that they lack depth, compartmentalize information, and fail to aid students in linking passages and discovering cause-effect relationships. Another charge is that they discourage hypothesis development and problem solving.

considerate (or friendly) texts

What characteristics specifically would make social studies texts seem **considerate or friendly** to a reader? Singer (1986) summarized the features of such texts into five categories: *text organization, explication of ideas, conceptual density, metadiscourse,* and *instructional devices* (see also Armbruster, 1984).

Text organization refers to statements of purpose and rationale, organization of material, suggestions concerning how to learn from the text, and the like, provided for the reader. Included are a uniform writing style throughout the text and consistent use and placement of questions and rhetorical devices. Other such aids would be time lines and cause-effect and comparison charts.

Explication of ideas refers to straightforward statement of facts and ideas. Included is the definition of new terms as they are introduced, the provision of necessary background information, and the relating of new knowledge to prior knowledge. Included also is the explication of some organizing point of view or theory for the text, if one exists.

Conceptual density refers to the number of new concepts, ideas, and vocabulary items that are included in the text. The greater the number and the fewer the explanations through the introduction of main ideas and examples, the more complex is the learning task for the student.

Metadiscourse has been likened to a conversation between the author and the reader about the text. The discussion may range over any topic and typically uses the first person form of narration.

Instructional devices refer to those features of a text that help the user better comprehend its meaning. Among these features are tables of contents, headings, cues, annotations in the margins, inserted questions, indices, and the like.

Researchers (Armbruster & Anderson, 1984; Armbruster, Anderson, & Meyer, 1991) also discovered strategies for helping students identify and use the organizing structures in their texts. They characterized these as **frames:** ways of visually conceptualizing significant content of texts.

frames

Frames represent important ideas and relationships in text and take many forms: data charts, tables, diagrams, and concept maps. When authors of texts do not provide frames, teachers and students have to create them. Once they are constructed, evidence suggests that frames facilitate learning from social studies texts (Armbruster et al., 1991), as well as other subjects.

Consider the following application of frames to a social studies text describing the American Revolution, as shown in Figure 10.7. The teacher has identified four major categories of information that structure the text's narrative concerning the colonists and the British: *goals*, *plans*, *actions*, and *outcomes*.

An example of a completed fifth-grade frame appears in Figure 10.8 (Armbruster et al., 1991). In constructing it, the instructors pulled together different sections of the text dealing with physical maps. They completed the first three columns and had the students identify pages in the "Examples" column to encourage application of the information.

FIGURE 10.7   Frame for the American Revolution

The American Revolution		
	The Colonists	The British
What were their goals?		
What were their plans?		
What actions did they take?		
What was the outcome of their actions?		

| FIGURE 10.8 | Example of a fifth-grade frame |

Using Physical Maps

Type of Map	Use	How to read	Examples (pages where maps appear)
relief map	shows landforms	uses shading to show the shape of landforms; unshaded areas are lower	p. 290 p. 218 p. 418
elevation map	shows heights of land areas; shows which way a river flows	color shows different elevations	p. 541
physical maps	show both relief and elevation; can show best travel routes	shading and color show shape and height of land	pp. 548-549

Source: From "Improving Content Area Reading Using Instructional Graphics" by B. B. Armbruster, T. H. Anderson, and J. L. Meyer, 1991, *Reading Research Quarterly, 26,* p. 399. Copyright 1991 by International Reading Association. Reprinted by permission of Bonnie B. Armbruster and the International Reading Association.

Reading Children's Literature

Pick up a basal elementary social studies textbook for any grade and read a sample chapter. Did it hold your interest?

Apart from their structural limitations, which we already have discussed, some of the most biting criticisms of social studies textbooks are that they are dull, lifeless, and disjointed, and that they lack a point of view. They also have been criticized for omitting the pageantry, myths, stories, issues, and anecdotes that are part of the vitality of social studies.

trade books   **Trade books** are an antidote to some of the textbooks' worst problems. A wealth of attractively illustrated trade books are available. Children's literature offers the promise of exciting and colorful portrayals of in-depth issues, ethical dilemmas, social models, events, persons, and places by some of the best children's authors and illustrators.

For studying history, Beck and McKeown (1991) suggested that one role for children's literature is to provide several accounts of the same event. In this way students can gain deep understanding and draw connections within information. When the accounts also differ in significant respects, they can provide the grist for discussions.

Biographies written for children are especially important forms of children's literature. "They are relatively short, and they provide enough background information to enable a child to make sense of the events described. Writers of

Units can be constructed around a series of trade books, or they can be used to supplement a basal text.

children's biographies do not assume that children are familiar with events that occurred before they were born; instead they fill in the missing information" (Zarnowski, 1988, p. 61).

At the same time, like their adult counterparts, biographies written for children often suffer from distortions, idealized portrayals, inaccuracies, misconceptions, and poor scholarship. Occasionally the deficiencies of some biographies persist through time. They eventually lead to the creation of stereotypes and myths that are difficult to destroy; witness the story that many of us learned concerning George Washington and the cherry tree he allegedly chopped down.

Students cannot possibly be kept from reading all biographies that suffer from such flaws, nor should they be. To attempt to "shield" students completely from all of these types of written material would be both undesirable and unrealistic. Doing so would not help them begin to deal with the same kind of deficiencies that abound in the mass media and the everyday world of experience.

As an alternative, teachers can engage students in exercises that involve comparative analyses of biographies. Unlike most adults, children, particularly younger ones, do not seem to find this task repetitive. In fact, they often may read the same book several times.

After reading several biographical accounts, children could discuss such questions as the following. Not all of the questions would be appropriate for younger children, but at least some of them could be used at any level.

1. What did each of the books say about the following things: person's child-hood, interests, major accomplishments, and important people in his or her life?

2. What things were similar in the books you read?

3. What things were different in the books you read?

4. If a friend asked you to tell him or her which *one* book he or she should read, which one would you choose? Why?

5. How would you sum up what you have learned from reading all of the books about _____'s life?

Zarnowski (1990) provided a detailed set of strategies for using biographies in social studies instruction in her book *Learning About Biographies*. One of the techniques she recommends is to draw relationships between the events in the life of the subject and those in history. After constructing a sequential time line of both sets of events, the children and the teacher brainstorm to construct two webs as shown in Figures 10.9 and 10.10. These webs then serve as reference points when students select the events about which they write.

FIGURE 10.9   A web showing the events in Dr. King's life

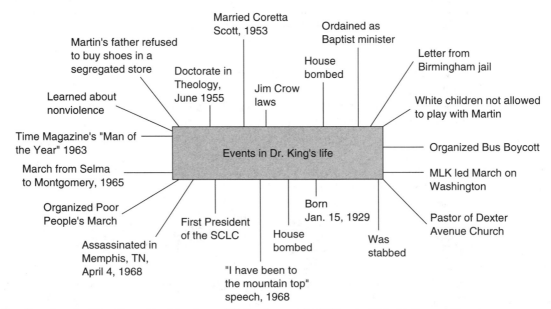

Source: From *Learning About Biographies: A Reading and Writing Approach for Children* (p. 67) by M. Zarnowski, 1990, Urbana, IL: National Council of Teachers of English. Copyright 1990 by the National Council of Teachers of English. Reprinted with permission.

FIGURE 10.10   A web showing events in history

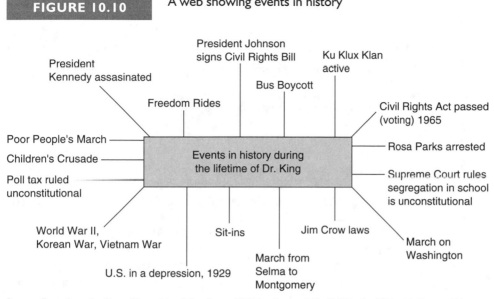

Source: From *Learning About Biographies: A Reading and Writing Approach for Children* (p. 68) by M. Zarnowski, 1990, Urbana, IL: National Council of Teachers of English. Copyright 1990 by the National Council of Teachers of English. Reprinted with permission.

In addition to Zarnowski's work, a number of excellent teacher reference works tell how to locate and use trade books that are appropriate for the social studies curriculum. Two examples are:

- Donna Norton, *Through the Eyes of a Child: An Introduction to Children's Literature*, 4th ed., Upper Saddle River, NJ: Merrill/Prentice Hall, 1995.
- K. Rudman, *Children's Literature: An Issue Approach*, New York: Longman, 1984.

To further help social studies teachers locate outstanding trade books, the National Council for the Social Studies (NCSS) has published *An Annotated Bibliography of Historical Fiction for the Social Studies, Grades 5 Through 12* (Silverblank, 1992); each year in the April/May of *Social Education*, the NCSS provides a list of notable children's trade books published in the field of social studies during the past year. The list includes works written for children in grades K through 8 that emphasize human relations and different cultural groups.

Three examples of items from a list ("Notable," 1991) are:

Diego. Jonah Winter. Illustrated by Jeanette Winter. Knopf. 40 pp. ISBN 0-679-81987-8. [For primary grades] This short biography of artist Diego Rivera, the famous mural painter who celebrated the Mexican people, chronicles events in Rivera's life that influenced his work as an artist. With text in English and Spanish, this book is boldly illustrated for young readers. (p. 253)

Cartons, Cans, and Orange Peels: Where Does Your Garbage Go? Joanna Foster. Illustrated with full-color photographs. Clarion. 64 pp. ISBN 0-395-56436-0. [For intermediate grades] This clearly written text tells exactly where garbage goes and argues that although the problems today outpace the solutions, alternatives do exist. Glossary. Index. (p. 255)

Fly Away Home. Eve Bunting. Illustrated by Ronald Himler. Clarion. 32 pp. ISBN 0-395-55962-6. [For primary grades] For a widower and his son, home is the airport until they earn enough money to pay for an apartment. This simple but powerful story describes how these two survive, cope with anger and despair, develop supportive relationships, and maintain their hope. (p. 254)

Increasingly, educators and publishers are recognizing the value of using children's literature in social studies instruction. Wooster (1991) provided a clear model of how trade books can be integrated into the social studies curriculum in the primary grades (see Figure 10.11). She stressed the importance of careful planning, good book selection, and student involvement in the planning and selection process.

McGowan, Guzzetti, and Kowalinski (1992) offered three concrete strategies for how literature studies can be blended successfully within a social studies program that emphasizes citizenship education. One of these strategies, which they call the **3-H Club technique,** creatively incorporates the construct that permeates this text—namely, that a social studies program should reflect some balance among matters of the head, the hand, and the heart.

3-H Club technique

The essence of the 3-H Club is a series of three basic steps. At the beginning of a unit, students make a selection from a list of books related to the unit theme. They then select one activity from each of the three categories that are spelled out in Figure 10.12. After completing the activities, students record their results in "literature logs."

Freeman and Levstik (1988) suggested that picture books with historical content can be used effectively with younger children in social studies instruction:

A number of picture storybooks present historical content appropriate for primary-age children (grades K–3). These books do not attempt to use sophisticated chronological history or to delve into all the complexities of historical issues. Instead, they generally provide a variety of time assists for readers who are just developing a sense of time. They also emphasize the daily lives of children and families and depend on illustration to convey at least an equal share of the historical data. (p. 332)

Although the use of trade books in social studies instruction has gained widespread support, some social studies educators have raised questions about their effectiveness. For example, based on a review of the research, McGowan, Erickson, and Neufeld (1996) cautioned: "Curiously, most advocates do not support their claims for the effectiveness of literature-based social studies teaching with research findings" (p. 203).

A counter example, dealing with metaphors in literature, however, suggests that even children in the primary grades are capable of rudimentary forms of metaphoric comprehension (Flynn, Dagostino, & Carofio, 1995).

FIGURE 10.11

Purposeful planning: A key to using children's trade books to teach social studies

Teaching social studies through textbooks with their neatly measured chapters divided into lesson-size bites is surely easier than constructing a social studies program using children's trade books. Happily, however, more and more teachers are moving toward literature-based social studies instruction. Trade books have a unique capacity to imbue content with value and attitude perspectives so important in teaching social studies. Literature has a motivational quality that is lacking in many other instructional materials.

There is no doubt trade books are an extraordinary vehicle for social studies education. However, all too often the power of excellent books to develop social studies content, concepts and skills is lost in learning experiences that are incidental and serendipitous rather than planned and purposeful. Some classroom examples may serve to illustrate approaches to using trade books deliberately to provide engaging and meaningful content, concept and skill development in social studies.

The study of the family had become increasingly challenging to one first grade teacher, many of whose students came from families undergoing profound trauma. Since focusing on the students' own families was often both too personal and painful, the teacher collected a large group of books that related to key ideas about families as a basic institution of societies. For example, he used Patricia Polacco's *Uncle Vova's Tree* (Philomel) and Elizabeth F. Howard's *Chita's Christmas Tree* (Bradbury) to help students understand that families share customs and traditions, though those traditions may vary from place to place, time to time, and group to group.

The first grade children explored generational issues and the interdependence of family members in Tomie de Paola's *Nana Upstairs and Nana Downstairs* (Putnam) and *Now One Foot, Now the Other* (Putnam). *The Chalk Doll* (HarperCollins) by Charlotte Pomerantz and *Amko and Efua Bear* (Macmillan) by Sonia Appiah extended the ideas of family interdependence to international settings. Students developed interest in maps and globes to locate places in their books, and correspond with pen pals to learn more about other people and places. In creating his literature-based program, this skillful teacher identified important social studies generalizations, selected relevant literature, and planned activities to help students develop specific content understandings.

A child-centered third grade teacher initiated the study of world communities by guiding her students to develop a list of questions they had about people in other times and places. Among the questions were
- What kinds of houses do they have?
- What special events do they celebrate and why?
- Who are their leaders?
- How do they have fun?

These questions, generated by the students became the focus of a year-long study of communities past and present. Students read, shared, charted and recorded their findings as they explored people and places around the world.

Both teacher and students combed library shelves and searched book lists to find excellent books such as Ann Grifalconi's *The Village of Round and Square Houses* (Little, Brown), Barbara Cooney's *Island Boy* (Viking), Oliver Dunrea's *Skara Brae: The Story of a Prehistoric Village* (Holiday House), Brent Ashabranner's *Gavriel and Jemal* (Putnam), and Riki Levinson's *Our Home Is the Sea* (Dutton). This alternative approach to the more traditional country-by-country approach capitalized on students' curiosity, developed the students' ability to ask meaningful social science questions and fostered important analytic habits of the mind. In addition, students were reading and enjoying fine literature, and incorporating writing and speaking into a rich interdisciplinary program.

Source: From "Purposeful Planning: A Key to Using Children's Trade Books to Teach Social Studies" by J. Wooster, 1991, *CBC Features*, July/December. Copyright 1991 by Children's Book Council.

FIGURE 10.12 A 3-H Club reading guide for sixth graders

The 3-H Club

As a citizen, you make *social decisions* (choices that influence others) every day. The following activities let you practice three tools citizens use to make social decisions: the **Head** (knowing and thinking about the world); the **Hand** (having skills to make social decisions); and the **Heart** (feeling concerned that a social decision should be made). Using information from the story you are reading or have just read, complete these activities in your literature log.

The Head

1. Tell when this story occurred, then describe how people lived during this time. What work did they do? What were their homes like? What foods did they eat? What games did they play? Compare and contrast this lifestyle to the way in which you live.

2. Briefly describe the story's setting. How does the setting influence how the characters must live? How is it similar to the setting in which you live? How is it different?

3. Select a major choice that the main character made during the story. Think this decision over carefully and discuss it with a classmate. Then, respond to these questions: Was it a wise decision? Would you have made the same or a different choice? What might you have done if you faced the same decision?

The Hand

4. Find a partner and locate the story's setting on a map or globe. Compute the setting's approximate distance from your community. Talk with someone who knows about transportation, (a travel agent, a pilot) then describe how you might travel to this place.

5. Determine the main events of the story, then construct a timeline showing the order in which they occurred. Underline the events which had the most influence on the progress of the story, and briefly explain their importance.

6. Copy terms from the story that you do not understand in the sentences in which they are used. Working with a classmate, consult dictionaries or other reference sources. Predict which meaning makes the most sense, then explain the meaning of the entire sentence in your own words.

The Heart

7. Tell if the story's characters have a particular cultural or ethnic background. Describe how their way of life might seem "different" from yours. How might you explain these differences? How is their lifestyle similar to the one you live?

8. Consider a major decision made by the story's main character. Did the character's religious beliefs, customs, or values influence this decision? In what ways?

9. Describe a pressing social problem that confronted the characters in this story (such as prejudice or poverty). How did you react to this problem as you read about it? Are there similar problems in your community? What might you do about these problems?

Source: From "Using Literature Studies to Promote Elementary Social Studies Learning" by T. M. McGowan, B. Guzzetti, and B. Kowalinski, 1992, *Social Studies and the Young Learner, 5*, p. 10. © National Council for the Social Studies. Used with permission.

Commercial publishers of basal texts also have begun to encourage the integration of literature studies within the social studies curriculum (Alleman & Brophy, 1991). As an illustration, consider the Harcourt Brace Jovanovich basal social studies textbook series (Harcourt Brace Jovanovich, 1990), which includes collections of children's literature for each grade, K through 6, as an integral part of the social studies program. For each grade, students have a basal textbook plus a series of trade books for each unit. An example for grades 3 through 6 is given in Figure 10.13.

Reading Newspapers and Periodicals

Newspapers and periodicals present many of the same problems as textbooks. On the one hand, they offer students a wealth of data on contemporary affairs and help bridge the gap between the real world and that of the school curriculum. To properly interpret and process the information that these media contain, however, most students—even good readers—need assistance.

Although they share many elements in common with textbooks, newspapers and periodicals present some special reading challenges. Effectively reading newspapers and periodicals includes being able to:

1. *Separate headlines from the substance of an article.* This involves a recognition that a headline is often an interpretation of what the article is about made by someone other than the author.

2. *Identify and correctly use common colloquialisms, metaphors, acronyms, and cryptic expressions.* This includes an awareness of how frequently such expressions are used.

3. *Locate new concepts in stories and dismantle sentences packed with difficult concepts.*

4. *Compare different accounts of the same event.* This involves searching for cause-effect relationships and separating what appears to be fact from opinion.

5. *Identify the big idea in a story.* This involves separating the important points from the peripheral or colorful but nonessential ones.

6. *Recognize how information is categorized and organized.* This includes identifying the structure of newspapers and periodicals, as well as recognizing the nature of the contents within each section.

Integrated Curriculum

Imagine studying about Mozart and his impact upon Western music without ever hearing any of his compositions or understanding how the Impressionists revolutionized art without viewing any of their works. Try to think about solving an important social problem without drawing on the insights of experts from many different disciplines.

FIGURE 10.13 An example of components in a basal social studies textbook series

Communities		GRADE 3
Unit 1	People and Communities	*Goodbye, My Island* by Jean Rogers
Unit 2	Communities Use Natural Resources	*Why People Work*
Unit 3	Community Governments and Services	*The San Diego Zoo*
Unit 4	Communities of Yesterday, Today, and Tomorrow	*The House on Maple Street* by Bonnie Pryor
Unit 5	Around the World	*Celebrations around the World*

States and Regions		GRADE 4
Unit 1	Our People, Our Land	*Paul Bunyan in Puget Sound* by Dell J. McCormick
Unit 2	The Shapes of the Land	*Animals in Our Country*
Unit 3	Regions of the United States	*US Territories and Puerto Rico*
Unit 4	America: A United Country	*Shh! We're Writing the Constitution* by Jean Fritz
Unit 5	Other Lands, Other People	*Protecting the Environment*

The United States: Its History and Neighbors		GRADE 5
Unit 1	The Geography of the United States	*The People, Yes* by Carl Sandburg
Unit 2	The First Americans	*American Indians Today*
Unit 3	Exploration and Settlement	*The Double Life of Pocahontas* by Jean Fritz
Unit 4	Life in the American Colonies	*A Visit to Williamsburg*
Unit 5	The American Revolution	*Americans for Freedom*
Unit 6	The New Nation	*Lucy Applegate on the Oregon Trail* by Michael DiLeo
Unit 7	The Nation Divided	*The Civil War at Sea*
Unit 8	Modern Times Begin	*How Business Works*
Unit 9	The Twentieth Century	*Charlie Pippin* by Candy Dawson Boyd
Unit 10	Canada and Mexico	*Hispanic Americans*

The World: Past and Present		GRADE 6
Unit 1	The Middle East, Past and Present	*Nefertiti Lived Here* by Mary Chubb
Unit 2	Europe, Past and Present	*How People are Governed*
Unit 3	Africa, Past and Present	*Roots* by Alex Haley
Unit 4	Asia, Past and Present	*The World's Economies*
Unit 5	The Western Hemisphere, Past and Present	*Secret of the Andes* by Ann Nolan Clark

Source: From *HBJ Social Studies, Making It Real* (p. 11) by Harcourt Brace Jovanovich, 1990, Orlando, FL: Author. Copyright 1990 by Harcourt Brace Jovanovich.

Roberts (1996) has defined integrated curriculum (or thematic instruction) as "both a way of teaching and a way of planning and organizing the instructional program so the discrete disciplines of subject matter are related to one another in a design that matches the developmental needs of the learners and that helps to connect their learning in ways that are meaningful to their current and past experiences" (p. 1). Integrated curriculum draws upon many different information sources to illuminate our understanding of people, places, and events. It also more nearly mimics the way individuals actually reference subject matter and construct knowledge in the world beyond the school walls (Hamston & Murdoch, 1996).

All subject matter has potential for linkages in integrated curriculum, but perhaps the most naturally allied subjects are social studies, humanities, and language arts. For example, in examining an issue such as the impact of poverty on individuals, data may be drawn from fiction, biographies, music history, psychology, and statistics, to name but a few areas. In addition, serious analysis of the issue will involve written and oral skills. Although all data sources, including basal textbooks, students' own experiences, and computer data bases, can contribute to integrated curriculum, trade books, such as those in Figures 9.3, 10.5, and 10.11, are especially rich sources of information.

Visual Literacy

Research data suggest that learning through imagery, such as pictures, often is easier than through other forms—especially for primary-age children. Pictorial data enliven lessons and spark interest in social studies activities. A variety of still pictures and visual materials is available for teaching social studies, including paintings, photos, slides, drawings, dioramas, and transparencies. Old magazines and newspapers, as well as commercially prepared materials, are treasure troves of visual materials that can be used as springboards for social studies lessons.

Pictures that children themselves draw, color, paint, or photograph and collages that they create are also rich sources of material for discussion. A child's picture can reflect feelings, as well as thoughts, and can serve as a medium of communication. For students to comprehend visual data with social data effectively, however, they need to understand how to *read* pictures.

Techniques for Reading Still Pictures.   Reading visual material effectively requires some of the same techniques that print reading does. It involves more than merely perceiving what is visually present. In reading visual materials, viewers try to answer a series of basic questions, including:

- What is presented? (Identifying which data the picture presents)
- Is this an actual or recreated version of reality? (Distinguishing whether the information represents fact or fiction)
- What bearing does this have on what is known already? (Relating the data to other information)
- What would be an appropriate title or caption for the item? (Summarizing the data)

In Chapter 7 other considerations for processing pictures and constructing meaning from them are discussed. This discussion encompasses an examination of the varieties of pictures that appear in the social studies, including political cartoons.

Metaphors and Other Figures of Speech

"The cold war has ended." "The United States can't be the world's police officer." Both social studies text materials and classroom discussions frequently employ such *figures of speech*. These are expressions that force students to go beyond the literal meaning of each concept in a statement to fathom the intent of the author (see Pugh, Hicks, Davis, & Venstra, 1992).

metaphors

The Nature of Metaphors.   Among the most common figures of speech that students encounter in social studies discussions are *metaphors* and *similes* (Mahood, 1987; Martorella, 1988). A **metaphor** is a phrase in which something well known is used to explain or expand the meaning of another item less well known—for example: "Reagan was the Teflon president." The familiar no-stick quality of Teflon serves to illustrate how criticisms of the president did not stick.

Similes function in a similar way. They also compare unlike sets of items, but use the terms *like* or *as:* "The president is *like* the captain of a ship."

Metaphors in Social Studies Instruction.   Metaphors are interwoven throughout texts, media reports, and discussions. Howard (1987) observed that metaphors are used to clarify points or to define a concept—for example: A revolution is an exploding volcano. Metaphors apparently act as a cognitive puzzle. To solve the puzzle, students need to discover the similarity between two seemingly dissimilar sets of concepts in the metaphor.

At least some evidence suggests that even children in the elementary grades are prepared to produce and comprehend some forms of metaphors (Flynn, Dagostino, & Carofio, 1995; Winner, 1988); these, in turn, are recognized as important tools for acquiring and restructuring knowledge. At the same time, it also is evident that teachers lack explicit instructional models that draw on relevant theory and research. For example, Readence, Baldwin, and Head (1987) concluded: "A survey of widely used basals will reveal that the typical instructional sequence involves defining a metaphor and then offering opportunities for practice in interpretation. The manuals provide little in the way of 'how to' suggestions" (p. 440).

Drawing on the work of researchers, it is possible to infer a general comprehension strategy that teachers could employ for teaching metaphors (Martorella & Spires, 1992). It might be hypothesized as follows:

1. Draw students' attention to the nonliteral meaning of the metaphorical statement. (Example: For the statement "A revolution is an exploding volcano," ask whether volcanoes actually explode during a revolution.)

2. Model your thinking for the students as you note that a nonliteral interpretation has been made intentionally by the author. (Example: Point out that the author described a revolution in an unusual way to draw attention to its unusual qualities.)

3. Assist the students in identifying the appropriate matching attribute in the topic and the vehicle. (Example: Let's list on the board some things we think of when we hear the word *volcanoes*. Now let's list some things we think of when we hear *revolutions*.)

4. Instruct students to disregard matching attributes that are trivial or inappropriate to comprehending the metaphor. (Example: Which items do we have in both lists? Which items do you think are most important?)

5. Provide ongoing feedback as students engage in each phase of the comprehension process.

Communicating Social Studies Subject Matter

In addition to *reading*, effective communications involve *listening*, *speaking*, and *writing*. These skills are central to productive and mutually satisfying interactions among citizens in a democratic society. In the home, the marketplace, at work, or at play, all of us are called on to read, listen, speak, and write effectively to achieve some of our most fundamental goals and to live in harmony with others.

Reading, listening, speaking, and writing are interrelated. "Each informs and supports the other" (Strickland, 1990, p. 20). Instructional approaches that attempt to integrate all of these elements into meaningful activities for children are often characterized as **whole-language approaches.** By integrating these four dimensions throughout the social studies curriculum, teachers can better help prepare students for their roles as citizens.

whole-language approach

Listening and Speaking

Much of children's early cognitive development depends on opportunities to engage in social discourse, which includes interactions within and presentations to groups, where feedback is available. As they engage in dialogue with others, children clarify and advance their own thinking, as well as influence and persuade others. Part of the social studies curriculum should assist students in becoming effective in communicating their ideas through listening and speaking to other individuals and interacting in small and large groups.

Some students, as they enter school, appear to be skillful listeners; they already have learned to wait quietly until another finishes speaking. Becoming a good listener, like becoming a good speaker, requires practice. The basic characteristic of good listeners seems to be that they allow senders to complete their messages without interruption and that they interpret correctly the senders' main points. Both conditions are necessary for effective listening.

In the classroom, helping students become good listeners includes teaching them to take turns in talking and to wait for acknowledgment before speaking. It also requires that the teacher delay calling on impulsive speakers. Posting a simple set of rules to encourage listening and speaking in structured teacher-led discussions can be a helpful reminder to children. An example of how this may be done is shown in Figure 10.14.

Other techniques that help foster effective listening and speaking are:

- Requiring all students periodically to restate or review what another said earlier
- Providing criteria for self-analysis of speaking abilities
- Emphasizing frequent oral reports and show-and-tell opportunities
- Creating games or role-playing enactments to provide practice in letting everyone speak and listen
- Asking older students periodically to take notes when others give reports or short presentations
- Having older students listen to public speakers or media figures and then quizzing them on what was said
- Encouraging older children to practice giving their reports at home by using a tape recorder or a video camera

A self-evaluation form that students may use to monitor their own discussion habits in groups is shown in Figure 10.15.

Integrating Writing Into the Social Studies Curriculum

Like reading, speaking, and listening, writing is an integral part of effective citizenship (Bragaw & Hartoonian, 1988; Center for Civic Education, 1991). Stotsky (1990) wrote:

FIGURE 10.14   Basic discussion rules

Group Discussion Rules

Rule 1.   Everyone must sit quietly and pay attention when another person is speaking.

Rule 2.   Only one person may speak at a time.

Rule 3.   In order to speak, each person must raise his or her hand and be recognized by the teacher or group leader.

Rule 4.   Everyone has a right to speak, but we must take turns.

| **FIGURE 10.15** | Pupil self-evaluation form for discussions |

What Do I Do in Discussions?

	Sometimes	*Always*	*Never*
1. Do I do most of the talking?	_____	_____	_____
2. Do I usually talk only a little?	_____	_____	_____
3. Can I follow the suggestions of others?	_____	_____	_____
4. Do I get angry when others do not agree with me?	_____	_____	_____
5. Do I interrupt others?	_____	_____	_____
6. Do I take turns talking?	_____	_____	_____
7. Do I stay on the subject?	_____	_____	_____
8. Am I a good listener?	_____	_____	_____

Writing has been as much a part of the history of democratic self government as reading, and is essential to public speaking. In the course of American history, as local self government developed, so too did the kind and amount of writing that people needed to do as citizens. . . .

Writing is also a vital support for the most direct way that citizens can express themselves and participate in civic or political life; as public speakers. Finally, writing for academic purposes can stimulate the moral reasoning and the independent reading and thinking that lie at the heart of both academic study and responsible public discourse. (p. 72)

Stotsky suggested some of the basic ways that students can use writing in their citizenship roles:

- To personalize civic relationships and/or express civic identity (e.g., thank-you letter to a civic official)
- To provide information or services
- To evaluate public services
- To advocate a position on a public issue

In addition to these types of civic writings, teachers could integrate the following types of writing into social studies activities: keeping journals, writing poems, constructing data retrieval charts, preparing information for databases in computer programs, creating captions for cartoons, note taking, and writing book reviews, reports, scripts for slide shows, advertisements, and newsletters.

Some roles and/or audiences that students might assume for their writing activities are listed below (Santa et al., 1988, p. 121):

ad agencies	journalists
administrators	lawyers
artists	movie stars
athletes	older or younger students
cartoonists	pen pals
chamber of commerce	politicians
characters in novels	salespersons
community figures	scientists
doctors	teachers
historical figures	television stations
hospital patients	

RAFT
technique

The RAFT Technique.   An example of a basic technique to make students more effective writers in the context of the social studies curriculum is the **RAFT technique,** developed by Vandervanter (cited in Santa et al., 1988). The technique helps students improve their essays by teaching them to consider four major dimensions in their writing:

- *Role* they are assuming, such as a woman in colonial times or the inventor of the polio vaccine
- *Audience* to whom they are writing, such as an employer or a patient
- *Format* for the written communication, such as a diary or an advertisement
- *Topic* (plus an action verb), such as to urge an industry to stop polluting a stream or to clarify a misunderstanding with a friend

An example of a student RAFT paper is shown in Figure 10.16.

Word Processing Tools in Writing

Among the tools that teachers have for assisting students in improving their writing are various types of word processing computer programs, which encourage children to experiment with language, sentence and paragraph structure, and the sequencing of ideas and to construct multiple drafts. Such programs also allow children to create individualized storybooks and to prepare banners and newsletters.

Examples of types of software that are appropriate for elementary children, grade 3 and up, are:

Bank Street Writer	Storybook Maker
Kidwriter	The Amazing Writing Machine
Print Shop	KidWorks

FIGURE 10.16 Fifth-grade history RAFT paper

R   A colonist in America in 1608
A   A friend in England
F   Letter
T   Conditions in America

Jamestown, December 3, 1608

Dear Sir Charles,

It has been 15 long, long months since we arrived in the New World. We have had terrible troubles since we arrived. Eighty-two men died during the cold winter season of diseases and starvation. If you would kindly send more food to the New World, we might survive. Also, please send more fire arms for hunting and self-protection. Indians inhabit our land, and I have a feeling they might attack us.

Thank you,

Geoffrey P.

Source: From *Content Reading Including Study Systems* by Santa et al. Copyright © 1988 by Kendall/Hunt Publishing Company, Dubuque, IA. Reprinted with permission.

Remembering Social Studies Subject Matter

An adjunct to helping students comprehend subject matter as they read text materials is to aid them in *remembering* such information (Torney-Purta, 1991). The subject of memory traditionally has suffered from association with the rote learning of nonfunctional information. In reality, students frequently are required, in social studies classes, to remember a great number of names, places, events, dates, and general descriptive information in order to clarify and link new knowledge in meaningful ways.

First-Letter Technique

A number of specific memory strategies, or **mnemonic techniques,** have application to social studies. Mnemonics involve imagery, verbal devices, or some combination of the two (Bellezza, 1981; Wittrock, 1986).

mnemonic techniques

Simple schemes that have produced significant memory retention in studies include mediators such as the **first-letter technique.** This technique involves taking the first letter of each word to be remembered and composing a word or sentence from these letters. With this mnemonic, words are remembered either by arranging their final letters in some form of alphabetical order or by creating a new word with the list of first letters. For example, to remember the list of American presidents in correct chronological order, one may remember a rhyme such as "*Watch a jolly man make* . . . " (Washington, Adams, Jefferson, Madison, Monroe).

Keyword Technique

Another mnemonic device, the **keyword technique,** which initially was used for learning foreign language vocabulary (Atkinson, 1975), has been applied to a variety of types of information, including social studies data. The keyword technique involves first identifying a word to be related to the one to be remembered and then generating an interactive image between the two words (Levin & Pressley, 1985).

To use the keyword technique in social studies, students might try to remember such items as the names of states and capitals by first forming images of each. Then they would create some linkage between the images. For example, *apple* might stand for Annapolis, and *marry* for Maryland. The images would be linked with a new image of "apples getting married."

Studies have shown that the keyword technique can be effective in remembering certain kinds of social studies information. From their extensive review of the related research, Pressley, Levin, and Delaney (1982) concluded: "The evidence is overwhelming that use of the keyword method, as applied to recall of vocabulary definitions, greatly facilitates performance" (pp. 70–71). Their conclusion was based on an analysis of studies in which both concrete and abstract words were the learning tasks and the subjects were of varying ages.

Imagery Technique

Creating an image associated with an element of subject matter also is a useful technique for facilitating the remembering of information (Bower, 1972; Richardson, 1980; Wittrock, 1986). This **imagery technique** involves creating an image related to the information you wish to remember. Students who wish to recall the various battles of the Civil War, for example, might visually imagine Bull Run as a bull, Gettysburg as a Getty gasoline station, and so on.

Group Activities

1. Select a social studies basal text for any grade, 4 through 8. Create (a) a graphic organizer for any chapter within the text, (b) a data retrieval chart for another chapter, and (c) a frame for another chapter. Compare your results.

2. Locate a fifth-grade social studies text and select any chapter within it. Then, using either the first-letter or keyword technique, develop a mnemonic device to help remember the names of important individuals, places, or events within the chapter. Compare your results.

Individual Activities

1. Identify five metaphors in newspapers or periodicals. Then explain how you would try to explain them to a child through use of the guidelines in the chapter.

2. Identify and read four children's trade books that address significant social issues. Pick two for the primary grades and two for the intermediate grades. List the author, title, publisher, and copyright date for each, along with a brief summary of the book and the issue it raises. To identify some appropriate works, consult the references in the chapter or the following sources: A. F. Gallagher, "In Search of Justice . . . ," *Social Education*, November/December, 1988, pp. 527–531; R. W. Evans and V. O. Pang, "Resources and Materials for Issues-Centered Social Studies," *The Social Studies*, May/June, 1992, pp. 118–119.

3. Work with an individual student and help him or her construct a concept map using any concept for the organizing theme.

References

Alleman, J., & Brophy, J. (1991). *Is curriculum integration a boon or a threat to the social studies?* East Lansing: Michigan State University, Institute for Research on Teaching.

Armbruster, B. B. (1984). The problems of "inconsiderate" text. In G. G. Duffy, L. R. Roehler, & J. Mason (Eds.), *Comprehension instruction: Perspectives and suggestions* (pp. 202–217). New York: Longman.

Armbruster, B. B., & Anderson, T. (1984). Structures of explanations in history textbooks, or so what if Governor Stanford missed the spike and hit the rail? *Journal of Curriculum Studies, 16*, 181–194.

Armbruster, B. B., Anderson, T. H., & Meyer, J. L. (1991). Improving content area reading using instructional graphics. *Reading Research Quarterly, 26*, 393–416.

Armbruster, B. B., & Gudbrandsen, B. (1986). Reading comprehension instruction in social studies programs. *Reading Research Quarterly, 21*, 36–48.

Atkinson, R. C. (1975). Mnemonotechnics in second language learning. *American Psychologist, 30*, 821–828.

Beck, I. L., & McKeown, M. G. (1988). Toward meaningful accounts in history texts for young learners. *Educational Researcher, 17*, 31–39.

Beck, I. L., & McKeown, M. G. (1991). Research directions: Social studies texts are hard to understand: Mediating some of the difficulties. *Language Arts, 68*, 482–489.

Bellezza, F. S. (1981). Mnemonic devices: Classification, characteristics, and criteria. *Review of Educational Research, 51,* 247–275.

Bower, G. H. (1972). *Human memory: Basic processes.* New York: Academic Press.

Bragaw, D. H., & Hartoonian, H. M. (1988). Social studies: The study of people in society. In R. S. Brandt (Ed.), *Content of the curriculum* (pp. 9–29). Alexandria, VA: Association for Supervision and Curriculum Development.

Camperell, K., & Knight, R. S. (1991). Reading research and social studies. In J. P. Shaver (Ed.), *Handbook of research on social studies teaching and learning* (pp. 567–577). New York: Macmillan.

Carr, E., & Ogle, D. (1987). K-W-L-plus: A strategy for comprehension and summarizing. *Journal of Reading, 30,* 626–631.

Center for Civic Education. (1991). *Civitas: A framework for civic education.* Calabasas, CA: Author.

Dole, J. A., Duffy, G. G., Roehler, L. R., & Pearson, P. D. (1991). Moving from the old to the new: Research on reading comprehension instruction. *Review of Educational Research, 61,* 239–264.

Duthie, J. (1986). The web: A powerful tool for the teaching and evaluation of the expository essay. *History and Social Science Teacher, 21,* 232–236.

Flynn, L. L., Dagostino, L., & Carofio, J. (1995). Learning new concepts independently through metaphor. *Reading Improvement, 32,* 201–219.

Freeman, E. B., & Levstik, L. (1988). Recreating the past: Historical fiction in the social studies curriculum. *Elementary School Journal, 88,* 329–337.

Hamston, J., & Murdoch, K. (1996). *Integrating socially: Planning integrated units of work for social education.* Portsmouth, NH: Heinemann.

Harcourt Brace Jovanovich. (1990). *HBJ Social Studies.* Orlando, FL: Author.

Howard, R. W. (1987). *Concepts and schemata: An introduction.* Philadelphia: Cassell.

Levin, J., & Pressley, M. (1985). Mnemonic vocabulary instruction: What's fact, what's fiction. In R. Dillon (Ed.), *Individual differences in cognition* (Vol. 2, pp. 145–172). New York: Academic Press.

Mahood, W. (1987). Metaphors in social studies instruction. *Theory and Research in Social Education, 15,* 285–297.

Martorella, P. H. (1988). Students' understanding of metaphorical concepts in international relations. *Social Science Record, 25,* 46–49.

Martorella, P. H., & Spires, H. A. (1992). Minding metaphors: Instructional strategies for production and comprehension. *Teaching Thinking and Problem Solving, 14,* 1, 3–5.

McGowan, T. M., Erickson, L., & Neufeld, J. A. (1996). With reason and rhetoric, building the case for the literature social studies connection. *Social Education, 60,* 203–207.

McGowan, T. M., Guzzetti, B., & Kowalinski, B. (1992). Using literature studies to promote elementary social studies learning. *Social Studies and the Young Learner, 5,* 10–13.

Notable 1990 children's trade books in the field of social studies. (1991). *Social Education, 55,* 253–260.

Novak, J., & Gowin, D. B. (1984). *Learning how to learn.* Cambridge, UK: Cambridge University Press.

Ogle, C. (1986). K-W-L: A teaching model that develops active reading of expository text. *The Reading Teacher, 39,* 564–570.

Pressley, M., Levin, J. R., & Delaney, H. D. (1982). The mnemonic keyword method. *Review of Educational Research, 52,* 61–91.

Pugh, S. L., Hicks, J. W., Davis, M., & Venstra, T. (1992). *Bridging: A teacher's guide to metaphorical thinking.* Urbana, IL: National Council of Teachers of English.

Readence, J. E., Baldwin, R. S., & Head, M. H. (1987). Teaching young readers to interpret metaphors. *The Reading Teacher, 40,* 439–443.

Richardson, J. T. E. (1980). *Mental imagery and human memory.* New York: Macmillan.

Roberts, P. L. (1996). *Integrating language arts and social studies for kindergarten and primary children.* Upper Saddle River, NJ: Merrill/Prentice Hall.

Santa, C. M., Havens, L., Nelson, M., Danner, M., Scalf, L., & Scalf, J. (1988). *Content reading including study systems: Reading, writing and studying across the curriculum.* Dubuque, IA: Kendall/Hunt.

Siler, C. R. (1986–87). Content analysis: A process for textbook analysis and evaluation. *International Journal of Social Education, 1,* 78–99.

Silverblank, F. (1992). *An annotated bibliography of historical fiction for the social studies, grades 5 through 12.* Dubuque, IA: Kendall/Hunt.

Singer, H. (1986). Friendly texts: Description and criteria. In E. K. Dishner, T. W. Bean, J. E. Readence, & D. W. Moore (Eds.), *Reading in the content areas: Improving classroom instruction* (2nd ed.). Dubuque, IA: Kendall/Hunt.

Stotsky, S. (1990). Connecting reading and writing to civic education. *Educational Leadership, 47,* 72–73.

Strickland, D. S. (1990). Emergent literacy: How young children learn to read and write. *Educational Leadership, 47,* 18–23.

Torney-Purta, J. (1991). Schema theory and cognitive psychology: Implications for social studies. *Theory and Research in Social Education, 19,* 189–210.

Winner, E. (1988). *The point of words.* Cambridge, MA: Harvard University Press.

Wittrock, M. C. (1986). Students' thought processes. In M. C. Wittrock (Ed.), *Handbook of research on teaching* (3rd ed., pp. 297–314). New York: Macmillan.

Wood, K. (1988). Guiding students through informational text. *The Reading Teacher, 41,* 912–920.

Wooster, J. (1991, July/December). Purposeful planning: A key to using children's trade books to teach social studies. *CBC Features.*

Young, T. A., & Marek-Schroer, M. F. (1992). Writing to learn in social studies. *Social Studies and the Young Learner, 5,* 14–16.

Zarnowski, M. (1988). Learning about contemporary women: Sharing biographies with children. *The Social Studies, 79,* 61–63.

Zarnowski, M. (1990). *Learning about biographies: A reading and writing approach for children.* Urbana, IL: National Council of Teachers of English.

Chapter

Harnessing Technology to the Social Studies Curriculum

Infusing Microcomputer Applications Into the Social Studies Curriculum

Telecommunications and Emerging Technologies

Identifying and Evaluating Appropriate Social Studies Software Programs

Interactive Multimedia in Social Studies Instruction

Distance Learning

Using Videotape and Television in Social Studies Instruction

Using Traditional Media Effectively

Technologies in the 21st Century

It is October 15, 2000, and we are about to visit Mr. Cornell's fifth–grade class in Angel Butte. It is already under way. The classroom is charged with energy and abuzz with activity. At first blush, however, to the untutored eye the class appears chaotic and lacking focus and structure.

Mr. Cornell spots us at the door and waves us into the room. He is hovering over a computer station, brainstorming with a small group of students who, he explains later, are working on an interdisciplinary unit. It deals with the social and biological effects of stream pollution, a hot issue in the small western community where the school resides.

The students, still in the preliminary stages of their research, first surveyed some basic reference materials such as the CD-ROM Encarta Encyclopedia School Edition and the online version of Encyclopedia Britannica. Now they are deep into the recesses of the Internet, using Netscape Communicator (formerly Netscape Navigator) to browse the World Wide Web for related information. They are floundering and need Mr. Cornell's help with identifying meaningful key words. He patiently explains how much trial and error is required for successful Web searches and he models some effective approaches. He also directs the students to Terry, the class Internet guru, for tutoring.

As we move about the room, we notice several other students recording notes for their group, using Bank Street Writer word processing software. They beckon to Mr. Cornell for assistance with a cranky printer that is causing font problems when they try to print a word processing file.

Nearby, two students are using a multimedia authoring system, HyperStudio. They are building the outline and structure that will be used to construct their unit report. A third member of the group is using a scanner to collect the images that will be required in the multimedia unit.

Suddenly, the class is joined by a noisy and animated group returning from the media center. With the help of the media parent volunteer, the students have located some excellent print and electronic trade books, as well as an extensive collection of database information.

In a quiet corner, a student with a portable phone is explaining the class's project to a state environmental official, who gives the student some contacts and telephone numbers. The official also volunteers to fax several sets of relevant charts and an important article describing the social costs of pollution.

At another spot in the back of the room, two other students are accessing the relevant electronic bulletin boards and attending to the daily review of e-mail messages. The students are frustrated because some of the messages are garbled and others were returned because of address errors. The designated e-mail experts try to sort out and repair the problems.

In the mini-media center, a small cluster of students are viewing the science laserdisc, Windows on Science. The group leader periodically stops the disc at individual frames for review or discussion. The teacher briefly joins the group to call attention to the list of important videodisc frames listed on the chalkboard and to raise questions.

About midway through the class, four students sign out to attend their 30-minute distance-education class housed adjacent to the media center. The session originates over 2,000 miles away and allows two-way communication between the remote instructor and the class. Today's program features a professor who is an expert on scientific and ethical concerns relevant to the group's project focus: the problem of water pollution in emerging nations.

Of the remaining students, one group is working with a preservice teacher-in-training to learn how to use ClarisWorks, a program that can be used to create a database for part of the project. All the students in the class, except this group, learned how to use the software the previous year.

In class Mr. Cornell uses a laptop computer for such tasks as note taking and PowerPoint transparency-like presentations. After school is over, he will take the computer home to preview new software and to assist in his planning. All the teachers at his school can check out laptops or other computers over the summer and vacation periods.

Infusing Microcomputer Applications Into the Social Studies Curriculum

All of the technologies employed in the school we have just described are, in fact, available and in use in schools and social studies classes across our nation, albeit not as extensively in individual classrooms. Mr. Cornell provides for his students a technology-rich environment that is highly functional in relation to his curricular goals. His students freely and comfortably use technology tools to access information and solve problems in school, as well as in the real world.

Although they have not yet engendered a revolution in our classrooms, computers have demonstrated that they can provide forms of instruction and reinforcement beyond the capability of alternative media. They have shown that with all ages and types of students, they can simulate patience, humor, excellent memories, personalized assistance, and immediate feedback on demand. In addition, they have extended our vistas concerning schools: "In the era of electronic learning, school is where the learner is" (Mecklenburger, 1990, p. 107).

In social studies classes, computers have proven that they can help students quickly access in structured ways great amounts of information to aid in hypothesis development and problem solving, simulate important social issues, and better organize their ideas and reports. Above all, computers can challenge and excite students.

With some exceptions, however, the full potential impact of computers on the array of required subjects and topics in the curriculum has not been fully realized (Mecklenberger, 1990). The newer computer-related technologies have yet to emerge as significant instruments of curricular change in our classrooms. The Office of Technology Assessment (1995, p. 2) reported in 1995, for example: "Despite technologies available in schools, a substantial number of teachers report they do not use computers and other technologies regularly for instruction."

Traditional technological tools such as overhead, film, and slide projectors and duplicating and xerography machines continue to dominate as the preferred electronic tools for facilitating social studies instruction. Increasingly, however, they will share a role with the developing computer-based technologies that have touched the lives of every American and forged a communications revolution outside of the classroom (Tyre, 1990).

Telecommunications and Emerging Technologies

By all accounts, the growth in telecommunications applications in recent years has been phenomenal. **Telecommunications** involves sending and receiving information, using some combination of a microcomputer, modem, communications software, and a telephone, satellite transmission, or cable. Through developing telecommunications teachers and students can exchange information around the world.

The Internet

Increasingly, telecommunications around the world are being sent along the *Internet*, a massive, giant electronic highway that speeds messages and information from networks of linked computers along to their destinations. No one is sure of the actual number of users on the Internet, since there is no central agency regulating it or keeping track of users.

Those who share access to the Internet may send messages, retrieve information and files from databases, and connect with thousands of other networks around the world. Telecommunications over the Internet can involve images, graphics, and sound, as well as text.

For a nominal fee, access to the Internet typically is arranged by a commercial service (e.g., America Online). It is often available at no cost through universities or other educational institutions. For example, the state of Massachusetts, through the Mass LearnNet, gives an Internet connection to any school within the state that requests it. TENET in Texas and VaPAN in Virginia have statewide networks for K through 12 teachers.

The Internet was created in 1969 by the Pentagon to help researchers and the military expedite the sharing of information around the world. Increasingly, however, it is being used by teachers and students to access and share information and break down the barriers between school and real-world learning (Martorella, 1997; Pawloski, 1994). The Internet also serves to reduce the isolation that many classroom teachers feel and increases the potential for collaborative activities (Kearsley, 1996).

The World Wide Web and Web Search Agents

One of the major components of the Internet is the **World Wide Web (WWW)**, a vast network of information nodes that are linked. Within the WWW, information is organized into "pages." By clicking on a button or a highlighted area on a page, the WWW lets you create a link to files on computers at sites across the world (Kearsley, 1996). You then can access the files from the web sites over the Internet.

Each web site has its own individual **Universal Resource Locater** (URL), which serves as its address. To illustrate, the URL for the NCSS web site is <http://www.ncss.org.online/wwwhome.html>(omit brackets when typing). In Figure 11.1, Cowan (1996) explains the various elements in the URL.

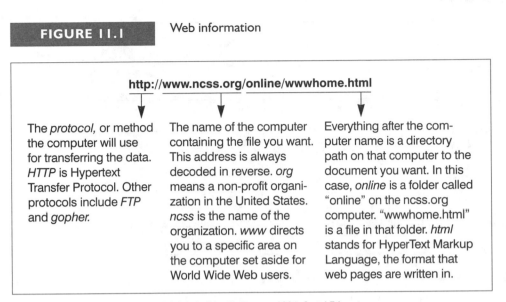

| **FIGURE 11.1** | Web information |

http://www.ncss.org/online/wwwhome.html

The *protocol,* or method the computer will use for transferring the data. *HTTP* is Hypertext Transfer Protocol. Other protocols include *FTP* and *gopher.*

The name of the computer containing the file you want. This address is always decoded in reverse. *org* means a non-profit organization in the United States. *ncss* is the name of the organization. *www* directs you to a specific area on the computer set aside for World Wide Web users.

Everything after the computer name is a directory path on that computer to the document you want. In this case, *online* is a folder called "online" on the ncss.org computer. "wwwhome.html" is a file in that folder. *html* stands for HyperText Markup Language, the format that web pages are written in.

Source: Adapted from "How the Web Works" by G. Cowan, 1996, *Social Education.*

Sites on the WWW also have **web home pages,** which may introduce the site, give directions for how to navigate it, provide links to other sites through the use of highlighted terms and buttons, or offer general information. WWW files can contain text, images, and audio and video clips. An example of the first or home page of one web site is shown in Figure 11.2. There is no cost for linking to most sites, but some are restricted and will deny access to users who do not have an account with the site.

web home pages

WWW Browsers.   The presence of an extensive body of information that continues to grow has spawned the creation of software tools, called **web browsers,** that can help us navigate the WWW. Browsers serve as our guides, accessing the WWW on demand to locate and read information we request. Then they display it one screen at a time in a form easily understood on any computer. Two of the most popular browsers are *Netscape Communicator* and *Internet Explorer.*

web browsers

Consider how Netscape works when you access its home page. If you click on the button that says "net search," it will take you to a selection of "search agents" (special software for searching on the Internet) that will conduct the search for the topic you wish to reference. At that point, you select from a list of choices an agent, say the one called *Yahoo!,* and click on its button.

When you do, you will be taken to a linked page and asked to provide Yahoo! with the key words of the item you wish to retrieve from the WWW— for example, you type "lesson plans," and then click the "search" button. This action will initiate a search for information relevant to your query. When the list of items from the search of web sites is assembled, it will be displayed, looking something like Figure 11.2.

FIGURE 11.2   Home page of a web site

Stock Quotes, News & Charts - Yahoo! Classifieds - Get Local - My Yahoo!

Also Free Call & Bug Tracking Software

Old-style, Alphabetical Format | Description of Enhancements

Categories - **Sites** - AltaVista Web Pages | Headlines - Net Events

Found **0** Category and **103** Site Matches for **lesson plans**.

Yahoo! Site Matches   (1 - 20 of 103)

Education: Teaching: K-12

- **Lesson Plans** Using Internet Web Sites - sample **lesson plans** using internet sites and information on creating your own **plans** and Bloom's taxonomy.

Science: Mathematics: Education: K-12

- Mathematics **Lesson Plans** - This site provides a collection of **lesson plans** for Secondary Mathematics teachers to use. Each **lesson** incorporates internet sites to be used into actual **lesson**.
- Big Sky Math **Lessons** - gopher site for K-12 **lesson plans**.
- Web Sites and Resources for Teachers: Math - links to **lesson plans**, activities and other resources on the web.

Entertainment: Music: Education: Teaching

- Music Educators' **Lesson Plans** - for educators to share **lesson plans** and ideas. Everyone is encouraged to contribute.

Education: K-12: Resources

- **Lesson Plans** Using Internet Web Sites - sample **lesson plans** using internet sites and

Source: Yahoo!

The search in our example identified 67 web sites to contact, but some look potentially more useful than others. We can link to and learn more about each by clicking on its highlighted area.

Online Databases

Through the Internet, students now have immediate *online* access to gigantic data bases that once were the exclusive province of the military, corporations, and scholars. The online provision refers to the fact that a user is actually interacting with a computer that may be several thousand miles or even continents away.

The computer is an ideal tool for those social studies topics that involve information retrieval, analysis, organization, and processing (Bilof, 1987; Hunter, 1985). These processes require accessing, creating, and manipulating *databases*. Ehman and Glenn (1987, p. 37) have called databases "one of the most powerful computer tools available for social studies instruction."

Among other features, a database can be used to access factual data (e.g., Who was our youngest president?); illustrate trends (e.g., Which were the 10 largest cities in the United States from 1950 to 1990?); and test hypotheses (e.g., Do countries with high infant mortality rates have a low or a high standard of living?).

The scope of existing databases extends to magazines, newspapers, biographies, photographs, wire news services, reference works, government publications, book reviews, recordings, consumer information, and much more. As an illustration, The New Deal Network, which is still growing, has a web site (<http://newdeal.marist.edu>) that contains a photographic archive of several thousand images of the Great Depression.

Many university and other libraries are converting their card catalogs to information retrieval systems that can be accessed online by schools and the general public. In North Carolina, for example, it is possible for anyone at a remote location to search online through the electronic list of holdings of the major universities in the state. Several other states make similar provisions.

The Library of Congress is engaged in a project that will make five million items from its holdings available online by the year 2000. The library will make accessible a vast array of primary sources, including photographs. Currently, it is field-testing use of the materials with students, including those in the intermediate and middle grades.

Resources for Social Studies Teachers and Students Available Over the Internet

Apart from files of data, the list of resources available without charge to users at WWW sites is enormous and growing by leaps and bounds. Consequently, published URL lists often are already out of date by the time they hit the newsstand. An excellent starting point for relevant web sites is *T.H.E. Journal's Road Map to the World Wide Web for Educators, 1996,* which contains hundreds of site addresses. The list is available online at <http://www.thejournal.edu>. To stay up to date, teachers can look to WWW references in the Instructional Technology: Internet section of *Social Education*, the official journal of the NCSS.

What follows is only a small sample of the varied materials on the WWW for social studies teachers and students. As you examine the list, recall that I noted earlier that each web site has a unique URL or address that we use to locate it.

Teacher Resources

Links to Social Studies Resources:
http://www.halcyon.com/howlevin/social.studies.html

K–12 World: http://www.k12world.com

Houghton Mifflin's Education Place, K–8:
http://www.eduplace.com

Top 10 Internet Learning Sites: http:/www.pierian.com

CUSeeMe Schools Using Videoconferencing:
http://www.gsn.org/gsn/cu/index.html

Links to Social Studies Sites: http://www.csun.edu/~hcedu013/

Database and Links to Social Studies Sites:
http://www.exepc.com/~dboals/k-12.html

IBM K–12 Teacher Resources: http://www.solutions.ibm.com/k12

Discovery Channel Resources: http://www.discovery.com

Resources for Teachers and Elementary- and Middle-Grade Students

U.S. Civil War Center: http://www.cwc.lsu.edu/

Planet Earth: http://www.nosc.mil/planet_earth/states.html

National Geographic Online: http://www.nationalgeographic.com

Books About the Native Peoples of Canada and the United States:
http://www.9to5.com/NBC/

Intercultural E-Mail Classroom Connections:
http://www.stolaf.edu/network/iecc/

Kids Creativity Cafe: http://www.creativity.net/ccafe/

CNN News: http://www.cnn.com

Global SchoolNet Foundation: http://www.gsn.org/

Library of Congress: http://www.loc.gov

Electronic Mail and Newsgroups

"Use of electronic mail in education has grown rapidly in recent years, reflecting proliferation of microcomputers, modems, networks, and easier-to-use software" (Updegrove, 1991, p. 37). One of the primary uses of the burgeoning

Internet is to support *Electronic mail* **(e-mail or email).** E-mail is a system of sending and receiving communications across great distances at relatively little cost. Once a school or classroom is set up for access to the Internet, the only direct cost for e-mail often is the price of a local phone call.

e-mail

Like the WWW, e-mail systems rely on a network of computers, one of which is a local contact. Networks exist all over the world. Typically, e-mail requires a computer, a modem, communications software, and access to a telephone line.

E-mail can be sent from individual to individual or from an individual to a group. Just as with web sites, each e-mail user (whether an organization or an individual) on the Internet is assigned an address. A social studies teacher who needed help with planning a unit on families around the world might contact the Educational Resources Information Center Clearinghouse on Information and Technology for help at the address <askeric@ericir.syr.edu>.

Across the country, teachers are using e-mail to extend the classroom (see <http://www.kidlink.org/>). In Vermont, teachers and students worked together over the Vermont Educators' Network to write a geography text for young children. Students at various remote locations do research for the text and send their data via e-mail to a central school that will organize and publish the collective results.

Using e-mail, a middle-grade class compared its ideas of what made up an ideal community with those of other students in the United States and abroad (Brehm & Waugh, 1993).

"Where on the Globe Is Roger?" (see Figure 11.3) is an illustration of how e-mail may be used in conjunction with the study of countries. Roger Williams, a retired pilot, invites students to join him and his truck, Bubba, electronically for his jaunts around the world. To date, he has visited two continents, seven countries, and the Americas, and is continuing his journey. The children who follow along through e-mail learn about history, geography, anthropology, and sociology.

E-mail holds out the promise of cross-cultural insights and sharing of information from regional, national, and international sites. It also affords students in social studies classes opportunities to obtain timely and reality-based data for research projects. In addition, it allows children to obtain multiple perspectives, including global ones, on an issue.

E-mail also can help students hone their communication skills. Since e-mail protocols promote focused writing (i.e., identifying audience and the purpose of the message), revising and editing before sending are important. Because the message will be sent out over a public forum to an unseen audience, students also tend to be motivated to produce an exemplary communication.

Similar to e-mail, **newsgroups** (also called "electronic bulletin boards") serve as a forum for the exchange of ideas. They provide an easy, low-cost way for individuals to interact with one another anywhere in the world using a computer, a modem, software, and the Internet. Users can post and receive written text messages about any subject (see Harris, 1993).

newsgroups

FIGURE 11.3   Where on the Globe Is Roger?

Introducing... Where on the Globe Is Roger?

Join Roger Williams, a global adventurer and raconteur, as he leaves South America and travels to South East Asia. Roger is driving around the globe in his 1982 Dodge truck and he wants to take you along on his trip—via your connection to the Internet. You can plot his travels on your global map; read his entertaining dispatches from the exotic places he visits; ask him questions; and make friends with the students in the places he visits.

Global SchoolNet Foundation is pleased to provide you with "free travel passes" to take a most amazing electronic journey with Roger!

Here is an invitation from Roger to all the school children around the globe.

Dear Boys and Girls,

I would like to introduce you to what I think will be a great adventure for us all and a chance to learn about countries around the world, first hand. My name is Roger Williams. I'm a retired Airline Pilot and U.S. Marine Corps Aviator. I was born on a ranch in Texas on October 3, 1936, graduated from High School in Austin, Texas, and then spent one year at the University of Texas.

My dream from the fourth grade on was to become a Marine Pilot. That dream was realized after many years of hard work in April 1962. While in the Marine Corps, I flew off aircraft carriers during the Vietnam War. I have always enjoyed traveling and I think this will be the ultimate trip as I drive my truck across every continent around the globe.

On the first leg of my journey. I departed from Southern California, on January 14, 1994, and drove through Mexico and all of Central America. I then shipped my truck from Panama to Northern Chile. From there I drove the full length of Chile and crossed into Argentina and proceeded to Tierra del Fuego. Upon completing my goal of reaching Tierra del Fuego by mid April 1994, I then proceeded north

---

Newsgroups are organized around themes. For example, there is a newsgroup called "k12.ed.soc-studies." The address for contacting the NCSS is <ncss-1@bgu.edu>. Lists of newsgroups are available over the Internet at various web sites. One such source, TILE.NET.LISTS (see Tile home page in Figure 11.4), can be found at the address <http:www.tile.net>.

Figure 11.5 describes a simulation dealing with local history that involves an electronic bulletin board (Nauss, 1992). Fourteen fourth-grade classrooms and seven school districts participated. Information was shared among schools through an electronic bulletin board.

FIGURE 11.3 *(Continued)*

through Argentina to Brazil and shipped my truck from Santos, Brazil, to Brisbane, Australia.

Throughout my travels, I visited local schools and helped the children communicate with kids back in the United States.

I am about to begin the next part of my journey. I am flying to Brisbane on August 1, 1994, to start my trip through Australia, Indonesia, Malaysia, Thailand, and possibly Burma—and, then on to China and Russia. I hope to be able to cross Russia then travel into Europe through Spain and Portugal. I will cross into Africa and finally return home sometime in late 1996 or early 1997.

As you can see, it will be a grand adventure and I hope you can join me through activities being coordinated by the Global SchoolNet Foundation. You see, challenge is an integral part of the human experience. Without it, life becomes very dull. We all have to challenge ourselves if we expect to grow and help make a better world for people to live in. Through participating in this adventure, I would hope you will be able to form life long friendships with other students around the world.

With better global human understanding, the possibility of violent conflicts diminishes. I am hoping all of us can contribute to a lasting World Peace.

I will be sending you summaries of my travels and when possible, digitized photos, using a special device called ComputerEyes that hooks up to my Apple laptop computer. I look forward to answering your questions and will do the best that I can. If my answers sometimes seem short and to the point, that is just the way I am—so just bear with me!

Sincerely,

Roger

Two-Way Videoconferencing Over the Internet

As we saw with the WWW, the Internet is able to transfer audio, video, and images. An application of this capability is **two-way videoconferencing** (sometimes known as **desk-top videoconferencing**), which works like a picture phone. Recall the class of fifth-grade students described in the introduction to this chapter. One group was using a piece of software called *Enhanced CUSeeMe*, commercial software (cost approximately $50), to construct an inexpensive interactive videoconferencing system.

two-way video-conferencing

desk-top video-conferencing

FIGURE 11.4   Source for lists of newsgroups

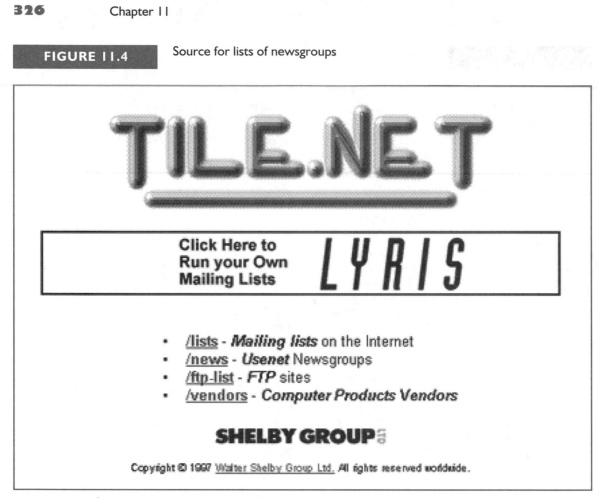

Enhanced CUSeeMe makes possible two-way transmission of sound and images in real time (i.e., as events are taking place) over the Internet. Using the software, the group will be able to see and speak with students at other schools who are working on similar projects and to share visual data and presentations. Schools can be anywhere in the nation or world where Internet access is available.

As we go to press, a free version of a similar program, *CUSeeMe*, also is available. For information on how to obtain it, contact Cornell University at the e-mail address: <CU-SeeMe-L@Cornell.edu>. Netscape and Macintosh are collaborating on developing a videoconferencing system called *CoolTalk for Macintosh*. It works with the browser Netscape, and currently it also is free.

Apart from the expenses related to the Internet telephone connection, software costs (if any), and the computer station, the total cost for a basic, nonelaborate videoconferencing system can be minimal. Images can be provided by a digital camera, regular video cameras that are connected to a video capture board, or a special inexpensive miniature video camera (e.g., QuickCam, cost approximately $95).

FIGURE 11.5 Pirates Ahoy!

Pirates Ahoy!

Pirates Ahoy is an integrated lesson designed to take four months or longer. Subject areas include Language Arts, Math, Art, Science, Social Studies, Research, Computer Skills, and Telecommunications. It is based on the search for Captain Kidd's treasure in the "Money Pit" on Oak Island, Nova Scotia, six miles from us—a search which is still in progress! The activity was designed for use with eight- and nine-year-old students, but fascination with pirates and buried treasure touches all ages, and provides its own motivation. Avast, landlubbers!

Objectives

Provide an active audience for writing to improve keyboarding, word processing skills, proofreading, and spelling skills. Provide a practical use for database development and searching, and to use scale in diagrams. Expand use of telecommunication from letter writing to a new method of sharing and learning.

Hardware and Software Needed

Computer, modem, communication program, word processor, graphics program, public domain *Flags* program.

Telecommunication Resources:

Local BBS.

Curriculum Areas

Language arts, art, social studies, computer literacy, math, research skills, interpersonal relationships, cooperation.

Grade Level:

Three.

Class Time Required

Four to five months, three forty-minute periods a week. The weekly time gradually decreases until only the time to keep the story moving is required.

Management Strategies

Computers are shared by a group of students. I have six groups because we are on a six-day cycle. Each child has a disk for their writing. On the day they use the computer they are required to do certain activities: spelling drill with words from that week's list, complete a word processor exercise, write their pen pal, do a math drill, copy and proof a story they have written, work on problem solving, or write a chapter for a continuing story. Other activities might include using a graphics program to produce a picture to go with a story, creating a map for a social studies lesson, or completing a reading activity. Class work is adjusted so students receive instructional time, but may be excused from the practical work or have only a portion of an assignment. I have not found this to cause difficulties with their progress.

Students are required to use consideration for members of the class who are not using the computer and to share with other group members. Failure to heed

FIGURE 11.5 *(Continued)*

the rules leads to loss of computer time. In my experience, the computer has been effective in improving and developing students' interpersonal relationships and social skills. It has improved writing, editing, and spelling skills, and it provides an active audience for writing.

Procedures/Activities

- Locate a class with whom you can exchange a story. Arrange a time frame and agree on a subject.
- Assign pupils to groups to gather information on types of ships, clothes, flags, weapons, and so on. During computer time, they record the information in note form, save it, and print it to make a reference booklet. Include information from "Oak Island and the Money Pit."
- On a map, label the nationalities of the pirates and draw a flag of their country. Use the program *Flags* to develop recognition of national flags during computer time.
- Brainstorm vocabulary lists of words and phrases: jolly roger, swab the decks, walk the plank, brig, and so on.
- As a group, write the initial chapter of the story. Type it and post it to the BBS.
- Find out where pirates were active, plot routes across the ocean to these areas, and determine the distances covered.
- Use scale to a diagram the money pit. Add to the story every other week, weaving in vocabulary and facts about Captain Kidd. Do this in groups or individually. The writing is typed, proofed, and sent to the BBS.
- Lessons using a pirate theme should incorporate information gained during research, designing pirate flags and illustrations.
- Students record information on pirates in a database. They will need to learn how to enter data and use search options.
- At the end of the story, students use a graphics program to design a cover and page layout. It is printed, illustrations are added, and copies are made for the other school, the library, and each child in the class.
- During this time I also read "The Hand of Robin Squires," by Joan Clark, and "The Teaser." This is still seen as a ghost ship today by many local residents. Include the story of how the women of Chester scared away an American privateer when their men were away.
- Invite one of the Oak Island workers to share what he knows about searching for Kidd's treasure on the island.
- Plan an excursion to visit the island and the museum.

Evaluating Achievement of Objectives

Compare writing at the beginning and end of the project. Check accuracy of scale drawing and map work, use of vocabulary, observation of keyboarding skills, ability to use editing commands on the word processor and to enter data and search to provide answers using the data base.

Source: Carol A. Nauss, 1992, *T.I.E. News,* 4.

Identifying and Evaluating Appropriate Social Studies Software

In addition to the vast resources available through the Internet, an assortment of software programs with individual lessons, exercises, and activities exists. However, teachers must select software carefully, choosing only programs that address important curricular objectives, regardless of their other merits.

Software programs often are categorized according to the instructional technique they employ (e.g., simulations, tutorials, drill-and-practice) or the functions they perform (e.g., word processing, database management, graphing). Throughout other chapters, where appropriate, specific software programs have been identified in relationship to activities.

However, note that new software is continually being developed and old titles retired or modified. For a list of current social studies titles, consult publications such as *Multimedia Source Guide* (1995–96) and *Only the Best: The Annual Guide to Highest Rated Education Software/Multimedia for Preschool–Grade 12* (Association for Supervision and Curriculum Development, 1995). The catalogs from commercial firms such as Educational Resources (1-800-624-2926) and Educational Software Institute (1-800-955-5570) list a large inventory of social studies titles.

Simulation Software

In Chapter 5, we considered *non*computerized simulations as an effective way to explore social issues in social studies classes. The increasing ability and speed of microcomputers in presenting complex simulations gives them a major edge over board-game counterparts.

Among other features, computer simulations afford students the opportunity to explore roles, positions, and opinions and obtain feedback in privacy. In addition, they can engage students in the kinds of challenges and opportunities for problem solving and success that the electronic games outside of the classroom present. Computer simulations also have the capacity to stimulate lively discussions, whether used as an individual, small-group, or whole-class activity with a large monitor.

An example of simulation software is *American Revolution CD* by Centrex, designed for grades 4 through 9, which immerses students in life during the Revolution by engaging them in roles related to such events as the Boston Tea Party and the writing of the Constitution. It also includes lots of graphics and video. For middle- and secondary-grade studies, Centrex has produced the simulation, *Civil War II*, which re-creates that period of our history. Two other popular and challenging simulations are *Crosscountry USA*, *Decisions, Decisions: Immigration* and *Where in the World Is Carmen Sandiego?*.

As with noncomputerized simulations, teachers need to carefully structure an activity and engage students in reflection and generalization. As a general procedure for effective use of a computer simulation, teachers should follow the five-step guidelines for enactments discussed in detail in Chapter 5:

1. Initiation and direction;
2. Describing the scenario;
3. Assigning roles;
4. Enactment; and
5. Debriefing.

Database and Spreadsheet Software

databases

In addition to accessing databases online, students can learn to create and analyze **databases,** which is possible with software programs such as *ClarisWorks*. These types of software are generic; that is, they contain no information but instead are "shells" that will operate with any type of data. Database shells allow students to create their own information systems (see Bilof, 1987; Mernit, 1991).

For example, suppose a class research project involves collecting basic data concerning the nature, scope, and seriousness of the problem of the homeless in America. The teacher has divided the class into 10 groups, each responsible for five states.

After some discussion, the teacher and the groups identify the basic questions they would like to have answered from the research.

- Who are the homeless (e.g., gender, number of children)?
- How extensive is the problem of the homeless (e.g., number)?
- Where is the problem of the homeless the greatest in the United States (e.g., states with highest percentage)?
- How much are local and state governments doing to solve the problem of the homeless (e.g., state expenditures, type of shelters provided)?

One group lists on a large sheet of paper the categories of data that it recommends the class collect and enter into the database according to the procedures specified in the software manual. The categories the students initially include in the database are shown in Figure 11.6.

Other groups make further recommendations. The teacher points out some changes in the categories that are required by the protocols of the database, for example, not using commas in recording numerical data. The class as a whole then finally adopts a common list of categories.

As a next step, students proceed to do research and mathematical calculations to identify the required information, then enter the data under each category. Once this is accomplished, students can use the database to answer their questions.

spreadsheet

Spreadsheet software engages students in social mathematics (Hannah, 1985–86). It enables them to make numerical tabulations quickly, make predic-

FIGURE 11.6	Categories initially included in the database

Name of state (abbr): _____   Total population of state: _____

Estimated number of homeless: _____

Homeless as % of total population: _____

Percentage of homeless who are males: _____   Females: _____

Percentage of homeless who are children (17 yrs. or less): _____

Annual state and local governmental expenditures for the homeless: _____

Types of shelters provided (select type from the list): _____

_____

tions from extrapolations, and show the impact of one variable on another (e.g., effects of increased cigarette taxes on the federal budget).

Within spreadsheets, numerical data are entered in columns and rows, and results may be represented as tabular data or in the form of graphs and charts.

Once data are entered in a spreadsheet, it can "crunch" the numbers to quickly answer questions. Although most spreadsheets appear foreboding and complex to use, some, such as *ClarisWorks* and *The Cruncher*, are suitable for students in the intermediate and middle grades. *The Cruncher*, for example, is designed for use by those in grade three and up.

Using Groups with Computer-Based Instruction

Teachers frequently have a small group of students work together with a single computer and software program. This may be due to an instructional decision (i.e., objective is best achieved through a group) or a resource constraint (i.e., not enough computers for the whole class). Some programs also are designed specifically to have students work cooperatively in small groups to solve a problem. This type of software is commonly referred to as **groupware.** *The Graph Club*, a graphing tool for children in grades K through 4, is an example of software that lends itself to group activities.

groupware

Roberts, Carter, Friel, and Miller (1988) have supplied an excellent example of how students can work effectively in groups on a sustained basis with a single computer using software called *Survey Taker.*

A fifth-grade class studying local town government decided to take a survey of the people's feelings about the quality of town services. Class members created the survey, typing into the computer the questions as they agreed upon them. The class wrote twenty questions and then decided to pilot the instrument with another fifth-

Computer software programs can encourage group interaction as well as allow students to work independently.

> grade class to see if the questions were clear and sensible. . . . The pilot suggested there were too many questions. . . . Based on the pilot, the class rewrote some questions, cutting the total number to fifteen. (p. 54)

The students then administered the refined survey to adults during parents' night. In doing do, the children separated the respondents into two categories: town employees and nonemployees. As a follow-up, the students spent several months in interviewing town officials responsible for public services.

In all cases, effective group work with computers requires some of the same skills and structures that were discussed in Chapter 5. It also involves procedures for ensuring that all students have access to the computer and have an opportunity to alternate roles in using it. Additionally, it demands that students have challenging and significant objectives to address.

Interactive Multimedia in Social Studies Instruction

Imagine a middle-grade class studying American history. A small group of students is huddled in front of a videodisc player, a computer, and a color monitor. In the player is one of the two discs in a program called *GTV: A Geographic Perspective on American History.* Each of the two discs contains one hour of video and audio data on various aspects of American history, including still photographs, graphs, maps, and music. In addition to the video data, students can access additional computer information on a range of topics, just a sample of which is shown below:

Colonization	The Industrial Revolution	Independence
Immigration	Westward Expansion	

As students select a topic from the menu by clicking a mouse, clear, crisp videodisc images appear on the color monitor within three seconds, providing visual data on the topic selected. After viewing the data, students may be queried on the computer screen concerning what they have seen. If they have questions, they have an opportunity to link to other related information in the computer program. They also may return to the menu of topics and select a new, related sequence of videodisc images or "browse" through the data.

Definitions abound, but essentially, the term **multimedia** refers to *some combination of video, sound, and images under the control of a computer.* "Interactive multimedia—the marriage of text, audio, and visual data within a single information delivery system—represents a potentially powerful tool for teachers and students throughout the curriculum" (White, 1990, p. 68). *Interactivity* refers to the fact that the user controls his or her path through a multimedia system.

multimedia

Increasingly, schools are incorporating interactive multimedia systems into social studies programs.

Social studies teachers can select from a growing number of commercially produced multimedia systems, such as the one just illustrated, that can incorporate sounds and images from CD-ROM discs and scanned drawings or pictures, video cameras, VCRs, digital cameras, microphones, records, and videodiscs. As an example, *Paths to Freedom*, an intermediate- and middle-grade supplementary history program, contains both videodisc and CD-ROM information.

Teachers and students also can create their own customized multimedia systems (Robinette, 1995). For instance, it is possible to produce an original instructional videodisc or CD-ROM disk. A number of commercial companies, including 3M, now provide mastering services; Kodak can create a special Photo-CD from your pictures produced by a regular 35mm camera.

For multimedia activities and projects, teachers and students can employ simple-to-use authoring programs, like HyperStudio and Digital Chisel. KidPix Studio is an authoring program especially appropriate for primary-grade children. Along with QuickTime, for the Macintosh, these tools can integrate text, motion, video, and audio.

To illustrate, picture a third-grade student using HyperStudio software to create a multimedia report. The theme is "ways to improve our community." The student elects to include edited clips of items within the community recorded with a digital camera (e.g., QuickTake), as well as some scanned documents. Some examples of other activities that lend themselves to student multimedia projects are biographies, family trees, time travels, and magazines.

Shown in Figure 11.7 are some sample pages from the electronic award-winning multimedia magazine created by students at Ligon Middle School in Raleigh, North Carolina. The magazine can be found at the URL address: <http://longwood.cs.ucf.edu/~MidLink/>.

CD-ROM Software

In recent years, sales of CD-ROMs have outpaced other multimedia components, such as videodiscs. Among other reasons, this is due to their large storage capacity and ease of use. CD-ROM disks are accessed by a computer connected to a special drive that plays the disks.

A disk is five inches in diameter and can hold approximately 550,000 pages of print information. This means that entire libraries of print, pictures, and sound can be stored on a few discs. The next generation of CD-ROMs will use both sides and hold about 26 times as much data as the current CDs. They also will be at least twice as fast.

CD-ROM applications increasingly are finding their way into social studies programs at all grade levels. Consider a cross section of CD offerings now available, for example, sound and video enhanced versions of encyclopedias, such as *Encyclopaedia Britannica*, *Compton's Interactive Encyclopedia*, and *Encarta*. Other reference works on CD-ROM with full sound and video on a single disk include Microsoft's *Bookshelf.*

| **FIGURE 11.7** | Midlink Magazine |

Also available in CD-ROM format are *Books in Print* and *Reader's Guide to Periodical Literature.* A CD offering by the National Council on Economic Education, *Virtual Economics, an Interactive Center on Economic Education,* includes items for both teachers and students (e.g., reference works, lesson plans, and film footage of presidents).

FIGURE 11.7 *(Continued)*

Civil War Research Projects

Preface by Jackie Brooks, AG social studies teacher

The Hyperstudio projects available at this address are the results of research conducted by my 8th grade social studies classes at Ligon Middle School, Raleigh, North Carolina. In pairs they researched a specific Civil War topic associated with North Carolina, focusing on primary sources.

To teach the information to other students and provide research material for the "Net", they designed these Hyperstudio projects. These programs provide rare Internet access to information about North Carolina's role in the Civil War and include bibliographies to help you pursue further research.

An Invitation

If you are studying a civil war in **any** country, we would be most interested in sharing your work and posting it here. Should you wish to share projects, ask questions, comment, or require assistance with your own project, please write to me.

Enjoy,
Jackie Brooks
jdbrooks@ligon.wake.k12.nc.us

Source: *Midlink Magazine*, Ligon Middle School, Raleigh, NC.

ICE Publishing has produced two programs for grades 4 and up that contain primary source materials, photographs, music, and video clips: *Ideas That Changed the World* and *Events That Changed the World*. For primary-grade youngsters, there is Rand McNally's *Children's World Atlas*. *The 3D Talking Globe: The See and Hear Atlas Gazetteer*, published by Now What Software, even provides pronunciations of place names by native speakers.

The National Geographic Society has placed all 108 years' of its magazine on CD-ROMs. Further, it produced a program for the intermediate and middle grades, *The Presidents: A Picture History of Our Nation*, that includes photos, video clips, time lines, and text. The society also has created a CD entitled *Picture Atlas of the World*.

The Voyager Company has developed *Who Built America*, which covers data from the period 1876 to 1914 taken from the American Social History Project. Additionally, the company has begun to produce full-feature films, as well as complete texts of books in CD-ROM format.

Also dealing with historical subject matter, the Bureau of Electronic Publishing has produced two discs: *U.S. History on CD-ROM* and *World History on CD-ROM*. Both include books, documents, photographs, and archive materials. For young children, there is *Dr. T's Sing-A-Long Around the World*, which examines other nations through their music and culture. MECC, a long-time producer of software, has expanded the classic simulation, *Oregon Trail*, and made it available in a CD version.

Multimedia technologies show promise of aiding social studies teachers in motivating students and translating abstract ideas into more concrete examples. The effective and full use of these electronic aids, however, will depend upon how skilled social studies teachers become in their applications. As Simon (1990) has underscored, "It is increasingly clear that as powerful new technologies and software proliferate, teachers will need to learn more about these new tools on a continuous basis" (p. 8).

The demand for multimedia instructional materials is likely to continue to grow. This should occur as programs become more sophisticated and states with textbook adoption policies become more flexible in how *text* is defined. Utah and Texas, for example, now permit adoptions of resources such as videodiscs in lieu of textbooks.

Distance Learning

At the beginning of the chapter, we noted a group of fifth-grade students who were about to converse with an expert at a remote site over 2,000 miles away from the students. The professor and students, who could see and hear each other via two-way audio and video, were engaged in *distance learning*, a process by which discussions, conferences, and courses can be transmitted in "real time" from locations remote to the classroom.

A growing number of states (e.g., Massachusetts, Texas, and Virginia) and school districts have established *distance learning* projects to enrich and broaden classroom instruction. In other cases, distance learning has provided elective courses, such as foreign languages, or accessed experts at university sites, as in our earlier example. Distance learning permits schools that otherwise lack the resources to enrich their curriculum.

An example of an extensive, diversified distance learning program is Mass LearnPike, which reaches over 200 Massachusetts school systems, as well as those in many other states. Mass LearnPike beams programs taught by experts to these systems from its Cambridge studios. It offers both programs on traditional social studies themes (e.g., *Ancestors: A Multicultural Exploration)* and **electronic field trips** (e.g., *The Lowell Mills*).

electronic field trips

Through electronic field trips, a museum or a historical site, such as Ellis Island, is brought to the students instead of the reverse. Local experts can focus on special features or artifacts and answer questions, much as they would during a conventional field trip.

Using Videotape and Television in Social Studies Instruction

VCRs and television, cable and standard, can be powerful technological allies of social studies teachers. Increasingly, information that once was provided to schools in the form of filmstrips and 16mm film is being offered on videocassettes. The rapid growth of video rental stores also has presented teachers with relatively inexpensive video materials, including tapes of documentaries or special television series.

Cable Programming

Further, within the copyright restrictions, a continuing body of contemporary television programming is at a teacher's disposal. Approximately two thirds of all schools now receive some form of cable television for classroom instruction. As we considered in Chapter 9, major cable networks provide news and other educational programs that may be taped free of charge under certain conditions. *Assignment Discovery*, produced by The Discovery Channel (1-800-321-1832), is an example of outstanding cable programming. It provides social studies programs via cable that may be taped for classroom use. Social studies and contemporary issues programs are aired on Tuesday and Friday during the school year at 9:00 a.m. (ET); past programs have included *Bill of Rights: Power to the People* and *How the West Was Lost*.

TLC Elementary School, produced by The Learning Channel (1-800-321-1832) provides via cable television social studies programs that may be taped free of charge for classroom use; tapes may be used for two full years. Programs are aired every Tuesday during the school year from 4:00 to 5:00 a.m. (ET). Examples of past offerings are *Zulei: Growing Up in West Africa* and *With Paper and Crayon: Houses*.

Teachers and students can collect and analyze video data from fieldwork, interviews, and other activities.

Teacher- and Student-Made Video Materials

Teachers and students also can collect on videotape and later analyze their own visual data from fieldwork, trips, interviews, and other activities. Bracey (1989), a teacher of a sixth-grade class, described in part how her students created a videotape designed around the five themes of geography that focused on their school.

> We began our project, *Where in the World Is Ashlawn School?* with shots of a globe and maps showing Ashlawn School's exact location. . . . [A student] interviewed the former owner of the land on which Ashlawn is built. We included some old photographs of the original dairy farm, and footage of the owner's home and the milk house. . . . We taped a visit to the Arlington Historical Society . . . and to the Arlington County courthouse. (Bracey, 1989)

Video media also can be used effectively in the classroom in other ways. Thomas and Brubaker (1972) have outlined a number of applications, including the following:

1. Demonstrating how a project is to be done by showing an example from the preceding year's class.
2. Evaluating a tape of student presentation as a means of focusing more specifically on certain points.

3. Aiding absentees by providing tapes of key classroom activities that the student missed and which could not be easily recaptured otherwise.

4. Informing parents about special classroom activities or projects.

Teachers may monitor their own teaching by using a video camera to tape social studies lessons. One effective technique for analyzing taped class sessions is to turn off the sound and concentrate on certain specific aspects of nonverbal behavior, such as eye contact, on each play of the tape. After a session has been recorded, a teacher might select a 15-minute segment for the analysis.

One suggested procedure for organizing and processing the data is to divide a sheet of paper into two columns. Label the left one "Nonverbal Behaviors," and list the series of distinct behaviors in the order in which they occurred over the time segment selected. In the right column, list and separate the corresponding reactions of the students, verbal and nonverbal, under the heading, "Student Responses."

Using Traditional Media Effectively

As I noted earlier in the chapter, traditional media continue to have an important place in instruction. Media in social studies classrooms have included filmstrips, photographs, artifacts, 16-mm films, transparencies, slides, records, audiotapes, and, more recently, videotapes. When used effectively, they function as vehicles for providing information in relation to some question, hypothesis, issue, or problem. They can either present or help resolve some puzzle that a student is to consider in the context of the curriculum.

They also can furnish primary source materials such as film clips of actual events or oral histories. In addition, they can help translate the abstractions of symbolic data in the social studies into concrete forms of expression that students can more easily comprehend and appreciate.

It is not the medium itself that necessarily makes it effective as an instructional vehicle, although visual media often transmit information more effectively than others. Rather, it is the teacher's understanding of how one form of data can serve an important instructional purpose and advance students' thinking.

Often, for example, it is more effective for instructional purposes that a teacher repurpose the media (use media in a way different from what its author intended). Consider a short film that shows people from a culture quite different from our own engaged in some typical activity. Initially the film might be shown with the sound track turned off. At the conclusion of the viewing, students might be asked a basic question: "What did you see?"

The class's responses could be recorded on a sheet and then covered with another sheet of paper. As a next step, the class could be subdivided into three groups. The first group would be asked to observe how *time* was used by the participants in the film. A second group would be asked to focus on the *people* and *what* each person did. The third group would be responsible for observing which *things* the people used and how.

The same film clip then would be shown a second time. After this viewing, each of the groups would be asked to summarize its members' individual observations and to report its findings to the class. Again the observations would be recorded on a sheet and then covered. At this point the teacher could elect to stop or to repeat the reviewing of the film, each time recording the latest round of observations of each group.

Typically, each new viewing will reveal additional observations that were missed in earlier sessions. The simple observational framework of time, people, and things corresponds to that used by anthropologists in ethnographic fieldwork. In a social studies class, the framework provides an interesting vehicle for systematically processing visual data.

Technologies in the 21st Century: The Challenge of the Future

What technological developments that can enrich the teaching of social studies loom on the horizon?

Mehlinger (1996) foresaw an especially rosy scenario for technologies such as desk-top videoconferencing. He prophesied that "technology will become faster, cheaper, more powerful, and easier to use. We can also predict that new devices that we can scarcely imagine today will be on the market before the end of this decade" (p. 45). At the same time, he warned: "Schools that expect to invest in a single computer system and then forget about technology purchases for several years will be surprised and disappointed" (p. 46).

We have entered the era where the lines between elements of technology are becoming blurred. Integrated sound and still and motion images of all types, all regulated by microcomputers with increasing capabilities have become the norm. CD-ROM technology continues to become more sophisticated and less expensive.

Both the memory and storage capacity of computers continue to grow, even as they shrink in size. High-capacity storage devices now are relatively inexpensive and readily available for all major computers, even notebook versions. Computers can recognize our handwriting and our voices.

Several further developments that are promising for schools seem likely. Multimedia systems increasingly will be used in many sectors of our lives, including the classroom. Videodisc and CD-ROM units that can *record*, as well as play audio and video data, will be more available to schools as the technology develops and costs per unit drop.

Software such as Apple's *QuickTime* will extend the powers of the teacher to incorporate visual information and create in a multimedia environment. Such software will make it possible to easily compress and store lengthy segments of still and motion video as digital (computer) files, then edit and move them into other files.

Gradually, too, more and more technological advances will be easier for teachers to apply and incorporate into their instruction. The telephone will become the standard of technological "user friendliness" that newer computer-based tools emulate. Telephone companies, now empowered to challenge cable companies, by the end of the decade will flood our homes with a smorgasbord of video data, from popular films to educational programs. All of these data will be easily stored in the new generation of computers.

Advancing cellular and radio technologies will permit each individual to have a personal telephone number that can be accessed anywhere on the globe. Satellite technologies and distance learning techniques will be refined and extended to all schools to further extend their access to information and reduce isolation.

The Internet or its successor will be faster and more easily accessible by all citizens; thereby our reach will extend beyond our borders to other nations of the world. This will make education truly global. Besides communicating over the Internet, students and teachers also will be able to tap into an expanding repertoire of comprehensive data bases.

Even our concepts of a book will undergo changes. Electronic books that fit in the palm of your hand, have clear resolution, and provide complete texts will inch their way into the schools. These new electronic tools will allow students to do key word searches, experiment with the text, or even create large print to compensate for poor vision.

The challenge for us as teachers of social studies is both exciting and demanding. We must determine which roles technology and the rich informal educational system beyond the school can play most appropriately in the development of reflective, competent, and concerned citizens.

Group Activities

1. Visit an elementary or middle school in your community that is reputed to use technology extensively. Make a specific list of the various items of technology that exist there and the ways that they are used in social studies instruction. Discuss those things that surprised or impressed you.

2. Visit a county or regional media center in your area to obtain an overview of the latest media materials for the social studies, including computer-related technologies. Discuss your finds and those things that surprised or impressed you.

3. Visit a local elementary and a middle-grade school media center or library and identify the media that are available in the area of social studies. Discuss those things that surprised or impressed you.

4. Contact a local media specialist in a school or a school system and ask him or her to identify a local school that is using electronic mail applications in the social studies program. Then visit the school to learn how the system works and is being used.

5. Access the Internet and locate 10 items from the list of social studies resources. Discuss the nature and merits of what you found, as well as any other interesting web sites you discovered.

Individual Activities

1. Examine and evaluate three social studies software programs: one for the primary grades, one for the intermediate grades, and one for the middle grades. Locate an evaluation instrument for software and assess the strengths and weaknesses of the programs.

2. Contact a company such as Optical Data Corporation to obtain more information on interactive multimedia social studies programs for elementary and middle schools.

3. Contact The Learning Channel at the 800 number given in the chapter to obtain more information on free social studies programs for the elementary grades.

4. Select one of the emerging technological applications discussed in the chapter, such as multimedia or CD-ROM systems, and read a related article that further explains its application. Identify the author and source and summarize what you learned.

5. Visit a large video rental store (such as a chain, Blockbusters). Identify a list of tapes and discs available for rental that might be used in social studies lessons.

References

Association for Supervision and Curriculum Development. (1995). *Only the best: The annual guide to highest-rated education software/multimedia for pre-school–grade 12.* Alexandria, VA: Author.

Bilof, E. G. (1987). How to design and use a culture area database with PFS:FILE and PFS:REPORT. *The Social Studies,* 35–41.

Bracey, B. L. (1989, Fall). Making a geography video—It's elementary. *Geography Education Update,* 4.

Brehm, B., & Waugh, M. (1993). The influence of telecommunications and classroom interactions on the problem solving behaviors of middle school students. Annual Meeting of the American Educational Research Association, Atlanta, GA.

Cowan, G. (1996). How the web works. *Social Education.*

Ehman, L. H., & Glenn, A. D. (1987). *Computer-based education in the social studies.* Bloomington, IN: ERIC Clearinghouse for Social Studies/Social Science Education.

Harris, J. (1993). Freedom of the (key)press: Internet-based discussion groups. *The Computing Teacher,* 52–55.

Kearsley, G. (1996, Winter). The World Wide Web: Global access to education. *Educational Technology Review,* 26–30.

Martorella, P. H. (Ed.) (1997). *Interactive technologies and the social studies curriculum: Emerging issues and applications.* Albany, NY: SUNY Press.

Mecklenburger, J. A. (1990). Educational technology is not enough. *Phi Delta Kappan, 72,* 105–108.

Mehlinger, H. D. (1996). School reform in the information age. *Phi Delta Kappan, 77,* 400–407.

Mernit, S. (1991, February). Black history month—Let your database set the stage. *Instructor,* 110–112.

Multimedia source guide. (1995–96). Justin, CA: *T.H.E. Journal.*

Nauss, C. A. (1992). Plan 2: Pirates ahoy. *T.I.E. News, 4.*

Office of Technology Assessment. (1995). Teachers & technology: Making the connection. Washington, DC: Author.

Pawloski, B. (1994). How I found out about the Internet. *Educational Leadership, 51,* 69–73.

Robinette, M. (1995). *Mac multimedia for teachers.* Foster City, CA: IDG Books.

Roberts, N., Carter, R. C., Friel, S. N., & Miller, M. S. (1988). *Integrating computers into the elementary and middle school.* Upper Saddle River, NJ: Prentice Hall.

Simon, M. (1990). Expanding opportunities for teachers to learn about technology. *Electronic Learning, 9,* 8–9.

Thomas, R. M., & Brubaker, D. (Eds.). (1972). *Teaching elementary social studies: Readings.* Belmont, CA: Wadsworth.

Tyre, T. (1990, May). Hypermedia: Practical platforms emerge. *T.H.E. Journal, 8,* 12, 14.

Updegrove D. A. (1991). Electronic mail in education. *Educational Technology, 31,* 37–40.

White, C. S. (1990). Interactive media for social studies: A review of *In the Holy Land* and *The '88 Vote. Social Education, 54,* 68–70.

Adapting Social Studies Instruction to Individual Needs

Matching Social Studies Instruction to Students' Developing Capabilities

The Nature of Concrete Social Studies Activities

Symbolic, Iconic, and Enactive Social Studies Activities

Constructivist Perspectives on Social and Cognitive Growth

Individualized Instruction and Individual Differences

Individual Differences Among Students

Organizing the Classroom for Individualized Social Studies Instruction

Computers

Multilevel Reading Materials

Learning Contracts

Learning Centers

Using Jackdaws and Teacher-Made Materials for Individualizing Instruction

Individual Styles of Thinking and Learning

Matching Thinking Styles to Instruction

Measures of Thinking Styles

Matching Learning Styles to Instruction

Measures of Learning Styles

Individualization and Cultural Diversity

Equity for Those with Disabilities

Public Law 94-142

Mainstreaming and Inclusion

Strategies for Mainstreaming Students for Social Studies Instruction

Equity for the Gifted

Societal Perspectives on the Gifted

Identifying the Gifted

Approaches to Gifted Education

Gifted Students in Social Studies Classes

Rasheed and Carlos are both attending their first day of school in kindergarten at Everett Elementary School. At first glance they look alike because they are approximately the same height and are wearing identical jeans and sneakers.

As they hesitantly enter their assigned classroom, Ms. Hardison, their teacher, greets them cheerily and asks their names. From that moment forward, their individual personalities and backgrounds will surface and affect in myriad ways the educational experiences they encounter throughout their school years.

Like Rasheed and Carlos, all students are unique in some way. In a democracy, a public educational system must be sensitive to this uniqueness and attempt to provide all students with equal opportunities for reaching their full potential. Ideally, this practice means that teachers should capitalize on students' special strengths and help compensate for their limitations. It also means that teachers should provide children who are grouped into categories—such as gifted, culturally different, less able, or those with handicaps—with different learning experiences appropriate for their capabilities.

In a pluralistic society, students often arrive at the school door more different than alike. Their differences may include languages, religious beliefs, intellectual abil-

FIGURE 12.1

Source: From "Pet Peeves" by Joel Pett, in *Phi Delta Kappan*, December 1991, p. 269. Copyright 1991, Joel Pett, *Phi Delta Kappan*. Reprinted by permission.

ities, physical and psychological impediments, traditions, and customs. Regardless of their race, religion, ethnicity, intellectual capabilities, gender, and other characteristics, all students are deserving of an equal chance to learn and succeed.

Exercising the responsibility to treat all students equitably begins with suspending judgment initially on what can be expected of each student regarding classroom performance, learning, behavior, and aspirations. When a teacher's preconceived expectations are that a particular individual will be industrious, bright, and well behaved, and will bring rich experiences and high learning ideals to the classroom, these views are likely to affect positively the teacher's behavior toward the student. By contrast, if the teacher associates negative labels with students, whatever those descriptors may be (e.g., retarded, lower-class, failure, lazy), the teacher's behavior toward the students may be negative.

Matching Social Studies Instruction to Students' Developing Capabilities

Treating children as individuals also requires providing them with social studies materials and activities that are appropriate for their growing capabilities. One of the clearest instructional implications of developmental psychology is the need for concrete learning activities and materials during the early years of social studies instruction.

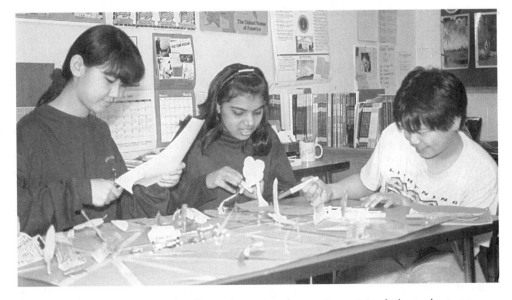

Hands-on activities, such as this three-dimensional mapping activity, help students translate abstractions into concrete examples.

The Nature of Concrete Social Studies Activities

Although the term *concrete* has many meanings in education, generally it refers to what can be perceived directly through one or more of the senses: smell, hearing, taste, touch, and sight. Thus a teacher who wishes to provide concrete learning experiences relating to the judicial system may take a class on a field trip to the local courthouse to observe a trial in action or have the class view a film of a trial. With a foundation of concrete learning, the students could follow up the lessons of the trip and the film with readings and discussions.

Children do use many *abstract* social studies concepts that cannot be perceived directly through the senses—for example, *love, fairness,* and *democracy*—in all stages of development. However, they often use these concepts in speaking or writing, without any clear understanding of their basic meanings. They quickly learn at home and, to an even greater degree, later in schools that the mere use of certain words in a situation will pass for learning and understanding. Students very early observe that the insertion and repetition of the correct words into the proper context will gain approval or rewards from the teacher and other adults in the school.

phony concepts

We may regard as **phony concepts** those abstractions not developed reflectively and internalized by children but rather learned through imitation or rote. Children often become quite proficient in using phony concepts in situationally correct ways without any real understanding of their conceptual meaning. Little Clara, for example, has learned from shrewd observation how to both ease her conceptual burden and gain teacher approval when asked a question in class such as, "What do you like best about our country?" Clara realizes that responding with the words *democracy* and *freedom of speech*, whatever they mean, will more than satisfy the teacher.

Symbolic, Iconic, and Enactive Social Studies Activities

Another way to view concreteness and abstractness is to consider the mode of representing information to students. Bruner (1973) identified three basic modes, each of which provides increasingly more concrete learning experiences:

symbolic mode
iconic mode
enactive mode

the **symbolic mode** (least concrete), the **iconic mode** (more concrete), and the **enactive mode** (most concrete). He argued that children gradually become more reliant on each of these three modes for learning as they progress developmentally.

Teachers can engage students in social studies activities through the enactive mode by having them actually do or simulate a task, such as build a shelter model or role-play an event. Providing experiences through the iconic mode necessitates the use of pictures, visual material, or imagery to represent information. These two modes of learning may be contrasted with the symbolic mode, which involves hearing or reading about something.

Teachers who wish to provide instructional alternatives in a class with students of differing levels of development could offer children experiences representing each of the three modes. To see how this might work, let us use the example of the concept of *assembly line*. Students could participate in a simulated assembly line for producing a simple product such as a paper hat (enactive mode); alternatively, they might be shown a filmstrip describing an assembly line (iconic mode). A third choice could be to read a trade book or textbook on the topic and then discuss the findings in a small group (symbolic mode).

Constructivist Perspectives on Social and Cognitive Growth

Constructivist perspectives on social and cognitive growth have underscored the importance of children's active involvement in the learning process.

> Teachers do not teach in the traditional sense of standing in front of a room of students and delivering instruction. Rather they use materials with which learners become actively involved through manipulation or social interaction. Activities stress students' observing, collecting data, generating and testing hypotheses, and working collaboratively with others. (Schunk, 1996, p. 209)

Regardless of the mode through which children acquire information, they require opportunities to communicate their findings and to raise questions. Social discourse involves children in sharing experiences, taking roles, discussing, disputing, and listening in small- and large-group activities. Strategies for conducting such activities are discussed in Chapters 5 and 8.

As a child increasingly interacts with others and begins to move away from egocentrism, he or she begins to internalize the existence and significance of alternative points of view. Social discourse in social studies instruction, whether in small groups or class discussions, also can be instrumental in refining and improving children's thinking. As children engage in verbal give-and-take and defend and explain their ideas, they not only share their thoughts but also test them out as well. In short, children's conversations in groups, when they have purpose and guidelines, stimulate both social and cognitive growth.

Individualized Instruction and Individual Differences

In its simplest form, **individualized instruction** is that which makes provisions for some set of differences among learners. There are many differences among students, and it would be impossible for a single teacher to consider all of them for any given learning task. Typically, teachers select some set of differences they regard as especially significant to recognize in the instructional program. They then consider the resources available and begin to develop strategies and materials for instruction.

**individualized
instruction**

Individual Differences Among Students

Some differences among students are relatively easy to address and involve only modest adjustments in classroom practices. An illustration is moving to the front center row a student who has slightly reduced visual acuity. Other adjustments may require major reorganization of the classroom or even of an educational system.

For example, it is widely accepted that all children enter kindergarten or first grade at approximately the same chronological age. Recognizing that developmentally, children differ widely in the ages at which they are ready to begin formal learning would challenge this common practice. It would require fundamental changes in both legal statutes and school admission policies.

Some differences among students that have been used in the past as a basis for individualizing instruction include the following:

Reading abilities	Prior knowledge
Developmental capabilities	Orthopedic problems
Learning and thinking styles	Attention spans
Motivational levels	Cultural experiences
Physical settings preferred for learning	Achievements
	Sight problems
Interests	Amounts of time needed to
Interpersonal skills	complete a task
Leadership abilities	Hearing problems

Whenever teachers select some set of these or other differences to address with special instruction, they engage in a form of individualized instruction.

Organizing the Classroom for Individualized Social Studies Instruction

Among the tools that social studies teachers have found especially useful for developing instruction that takes account of individual differences are *computers*, *multilevel reading materials*, *learning contracts*, and *learning centers*. Each offers students an opportunity to learn through a medium or environment that is responsive to individual needs or strengths.

Computers

As I note at some length in Chapter 11, computers have the capacity to enliven social studies instruction in many ways. Students can work individually or in small groups and at their own pace. For children who have been absent from class, computers can be used for reviews of material. Others can use the computer to practice skills or to extend their understanding of a topic.

Appropriate software can accommodate a range of attention spans, motivational levels, and learning paces of students. New peripherals and software, such as videodisc players and videodiscs and CD-ROM units and compact discs, offer access to an enormous range of sophisticated data, as does the Internet.

Multilevel Reading Materials

The individual differences in the levels at which children read in the elementary level are often vast. They become even more pronounced in the intermediate and middle school grades than in the primary ones. This phenomenon is an especially serious obstacle to learning in the area of the social studies, where much of the subject matter in schools typically is available in written form.

In Chapter 10 we consider in depth how providing students with varied reading materials and strategies for comprehension affords them opportunities for success even though their individual reading abilities may vary considerably. If a rich mix of different reading materials is available on the same topic, students can seek their own levels of proficiency and challenges, progressing as their comprehension and self-confidence grow. Where multilevel children's trade books are used, the basal textbook can serve as a basic reference work, consulted as needed.

Learning Contracts

Learning contracts are a simple way to provide students with individualized learning tasks, while clarifying the objectives of an activity. They also help students learn to establish reasonable deadlines and work schedules. Contracts can help teachers with the managerial problems of keeping track of different students working at different rates on different tasks.

There is no set format for a learning contract. Typically, it spells out (a) what a student agrees to do, (b) which resources will be used and in what ways, (c) how to determine when each phase of the activity has been completed, and (d) when the activities will be completed. An example of a basic learning contract is given in Figure 12.2.

Learning Centers

Learning center, or activity center, approaches can be incorporated into any pattern of organizing instruction. They are a flexible form of individualization because they can accommodate provisions for attending to many types of differences, such as *interests, rates of learning, reading levels, prior learning, learning and thinking styles, attention spans,* and *interpersonal skills.* Learning centers also can incorporate the use of computers, multilevel reading materials, and learning contracts.

learning contracts

learning centers

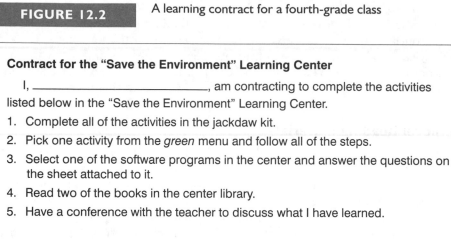

FIGURE 12.2 A learning contract for a fourth-grade class

Contract for the "Save the Environment" Learning Center

I, _____, am contracting to complete the activities listed below in the "Save the Environment" Learning Center.

1. Complete all of the activities in the jackdaw kit.
2. Pick one activity from the *green* menu and follow all of the steps.
3. Select one of the software programs in the center and answer the questions on the sheet attached to it.
4. Read two of the books in the center library.
5. Have a conference with the teacher to discuss what I have learned.

Student's Signature: _____ Date: _____

Teacher's Signature: _____ Date: _____

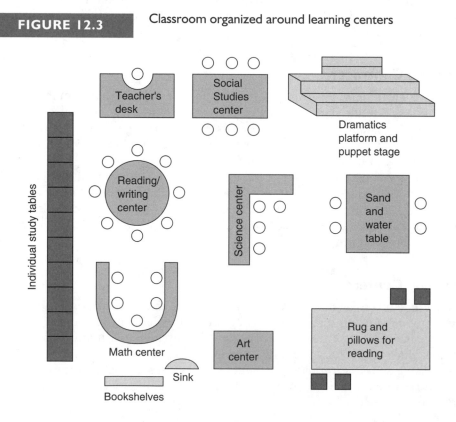

FIGURE 12.3 Classroom organized around learning centers

In typical classroom applications, one or more social studies centers are designated at certain locations and are attractively designed. Figure 12.3 is an illustration of how an entire classroom area might be organized around learning centers.

A center should have provisions for either individuals or small groups to work there. The types of materials in a social studies center might include some combination of these items:

Technology Tools

Listening post with multiple sets of headphones

Filmstrip projector with screen

Record player

Slide projector

Tape player

Microcomputer and peripherals such as a printer and a modem

Videotape machine

Videodisc player

Compact disc player

Overhead projector

Multimedia and Print Materials

Collections of photographs and pictures

Globe and maps

Models

Dioramas

Flannel boards

Tapes, records, films, filmstrips, videodiscs, slides, compact disks, computer software, and video cassettes

Study prints

Simulation games

Artifacts

Compasses

Posters

Magazines and newspapers

Historical works of fiction

Nonfiction and biographical informational books

Textbooks

Reproductions of historical documents

Time lines

Teacher-made materials

Study kits

Reference works

Activity sheets and cards

Cartoons

Charts, graphs, and tables

Travel folders

Catalogs

Yellow Pages

Atlases

Bulletin boards

Implementing Learning Centers.   Ideally, centers should contain all of the materials needed to complete activities, including instructions and checklists to indicate progress or completion of tasks. Generally a center focuses on a single theme and provides a number of options for exploring it. Any of the various topics discussed in earlier chapters for units, such as in Chapter 4, are suitable for center themes.

A learning center should include a mix of activities to explore a single theme.

Topics may be interdisciplinary and can be integrated with other subjects, such as science, mathematics, art, and language arts. The contents and subjects for centers should be changed periodically to heighten interest. Students also may be encouraged to participate in the creation and development of a center.

The learning activities within the center may include a mix of open-ended and structured tasks. In either case, they should emphasize active learning where students are called on to interact with and manipulate the materials in the center and then have an opportunity to discuss their experiences. Teachers also should make some provisions for working with individual students who need to be challenged or assisted. Simple color-, number-, letter-, or picture-coding schemes should be used to help students locate and cross-reference activity cards, instructions, and materials.

Sample Learning Center.   An example of a learning center is the set of materials designed by Weber (1992) and based on the book *Seeds of Change* (Hawke & Davis, 1992). The theme for the center was "Bittersweet Sugar" (the role that sugar cane played in the introduction of slavery into the Americas). The center has five interrelated components, each represented by different color-coordinated cards and a set of related readings, activities, and instructional materials. For each card, there also is a brief description of the objectives and the evaluation procedures.

FIGURE 12.4 Outline of the Bittersweet Learning Center

Bittersweet Sugar Learning Center

   General Instructions. This learning center has five sections. Each section has a different color, which is on the laminated instruction card: red, orange, yellow, white, and blue. Each section also has a set of readings and materials for you to examine. You will need them to complete the activities in each section.

When you begin work in the center:

1.   Start by completing the activity in the blue section and recording your responses in your social studies journal.

2.   Next select any *two* activities in the white section.

3.   Choose *one* activity in the red section. After you have completed it, have a conference with the teacher.

4.   Complete all of the activities in the orange section.

5.   The yellow section is optional. You may complete any activities that interest you, if you have time.

6.   Place your social studies journal and all written work in your folder.

Source: From *Seeds of Change Learning Centers* by M. Weber, 1992, Unpublished manuscript.

The outline of the Bittersweet Sugar Learning Center is shown in Figure 12.4. A sample objective, activity card, and assessment item for the blue section of the center is illustrated in Figure 12.5.

Using Jackdaws and Teacher-Made Materials for Individualizing Instruction

Individualizing instruction usually requires the use of some activities and materials that are designed or modified by the teacher for use with a particular class. One example is the use of **jackdaws** (Dowd, 1990; Rasinski, 1983). Loosely defined, *jackdaws* are kits of various kinds of materials built around a single theme, with the focus being an individual, a document, an event, an issue, or a place. Some examples are:

jackdaws

- Thomas Jefferson
- The Battle of Gettysburg
- The Bill of Rights
- The Columbian Quincentenary
- Philadelphia
- Great Inventions

| FIGURE 12.5 | Sample activity card for the Bittersweet Sugar Learning Center |

Blue Section

Slave Passages Activity Card

Objective. The student will describe in writing in his or her social studies journal everything he or she sees in the picture "Bittersweet Sugar, the Root of Slavery."

Related Assessment. The student will make at least a one-page journal entry about what was observed.

Activity Directions. Everyone working in the Center must complete this activity first. Form a group of four. The person whose last name begins with the letter of the alphabet closest to "A" should read aloud the passage below. Everyone should examine the drawing. Notice that the slaves are right below the main deck.

After reading the passage, the group should do the activity and then discuss the questions. After the discussion is finished, write your answers in your *social studies journal*. You should have at least one page of observations.

In addition to being chained together, slaves were tightly packed between the decks of slave ships. Study the drawing of the slave ship. As the enlarged area [bottom drawing] shows, slaves were required to sit in a space three feet, three inches in height. This is a little more than the height of the space under a table.

With three or four classmates, crawl under a table and sit the way the slaves are sitting in the picture. How long could you comfortably sit in this position? How would you feel if you had sat in this position almost twenty-four hours a day for four to six weeks, as African slaves had to do? (Hawke & Davis, 1992, p. 74)

- Women in the American Revolution
- Houses Around the World
- Our Community
- Slavery in the United States
- The Great Depression

Typical jackdaws are housed in an attractive and sturdy container or box that holds all of the relevant materials. These may include some combination of artifacts and three-dimensional objects such as clothes, utensils, models, and coins; copies of primary source materials, such as historical documents, advertisements, maps, legal documents, birth certificates, and letters; books, magazines, articles, charts, and pictures; and teacher-produced items such as dioramas and drawings (Dowd, 1990).

As an illustration, Dowd (1990) noted that a jackdaw created by the Institute of Texan Cultures in San Antonio with the theme "Early Texan Frontier Life" was housed in an old pioneer trunk that contained a washboard, a quilt, a bonnet and dress, a coffee pot, and lye soap. She also provided an example of how a jackdaw for primary-grade children might be built around a theme and a book, *Leonardo da Vinci: Artist, Inventor, Scientist*, by Alice and Martin Provensen. Dowd suggested the jackdaw might include photographs or reproductions of *Mona Lisa* and *Last Supper*, maps of Italy and the solar system, botanical and anatomical drawings, a plastic skeleton, a diorama of an Italian town square, and facsimiles of Leonardo's backward and left-handed handwriting.

Both teachers and students can contribute items to a jackdaw kit. Some excellent commercial jackdaws also are available (see Figure 12.6), but most of these have been designed for middle grades and secondary students and are limited in the types of materials they contain.

Jackdaws should be designed to be self-instructional and for the use of a single student or a small group of two or three students. They should accommodate individual student needs and allow them to explore freely all of the materials in the kit. They should include structured cues and tasks to help students focus on

---

FIGURE 12.6   Commercially produced jackdaw

The Depression

On October 29. 1929, the New York stock market crashed and heralded the onset of the great Depression. It has been estimated that between twelve to fifteen million workers were unemployed by 1933. What were conditions really like in the cities? What problems were faced by the farmers? How was the discontent of the nation manifested?

In a format designed for both personal enjoyment and classroom participation, this Jackdaw puts the evidence directly in the reader's hands. Through the use of primary materials—newspapers, pictures, flyers, posters, etc.—the reader can sense the feelings of fear, discouragement, futility and anger as the people attempted to survive the black days of the Depression. Historian: Andrew Bronin.

Primary Source Exhibits:
- Page 1 of *Variety*, Wednesday, October 30, 1929.
- The Depression: A Family Album.
- Sign: "Unemployed—Buy apples 5¢ each."
- Depression Scrip.
- A&P Advertising Flyer, 1933.
- Auction sale poster for farm equipment, North Dakota, 1933.
- Page 1 of The Emporia Gazette, May 11, 1934.
- Photo Sequence: A Texas Dust Storm.
- Page 1 of *The Daily Worker*, Monday, January 27, 1930.
- Broadside: "Veterans March to Washington," 1932.
- Campaign flyer: "Closing-Out Sale of the G.O.P. Party," 1932.
- Poster: "NRA—We do our part."

Source: From *Jackdaws: Portfolios of Primary Source Documents* (p. 25) compiled by A. Bronin, 1993, Amawalk, NY: Golden Owl. Copyright 1993 by Golden Owl Publishing Company. Reprinted by permission.

salient points and issues. To simplify analyses, different-colored sheets should be used for different types of information.

In addition to the collection of materials, jackdaws should contain the following:

- A sheet that lists all of the items in the kit (see Figure 12.7)
- Any special instructions on how the materials are to be examined
- A set of questions designed to stimulate students' thinking as they examine the materials
- Commentary sheets that provide appropriate background or context for the materials included
- A set of activities to be done in conjunction with an examination of the materials
- A list of references and readings for students
- Special instructions for how to divide tasks if a small group is to use the kit

Individual Styles of Thinking and Learning

A further element for teachers to consider in individualizing social studies instruction is the dominant pattern or *style* students employ for acquiring new information. Taking into account students' preferred styles for acquiring information involves providing alternative ways and learning environments through which to approach an assignment, acquire knowledge, or solve problems. Teachers who are sensitive to students' styles try to find the best match between the learning task and the style of individual students.

thinking styles

The term **thinking (or cognitive) style** refers to the pattern we typically follow in solving problems, engaging in thinking, and generally processing information. Individuals may vary their thinking style from one task to another, but one style usually is dominant and stable over a period of years (Witkin, Moore, Goodenough, & Cox, 1977). Researchers report that thinking styles develop early in life and influence not only the ways we learn but also our career choices (Witkin et al., 1977).

learning styles

Learning styles are similar to thinking styles in that they represent patterns we typically follow in learning. *Learning styles* are the set of preferences we express about the conditions under which we like to learn something. Certain learning style differences appear to be biological, whereas others are developed through experience (Dunn, Beaudry, & Klavas, 1989).

Matching Thinking Styles to Instruction

Some of the number of systems for classifying thinking styles are quite complex. One system that has been applied to classroom instruction is based on the

FIGURE 12.7   Jackdaw contents

1 Outline of Cherokee dates and events. Taken from J. Ed. Sharpe's book *The Cherokees Past and Present.*

2 Map of the boundaries of Cherokee country. Taken from *The Cherokees Past and Present.*

3 Broadsheet on Cherokee origin and history.

4 Broadsheet on Cherokee government.

5 Symbol of the seven clans of the Cherokee. Taken from *The Cherokee Past and Present.*

6 Broadsheet of the Cherokee religion.

7 Cherokee poem "The Corn Maiden." Taken from Mary Newman Fitzgerald's book *The Cherokee and His Smokey Mountain Legends.*

8 Carved wooden figure of the Eagle Dancer. Taken from Rodney Leftwich's book *Arts and Crafts of the Cherokee.*

9 Broadsheet of the Cherokee Language.

10 Cherokee Alphabet. Taken from Samuel Carter III's book *Cherokee Sunset: A Nation Betrayed.*

11 Cherokee glossary. Taken from *The Cherokees Past and Present.*

12 Clipping from the Cherokee newspaper, the *Cherokee Phoenix*. Taken from *Cherokee Sunset: A Nation Betrayed.*

13 Broadsheet on Cherokee dwellings.

14 Arts and crafts of the Cherokee. Taken from *The Cherokee Past and Present.*

15 Cherokee crafts.

16 Arrowheads.

17 Cherokee Memorial to U.S. Congress, December 29, 1835. Taken from the *American Heritage Book of Indians.*

18 Various photographs dealing with the "Trail of Tears."

19 Map of the "Trail of Tears." Taken from *Cherokee Sunset.*

20 Map of the Cherokee Reservation in Oklahoma. Taken from *Cherokee Sunset.*

21 Photo of John Ross.

22 The story of Tsali, a Cherokee hero. Taken from *The Cherokee and His Smokey Mountain Legends.*

23 Broadsheet on the contributions of the Indians. Taken from *The Cherokee and His Smokey Mountain Legends.*

Source: From *The Cherokee Indians* by J. Allen, 1991, Unpublished manuscript.

field-
dependent
individuals
field-
independent
individuals

work of Witkin and his associates (1977). They identified two basic thinking styles: **field-dependent** and **field-independent.** Some of the salient comparative characteristics of each type are summarized below.

Field-Independent Individuals:

- Can deal effectively with unstructured problems
- Are task oriented
- Are relatively unconcerned with social interaction
- Can deal effectively with abstract thinking
- Are intrinsically motivated

Field-Dependent Individuals:

- Are relatively effective in remembering information that has social content
- Prefer group activities
- Prefer highly structured tasks and activities
- Are extrinsically motivated

Teachers who wish to adapt their social studies instruction to account for differences in thinking styles among students could offer alternative choices such as structured (dependent) versus unstructured (independent) assignments (Guild & Garger, 1985). Similarly, teachers could offer guidelines for activities that provide open-ended (independent) versus specific and detailed (dependent) instructions.

They also could ensure that alternatives in instructional strategies are available, such as discovery (independent) versus expository (dependent) approaches. Further, they could offer students choices between working alone (independent) or in groups (dependent) on tasks.

Measures of Thinking Styles

More detailed information on the characteristics of the two types of thinking style is available, as well as on paper-and-pencil measures that are easy to use and score. One test, available in two forms (group and individual) for elementary-school children, is called the Embedded Figures Test. It is available from Consulting Psychologists Press, 577 College Avenue, Palo Alto, CA 94306.

Matching Learning Styles to Instruction

In contrast to our thinking style, our learning style may vary over time and from task to task. It also may include a host of visual, auditory, and kinesthetic factors that influence how we learn. To illustrate, applying Bruner's theory of the three modes of learning (discussed earlier in the chapter), we may prefer to learn something by *observing* two- or three-dimensional items (iconic mode).

Alternatively, our preference may be to rely on the *spoken or written word* (symbolic mode). A further preference might be for *hands-on* activities that emphasize learning by doing (enactive mode).

Our learning style may involve conditions such as the temperature or ambience within a classroom, seating arrangements, our mood and motivations, our physical state, the sounds around us, and the time of day that is optimal for learning (Dunn et al., 1989). It may even include the hemisphere of our brain that appears to be the dominant one in processing information (McCarthy, 1990).

A basic approach to adapting instruction by matching learning styles involves an analysis of the conditions in the school environment that the teacher can actually control. The next step is to decide for which of the conditions it is practical or productive to provide students with options in social studies instruction.

Further, the teacher should identify the objectives and activities for which options are to be included. Two additional steps are to survey student preferences concerning the options the teacher is prepared to offer and to develop the actual instructional alternatives for the students.

The 4MAT System. Other approaches focus upon providing alternative instructional strategies that are responsive to students' dominant preferences. The **4MAT System,** for example, assumes that there are four major learning styles, all equally valuable (McCarthy, 1990):

4MAT system

- Style One: learners who are primarily interested in personal meaning
- Style Two: learners who are primarily interested in understanding facts
- Style Three: learners who are primarily interested in how things work
- Style Four: learners who are primarily interested in self-discovery

McCarthy contended that students need to learn through all four styles, not just their preferred one. She also stated they should engage in activities that draw upon both hemispheres of the brain.

Multiple Intelligences. In a similar vein, Gardner (1991, 1993) has developed a theory of **multiple intelligences** (MI), which postulates that individuals learn through at least *eight* comprehensive modes or intelligences.

multiple intelligences

1. Bodily-Kinesthetic Intelligence: ability to use our bodies to indicate ideas and emotions
2. Interpersonal Intelligence: capacity to distinguish emotions, feelings, and motives of others
3. Intrapersonal Intelligence: ability to introspect and act flexibly on self-insights
4. Linguistic Intelligence: ability to communicate effectively either orally or in writing

5. Logical–Mathematical Intelligence: capacity to reason clearly and facility with mathematical operations

6. Musical Intelligence: ability to distinguish, manipulate, and communicate musical elements

7. Spatial Intelligence: capacity to distinguish and manipulate spatial and visual elements

8. Nature Intelligence: affinity for plants, animals, and natural things

In 1991, Gardner wrote: "we all are able to know the world through language, logical mathematical analysis, spatial representation, musical thinking, the use of the body to solve problems or make things, an understanding of other individuals, and an understanding of ourselves" (p. 12). Later, he added an eighth form of intelligence: Nature Intelligence. Where individuals differ, he maintains, is in the relative strengths of each MI and in the ways we use them to accomplish various tasks.

His ideas have been put into practice at the Key School, an inner-city public elementary school in Indianapolis, Indiana. Each day, every student has at least one experience designed for each of the types of intelligences.

Developing special instructional strategies for identifying learning styles, such as in the 4MAT system, requires special training and some assistance and practice. However, all teachers can adapt their instruction in some ways to accommodate differences in students' learning styles.

Benson (1995) has provided an illustration of a lesson for middle-years students, using an MI approach (see Figure 12.8). The example includes activities that address each of the seven earlier types of MI.

Measures of Learning Styles

A number of learning-style inventories already have been developed and are marketed commercially. These employ paper-and-pencil measures that ask students to indicate their preferred conditions for engaging in learning activities.

One measure widely used is the Learning Style Inventory (Dunn & Dunn, 1992). The authors organized learning style preferences into five categories: *environmental*, *sociological*, *emotional*, *physiological*, and *psychological*. These include an assortment of specific preferences, such as whether students like sound or quiet when they are learning, whether they like to eat while doing some task, whether they prefer to remain stationary or move about the classroom, and whether they like to work alone or in some way with others (Dunn & Dunn, 1992). This instrument, which is used for identifying learning styles of students in grades 3 through 12, is available from Price Systems, Box 1818, Lawrence, KN 66044-1818.

A similar measure that covers 23 categories of conditions, the Learning Style Profile, has been developed by the National Association of Secondary School Principals (NASSP) (Keefe & Monk, 1986). It can be used with middle-grades students and is available from NASSP, 1904 Association Drive, Reston, VA 22091-1598.

FIGURE 12.8 Sample lesson for middle grades using a multiple intelligences approach

Level:	7th grade
Subject:	Social Studies
Objective:	To understand the importance of loyalty and duty in the Japanese culture.
Monday:	(Linguistic Intelligence): Students will listen to the importance of philosophy in the Japanese society. Students will listen to some of Confucius' sayings concerning family and duty to that family. Students will listen to the importance the Shinto religion places on the spirits of the dead which are found in all of nature. Students will listen to the Buddhist value of ancestors.
Tuesday:	(Spatial Intelligence): Students will observe art that demonstrates the importance the Japanese place on family loyalty and duty. Students will watch a film on the history of Japanese culture.
Wednesday:	(Bodily-Kinesthetic): The students will learn how to do four moves in Judo, one of the martial arts used in Japan. The students will be taught that the proper way to begin any martial art is with great respect. It is considered a duty to do so.
Thursday:	(Musical Intelligence): Students will listen to a demonstration of Japanese music played by three of the members of a musical group from Japan who attend the University here.
Friday:	(Logical-Mathematical Intelligence): The students will classify the different philosophies and religions of Japan to see a clear history of cultural belief in duty and loyalty.
Monday:	(Interpersonal Intelligence): The students will divide into four groups. Each will study and discuss a separate philosophy and/or religion of Japan which has influenced the presence of duty and loyalty in their culture. They will select one student from their group to present the results of their study and discussion to the class.
Tuesday:	(Intrapersonal Intelligence): The students will write about how they think they would feel when the atomic bomb fell on Hiroshima if they were Japanese and their mother was caught under fallen rafters. They could escape if they left her and possibly not escape if they helped.

Source: From *Planning for Multiple Intelligences* (p. 2) by L. Benson, 1995, Raleigh, NC: Department of Curriculum and Instruction, North Carolina State University. Reprinted with permission.

Individualization and Cultural Diversity

As we consider in Chapter 9, we are an increasingly pluralistic society and our classrooms reflect this fact. More than 20 million people in our nation have a native language other than English. In California, for example, during 1988 one in six students was foreign born (Olson, 1988). In some areas of that state, it is not uncommon to find more than 20 languages spoken in a single elementary school.

Classrooms in urban areas across the United States house a mix of cultural groups representing immigrants, refugees, and illegal aliens, as well as diverse populations of native-born citizens, all speaking in many different tongues. Further, the cultural expectations of parents within these groups often clash with those of the school, as illustrated in Figure 12.9.

The unprecedented challenges these students present have been overwhelming for many school districts, particularly in urban centers. As Olson (1988) noted, "Most schools are reeling—aware that changes need to be made but unsure what should or can be done and lacking the resources, direction, and support needed to try to deal with the problems" (p. 212). Teachers have the difficult responsibility of trying to ensure that the diversity their students bring to the classroom enriches, rather than impedes, all students' learning.

| FIGURE 12.9 | Incongruities between American teachers' expectations and Asian parents' expectations |

American Teachers' Expectations	Asian Parents' Expectations
Students need to participate in classroom activities and discussion.	Students are to be quiet and obedient.
Students need to be creative.	Students should be told what to do.
Students learn through inquiries and debate.	Students learn through memorization and observation.
Asian students generally do well on their own.	Teachers need to teach; students need to "study."
Critical thinking is important. Analytical thinking is important.	It is important to deal with the real world.
Creativity and fantasy are to be encouraged.	Factual information is important; fantasy is not.
Problem solving is important.	Students should be taught the steps to solve problems.
Students need to ask questions.	Teachers are not to be challenged.
Reading is a way of discovering.	Reading is the decoding of new information and facts.

Source: Reprinted from *Assessing Asian Language Performance* by L. L. R. Cheng, p. 14, with permission of Aspen Publishers, Inc., © 1987.

Equity for Those With Disabilities

Of all the categories of students vying for individualized instruction in our schools, those with disabilities have received the most attention in the past decade. The basic issue is how to provide instruction appropriate to their special needs.

In recent years considerable progress has been made in addressing the needs of special students (see Figure 12.10). Once their level of awareness toward those with disabilities was raised, many organizations and businesses voluntarily changed policies and procedures that created hardships. The passage of federal, state, and local laws also has expanded access to public facilities through

FIGURE 12.10	Ten commandments for communicating with people with disabilities

1. Speak directly rather than through a companion or sign language interpreter who may be present.
2. Offer to shake hands when introduced. People with limited hand use or an artificial limb can usually shake hands and offering the left hand is an acceptable greeting.
3. Always identify yourself and others who may be with you when meeting someone with a visual impairment. When conversing in a group, remember to identify the person to whom you are speaking.
4. If you offer assistance, wait until the offer is accepted. Then listen or ask for instructions.
5. Treat adults as adults. Address people who have disabilities by their first names only when extending that same familiarity to all others. Never patronize people in wheelchairs by patting them on the head or shoulder.
6. Do not lean against or hang on someone's wheelchair. Bear in mind that disabled people treat their chairs as extensions of their bodies.
7. Listen attentively when talking with people who have difficulty speaking and wait for them to finish. If necessary, ask short questions that require short answers, a nod or shake of the head. Never pretend to understand if you are having difficulty doing so. Instead repeat what you have understood and allow the person to respond.
8. Place yourself at eye level when speaking with someone in a wheelchair or on crutches.
9. Tap a hearing-impaired person on the shoulder or wave your hand to get his or her attention. Look directly at the person and speak clearly, slowly and expressively to establish if the person can read your lips. If so, try to face the light source and keep hands, cigarettes and food away from your mouth when speaking.
10. Relax. Don't be embarrassed if you happen to use common expressions such as "See you later," or "Did you hear about this?" that seem to relate to a person's disability.

Source: From National Center for Access, Chicago, IL.

requirements for provisions such as ramps at sidewalks or Braille instructions in elevators.

Public Law 94-142

Schools, like other institutions in our society, have been affected by governmental statutes and regulations concerning those with disabilities. The most significant of these was the Individuals with Disabilities Education Act, usually referred to as **PL 94-142,** which was passed in 1975. It stated, in effect, that if any school system in the United States wished to receive special federal funding, it had to make provisions by 1980 for "free, appropriate, public education."

PL 94-142 affected all children with disabilities, regardless of the types of impairments or disabilities they had. Disabilities, as the term is used in practice, include the following:

Speech impairment	Orthopedic impairment
Hearing impairment	Emotional disturbance
Learning disability	Physical impairment
Visual impairment	Behavioral disturbance
Mental retardation	

In practice, however, the vast majority of mainstreamed students with disabilities are classified in four categories as having a learning disability, emotional disturbance, speech impairment, or mental retardation.

One of the lingering controversies concerns the labeling or classifying of special students. The issues center on the validity of the process, particularly where considerable weight is given to scores on IQ tests. Critics of current practices contend that, given the normal variance in such tests and their dependence on culturally bound references, it seems likely that many students have been labeled improperly (refer to Figure 12.1).

The category of learning disability is particularly susceptible to misapplication; the actual criteria used to classify students as having learning disabilities often are difficult to distinguish from those that teachers informally use to describe a student as a "slow learner" or "not working up to potential." Many teachers who struggle with entire classes of students with low motivational levels, poor self-concepts, and a variety of educational, social, and economic deficits would argue that labels are less meaningful than specific strategies that attempt to match instructional programs with the needs and abilities of individual students.

A Least Restrictive Educational Environment.   One of the significant provisions of PL 94-142 for social studies teachers was that children with disabilities had to be educated with nondisabled ones to the maximum extent possible and in the "least restrictive" educational environment. What this last provision means in practice has been the subject of considerable debate and varying interpretations. Many different implementations of the provision exist in schools across the nation.

Individualized Educational Programs.   In addition to the provisions already mentioned, PL 94–142 contained a section requiring for each student the development of an **individualized educational program (IEP).** An IEP is a written plan with specific details concerning a student's present level of educational performance, the educational program to be provided for the student, and the criteria that will be used to measure progress toward the objectives. The student's parents and the student, where appropriate, are to be involved in the development of an IEP. The teacher also may participate in a conference. An IEP may take any form, but by law it must include the basic components indicated.

individualized educational program (IEP)

Many states and local school districts have developed sample formats for developing an IEP. Figure 12.11 is an example of one such format. The figure represents the major portion of an IEP that would be drawn up to specify the educational program for an elementary- or a middle-school child.

Mainstreaming and Inclusion

School practices associated with the provision for a least restrictive educational environment often are referred to as **mainstreaming.** This means bringing students with disabilities into the mainstream of public education by placing them in regular classrooms for at least part of their education. An assumption of PL 94–142 is that children with disabilities will advance socially, psychologically, and educationally when they are not isolated from other children and that they will be better prepared for the realities of the world if they have to function in normal environments. The law also assumes that the experiences of nondisabled children with disabled children should help break down stereotypes and negative attitudes.

mainstreaming

Integrating students with disabilities into the regular classroom provides opportunities for all students to share experiences and break down stereotypes.

FIGURE 12.11   Sample format for developing an IEP

Individualized Education Program/Service Delivery Plan
(To be completed after Part 1 of the IEP is developed)

Student: _____

School: _____

ID#: _____   Grade: _____

Check Purpose
[ ] Initial Entry   [ ] Change in Placement
[ ] Annual Review   [ ] Change in Identification
[ ] Reevaluation   [ ] Other: _____

I. AREA OF IDENTIFICATION (ELIIGIBILITY) (mark only primary condition)*
[ ] Academically Gifted
[ ] Autistic
[ ] Behaviorally-Emotionally Handicapped
[ ] Deaf-Dlind
[ ] Hearing Impaired
[ ] Mentally Handicapped
   [ ] EMH   [ ] S/PMH   [ ] TMH
Other Needs: _____

[ ] Multihandicapped
[ ] Orthopedically Impaired
[ ] Other Health Impaired
[ ] Specific Learning Disabled
[ ] Speech-Language Impaired
[ ] Traumatic Brain Injured
[ ] Visually Impaired

II. RELATED SERVICES
[ ] None
[ ] Audiology
[ ] Counseling Services
[ ] Occupational Therapy
[ ] Physical Therapy
[ ] Speech-Language
[ ] Transportation
[ ] Other _____

*Child meets the eligibility criteria of the State Board of Education and is in need of special education.

III. LEAST RESTRICTIVE ENVIRONMENT (PLACEMENT)
A. AMOUNT OF TIME IN EXCEPTIONAL EDUCATION:

Type of Service	Sessions per Wk./Mo./Yr.	Min. Per Session	Hours Per Wk.
Consultation	_____	_____	_____
Direct Special Education	_____	_____	_____
Related Services	_____	_____	_____
_____	_____	_____	_____
_____	_____	_____	_____
Total	_____	_____	_____

B. CONTINUUM OF SERVICES: Check the services considered by the committee, and circle the decision reached. Give reason(s) for options rejected and the decision reached. A continuum of services must be considered.
[ ] Regular - Less than 21% of day (up to 1 hour 15 min.)
[ ] Resource - 21% - 60% of day (1 hr. 15 min. to 3 hrs. 30 min.)
[ ] Separate - 61% or more of day (excess of 3 hrs. 30 min.)
[ ] Public Separate School - 100%

[ ] Private Separate School - 100%
[ ] Public Residential - 100%
[ ] Private Residential - 100%
[ ] Home/Hospital - 100%

PRESCHOOL
[ ] Regular* - Up to 6 hours per week
[ ] Resource* - 6 to 18 hours per week
[ ] Separate* - more than 18 hours per week
[ ] Public Separate School - 100%
   *Applicable only in a classroom setting

[ ] Private Separate School - 100%
[ ] Public Residential - 100%
[ ] Private Residential - 100%
[ ] Home/Hospital - 100%
[ ] Home/Family - minimum 1 hour per week

AGENCY: Check where the student is receiving special services.
[ ] 1. LEA/School in Attendance Area   [ ] 3. Another LEA
[ ] 2. LEA/School Not in Attendance Area   [ ] 4. Other _____

Reason(s) for options rejected _____
_____

Reason(s) for decision reached _____
_____

C. REGULAR PROGRAM PARTICIPATION: Circle the regular class(es) in which the student is enrolled and list the letter(s) for any modification(s) in the blank provided.

____ Reading	____ Library	____ History	____ For. Lang.	____ Vocational
____ English	____ Music/Art	____ Science	____ Physical Educ.	____ Recess
____ Spelling	____ Economics	____ Health	____ Chapter 1	____ Homeroom
____ Math	____ Social Studies	____ Writing	____ Remediation	____ Other
____ Language Arts	____ Lunch	____ Assemblies		

Appropriate classroom modification(s), if any:
a. Grading
b. Peer Tutoring
c. Oral Test
d. Abbreviated Assign-ments

e. Alternative Materials
f. Extended Test Time (Tchr. Test)
g. Large Print Books
h. Audio Tapes
i. Tape Recorder

j. Interpreter
k. Auditory Trainer
l. Assistive Devices
m. Computer/Typewriter/ Word Processor

n. Other _____
_____
_____
_____

Source: From Wake County Public School System, Raleigh, NC, 1993.

In many schools some children with disabilities always have been mainstreamed. Children in wheelchairs, with poor eyesight, with hearing problems, or with psychological disorders, for example, had been assimilated into many classrooms long before legislation required it. Among other things, what PL 94-142 attempted was to increase both the scope of disabilities and the number of children who would be mainstreamed. It also sought to establish the legal right of all students to such education, whether the schools wished to provide it or not.

The basic social intent of PL 94-142 was to bring all individuals with disabilities, as fully as is possible, into the mainstream of society, including its schools. The "least restrictive environment" provision of PL 94-142 did *not* require that all children with disabilities be placed in regular classrooms or that all aspects of their education occur there. It *did*, however, place on school districts the burden of proof to show that some part of these students' education cannot take place in a regular classroom setting.

In recent years, advocates for increased special education services have argued for the principle of full **inclusion**, that is, including all handicapped children in regular classrooms, regardless of the nature of their handicap (Shanker, 1995). This proposition has spawned an unresolved controversy over how to best serve and offer individual instruction for all children.

inclusion

Consider the case of Mary, a third grader, who has been labeled "handicapped." What is the most appropriate type of placement for her?

> Mary has Down Syndrome and has significant delays in fine motor and language skills. In traditional service delivery, Mary would be educated in a classroom for students labeled as educable mentally handicapped (EMH). In that class, Mary would have instruction in segregated resource rooms and be taught by a special education teacher. In these classes, the focus would be largely on reading and math where she could repeatedly practice those skills. The curriculum would consist of many repetitive worksheets and exercises.
>
> In third grade, Mary needs supports and modifications to participate in social studies. The objectives for a project on world history were to work in groups to research any country, group of people, or period of time. Once placed in a cooperative peer group, many of the supports and modifications occurred naturally. The groups were required to select roles for each group member. Mary was assigned the role of supervisor and designer. (Freagon et al., 1995, p. 17)

Strategies for Mainstreaming Students for Social Studies Instruction

Glazzard (1980) developed a list of 44 specific suggestions for adapting classrooms for mainstreamed students; her suggestions cover six categories of disabilities. A number of instructional strategies can facilitate mainstreaming of special students for subject matter instruction (see Curtis, 1991; Ochoa & Shuster, 1981). Some of the most successful approaches have involved cooperative learning techniques (Margolis, McCabe, & Schwartz, 1990), such as those discussed in Chapter 5.

Examples of how the *physical environment* of the classroom might be adapted to accommodate various disabilities include removing barriers to facilitate easy movement and seating special students near the chalkboard and/or doors. Other ways to assist students involve tape-recording and providing outlines and notes of lessons and attaching Braille labels to materials (Barnes, 1978). Additional strategies include allowing students to answer test questions orally and letting those who have orthopedic impairments be dismissed a few minutes early for their next classes.

Sanford (1980) offered a number of strategies and guidelines that are specific to social studies instruction in a mainstreamed classroom. To aid students with visual problems in geography instruction, for example, he advocated the use of tools such as Braille atlases, relief maps and globes, dissected maps of continents and countries, and landform models featuring three-dimensional tactile maps.

Bender (1985) advocated extensive use of visual materials, such as various graphic organizers (see Chapter 10), with special students in social studies classes. He observed that many students with disabilities learn better when subject matter is presented through some visual representation.

For administering social studies tests to mainstreamed children with mild disabilities, Wood, Miederhoff, and Ulschmid (1989) made a number of suggestions. Their recommendations included the following:

1. Give examples of how children are to respond.
2. Provide directions both orally and in writing.
3. Offer alternative ways to test the same item (e.g., orally or written).
4. To reduce errors, let students circle correct answers, rather than use answer sheets.
5. Use only one type of question (e.g., multiple choice) per sheet.
6. If a modified test is required for a mainstreamed student, design it to look like the regular one.

In some cases, materials for children with certain disabilities are available through special agencies. For example, students with visual and hearing disabilities are served by several agencies that provide special media social studies materials, such as captioned films and filmstrips and audio recordings of texts, on a loan basis. Many community agencies offer the use of these materials, or they may be secured from the following organizations:

American Foundation for the Blind
15 West 16th Street
New York, NY 10011

American Printing House for the Blind
1839 Frankfurt Avenue
Louisville, KY 40206

Captioned Films for the Deaf
Special Office for Materials Distribution
Indiana University Audiovisual Center
Bloomington, IN 47401

Equity for the Gifted

gifted

Another category of special students in our schools is the **gifted.** As it passed the Gifted and Talented Children's Act in 1978, Congress asserted boldly, "The nation's greatest resource for solving national problems in areas of national concern is its gifted and talented children."

The gifted are arguably one of our nation's most valuable natural resources. They enrich and enlighten our world through their contributions to literature and the visual and performing arts. They produce our scientific breakthroughs and new technologies. Our societal problem solvers, national leaders, great artists, and top scientists come from their ranks.

In these and a host of other ways, gifted and talented individuals are an important national resource. Whether we nurture and use this resource wisely depends, in great measure, on what special provisions our educational systems offer.

Societal Perspectives on the Gifted

American society historically has existed in a state of tension concerning the gifted student (Delisle, 1991; Laycock, 1979). One school of thought maintains that the gifted are an elite who are well qualified to look out for themselves without any special help. This perspective reasons that schools filled with average students and those with special problems should focus their limited resources on the majority, not on the gifted minority.

At the same time, our society promotes the notion of excellence and the ideal that each individual should strive to achieve all that his or her abilities allow. Schools are alternately chided and prodded when they ignore this societal goal. We exhort our schools to help in the competition to produce exceptional individuals who will keep our nation in the forefront of the world in areas like technology, industrial productivity, space, the arts, peacekeeping, human rights, and standards of living. When we seem to lag or fall behind, as in the 1950s in the space race with the Soviet Union, we initiate national crash programs and offer special incentives to stimulate the education of talented individuals.

Identifying the Gifted

Who are the gifted? Definitions of *gifted* vary considerably, but most include some combination of the following characteristics (Marland, 1972):

Special academic aptitudes   Artistic abilities
General intellectual abilities   Leadership abilities
Creativity   Psychomotor abilities

Some states and local school districts have created operational meanings for the characteristics they use to define gifted students. For example, a school may consider a score of 130 or above on an individual IQ test as an indicator of general intellectual ability. Such procedures, however, have come under attack on the grounds that they are too limiting and favor students reared in the mainstream culture (Baldwin, 1978; Frasier, 1989). The critics favor alternative procedures and instruments to identify giftedness in students whose backgrounds are dissimilar to the majority of students (Sisk, 1987).

Approaches to Gifted Education

Schools that provide for the special needs of the gifted usually employ some variation of three organizational approaches to their programs (Maker, 1982; Renzulli, 1968; Sisk, 1987). One approach is to group students in one or more subjects by *ability*. For example, students judged to be gifted in social studies might be placed together either by grades or across several grades. A variation of this approach is to place together for all subjects all students designated as gifted.

A second approach is to keep students within a regular classroom setting but to provide *enriched* learning experiences in one or more subjects. Enrichment may be provided within the regular classroom setting or through so-called pull-out programs, for which gifted students are taken from their classrooms to special programs one or more times per week.

The third basic approach emphasizes *accelerating* students' progress in mastering subject matter. Through special in-class activities or other types of special programs, students advance as rapidly as they are capable of through the study of a subject. When a "grade" of subject matter has been mastered, a student advances to the next grade. Under the accelerated approach, for example, a gifted student might complete three years of the social studies program in a single year.

Gifted Students in Social Studies Classes

Sisk (1987) observed that the "social studies, more than other subjects, offers the gifted student a chance to deal with real problems in the world, problems that have their roots in the past, direct application to the present, and implications for the future" (p. 171). Several sets of characteristics that seem to distinguish general giftedness in social studies have been identified (National Education Association, 1960; Plowman, 1980; Sisk, 1987).

Consider a sixth-grade class composed of students who have demonstrated exceptional *cognitive abilities* in the area of social studies. Signs of such cognitive abilities in the area of social studies might include the following:

With respect to *verbal ability*, the student exhibits signs of:

1. A high level of language development
2. A vast store of information
3. Advanced comprehension
4. Facility in speaking and expressing complex ideas
5. Asking many and often original questions
6. Unusual curiosity and originality in questions
7. Ability to engage in sustained, meaningful, give-and-take discussions
8. An exceptional memory
9. Large vocabulary
10. Varied interests

With respect to *written work*, the student exhibits signs of:

1. An unusual capacity for processing information
2. A special knack for seeing unusual or less obvious relationships among data
3. A pattern of consistently generating original ideas and solutions
4. Unusual examples of cause-and-effect relationships, logical predictions, and frequent use of abstractions
5. An unusual ability to synthesize accurately large bodies of information
6. The capacity to use with ease a number of different reference materials in solving problems and testing hypotheses
7. Advanced reading ability
8. Unusual ability to understand alternative points of view or to place oneself in another's shoes
9. A large storehouse of information
10. Creativity

Among the ways special social studies programs for the gifted have been provided to address the special cognitive abilities described above are:

- *Using Alternative Materials at Advanced Reading Levels.* Example: Using eighth-grade and above materials on American history to supplement or replace normal fifth-grade American history text and program.
- *Using Exclusively Discovery Approaches and Simulations and Role-Playing Techniques.* Example: Substituting the usual narrative expository study of a topic with a series of discovery lessons and simulation and role-playing activities that are open-ended and require consideration of alternatives and problem solving.

- *Using a Special, Alternative Curriculum.* Example: Substituting a year's course of study in geography, economics, or anthropology for the standard basal text in the first grade.

- *Employing Mentors Specializing or Working in Areas Related to the Social Studies Curriculum.* Example: Under the guidance of a mentor specialist, having a student conduct a project to obtain data regarding the ethics of seal hunting (see Figure 12.12).

- *Emphasizing Problem-Solving Assignments and Activities.* Example: Reorganizing the second-grade curriculum around a series of learning centers that involve problem-solving tasks.

- *Focusing on Research as Conducted by Social Scientists.* Example: Organizing several units around the use and analysis of primary and secondary source materials.

- *Studying Cutting-Edge Issues and Developments.* Example: Spending the entire sixth-grade year examining the state of current computer technology and the microprocessor revolution and how different countries have been affected by it. Then determining what the projections for the future indicate and developing alternative scenarios for how the world of the future will be different because of the computer.

- *Use of Student Projects.* Example: As an alternative to studying about communities in the basal text, students design, carry out, and evaluate, with teacher assistance, a series of projects to better understand their local community.

Group Activities

1. Develop a plan for a social studies learning center for grade 5. Select any theme you wish. Be as specific as possible about what sorts of things you would include in the center. Compare your plans.

2. Visit a classroom in either an elementary or a middle-grade school that includes a mix of cultural groups. Identify all of the ways the classroom is culturally diverse and the procedures the teacher follows to be responsive to the diversity. Discuss your findings.

3. Visit a primary- and an intermediate-grade classroom. Draw a map of each, locating all of the desks, facilities within the room, materials areas, centers, assorted work areas, and collections of social studies materials. On your maps, note the grade level and label each item in the room. (You also may use a legend.) After drawing these maps, construct a third one showing *your* idea of how a classroom should be organized (any grade level). Add any necessary explanations. Also discuss how your design for a classroom reflects your ideas about teaching.

FIGURE 12.12   Plan for a mentorship activity

Finalized Plan for a Community-Based "Mentor-Directed Enrichment Project"

Mentor's Name ___Jeannie G.___   Pupil's Name ___Grania M.___

Project Topic ___Sealing: Right or Wrong?___

Project Meeting Time ___Friday Afternoons 1:00-3:00 or longer___

	Week # Learning Activities (Including Resources)	Related Learning Outcomes
Phase I Planning proposal	1. (a) Mentor writes up proposed project in his or her area of expertise (b) University instructor and enrichment teacher use proposal to match mentor to an interested pupil	(a) Preparing for first meeting with pupil
Phase II Agreeing on finalized project plan	2. (a) Introduce proposal and topic (b) Find out what Grania knows about seals and sealing, and what her attitudes are (can change project plan if necessary) (c) Prepare questionnaire for next week's interview, and role-play an interview using tape recorder (d) Make "thank you" card	(a) Increasing intrinsic motivation (b) Planning an enrichment project (c) Posing answerable questions (d) Interviewing skills (e) Practicing courtesy
Phase III Carrying out the project plan	3. (a) Visit Vancouver Aquarium to observe seals (b) Interview (tape record) seal trainer discussing what seals are like (c) Take slides of seals; sketch them	(a) Observation skills (b) Interviewing skills and confidence (c) Background knowledge about seals (d) Artistic skills
	4. (a) At school, Grania decides which sketches, slides, and information are to be used in her presentation (b) Read materials on seals and compare to observations made at aquarium	(a) Decision-making and organization skills (b) Comparing and contrasting
	5. (a) Assess project thus far (review) (b) Prepare and rehearse questions for next week's interview with Gordon Rogers (a "pro-sealer" from Newfoundland) and the following week's interview with someone from the Greenpeace organization (anti-sealing)	(a) Grania has greater voice in preparing questions (b) Brainstorming imaginative questions
	6. (a) Interview Gordon Rogers (b) Obtain leads to other pro-sealing sources	(a) Gain a "pro-sealer's" point of view firsthand (b) Refine interviewing skills
	7. (a) Interview spokesperson from the Greenpeace organization (b) Obtain leads to other anti-sealing resources (c) Obtain materials to be used in presentation (including visuals)	(a) Gain an anti-sealing point of view firsthand (b) Refine interviewing skills
Phase IV Completing and presenting the project	8. (a) Organize the material to be used in the class presentation (b) Mount Grania's sketches (c) Mould clay seals; paint them (d) Prepare posters to display pro and con information obtained	(a) Decision-making and organization skills (b) Lettering posters (neatness)
	9. (a) Role-play the class presentation (mentor demonstrates; pupil practices) (b) Objectively present both pro and con information to allow class members to decide for themselves if sealing is right or wrong	(a) Speaking skills and self-confidence (b) Objective reporting of controversial information
	10. (a) Pupil gives class presentation and answers questions about what she liked best about her project, and so forth.	(a) Public speaking skills (b) Thinking "on one's feet" while answering questions

Source: From "Mentor-Assisted Enrichment Projects for the Gifted and Talented" by W. A. Gray, 1982, *Educational Leadership, 40*, pp. 19–20. Copyright 1982 by Association for Supervision and Curriculum Development. Reprinted by permission.

Individual Activities

1. Select any elementary social studies basal textbook, grades 2 through 4. Pick a topic or a sample of subject matter that is part of the text narrative (symbolic mode). Develop a sample activity to illustrate how the same material could be taught through the iconic mode. Repeat the process for the enactive mode.

2. Construct a jackdaw for either grade 5 or 6, dealing with any social studies topic. Follow the directions and suggestions from the chapter.

3. Arrange with a local elementary school to examine the type of IEP it uses. Compare the format used by the school with the one shown in this chapter. Identify the information provided for each student and the extent to which students are mainstreamed. Note particularly whether any provisions for social studies activities are included in the school's IEP.

4. Gain access to the Internet and search for information on "intelligent agents (tutors)." What are their capabilities? their limitations? For which social studies topics would the agents be most useful?

References

Allen, J. (1991). *The Cherokee Indians.* Unpublished manuscript, North Carolina State University, Department of Curriculum and Instruction, Raleigh.

Baldwin, A. Y. (1978). *Educational planning for the gifted: Overcoming cultural, geographical, and socioeconomic barriers.* Reston, VA: Council for Exceptional Children.

Barnes, E. (1978). *What do you do when your wheelchair gets a flat tire? Questions and answers about disabilities.* New York: Scholastic Book Services.

Bender, W. N. (1985). Strategies for helping the mainstreamed student in secondary social studies classes. *The Social Studies, 76,* 269–271.

Bruner, J. (1973). *Beyond the information given.* New York: Norton.

Cheng, L. (1987). *Assessing Asian language performance.* Rockville, MD: Aspen.

Curtis, C. K. (1991). Social studies for students at-risk and with disabilities. In J. P. Shaver (Ed.), *Handbook of social studies teaching and learning* (pp. 157–174). New York: Macmillan.

Delisle, J. R. (1991). Gifted students and social studies. In J. P. Shaver (Ed.), *Handbook of social studies teaching and learning* (pp. 175–182). New York: Macmillan.

Dowd, F. S. (1990). What's a jackdaw doing in our classroom? *Childhood Education, 66,* 228–231.

Dunn, R., Beaudry, J., & Klavas, A. (1989). Survey of research on learning styles. *Educational Leadership, 46,* 50–58.

Dunn, R., & Dunn, K. (1992). *Teaching elementary school students through their individual learning styles.* Boston: Allyn & Bacon.

Frasier, M. M. (1989, March). Poor and minority students can be gifted, too! *Educational Leadership, 44,* 16–18.

Gardner, H. (1991). *The unschooled mind: How children think and how schools should teach.* New York: Basic Books.

Glazzard, P. (1980). Adaptations for mainstreaming. *Teaching Exceptional Children, 13*, 26–29.

Gray, W. A. (1982). Mentor-assisted enrichment projects for the gifted and talented. *Educational Leadership, 40*, 19–20.

Guild, P. B., & Garger, S. (1985). *Marching to different drummers*. Alexandria. VA: Association for Supervision and Curriculum Development.

Freagon, S., Best, R., Sommerness, J., Usilton, R., West, J., Cox, K., & Reising, P. (1995, April/May). Inclusion of young learners with disabilities in social studies. *Social Studies & the Young Learner*, 15–18.

Hawke, S. D., & Davis, J. E. (1992). *Seeds of change: The story of cultural change after 1492*. Boston: Allyn & Bacon.

Jackdaws: Portfolios of primary source documents. (1993). Amawalk, NY: Golden Owl.

Keefe, J. W., & Monk, J. S. (1986). *Learning style profile: Examiner's manual*. Reston, VA: National Association of Secondary School Principals.

Laycock, F. (1979). *Gifted children*. Glenview, IL: Scott, Foresman.

Maker, C. J. (1982). *Teaching models in the education of the gifted*. Rockville, MD: Aspen.

Margolis, H., McCabe, P. P., & Schwartz. E. (1990). Using cooperative learning to facilitate mainstreaming in the social studies. *Social Education, 54*, 111–114, 120.

Marland, S. (1972). *Education of the gifted and talented*. Washington, DC: Government Printing Office.

McCarthy, B. (1990). Using the 4MAT system to bring learning styles to schools. *Educational Leadership, 48*, 31–37.

National Education Association. (1960). *Project on the academically talented student*. Washington, DC: English for the Academically Talented Student.

Ochoa, A. S., & Shuster, S. K. (1981). Social studies in the mainstreamed classroom. In T. Shaw (Ed.), *Teaching handicapped students social studies: A resource handbook for K–12 teachers* (pp. 8–20). Washington, DC: National Education Association.

Olson, L. (1988). Crossing the schoolhouse border: Immigrant children in California. *Phi Delta Kappan, 70*, 211–218.

Plowman, P. (1980). *Teaching the gifted and talented in the social studies classroom*. Washington, DC: National Education Association.

Rasinski, T. (1983). *Using jackdaws to build background and interest for reading*. Washington, DC: U.S. Department of Education, National Institute of Education. (ERIC Document Reproduction Service No. ED 234351)

Renzulli, J. (1968). Identifying key features in programs for the gifted. *Exceptional Children, 35*, 217–221.

Sanford, H. (1980). Organizing and presenting social studies content in a mainstreamed class. In J. G. Herlihy & M. T. Herlihy (Eds.), *Mainstreaming in the social studies* (Bulletin 62, pp. 42–50). Washington, DC: National Council for the Social Studies.

Schunk, D. H. (1996). *Learning theories* (2nd ed.). Upper Saddle River, NJ: Merrill/Prentice Hall.

Shanker, A. (1995). Full inclusion is neither free nor appropriate. *Educational Leadership, 52*.

Sisk, D. (1987). *Creative teaching of the gifted*. New York: McGraw-Hill.

Weber, M. (1992). *Seeds of Change Learning Centers*. Unpublished manuscript, North Carolina State University, Department of Curriculum and Instruction, Raleigh.

Witkin, H. A., Moore, C. A., Goodenough, D. R., & Cox, P. W. (1977). Field-dependent and field-independent cognitive styles. *Review of Educational Research, 47*, 1–64.

Wood, J. W., Miederhoff, J. W., & Ulschmid, B. (1989). Adapting test construction for mainstreamed social studies students. *Social Education, 53*, 46–49.

Chapter

Evaluating and Assessing Student Learning

What If . . . A Vision of Educational Assessment in California

"**What if** students found assessment to be a lively, active, exciting experience?

What if they could see clearly what was expected of them and believed that the assessment provided a fair opportunity to show what they had learned?

What if they were challenged to construct responses that conveyed the best of what they had learned—to decide what to present and how to present it—whether through speech, writing, or performance?

What if they were educated to assess themselves to become accurate evaluators of the strengths and weaknesses of their own work, and to prescribe for themselves the efforts they must make to improve it—ultimately, the most important form of assessment available to our students?

*What **if** the assessment allowed students to use their own backgrounds and indicated ways of building on their strengths for further learning?*

*What **if** their learning were recognized by the school and the community when they had made outstanding progress—regardless of their initial level of achievement?*

*"**What if** teachers could look at the tests and say, 'Now we're talking about a fair assessment of my teaching;*

*   **one that** focuses on the essence of the student outcomes that I am striving for—not one that focuses on the peripheral skills or the isolated facts which are easiest to measure;*

*   **one that** shows they can produce something of value to themselves and to others—an argument, a report, a plan, an answer or solution; a story, a poem, a drawing, a sculpture, or a performance; that they can conduct an experiment, deliver a persuasive oral presentation, participate cooperatively and productively in groups;*

*   **one that** is accessible to all my students, yet stretches the most capable students as well—not one that measures some mythical minimum competency level;*

*   **one that** matches the assessment that I use on a day-to-day basis to guide my teaching and that guides my students in their learning—not one that takes an artificial form and then naively expects students to give a natural response in an artificial situation;*

*   **one that** doesn't take valuable time from the teaching/learning process, but is an integral part of that process;*

*   **one that** doesn't treat me as a "Teller of Facts," providing and prescribing the concepts and the content that students are to study—but rather as a coach and a fellow learner, helping my students to become active learners who are prepared to discover what is important to them now and enthusiastic about learning in the future?"*

*"**What if** the new assessments led parents, taxpayers, legislators, and the business community to exclaim:*

*   '**I can see** that the schools are focusing on the important things—that students are achieving levels of academic excellence which truly prepare them for the future.*

*   **I can see** that students are learning what they need to fulfill themselves as individuals, to become concerned and involved citizens and workers who can adapt to the changing demands of our world—creative people who can think and take initiative, who care about what they do, and who can work with others to solve problems.*

*   **I can see** the results in the newspapers, which give me the information I need in terms I can understand, which show me the progress our schools are making on assessments that really matter, and where they need my help and support.'?" (Reprinted by permission of the California Assessment Program, California Department of Education, 1990)*

More and more often, schools are being asked to provide specific indicators of student learning and comparisons with their classmates' achievements in social studies. Tests, grades, assessment, and evaluation have become an integral part of the process of schooling. Teachers are expected to provide reasonable and clear answers to basic parent questions such as, "What did my youngster—not the class—learn in social studies this year?"

The Dimensions of Evaluation

Evaluation can be seen as a way of making a decision about the value of something based on some systematically organized data. Literally the term means "to
determine or judge the value or worth of something or someone." Parents and
other societal groups look to educators for evaluations of how successful our
schools have been in achieving their objectives. Students, more basically, wish to
know simply, "How am I doing?"

evaluation

Evaluation has many objective and subjective dimensions; it involves much
more than "giving tests" and labeling students. The National Council for the
Social Studies (NCSS) stated: "To gauge effectively the efforts of students and
teachers in social studies programs, evaluators must augment traditional tests
with performance evaluations, portfolios of student papers and projects, and
essays focused on higher-level thinking" (NCSS, 1991, p. 285).

We first consider some of the nuances, issues, and mechanics associated
with different dimensions of evaluation and then move beyond them to examine
how a teacher develops an evaluation framework. This framework is what
guides teacher decisions about what is important in the curriculum and how
best to assess what students have learned.

Grades, Assessments, and Standards

Grades are one of the shorthand ways of communicating the results of an evaluation. "Rodney got an A in social studies" means that the teacher evaluated his
performance and decided it was exceptional. In the absence of a grade, a sentence, a symbol, or other means could have served the same purpose. Grades,
however, are widely used because they are easy to record, to communicate to
others, and to compare.

grades

Perhaps most significantly, grades can be reduced to quantifiable terms: Separate evaluations from different subjects, each totally unrelated, may be merged and
used to form a new, single evaluation; for example, "Reba was a 3.35 student."

In contrast to grades, **assessments** are the systematic ways we use to collect our data. They encompass such measures as simple charts for keeping track
of the number of times a student asks questions in a social studies class and
comprehensive collections of student work. Assessments also may include
paper-and-pencil measures, such as tests to measure how much subject matter
a student has learned.

assessment

Standards, which are related to both assessment and evaluation, are the
criteria teachers use for making judgments. Standards determine what should
be placed on a test, how carefully something should be assessed, and what is
satisfactory performance. Teachers' standards determine whether they are
regarded as "easy" or "tough" graders.

standards

The ultimate purpose of grades, assessments, standards, and evaluation
should be to validate and improve teaching and learning; therefore, assessment
should be an ongoing part of social studies instruction, rather than a culminat-

ing activity. The opening extract, an excerpt from a California Assessment Program document (California Department of Education, 1990) summarizes nicely what an ideal evaluation program might encompass.

The Use and Misuse of Tests

Testing has assumed a large role in our society during the past half-century. Tests and testing probably will dog students throughout at least the early part of their lives and occupational careers. It is safe to say that children who enter a public school in the United States will take countless tests of all types before they graduate. College and the world of work likely will present yet another battery of tests for the student to take.

Although tests can aid the teacher in some aspects of evaluation, they often are inappropriate measures of what a student has learned. Tests, especially paper-and-pencil tests, sometimes are used on occasions when other tools would be more efficient or suitable. It seems obvious, for example, that a paper-and-pencil test dealing with art would be inappropriate to use in discovering whether students are exceptional artists. Rather, we likely would have a qualified artist or panel judge their artwork. So it is with many aspects of achievement in the social studies. If we wish to evaluate how well students can use data to solve a problem or to determine how effectively they apply techniques of research, for example, student productions or projects probably are more appropriate than a test.

Critics of existing testing practices also point to their potential negative consequences (e.g., Darling-Hammond & Lieberman, 1992; Mitchell, 1992). One particularly penetrating criticism of many tests is that they are biased with respect to ethnicity, social class, and gender. In addition, Darling-Hammond and Lieberman also charged:

> Because of the way in which the tests are constructed, they place test-takers in a passive, reactive role, rather than a role that engages their capacities to structure tasks, produce ideas, and solve problems. . . . Teaching has been geared to the tests, reducing students' opportunities for higher-order learning. . . . Many studies have found that because of test-oriented teaching, American students' classroom activities consist of listening, reading textbook sections, responding briefly to questions, and taking short-answer and multiple-choice quizzes. They rarely plan or initiate anything, create their own products, read or write something substantial, or engage in analytical discussions or in projects requiring research, invention, or problem solving. (p. B1)

Norm-Referenced Tests

Two basic types of social studies tests that students typically are required to take throughout their elementary school careers and beyond are *norm-referenced* and *criterion-referenced* tests. **Norm-referenced tests** allow teachers to compare their students with the norms or results obtained from the performance of a

norm-referenced testing

sample group of students on the same test (Williams & Moore, 1980). Such tests provide answers to a question such as "How does the performance of my fifth-grade students compare with that of other fifth graders?"

Standardized Social Studies Tests.   So-called **standardized tests**, such as the California Achievement Tests, have standardized sets of instructions for administering the tests to ensure uniform test-taking procedures. They have been administered to a specified population and contain scores and percentiles. Usually the items on a standardized test have been refined over time. For example, three types of questions have been eliminated through field tests and trials: (a) those that are poorly worded or ambiguous, (b) those that most students answer correctly, and (c) those that most students answer incorrectly.

Major sources of information on all of the standardized tests currently available, including those in the area of social studies, are the *Mental Measurement Yearbooks* and *Tests in Print.* They are available in most college libraries and contain information such as a description of a test, where it can be purchased, and one or more critiques of its strengths and weaknesses. Examples of standardized tests for the social studies are California Achievement Tests, Iowa Tests of Basic Skills, and Sequential Tests of Educational Progress.

Teachers should realize that the subject matter sampled in standardized tests *may not correspond to what is being studied in any individual classroom*, because the specific subject matter and curriculum for a given grade level may vary from district to district. As a consequence, standardized tests often exclude social studies information and skills that are considered to be important to teachers. Further, as Darling-Hammond and Lieberman (1992) cautioned, "They are inappropriate tools for many of the purposes that they are expected to serve, including tracking students, determining promotions, and allocating rewards and sanctions to students, teachers, and schools" (p. B1).

In sum, as they use and interpret the results of standardized tests, teachers should consider carefully whether what they measure matches with the objectives of the classroom social studies program. Unless a clear match exists, the standardized test is useful only as a general diagnostic measure of what students know.

Criterion-Referenced Tests

In comparison to norm-referenced tests, **criterion-referenced tests** allow teachers to compare the performance of their students against some standard of what they should know (Popham, 1988). To develop large-scale criterion-referenced tests, school districts contract with test publishers to develop suitable materials for the school's curriculum. Such tests provide answers to questions such as "How does the performance of our fifth-grade students compare with the criterion of what we expected them to know or demonstrate?" An example of a criterion: Given an unlabeled globe of the world, a student will be able to identify correctly 80% of the world's major waterways.

Margin notes: **standardized tests**

criterion-referenced testing

The National Assessment of Educational Progress

In 1969, after six years of gestation, a consortium of states embarked on a national project known as the **National Assessment of Educational Progress (NAEP),** which is still in existence. The NAEP was an attempt by states to begin collecting evaluation data across the various participating states. It now attempts to measure student growth in various areas of the school curriculum, including areas of the social studies.

Samples of students from across the United States have been included in the ongoing NAEP project. Findings have been reported for ages 9, 13, and 17. Tests are repeated on a cyclical basis, and results are published and made available to the general public, as well as to participating school districts.

National Standards and National Testing

In recent years some groups both separate from and within NAEP have called for the establishment of **national standards** for each of the subjects within the curriculum. These standards would establish what all students in the United States should know and when they should know it.

In Chapter 3, we considered in detail the recommendations of four groups addressing standards for the social studies curriculum. Their efforts are represented in the History Standards Project; the Geography Standards Project; the National Standards for Civics and Government Project; and the NCSS Curriculum Standards Project, which addresses the social studies as a whole.

Two sample assessment items from the projects outlined in Chapter 3 are:

1. Use layers of colored paper, transparencies, and other graphics to identify political units at different scales, local to global (e.g., precinct, census district, school attendance zone, township, metropolitan area, county, state, and nation).
2. Research daily life in the Spanish colonies in the Americas. In an illustration, draw yourself and your friends doing what you would be doing if you lived in one of the Spanish colonies during the colonial period.

A related but separate movement is afoot to establish a national test in each subject area at various grade levels. Who would administer such a test is uncertain because, as discussed in Chapter 1, the federal government plays only a limited role in the regulation of local schools. A national test would require national standards, but the reverse is not necessarily true. Various educational agencies could be involved in developing and sharing assessment procedures based on a set of national standards.

Proponents of one or both proposals argue that they would serve to improve education by establishing common goals for all schools. They point to the fact that many other nations employ such approaches. Critics, however, maintain that the proposals would work to the disadvantage of poor and minority stu-

Performance assessment can help measure a student's skill in handling specific tasks and processes.

dents, who have special curricular needs. They argue further that national standards or testing would tear at the fiber of local school curricular autonomy and destroy diversity and creativity.

Performance Assessments

Proposals for national standards and testing frequently embrace the use of **performance (authentic) assessments** as part of an overall program of evaluation. They are a way of measuring student learning that requires the active construction of responses in the context of performing real (sometimes called "authentic") tasks (Perrone, 1991). Among other features, performance assessment approaches typically tap multiple sources of information to determine what students have learned in every phase of the social studies program (McTighe, 1997).

performance (authentic) assessments

Although performance assessments may employ paper-and-pencil tests, these have a limited role in the total evaluation process. Because tests that merely assess knowledge of social studies subject matter typically pass over knowledge of processes and skills, they cannot provide thorough and comprehensive measures of social studies learning.

Among the types of learning that such tests typically ignore in the social studies are the ability to:

- Identify, clarify, and solve an open-ended problem.
- Use spatial tools such as maps, globes, and compasses to locate objects.

- Identify cause-and-effect relationships among social data.
- Develop, execute, and critique an oral presentation to argue on behalf of a position or valued principle.
- Generate and test hypotheses and generalizations.
- Apply and relate concepts.
- Take and defend an ethical position.
- Organize a large body of related information into a graph, a chart, or a table.
- Conduct an interview to gather social data.
- Write a report summarizing important similarities and differences among issues, events, and individuals.
- Evaluate the evidence presented in competing arguments.

Social Studies Performance Assessments and Portfolios

portfolios

To redress the limitations of traditional measures of achievement, teachers frequently employ performance assessment techniques and **portfolios,** which emphasize student productions. Portfolios consist of samples of a student's work accumulated in a folder over a period of time. Additionally, they may include observations and evaluations by parents, the teacher, and the student.

Portfolios are intended to provide a holistic view of a student's capabilities in social studies. Optimally the student and the teacher should review portfolios periodically throughout the year to chart progress.

Student productions might include the following types of items:

- Written essays, papers, projects, and exercises
- Skits, debates, oral reports, panels, and role-playing enactments
- Cooperative learning group outcomes
- Skill demonstrations (e.g., using reference materials and interviewing techniques)
- Creations of products (e.g., dioramas, oral history collections, exhibits, videotapes, artifacts, bulletin boards, posters, card sorts, time lines)
- Checklists, rating forms, and observation forms
- Diaries and logs
- Experiments
- Teacher anecdotal records
- Teacher interviews

Sample applications of these types of measures to social studies instruction follow. The first example shows how a basic rating form was used to assess the quality of students' oral reports. Each student was judged by using the following questions:

Did the student

speak so that everyone could hear?
finish sentences?
seem comfortable in front of a group?
give a good introduction?
seem well informed about the topic?
explain ideas clearly?
stay on the topic?
give a good conclusion?
use effective costumes, pictures, or other materials to make the presentation interesting?
give good answers to questions from the audience? (Maeroff, 1991, p. 279)

Note how instruction and assessment are *interrelated* in this example; that is, the results of the assessment would give students relatively clear directions for what they need to do to improve their work.

In the second example (Figure 13.1), a diary format is used. It serves to tap into students' insights concerning an event and a historical figure.

FIGURE 13.1

Assessment item: Historical diary entry

Source: From *America Past and Present*, Teacher's Edition Workbook, by Joan Schreiber, et al. Copyright © 1983 by Scott, Foresman and Company. Reprinted by permission.

Writing a Diary Entry

Your textbook records the thoughts of one sailor on October 11, 1492—the day that Columbus's crew sighted land. It was a day of joy and new hope.

But what of October 10th—the day before? Imagine that you are that same sailor, aboard the tiny Santa Maria. You have been at sea over two long, lonely months. You see no signs of land; you have no hope. What would you have written that day?

Below is a diary entry dated October 10th. Read the beginning and ending of the entry carefully. Then on the blank lines write what the tired and angry sailor might have written.

Columbus—bah! I remember his two "great" promises--made two long months ago. First, _____

_____
_____
_____
_____
_____

All those promised riches and all that promised glory—where are they now? At the bottom of this cursed dark ocean, where our captain may soon find himself.

The third example (Figure 13.2) illustrates how pictures may be used in assessment. It employs a picture card to assess young children's grasp of chronological sequences. Items such as these three examples could be accumulated in students' portfolios.

FIGURE 13.2   Assessment item: Picture card sort

Tell a story with these pictures. Which picture comes first? Which one next?
Which one next? Which comes last?

Source: Adapted from *Looking at Me: Webstermaster Activity Sheets* (p. 42) by P. H. Martorella, L. Martelli, and A. Graham, 1983, New York: McGraw-Hill. Copyright 1983 by McGraw-Hill Book Company.

Teacher-Made Paper-and-Pencil Tests

Teacher-made paper-and-pencil tests often include features and items that resemble those found in norm-referenced and criterion-referenced tests. They differ from commercially prepared tests in the uses to which they are put and in the procedures used to develop them.

Teachers of primary-age children are, understandably, less likely to construct formal tests than those with older students. However, as the earlier example illustrated, some simple tests can be constructed even for younger children and nonreaders. Tests for these children should rely heavily on such visual materials as pictures, posters, drawings, filmstrip frames, and slides. Children may be asked to respond to a question either orally or with a drawing, rather than in writing.

Posttests and Pretests

As one dimension of evaluation, teachers typically give tests after students have studied a subject. These tests often are referred to as **posttests.** Tests also can be used as diagnostic measures to determine what students know before they begin study of a topic. Used in this fashion, such measures are called **pretests.**

posttests

pretests

Pretests can provide direction for the shape of a unit by identifying students' interests and gaps or misconceptions in their knowledge. Comparison of scores with those on posttests also can be an indicator of how much students actually have achieved as a result of instruction. The *K-W-L technique*, described in Chapter 10, is an illustration of how this comparison can be done.

A number of specialized books, materials, and guidelines can help teachers construct teacher-made tests (e.g., Airasian, 1991; Popham, 1988; TenBrink, 1994). Once a teacher has determined that student achievement can be measured best through a teacher-made test, several basic choices must be made. These generally consist of identifying or creating *essay* and *objective* test items.

Constructing Essay Test Items

Essay questions are an especially effective way to measure students' ability to organize, analyze, apply, synthesize, and evaluate, in their own words, information they have learned. Such questions provide students with the freedom to think broadly and to express themselves in different ways. Student essays, however, often are difficult to assess with objectivity. Further, of necessity, they can cover only a narrow range of objectives in a short period of time. They also are time consuming to score and allow students to digress.

In some cases essay questions also penalize the student who has, in reality, learned a great deal but has trouble expressing himself or herself in standard English. Translating concrete objects and ideas into abstractions represented by answers to essay questions is a cognitive task related to both development and language facility. Those for whom English is a second language, for example, often have more difficulty in stating something in their own words than in demonstrating learning by selecting, identifying, applying, or demonstrating among alternatives.

General Guidelines.   Two basic guidelines for constructing well-designed essay questions are:

1. Use clear, specific, and simple language.

   Yes: Describe two major ways in which urban and rural neighborhoods are alike.

   No: Tell me what you know about urban and rural neighborhoods.

2. Limit the scope of the question and the expected answer as much as possible.

   Yes: Give three ways in which the United States differs geographically from Mexico.

   No: How are the United States and Mexico different?

Before a teacher presents essay questions to students, he or she should construct a model answer for each question. The model should list the major points, items, or type of discussion the teacher will accept as correct, partially correct, or satisfactory (TenBrink, 1994). It also should indicate the relative weights that will be assigned to each element in the answer.

For example, notice the short-answer essay question given in Figure 13.3. Let us assume that the question is worth a total of 7 points and that the correct answer has seven elements, each worth 1 point. The teacher will accept the following three elements as correct for the middle area: both were important men; both wanted to govern wisely; and both led political parties.

Under "Jefferson's Views" the teacher will consider as correct any two of the following three items: as little government as possible is best, common people should have power, and farming should be a major industry. For "Hamilton's Views" the teacher will accept any two of these items: strong federal government is best, wealthy should have power, and strong businesses are necessary.

holistic scoring   An alternative approach in scoring an essay question is to use **holistic scoring.** Using this technique, the teacher reads the answer quickly and scores it as a whole without analyzing the components of the answer. Each essay is given a rating that reflects the teacher's assessment of its overall quality.

Constructing Objective Test Items

The term *objective* in the context of testing refers to the way responses to a question will be graded, not to the nature of the question itself. Deciding to include one item instead of another on a test to represent learning is a *subjective* judgment of the teacher.

FIGURE 13.3

Assessment item: Short-answer essay

Source: From *America Past and Present,* T. E. Workbook by Joan Schreiber, et al. Copyright © 1983 by Scott, Foresman and Company. Reprinted by permission.

Diagramming Two Different Views

Thomas Jefferson and Alexander Hamilton were both very important men during the beginning of the United States. Both men wanted the country to be governed wisely, but each had views that were very different.

While Hamilton felt that the federal government should be strong, Jefferson believed that as little government as possible would be best for the people. Hamilton felt that the wealthy should run this government. Jefferson believed that common people should have the power.

Jefferson wanted farming to be the country's main industry. Hamilton felt that strong businesses that provided many jobs were necessary. Both men led political parties that supported their own beliefs. Jefferson and his followers became known as Republicans. Hamilton and his followers became known as Federalists.

Complete this Venn diagram. In the middle area, summarize three things that Jefferson and Hamilton shared in common. Then summarize each man's differing views below his name.

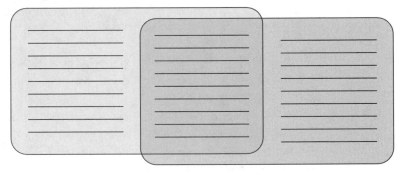

Objective test items are relatively easy to grade quickly and are not susceptible to teacher bias in scoring. They also permit many objectives to be addressed in a short period of time and do not penalize students who lack verbal skills. However, objective items encourage guessing and are often more difficult and time consuming to construct than essay questions. They also afford students no opportunity to demonstrate divergent thinking.

Types of Objective Test Items.   Types of objective test items most appropriate for use in the social studies are *multiple-choice, alternative response (true/false),* and *matching* questions; each form has many variations. Several of the references cited at the end of the chapter provide comprehensive instructions on constructing each of these types.

A fourth form of objective test item, *completion* or *fill-in-the-blank,* also is used by some social studies teachers. Typically, however, its use in social studies is fraught with problems. Clear and unambiguous items are difficult to construct; students often can respond with many reasonable completion items, besides the correct one.

Consider, for example, this poorly constructed question: "_____ _____ was the author of the _____ of _____ ." The correct answer expected is the set of four words, *Thomas*, *Jefferson*, *Declaration*, and *Independence*. In reality, however, myriad plausible alternative sets of answers are equally correct (e.g., *John*, *Steinbeck*, *Grapes*, and *Wrath*).

An example of each of the three types of objective items recommended—multiple-choice, alternative response, and matching questions—follows, accompanied by some guidelines on the writing of the item.

Multiple-Choice Questions

The smallest of the 50 states in terms of land area is which of the following?

a. Wyoming
b. Delaware
c. West Virginia
d. Rhode Island

Some basic guidelines for writing multiple-choice questions include the following:

- The stem (the first part) should state the question or issue.
- All of the choices should be plausible, related, and, ideally, approximately the same length.
- Use four options and avoid use of the options "All of the above" and "None of the above," which often are confusing to students.
- Preferably the stem should be stated in a positive form, avoiding the use of terms such as *not* and *never.*
- Organize the stem around one idea only.

Alternative Response Questions

All of the statements below deal with the map you have been given. If the statement is true according to the map, circle the T next to it. If it is false, circle the F.

T   F   The country has a large city near a port.

T   F   There are mountains in the country.

T   F   It probably is very cold there.

Some basic guidelines for writing alternative response questions include the following:

- Each statement should include a single point or issue.
- Statements designed to "trick" or mislead students if they do not read carefully should be avoided.
- Avoid terms such as *always*, *never*, *all*, *generally*, *occasionally*, and *every*, which signal the correct answer.

Matching Questions

Look at the two sets of items below. The set on the left lists cities and the one on the right lists states. In front of the set of cities is a blank space. Write in each space the letter of the state that belongs with the city.

_____	Milwaukee	a. Ohio
_____	Pittsburgh	b. California
_____	Cleveland	c. Wisconsin
_____	Boise	d. Pennsylvania
_____	San Francisco	e. Idaho
_____	Portland	f. Texas
		g. Minnesota
		h. Maine

Some basic guidelines for writing matching items questions include the following:

- The items in each column should be related.
- The directions should state clearly what the student is to do and any special limitations on the use of choices (e.g., whether items may be used more than once).
- Generally there should be more choices than can be matched.
- The order of the items in each set of choices should be either alphabetical or random.
- The number of items in the shorter column should be fewer than 10 to avoid students wasting time by searching through long lists.

Test Software

Publishers of basal textbook programs now include computer software with banks of test items correlated with the subject matter of the text. This type of software allows easy modification of tests and duplication for sharing. A number of commercially developed software programs also make it possible for teachers to create their own tests. Examples are Test Generator, Test Quest, and QuickTests.

Evaluating Reflection, Competence, and Concern

Effective, meaningful evaluation is transacted for some significant purpose. We conduct evaluations to determine the relative effectiveness of significant components of our instructional program and to validate student achievement.

It has been suggested throughout this text that, in social studies, our ultimate goal should be the development of reflective, competent, and concerned citizens. Correspondingly, the evaluation system and the assessments we devise should tap each of these three dimensions of the effective citizen. Moreover, our objectives and our curricular programs should guide the character of our evaluation and assessment system, rather than the reverse.

In the preceding sections, we considered issues associated with evaluation and a repertoire of assessment strategies that can aid in the evaluation process. We now examine sample assessment items specifically related to measuring the dimensions of reflection, competence, and concern. The items illustrated include a mix of the following types of performance assessments:

test items	role-play enactments
cooperative learning outcomes	anecdotal records
research sheets	checklists
creation of products	rating scales
teacher interviews	

Results from each of these forms of assessment may be accumulated in individual students' folders. These products, or illustrative samples of them, can be reviewed periodically to evaluate student progress.

Assessing Reflection

We have characterized reflective citizens as those who have knowledge of a body of facts, concepts, and generalizations. Reflective citizens are capable of channeling that knowledge into action in the form of problem solving and decision making. The achievement of instructional objectives related to the development of these characteristics can be measured in a variety of ways. Let us consider some sample items. For each item, the dimension of reflection that it attempts to assess is listed, followed by the type of assessment and an example.

1. *Dimension of Reflection:* Identification of examples and nonexamples of the concept.
Type of Assessment Procedure: **Creation of a group product.**
Example: In your group, look at all of the items in the picture box. Place on the bulletin board under the label "transportation" all of the pictures that are examples of transportation. Put under the label "not transportation" all of those you think are not examples.

If you are not sure about a picture, discuss it in your group. Tell why you think the picture does or does not show transportation. If you can't make up your mind, put the picture on the board under the label "not sure."

2. *Dimension of Reflection:* Developing a generalization from facts.
Type of Assessment Procedure: **Interactive multiple-choice test question.**

Example: At the testing station, you will see charts and graphs that go with the questions on your sheets. The number of the chart or graph is the same as the number of the question. For example, Graph 1, showing how unemployment and inflation are related, goes with Question 1. After you examine each chart or graph, circle the correct answer on your sheet.

Which of the following statements best summarizes what Graph 1 shows?

a. Unemployment increases as inflation decreases.
b. Unemployment decreases as inflation decreases.
c. Unemployment increases as inflation increases.
d. Unemployment and inflation are not related.

If you think the graph also shows some other relationships, write your ideas on the answer sheet next to the question.

3. *Dimension of Reflection:* Forming a hypothesis.
Type of Assessment Procedure: **Essay test question.**
Example: Look carefully at the large picture taped to the front chalkboard to answer the question: Why do you think the little boy is crying? Give two hypotheses that might explain why he is crying.

4. *Dimension of Reflection:* Identifying cause-and-effect relationships.
Type of Assessment Procedure: **Group role-play enactment.**
Example: In your small group, read the instructions for developing a role-play activity that shows what would happen if one of the parents in a family lost his or her job. One member of your group should be the father, another the mother, and the rest the children.

After you identify the members to play each role, brainstorm all of the things you think might happen when the parent loses the job. Then follow the directions for getting started.

If you need help or more details, ask the teacher to meet with your group. Otherwise, when you are ready to begin, let the teacher know.

5. *Dimension of Reflection:* Relating facts and generalizations.
Type of Assessment Procedure: **Research sheet.**
Example: The end of the Civil War caused major economic, social, and political changes in the United States. Identify five sets of facts that support this generalization. Record each set of facts by using the procedure sheet that you were given for this report.

For your references, consult the books that have been set aside in the library. After you have completed the research sheet, place it in your social studies portfolio.

Assessing Competence

Competent citizens were described earlier as having a repertoire of talents that include social, research and analysis, chronology, and spatial skills. Paper-and-pencil tests often are sufficient to measure such skills; however, as with many other skills in life, some citizen competencies can be demonstrated best through actual performance.

Checklists are inventories that show, from demonstrations with real tasks, which skills students have mastered. They may be completed by the teacher or the student and are especially useful for objectives that are either-or types (either the student achieved the objective or not).

rating scales

Rating scales appear in many forms (e.g., attitude inventories introduced in Chapter 8). Unlike checklists, they can be used to measure the *degree of progress* students have made. For example, a teacher may assess whether a student has demonstrated considerable or minimal growth in an area, rather than merely check "has made progress" or "has not made progress."

Let us examine some sample assessment items that include checklists and rating scales. For each item, the dimension of competence that it attempts to measure is listed, followed by the assessment procedure and an example.

1. *Dimension of Competence:* Demonstrating map-making skills.
Type of Assessment Procedure: **Creation of a product.**
Example: Create a map that shows someone who is traveling by car from our school how to get to the Crossroads Shopping Mall. In your map, include the features listed on the attached sheet. Also consult your compass and use it in constructing the map.

After you have completed the map, ask two people who can drive if they could locate the mall by using your map. From their answers, make any final changes that are needed. Then place the map in your social studies portfolio.

2. *Dimension of Competence:* Use of reference materials.
Type of Assessment Procedure: **Checklist.**
Example: A checklist similar to the one in Figure 13.4 could be constructed to assess students' use of basic reference materials. After a student working in a group has demonstrated each of the skills satisfactorily, a check is made next to the student's name.

3. *Dimension of Competence:* Group skills.
Type of Assessment Procedure: **Rating scale.**
Example: Each student would be rated on each of the characteristics on a sheet such as that shown in Figure 13.5.

4. *Dimension of Competence:* Construct a time line organizing major events.
Types of Assessment Procedures: **Creation of a product and teacher interview.**
Example: Make a time line that shows what you think are the major events that occurred during 1929 and 1942 in the United States. Then be prepared to explain to the teacher in a conference why you thought these events should be included.

5. *Dimension of Competence:* Establishing factual claims.
Types of Assessment Procedures: **Cooperative learning technique and creation of a product.**

| FIGURE 13.4 | Sample checklist for reference sources |

Reference Sources Checklist

	Mircea	Ramesh	Tara	Fred	Jo
1. Uses picture captions and titles to organize information	—	—	—	—	—
2. Uses glossaries and dictionaries to identify word meaning	—	—	—	—	—
3. Uses dictionaries as aids to pronunciation	—	—	—	—	—
4. Uses a variety of reference works	—	—	—	—	—
5. Uses an atlas	—	—	—	—	—
6. Uses the telephone directory and the Yellow Pages as sources of information	—	—	—	—	—
7. Uses an index to locate information	—	—	—	—	—
8. Uses newspapers and magazines as sources of information	—	—	—	—	—
9. Writes letters to obtain information	—	—	—	—	—
10. Constructs computer databases	—	—	—	—	—

Example: Students are assigned to a Jigsaw II cooperative learning group (see Chapter 5). Each expert is given a different sheet of factual claims that have been made concerning the Columbus voyages and their impact. Each expert is required to research the information on his or her sheet and to determine what the best evidence suggests. Following the Jigsaw II procedures, each expert briefs the other members on the findings. Each group then creates a poster that lists "claims" and "facts."

Assessing Concern

We have characterized concerned citizens as those who are aware of and exercise fully and effectively their rights and responsibilities as members of our society. They also are aware of and responsive to the larger social world around them. In addition, they are willing to make commitments and to act on social issues at the local, regional, national, and international levels. Concerned citizens also establish personal priorities and make ethical decisions with respect to significant values and issues of greatest concern to them.

In assessing students' progress toward developing dimensions of concern, teachers may find such tools as checklists, research sheets, anecdotal records, and rating scales especially helpful. These instruments can be equally valuable as pretests or posttests.

FIGURE 13.5

Group participation rating sheet

Student's Name _____ Date _____

Group Members _____

Date Group Formed _____

Each of the characteristics of group participation will be rated as follows:

    5 = Consistently Exhibited
    4 = Frequently Exhibited
    3 = Occasionally Exhibited
    2 = Seldom Exhibited
    1 = Not Exhibited

Characteristics   *Rating*

1. Accepts ideas of others   ___

2. Initiates ideas   ___

3. Gives opinions   ___

4. Is task oriented   ___

5. Helps others   ___

6. Seeks information   ___

7. Encourages others to contribute   ___

8. Works well with all members   ___

9. Raises provocative questions   ___

10. Listens to others   ___

11. Disagrees in a constructive fashion   ___

12. Makes an overall positive contribution to the group   ___

                                          Total Rating   ___

Additional Comments:

Let us consider some sample items. For each item, the dimension of concern that it attempts to measure is listed, followed by the type of procedure and an example.

1. *Dimension of Concern:* Perspective-taking.
Type of Assessment Procedure: **Research sheet.**
Example: From your study of the colonial period, what can you say were the attitudes of these different groups toward their experiences? Refer to your text and the set of books in the learning center. List as many things as you can for each group. Then try to put yourself in the shoes of the English, the Africans, and the Native Americans. Offer some reasons why they might have felt this way (see Figure 13.6) (adapted from Wallen, 1974, p. 37).

2. *Dimension of Concern:* Taking a stand on ethical dilemmas.
Type of Assessment Procedure: **Essay test question.**
Example: Think about the dilemma that was presented in the filmstrip. What course of action would you take? Write out your position.

Then suppose you had taken the opposite position. What are some reasons you might have given for taking the other position? Write out your answer.

FIGURE 13.6   Sample research sheet

How the English Felt	Why They Felt This Way
_____	_____
_____	_____
_____	_____
How the Africans Felt	Why They Felt This Way
_____	_____
_____	_____
How the Native Americans Felt	Why They Felt This Way
_____	_____
_____	_____
_____	_____

FIGURE 13.7	Checklist of student behaviors related to sensitivity for alternative points of view

	Chang	Abe	Keesha	Rea
1. Is open to new ideas	___	___	___	___
2. Listens while others speak	___	___	___	___
3. Is willing to change his or her mind	___	___	___	___
4. Does not ridicule others' ideas	___	___	___	___
5. Does not engage in name calling	___	___	___	___
6. Does not reject those who disagree	___	___	___	___
7. Supports others' rights to speak	___	___	___	___
8. Is curious about ideas different from his or her own	___	___	___	___

After everyone is finished, we will break into groups to discuss your answers.

3. *Dimension of Concern:* Developing sensitivity to alternative points of view.
Type of Assessment Procedure: **Checklist.**
Example: A checklist similar to the one in Figure 13.7 could be constructed for individuals working in a group. If a student has demonstrated the behavior, a check is made next to his or her name.

4. *Dimension of Concern:* Attitudes toward schoolwork.
Type of Assessment Procedure: **Rating scale.**
Example: Using a feelings chart (shown in Figure 13.8), each student would record his or her feelings about the day's experience (see also evaluation thermometer, in Chapter 8).

5. *Dimension of Concern:* Open-mindedness and tolerance.
Type of Assessment Procedure: **Anecdotal record.**
Example: During a 9-week period, a teacher compiled anecdotal records of students' behavior relating to open-mindedness and tolerance. On a small card, instances of related behavior were recorded, along with the date and the context of the behavior. A sample card is shown in Figure 13.9.

A Framework for Evaluating the Outcomes of Social Studies Instruction

To this point, we have been examining assessment techniques associated with evaluation. Let us now consider a scenario in which a teacher, Mr. Halpern, armed with these techniques, develops an evaluation plan from the ground up. Suppose that, at the beginning of the year, he is engaged in designing an evaluation framework for the first report card period.

FIGURE 13.8

Assessment item: Feelings chart

February						
Sunday	Monday	Tuesday	Wednesday	Thursday	Friday	Saturday

Children place one of the following figures on the calendar
to show how they felt about school each day:

Happy

Unhappy

OK

FIGURE 13.9

Sample anecdotal card

Samantha Wilcox—12/3

Overheard several students talking during their free period about a TV show that
had a gay character. One student made a disparaging remark about gays.
Samantha chided him and defended people's rights to be different and not be
ridiculed. After she spoke, the other students didn't contest her point and then
dropped the subject.

After some reflection about his students, he decides the following assessment procedures will be appropriate and adequate as measures of their learning in social studies.

- Scores from teacher-made tests
- Anecdotal records of class interaction
- Checklists of group participation skills
- Ratings on individual projects
- Ratings on oral reports
- Scores from a standardized test
- Checklists of written assignments

The further decision he makes is related to the percentage of the total evaluation that should be assigned to each of the seven measures. Again he made a subjective judgment; that is, Mr. Halpern decided which indicators would be more important than others in determining student progress.

He decided that ratings of individual projects should receive the greatest weight. His rationale was that a great deal of class time during the evaluation period would be spent on project activities. Correspondingly he assigned the smallest percentage to a standardized test because only one would be given and it would cover only a small set of subject matter objectives addressed by the course.

The sizes of the remaining five pieces were determined on a similar basis. If Mr. Halpern had deemed it appropriate, all of the pieces could have been of an equal size or of some other proportion. Once he had made his decisions about the relative importance of the different components of the course, his evaluation framework, as shown in Figure 13.10, was established.

Matching Evaluation and Instructional Goals and Objectives

In making his evaluation decisions, Mr. Halpern looked to the goals and specific instructional objectives he had established for the social studies program. The seven elements of his evaluation framework addressed all aspects of the program considered to be important for the time period in question. They also took into account those areas in which the class would spend most of its time during the evaluation period.

Developing an evaluation pie chart similar to the one in Figure 13.10 allows a teacher to separate, in some measure, subjective and objective aspects of evaluation. Determining how the weight of each element in the evaluation will be distributed is a *subjective* process. It involves a *value judgment* that certain elements should make up the evaluation and each should be weighted in a particular way.

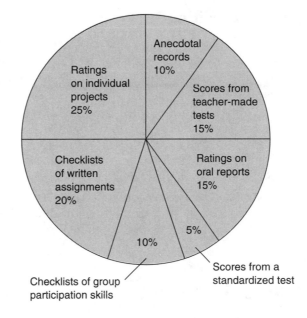

FIGURE 13.10

An evaluation framework

In addition to an evaluation pie chart, an **evaluation grid** sometimes is useful for determining whether all of the teacher's goals or objectives have been reflected in the evaluation framework and in which ways. It involves listing in one column all of the instructional goals or objectives that the teacher considers to have been important. In the next column are matched those ways in which student achievement of the goals or objectives are to be measured (e.g., through ratings on an oral report). A portion of a sample evaluation grid is shown in Figure 13.11.

evaluation grid

FIGURE 13.11   Evaluation grid

Evaluation Grid	
Important Goals	How Achievement of the Goals Will Be Assessed
Identify major ethnic groups within the United States and some of the traditions associated with each of them.	Ratings on an oral report Individual projects A teacher-made test
Learn research techniques associated with locating information from written materials.	Skill demonstrations Samples of individual student papers Anecdotal record

Group Activities

1. Identify several teachers in grades 4 through 8. Show them the example of an evaluation framework (Figure 13.10) and ask them to share their frameworks. Also ask them to discuss the rationale for their decisions. Compare your findings.

2. Examine a commercially produced test for elementary or middle-grade social studies. If possible, obtain the computer-based version. Note its name, the publisher, the copyright date, and the grade level. Also identify the different forms of questions that are included (e.g., multiple-choice) and the topics or subjects it covers. Discuss your findings and reactions.

3. Locate samples of report cards or report statements used by local schools. Determine how well they assess the dimensions of the schools' social studies programs. Discuss your findings and conclusions.

Individual Activities

1. Consult the section in the chapter on essay tests and design an essay question for any aspect of a fifth-grade American history course. Also construct a model answer with weights for each portion of the answer.

2. Covering the same topical area as in the previous activity, construct a multiple-choice, alternative response, and matching question. If you need further assistance, consult one of the reference works cited or a similar source from your school library.

3. Develop either a checklist or a rating scale to assess whether students have acquired some set of research and analysis, spatial, or chronology skills that you have identified as appropriate for an elementary-grade student. Refer to Chapter 7 for a list of skills keyed to grade levels.

4. Pick any grade and a unit from a corresponding social studies basal text. Develop three performance assessments that would be appropriate for assessing how well students had learned the information in the text.

References

Airasian, P. (1991). *Classroom assessment.* New York: McGraw-Hill.

California Department of Education. (1990). *California: The state of assessment.* Sacramento: Author.

Darling-Hammond, L., & Lieberman, A. (1992, January 29). The shortcomings of standardized tests. *Chronicle of Higher Education,* B1–B2.

Maeroff, G. I. (1991). Assessing alternative assessment. *Phi Delta Kappan, 73,* 272–281.

Martorella, P. H., Martelli, L., & Graham, A. (1983). *Looking at me: Webstermaster activity sheets.* New York: McGraw-Hill.

McTighe, J. (1997). What happens between assessments? *Educational Leadership, 54,* 6–12.

Mitchell, R. (1992). *Testing for learning: How new approaches to evaluation can improve America's schools.* New York: Free Press.

National Council for the Social Studies (NCSS). (1991). *Testing and evaluation of social studies students.* Washington, DC: Author.

Perrone, V. (Ed.). (1991). *Expanding student assessment.* Alexandria, VA: Association for Supervision and Curriculum Development.

Popham, W. J. (1988). *Educational evaluation* (2nd ed.). Englewood Cliffs, NJ: Prentice Hall.

Schreiber, J., et al. (1983). *America past and present: Teacher's edition workbook.* Glenview, IL: Scott, Foresman.

TenBrink, T. D. (1994). Evaluation. In J. Cooper et al., *Classroom teaching skills* (5th ed.). Lexington, MA: D. C. Heath.

Wallen, N. E. (1974). *Getting together with people.* Reading, MA: Addison-Wesley.

Williams, P. L., & Moore, J. R. (Eds.). (1980). *Criterion-referenced testing for the social studies* (Bulletin No. 64). Washington, DC: National Council for the Social Studies.

Index